Bilingual Education Series

GARY D. KELLER, *Editor*

GUADALUPE VALDÉS, ANTHONY G. LOZANO, and
RODOLFO GARCÍA-MOYA, editors
*Teaching Spanish to the Hispanic Bilingual:
Issues, Aims, and Methods*

JOSHUA A. FISHMAN AND GARY D. KELLER, editors
*Bilingual Education for Hispanic Students
in the United States*

FLORENCE BARKIN, ELIZABETH A. BRANDT, and
JACOB ORNSTEIN-GALICIA, editors
*Bilingualism and Language Contact:
Spanish, English, and Native American Languages*

MAE CHU-CHANG, editor
*Asian- and Pacific-American Perspectives
in Bilingual Education: Comparative Research*

GARY D. KELLER
Leo y entiendo, a Spanish-language reading program
for kindergarten through grade 3

THERESA H. ESCOBEDO, editor
*Early Childhood Bilingual Education:
A Hispanic Perspective*

EUGENE E. GARCÍA, FRANCISCO A. LOMELÍ, and
ISIDRO D. ORTIZ, editors
Chicano Studies: A Multidisciplinary Approach

MICHAEL A. OLIVAS, editor
Latino College Students

Latino
College Students

Edited by

MICHAEL A. OLIVAS

Teachers College, Columbia University
New York and London

Published by Teachers College Press, 1234 Amsterdam Avenue, New York, N.Y. 10027

Library of Congress Cataloging in Publication Data

Latino college students.

  (Bilingual education series)
  Includes index.
    1. Hispanic Americans—Education (Secondary)—United States—Congresses. 2. Hispanic Americans—Education (Higher)—United States—Congresses. 3. Educational equalization—United States—Congresses. 4. Universities and colleges—United States—Entrance examinations—Congresses. I. Olivas, Michael A. II. Series: Bilingual education series (Columbia University. Teachers College)
LC2670.4.L37 1986   378'.1982   86-5697

ISBN 0-8077-2798-9

Manufactured in the United States of America

91 90 89 88 87 86   1 2 3 4 5 6

Contents

I | The Transition from High School to College

II | Hispanic Student Achievement

III | Economics and Stratification

Foreword

GREGORY R. ANRIG

When Michael Olivas invited Educational Testing Service (ETS) to co-sponsor the conference on Latino College Students, we were delighted to give our support and even more delighted with the outcome. The conference participants at the ETS Conference Center witnessed a showcase of talented young scholars who reviewed the condition of higher education for Hispanics from multiple perspectives. The participation by Richard Durán, Luis Laosa, and María Pennock-Román, former and current research scientists at ETS, gives us special pride as an organization. We celebrate the emergence of this volume because it enables a far larger audience to benefit from the papers.

Although much research has documented the common obstacles that minority students encounter in obtaining a quality education, relatively few studies have focused specifically on students of Hispanic descent, the most rapidly growing segment of the U.S. population. This focus is needed because the educational consequences of characteristics unique to Hispanics—such as language background and the immigration histories of the various groups—deserve close attention. Most of the papers in this volume are derived from data bases that have emerged in the last six years. Furthermore, this text provides an overview of key stages and turning points in the educational process for Hispanics that is unusually complete. Thus, the present volume fills an important gap, and readers will find it useful in more than one respect.

The allocation of three chapters to tests and their uses in selective admissions underscores the importance of these topics. Given unevenness in the quality of high schools, selective universities find that grades alone are inadequate for choosing their incoming freshmen. Without tests to provide a common indicator of academic performance, admissions committees would need to rely more heavily on more subjective information, such as their knowledge of the reputation of the students' high schools, individual interviews, and teacher references, as supplements to what still is the best indicator of success in college—the transcript of grades earned and courses taken over four years in high school. Despite their limitations, if judiciously used, tests can help to identify talented students who have the ability to succeed in college whether or not they had the opportunity to attend an elite high school. Unfortunately, as shown by Durán's review, predicting which Hispanic students are potentially most successful presents special problems. Not only are tests less predictive for Hispanics, but high school grades are also significantly less related to college grades for Hispanics than for other groups. This means that the college performance of some Hispanics falls below expectations based on traditional academic credentials, whereas others surpass these expectations to a greater extent than majority students. These findings need to be more broadly understood throughout the educational community and need to be carefully considered in determining admissions policies in higher education.

One encouraging note pointed out by Pennock-Román in her chapter on selective admissions is that overall increases in minority student admissions can be obtained without substantially lowering the success rates of those who enroll. This result, predicted by theory, is substantiated by empirical findings in schools of law and medicine among other institutions. Apparently, many admissions committees are wisely relying on a variety of information to identify successful students. Such news is very good indeed, although the numbers of Hispanics who apply and are admitted to higher education institutions are still far too few.

Thus, our commitment to widening the applicant pool and searching for better instruments to assess college applicants must continue. While it is vital to intensify our efforts to improve testing procedures, investigation of the situational aspects of the college experience that best promote the realization of Hispanic students' potential is also necessary. Researchers at ETS are continuing the research on test-item discrepancies reviewed in this volume. In addition, we are currently conducting a survey of Hispanic freshmen to study further the relationship between college achievement, admissions tests, language background, and the college environment.

This current volume documents the dialogue among an extraordinary group of able researchers from diverse disciplines that took place in the Conference on Latino College Students. The interdisciplinary nature of the exchange will enrich research efforts in a critical area of education, and we hope that forums of this type will be repeated in the future.

Foreword

ARTURO MADRID

Our history, or that part of it within the American community, has all too frequently been one of inability to speak up, to speak out, or to speak at all on the issues that concern us. Specifically, our exclusion from the institutional life of American society and from the forums it provides has kept us from being heard, even when our voices have been loud and our concerns compelling. Denied access to power, especially the power to define, we have had to suffer in silence the denial, distortion, and trivialization of our historical experience. Most damagingly, we were seduced into believing that the fault lay in ourselves and not in the constellation of institutions that govern our lives.

Over the past two decades our voices, although still muted, have begun to ring out. Access to American institutions, and in particular to institutions of higher education, has provided us with podiums from which to offer dissenting views and the training and research that makes possible the adducing of evidence to sustain them.

Nowhere have we felt the burden of institutional oppression nor the weight of responsibility more heavily than in education. This supposedly enlightened institution is seemingly also one of the most retrogressive. The educational system continues to blame the victim for its own failures, rather than to adapt its methods and policies to the differing populations and changing circumstances with which it is constantly confronted.

Thus, the 1983 Conference on Latino College Students was a signal event, as is this volume of essays issuing therefrom: signal in its focus; signal in its range; signal in its depth. Only recently has the study of Latino students become feasible, since there were so few prior to the 1970s. Moreover, comprehensive, disaggregated record-keeping on this population is a new and still inchoate phenomenon. Our earlier challenges to the reigning ideological constructs were limited by inadequate methodologies and insufficient data. Of course, depth comes with experience and is a product of good training, of adequate data, of sustained work, and of scholarly debate.

The various essays that constitute this volume are at the cutting edge of this field of study. The introductory essay by the conference organizer and editor, Michael Olivas, provides an exceptionally comprehensive, insightful, and intelligent introduction to the subject. He facilitates the reading of the book and the overall conceptualization of the field by categorizing research on Latino students, by reviewing the various chapters of the book and showing how each chapter fits into the volume's three major parts ("The Transition from High School to College," "Hispanic Student Achievement," and "Economics and Stratification"), and by offering expert opinion on the most valuable directions for future research.

The research categories which have emerged include the vital characteristics of Hispanic students themselves, the financing of education, and governance research. Olivas remarks frankly that the application to Hispanics of test instruments derived from studies of majority students are inappropriate, and he reviews the difficulties Hispanics face in financing a higher education. A fourth area of research, that of Hispanic education perceived from the model of "internal colonialism," focuses on the use of ameliorative tactics, such as affirmative action programs, which, Olivas notes, can coopt Hispanic concerns by "specialized minority hiring to fill minority slots, thereby relieving the institutions of the need to integrate throughout their ranks."

Olivas provides a candid assessment of certain prevailing negative behaviors toward Hispanics in the United States, wherein "institutional practices that methodically exclude Hispanic participation present a far more serious and systematic barrier" to equal status than do the more obvious negative behaviors, such as anti-immigration attitudes. His summary statement notes that educational reform will not be accomplished to any large extent "without more comprehensive social and economic reform."

Vilma Ortiz bases her chapter on an analysis of data gathered in the first year (1979) of the five-year National Longitudinal Survey of Labor Market Experiences, conducted by Ohio State University. She uses techniques of multivariate analysis to compare first, second, and third generation Hispanic youth with non-Hispanic white youth. Initially, the data indicated that Hispanic youth are more than twice as likely to be delayed in school (20 percent to 9 percent) and to have dropped out of high school (30 percent to 12 percent) than non-Hispanic white youths.

As in many prior studies, this one finds that second generation Hispanics stand out in school achievement when compared to first and later generations. Ortiz opines that "immigrant parents provide more encouragement and hold higher expectations for their children than do non-immigrant parents," thus partly explaining this variation.

Ernesto Ballesteros reviews the literature on the characteristics of Chicano students and presents his own analysis of data collected through the Cooperative Institutional Research Program and the University of California at Los Angeles. This sample included Chicano students who entered four-year colleges and universities as first time freshmen in the fall of 1975. His conclusion, presented within a detailed outcome model which considered inputs (such as high school curriculum, parental income, and so forth) and outputs (ultimately, the grade point average achieved in college) is that social class status and placement in a college preparatory program in high school seem to explain a significant proportion of the variation in school outcomes.

In discussing his findings, Ballesteros asserts that equal educational opportunity is not a reality for Hispanics and proposes that all high school students, regardless of other factors, should be required to take college preparatory courses. "The existence of one classical secondary school curriculum," he writes, "as had originally been the case, represented a more equitable situation, in that every child had access to the same resources and, therefore, had an equal opportunity to garner all the benefits of schooling."

Ballesteros further recommends "massive remediation" in the early school years in order to "ensure that children acquire sound learning and communication skills." Moreover, remediation, tutoring, and counseling may also be indicated even at the college level.

François Nielsen presents a particularly cogent paper, based in part on the national survey of students in the tenth and twelfth grades, *High School and Beyond* (HS&B), but paradigmatic in its discussion and organization. Nielsen reviews many of the typical distributional outcome measures which have been used to compare subpopulations of the HS&B survey. Delay rates for Hispanics, for example, are substantially greater than for non-Hispanic whites, and the delay increases as a function of the frequency of Spanish used in the home (although use of Spanish in the home is positively correlated with most other achievement measures). Nielsen discusses the school retention measure with respect to "pullout" mechanisms, whereby students may leave school because more attractive "economic opportunities" are available to them, and even suggests the consideration of the illegal sector as an integral part of the structure of such opportunities outside of school.

Nielsen makes some further points about the role of Spanish language proficiency in school achievement, but notes that the HS&B data are limited because of lack of experimental controls (specifically, no pre-test of early abilities) and because placement into high school bilingual programs has been neither random nor systematic, but haphazard. He suggests a "triangulation strategy" in using the HS&B data, whereby two or more additional, independent measures are utilized either to support or negate the HS&B data on various topics of interest to minority researchers.

Richard Santos refers to the same data source cited by Vilma Ortiz in the earlier chapter, that is, the National Longitudinal Survey of Youth Labor Market Experience. Santos here focuses on youth sampled in 1981 who graduated from high school between 1975 and 1979. High school graduates are examined with respect to their subsequent choices, including college attendance, military service, training experience, and work experience. The choices are, of course, not mutually exclusive.

Santos evaluates the data with respect to the subpopulation selecting each of the four major post-graduation options. With regard to those selecting college, for example, he notes that important variables included gender, enrollment in a college preparatory program, knowledge of the world of work, educational aspirations, and the educational aspirations of friends. On the other hand, Santos found that Hispanic-related variables such as nativity or language did not significantly affect the probability of college attendance for Hispanic high school graduates. He finds further that two-year colleges are the mode for Hispanics in comparison to four-year colleges among other youth. In conclusion, Santos brings the reader's attention back to the high proportion of youth who are not in a position to make any of the choices because they never graduate from high school.

The well-written, well-organized chapter by Daniel Muñoz presents the results of an interview survey conducted by the author and his co-workers with Chicano and Anglo undergraduates of both sexes. The study presented here had been preceded by similar work in which Muñoz found that ". . . Chicano undergraduates of both sexes reported much greater stress than did Anglo students," and that Chicanas reported significantly more than their male counterparts. For both groups, the principal source of stress was financial. In extending his work, Muñoz suggests that stress impairs the student's ability to persevere and finish college; in his view, this accounts for the higher dropout rate of Chicano undergraduates compared to Anglos.

The interviews conducted for this study included one-on-one structured questions on attitudes, perceptions, and coping styles, as well as the College Environmental Stress Index. In general, the results supported the earlier study. "The lack of money and the uncertainty of obtaining it are the two highest sources of stress for Chicano students." This financial stress was related to the lower socioeconomic levels of Chicanos, such that parental financial support was less for Chicanos. Chicanas reported more stress than any other group, and Muñoz notes that ". . . cultural background, specifically sex-role socialization, provides significant discontinuity for the Chicana in higher education." In view of these findings, Muñoz recommends that minority professionals, educators, and counselors help students by "shedding facades of invulnerability and sharing with students the problems they have had," and by pointing out the positive aspects of certain types of stress.

José P. Mestre reports the results of a series of studies conducted with Hispanic collegians enrolled in science and engineering. The theme of all the studies is the interplay of language and problem-solving ability. In this context, several possible language variables are examined with respect to their impact on problem-solving. These include bilingualism itself, of which Mestre presents three categories: semilingualism, in which neither language is used proficiently; dominant bilingualism, in which one language is used with more proficiency than the second; and additive bilingualism, in which both languages are mastered well and seem to enhance each other. Other factors studied include academic preparation prior to college, verbosity (or "wordiness") of problems presented, the use of double negatives, speed of performance, and other socioeconomic or motivational factors.

Although Mestre notes that the small samples utilized in these studies prevent wide generalization to other populations, he concludes that Hispanic college students are underprepared in technical areas compared to Anglo college students. Specific areas of deficiency for the Hispanic group include algebraic skills, language skills, and problem-solving skills in which substantial amounts of linguistic processing are required.

Mestre proposes that microcomputers be put to use in elementary and higher grades to help students improve vocabulary, reading speed and comprehension, and mathematical problem-solving skills. Microcomputers are especially useful because they are economically feasible and because they eliminate the embarrassment underprepared students may feel in dealing with remedial teachers or tutors.

The first of two chapters by Maria Pennock-Román stands out as an effort that will increase the reader's understanding of the definition and measurement of test bias. She has presented an exceptionally comprehensible overview of a difficult, statistically-oriented methodology, and has reviewed the utility and validity of certain tests developed by the Educational Testing Service for use with bilingual, Hispanic populations.

The author emphasizes the important distinction between discrepant test items and unfair test items. An item is discrepant "if individuals with equal ability, but from different groups, have different probabilities of answering the items correctly." Discrepant items are not necessarily unfair, nor are unfair items necessarily discrepant. When differences occur which are unrelated to the skill being measured, they are clearly related to unfairness (or bias) in a test item.

Pennock-Román provides a highly readable discussion of the most significant of the several statistical methods proposed for the detection of discrepancy. Few existing studies have focused on test-item discrepancy with respect to Hispanics, although it has been found that the standard college aptitude tests have less predictive validity for Hispanics than they do for whites, as discussed in the chapter by Durán. In such circumstances, statistical discrepancy analyses must be combined with *a posteriori* "judgment" analyses to ascertain which items are truly unfair. As the author notes, "The inescapable fact is that fairness in all aspects of testing is ultimately a question of values."

Richard P. Durán reviews available data on college achievement among Hispanics: "The weight of the current findings suggests that high school grades and admissions test scores do not do as good a job at predicting Hispanics' college grades as is the case for non-minority students." Yet, most four-year colleges rely heavily on these factors to determine who will be admitted each year.

Durán finds, moreover, that the admissions process at most colleges is rarely based solely on rational decision-making. He suggests that an improved, more predictive model be developed for Hispanics, based on factors other than grades and test scores, but admits that, "In no small part, the attempt to derive an improved framework for prediction of Hispanics' college achievement is a sociopolitical one."

At the same time, Durán feels that measures of college achievement may be inadequate in the case of Hispanic students, and suggests that personal growth characteristics be incorporated into the existing definition of achievement in order to reflect better the progress through college by Hispanics. It would also be important to understand better those institutional characteristics, such as financial aid, study assistance, counseling, and so forth, which help to create a sociocultural climate on the college campus which is more or less congenial to the Hispanic student, and which is of critical importance in achievement by Hispanics.

Next, Pennock-Román discusses the theory and practice of college admission policies. Various justifications for selective admissions are cited and fair selection models are described. These models range from the single-group regression type, in which a predictor such as high school grade-point average is used as the selection criterion without regard to group membership; to the "quota" model, in which specified proportions of majority and minority group candidates are selected for admission, regardless of criterion scores across groups.

Pennock-Román asserts that all current selection strategies are oversimplistic, because they rely on a unidimensional dependent variable, usually high school grade-point average. She writes: "Ideally, future research should challenge the view that academic performance is the only criterion for success by developing measures of competence other than grades ... the selection problem would become a multivariate multiple regression paradigm where several measures of quality are to be predicted. Cutting scores could then be set to maximize these qualities simultaneously." In comparing actual admissions with the predictions from the various models, Pennock-Román found that some colleges admit greater numbers of minorities than prescribed by even the most liberal selection models, but that this was not the case for women, who were admitted less often than prescribed by the models.

Pennock-Román places emphasis on "self-selection" by Hispanics, in contrast to selection by college admissions committees. Hispanics often eliminate themselves from the entire admissions process by failing to take the standardized tests at all, or by failing to submit complete applications. "Research should concentrate," writes Pennock-Román, "on ways to counsel minority students to take standardized tests and apply to higher quality institutions."

In a brief chapter, Olivas describes his own study designed for the purpose of establishing "baseline data on receipt of financial aid by disadvantaged Hispanic students." He notes that financial packaging to date has been a field rarely studied and without any theoretical underpinnings.

In the study project, files from the federally-funded counseling program, Hispanic Talent Search, were examined. A total of 521 files of Mexican American and Puerto Rican fulltime, first-time students were selected from the 1979-80 cohort. Olivas found that over 60 percent of Hispanic students received only one source of aid, namely, the Pell Grant (formerly, the Basic Educational Opportunity Grant). Olivas considers this reliance on one source of financial aid to be a significant problem for Hispanic students. The concentration of Hispanics in two-year colleges and less prestigious four-year colleges is noted. Olivas discusses his findings in terms of "packaging scenarios," in which several ideas about financial aid are illustrated. These range from the "individual good" scenario, in which students are expected to work, borrow, or use personal resources to fund education; to the "community contribution" scenario, in which educational subsidy is all-encompassing, including even lost or deferred wages resulting from school attendance.

Olivas concludes by reminding the reader that his study involved only students already enrolled in college. He poses the question of how many students were discouraged from attending college because of their inability to procure financial aid or information about aid.

The following chapter by Chacón and her colleagues is based on a multivariate analysis of a sample of Mexican-Americans, 508 women and 160 men, attending five different California colleges. The "program progress" toward the end-goal, either a degree or a vocational certificate, was measured for each student and correlated with several variables. Of the variables chosen for consideration, several were significantly correlated with program progress. Age, hours of domestic work, and hours of paid work were negatively correlated with program progress, while socioeconomic status and "freedom from academic difficulty" were positively correlated with program progress. Chicano males are significantly more likely than are Chicanas to report that their parents were very supportive of their college attendance.

The authors note, on the one hand, the close relationship between individual demographic characteristics and fixed time costs and, on the other, variables pertaining to institutional climate and school policies. They also note the difficulty in separating the two types of variables.

Although the data of this study were limited by the dependent variable, which was self-reported, and by the fact that measures were taken only once, nevertheless, the authors draw several strong conclusions from the study. They report that the study is the first to detect the impact of domestic labor on persistence in higher education, and conclude that attendance at a four-year college is a far better investment than attendance for four years beginning with the community college. Chacón and her colleagues further recommend that schools provide "funds to launch intensive programs of writing and reading comprehension for language minority youth who want to attend college but who clearly lack the requisite skills." They strongly oppose "tracking," however. They conclude with the hopeful observation that "policy research of this kind can be an effective tool for sensitizing and educating decision-makers."

Richard R. Verdugo reviews the sociological literature on racial and educational stratification, with special reference to Hispanics. He emphasizes the interplay between racial stratification in the larger society and segregation or tracking in the educational system. He distinguishes also between "ideological" and "structural" mechanisms of stratification, which reinforce one another and "serve to justify and maintain a given social order. . . . In short, the educational system reproduces a social order stratified by class, gender, and race found in larger society."

Racism can enter the school curriculum through written texts which depict minorities negatively or ignore them all together. Intelligence tests may be considered a form of racism, since they measure one's knowledge of middle class culture. "Until the predictive power of such tests is conclusively proven," writes Verdugo, "they should not be used." The result of racism in the educational system is continued segregation of Hispanics, as documented recently by Orfield (1982), and as demonstrated also by the concentration of Hispanics in two-year colleges as opposed to four-year colleges. Writes Verdugo: "Community colleges . . . are institutions which, by and large, perpetuate and reinforce existing stratification systems." Verdugo concludes by suggesting that the problem of segregation in the educational system has not been resolved because Hispanics, rather than the system itself, have been targeted for change.

In all, this book is a fine collection of highly relevant essays, the value of which lies not only in the questions answered but also, especially, in the questions raised. The volume testifies to the existence of a core of talented and well-trained scholars who are interested in the field of Hispanics in higher education.

There is yet much work to be done. We have not yet captured the sustained attention of educational policy-makers, and consequently our impact on them has been limited. Our voice is now loud, clear, and eloquent, but it is yet a voice often unheard. Having finally gained access to the appropriate communication channels, we must now press forth to bring influence to bear on the decision-makers who determine the future of our educational experiences. It is this challenge which confronts every individual concerned with the status of the Latino population in the United States. Its pursuit must be pressed with a tenacity equal to that which has finally brought about our access to the media of communication, as evidenced in this volume.

Preface

This book, like many other edited volumes, is a collaborative work indebted to many persons. Although the idea for *Latino College Students* was mine, it was hardly an original thought, but rather one that had its roots in many formal and informal discussions. The poor state of the art in this area of research led me quickly to conclude that any such volume would have to draw upon several disciplines and sets of colleagues in order to survey the field and result in a comprehensive work. This work, therefore, was conceived as a collegial enterprise that would enlist the most talented colleagues I could encourage into participating.

I knew many of the participants through previous professional activities, although several authors I knew only by reading their research. Inasmuch as significant scholarly work on Latino students is a relatively recent research interest, these colleagues tended to be junior scholars, the majority not yet tenured or senior professors. This has meant that the volume has been the fortunate beneficiary of fresh insights, not merely glosses on traditional studies. It has also meant that many of these articles call into question traditional approaches to the study of students; not content merely to question why Hispanics do not more closely resemble their Anglo counterparts, the writers criticize an educational system that systemically fails Hispanic communities.

It is only now, with the twenty-twenty hindsight of having edited and contributed to this volume, that I can see the lacunae, the gaps to which I can direct future researchers. Length considerations have necessitated giving short shrift to law and history. I concede that neither law nor history is as evident in these chapters as its contributions undoubtedly merit, and the mixture of psychologists, sociologists, economists, and policy analysts would surely have been enriched by the addition of lawyers and historians. In truth, however, this book is more likely to be provocative for what it includes than for what space limitations or lack of vision have caused to be omitted. For the first time, to select only a few examples, Chicana disadvantage has been quantified and partially identified as domestic time on task (by María Chacón, Elizabeth Cohen, and Sharon Strover); predictive validity for standardized test scores is shown to be substantially lower for Hispanic test takers (by Richard Durán); Chicana and Chicano students' stress is seen as measurably different from the stress encountered by Anglos (by

Daniel Muñoz); and Hispanic financial-aid packages are found to be considerably different from those assembled for Anglo students (in my own essay).

These are profoundly disturbing, deeply evocative social science findings; each is painstakingly documented and carefully analyzed. One reviewer called this volume "eerie, as if each author was trying not to declare an emergency even though one clearly exists. We should not trample each other to escape the fire in the theater, but we must make the proprietors aware that there *is* a fire." As any fair reader must concede, this does not mean that these papers are dispassionate or bloodless. Rather, each author has marshaled the evidence to let readers draw their own inferences. Most will conclude that if we allow the extraordinary wastage of Hispanic attrition to continue, we will have doomed an entire generation to persistent poverty and hopelessness. This urgency permeates all the articles, making them more than dry recitations of facts.

Documenting a problem is the first step toward rectifying it, so this volume should provide hope for the many educators and parents who know firsthand the failure of the system for Hispanic students. The papers analyzing national data bases can, for the first time, draw upon data with large Hispanic subsamples. Despite recent federal cutbacks in racial data-gathering efforts, scholars have data proving what Hispanic communities have known intuitively. The development of del statistics and other sophisticated methodological techniques (chronicled by María Pennock-Román) augurs well for future studies, as does the growing and important work by Hispanic scientists (José Mestre, for example, is trained as a physicist). This volume should point to many promising areas for future work and provoke action in the Hispanic scholarly community as well as in the larger policymaking arena.

In any collaborative effort, many persons provide support, and this one was no different. While the list is longer than this space allows, acknowledgment must be made to those whose selfless work made this volume possible for me and the coauthors. Chief among these colleagues are Educational Testing Service persons whose support made the book possible: Gregory Anrig, Robert Solomon, Eleanor Horne, Sherril Lord Frazer, and Paulette Harris. I received valuable advice from colleagues who served as reviewers and sounding boards: Arturo Madrid, Melba Vásquez, Edward Rincón, John García, Isaura Santiago, Tony Evans, Rafael Magallan, and Luis Laosa. Teachers College Press personnel (including Carole Saltz, Lois Patton, and Susan Liddicoat) and, above all, Gary Keller have been very helpful. University of Houston staff, particularly George Magner, Jarry Booth, and Tessa Smith, have given a great deal of time and assistance. The staff of the Institute for Higher Education Law and Governance includes such unfailingly helpful colleagues as Marilyn Nerem and Carolyn Winter. Augustina Reyes and Inez Cardozo-Freeman encouraged this book. Finally, George Sánchez and Tomás Rivera inspired all of our work. Teachers have always been revered in our communities, and none so much as these two. All of us have profited, whether or not we know it, from the examples of George Sánchez and Tomás Rivera. It is to them that these Latino students dedicate the book.

Latino College Students

Introduction

Research on Latino College Students: A Theoretical Framework and Inquiry

MICHAEL A. OLIVAS

Hispanic education issues have not been sufficiently examined, even by equity researchers or bilingual educators, because the systemic and structural disadvantages facing Hispanic students are so great at all levels of education and so intertwined with the politically powerless status of Hispanics that neither the nature nor the severity of the disadvantage is fully understood. It may be impossible to disentangle the educational problems stemming from Hispanic political disenfranchisement, inasmuch as educational policy is political at both local and higher levels. Hispanics do not control political institutions at any level, even in geographic areas where they constitute a majority. The focus of this inquiry, however, is on the inability of school districts to educate Hispanic children, rather than on the scarcity of Hispanic-elected school board members, and on the failures of federal education-equity legislation, rather than on the small number of Hispanic legislators.

THE CONDITION OF HISPANIC EDUCATION

In 1982 Hispanic children attended schools that were more segregated than in 1970. Data[1] showing dramatic national and regional trends reveal that a high percentage of Hispanic students now attend schools in which minority children are the majority of the student body. More than two-thirds of all Hispanic students are enrolled in public schools in which 50 percent of the enrollment is minority. Understandably, many Hispanic families feel that desegregative racial assignments without regard to a child's linguistic competence will dilute bilingual programs and render both desegregation and bilingual education ineffective (Arias, 1980).

Hispanic students are far less likely than majority or even most minority students to complete high school or graduate with their age group. Attrition

1

rates, which tend to understate the extent of dropout, show that 1978 high school completion rates for Mexican Americans who were twenty-five years or older were 34.3 percent compared to 67.1 percent for non-Hispanics over twenty-five. Hispanic students who did remain in school fell behind until 24 percent of the fourteen-to twenty-year-olds were enrolled two grades behind their classmates. Only 9 percent of the Anglo students were two years behind their same-age peers.

Moreover, bilingual education programs remain inadequate in most states, both in the diagnosis of linguistic competence and in the provision of bilingual curricula and personnel. Tests and other instruments have not been widely used to measure the cognitive abilities and English-speaking abilities of linguistic-minority children. However, even when Hispanic children are diagnosed as "limited-English" or "non-English proficient," fewer than half are enrolled in bilingual programs. Further, few classrooms have Hispanic teachers: In 1976, less than 3 percent of all public school employees were Hispanic, with nearly as many Hispanic service workers (custodians) as Hispanic teachers. Until the number of Hispanic educators is increased, bilingual programs and school systems will continue to be unresponsive to bilingual children's needs.

The failures of school systems to meet the needs of Hispanic communities are mirrored in postsecondary institutions. Here, issues of limited access, discriminatory employment practices, and high attrition disproportionately affect Hispanic students. Although there is a public perception that Hispanic enrollments have increased greatly in recent years, the reality is very different. Hispanic students have neither entered a broad range of institutions nor dramatically increased their numbers throughout the system. For example, from 1970 to 1984, full-time Hispanic undergraduate students increased only from 2.1 percent of the total to 3.5 percent. Even more dramatic is the decline of the percentage of Hispanic high school graduates attending college, from 35.4 percent in 1975 to 29.9 percent in 1980. It thus becomes clear that Hispanic matriculation has not shown the growth one would have expected from affirmative action, governmental, or institutional programs and efforts to increase minority-student enrollments.

While these figures reveal that Hispanic entry into postsecondary institutions has not been deep, distribution data show that access also has not been widespread. Hispanics are concentrated in the less prestigious and less well funded institutions, and, indeed, in very few four-year institutions. In 1984, only 23 percent of white full-time students attended two-year colleges, while fully 46 percent of Hispanic students attended such institutions. This uneven distribution of Hispanics within the system indicates that a large cadre of Hispanic students seeking a full-time, traditional learning experience is doing so in institutions established for part-time commuter students. While two-year institutions have increased Hispanic access, they suffer from the inherent problems of student transfers, part-time faculty, commuter programs, and funding patterns. Moreover, Hispanic students do not even enjoy full access into open-door institutions: A mere twenty-one colleges in the mainland United States enroll 24 percent of all mainland Hispanic students; when the thirty-four Puerto Rican institutions are included, these fifty-five colleges collectively enroll 43 percent of all U.S. Hispanic students. Additionally, unlike other minority students who benefit from historically black or tribal colleges, Hispanic students do not have access to a network of traditionally Hispanic colleges. Therefore, Hispanic students are disproportionately concentrated in fewer than 2 percent of the more than 3,100 colleges and universities in the country and in institutions that lack historical missions to serve Hispanic students.

To note that the leadership of these schools is non-Hispanic is an understatement. In the summer of 1985, there were six Hispanic four-year-college presidents and twenty Hispanic two-year-college presidents. A survey of two-year-college trustees revealed that only .6 percent were Hispanic, while a study of postsecondary coordinating boards found 1.1 percent of the commissioners to be Hispanic. At another level of leadership, there is little evidence to suggest that significant leadership will be drawn from faculty ranks, because only 1.4 percent of all faculty (and 1.1 percent of all tenured professors) are Hispanics, including faculty members in Spanish and bilingual education departments. With many Hispanics employed in special assistant or affirmative action and equal-employment-opportunity staff capacities, even fewer will hold important policymaking positions. Confronted with these data, one is forced to concede that Hispanics have not entered American institutions of higher education in any significant fashion.

RESEARCH ON HISPANIC STUDENTS

Any comprehensive review of research findings can only conclude that little is known about Hispanic students. As a result, program-evaluation researchers measure Hispanic children with instruments and methodologies evolved from studies of majority students. More often than not, such studies predictably find evidence that educational programs are not accomplishing the goal of improving Hispanic student performance. In questioning the value of research on Mexican American children, Carter and Segura (1979) have noted:

> Little had been written about the interaction of cause and effect among the three important variables—the school, the social system, and the Mexican American subcultural group. The available literature, however, clearly demonstrated that

Mexican Americans often do poorly in school, drop out early, speak Spanish, and are poor. These four factors are usually seen as causal and circular: Chicanos do poorly in school because they are poor, speak Spanish, and are culturally Mexican; or Mexican Americans are poor, speak Spanish, and carry a traditional folk culture because they do poorly in school. Most research slighted the socioeconomic influence; the nature and outcomes of school programs, policies, and practices; and the more recent considerations of school social climate. There was little analysis of school intervention in the apparently self-perpetuating cycle of poverty-school-failure-poverty. (P. 7)

Although their criticisms addressed research on Chicanos in the southwestern United States, the authors might well have noted that, by the same token, research on Puerto Ricans and other Latinos has ignored them or blamed them for the condition of their education.

The research findings on elementary and secondary Hispanic students have been summarized by several commentators and do not merit detailed repetition here. However, the bulk of this literature falls into two conceptual categories: studies that blame Hispanics for their own school failures and studies that articulate a deficiency model of minority education, a model of remediation, or one of compensation. In the first view, minority communities are themselves to blame for not encouraging their children to do better in school and for not providing a more learner-centered home environment. In the second, a corollary view is offered to explain why these children do not act like children from the middle class and therefore require remedial efforts to overcome their cultural deprivation.

This record of poor evidence on Hispanic elementary and secondary student characteristics has severely limited research on Hispanic college populations. In particular, the K–12 attrition rates and disproportionate Hispanic attendance at two-year institutions create major problems for population validity and college entrance measures, which most frequently have been normed on Anglo or black cohorts. Breland (1979), for instance, has noted: "Although a few studies have been made of Hispanic groups, these are not sufficient to allow for any sound generalizations. Hispanics are often grouped with blacks to construct a minority population. Given the possibility of important linguistic influences, it seems essential that more studies be made—both in prediction and in internal analysis—for groups having had substantially different linguistic and cultural experiences" (p. 49).

Our understanding of Hispanic college students is not significantly increased by the available student literature. A major summary of research on college students published in 1973 reported no studies on Hispanic students (Feldman & Newman, 1973). This book is the first on Hispanic college students. However, one unpublished study of Chicano students in the University of California and California State University systems does suggest a methodologically and conceptually appropriate approach to understanding Hispanic undergraduates—that of analyzing the stress encountered. The research, updated in this book and originally reported in *A Study of the Chicano Experience in Higher Education* (Muñoz & García-Bahne, 1977), employed three instruments, two of which were designed specifically to test the minority experience in majority institutions. The first was a structured interview format, adapted from a study of black students in white colleges. The second was a general demographic questionnaire designed to test language and family characteristics. Finally, a standardized test to measure stress, the College Environmental Stress Index (CESI), was administered. The results revealed that

1. Chicanos and Chicanas reported greater stress levels than did their Anglo counterparts;
2. Anglo men and women were very similar regarding the intensity of stress they perceived;
3. Chicanos and Chicanas reported vast differences regarding the intensity of stress experienced, with Chicanas scoring higher at every level;
4. There were significant differences between Anglo women and Chicanas, which suggest that socioeconomic and cultural differences were more influential than their gender identity; and
5. Chicanas reported greater stress scores than did Chicano men, Anglo men, and Anglo women. In spite of their higher stress scores, however, Chicanas did not appear to have a higher attrition rate than Chicanos. Furthermore, Chicanas performed academically at a higher level than did Chicanos. Primary support systems for Chicanas seemed to be Chicano campus organizations and Chicana discussion groups. Chicanas and Chicanos were significantly more similar than any other groups in ranking events from most to least stressful, although they differed considerably with respect to the intensity of stress perceived (Muñoz & García-Bahne, 1977, pp. 9–18, 131–132).

While these findings do not surprise Hispanic educators, they reveal a marginalization of the students within a system that accommodates them only reluctantly, and they suggest the extent to which K–12 systems alienate Hispanic students—even the elite who graduate from high school and attend college. It seems clear that much work is needed on Hispanic student characteristics and achievement. The disappointing quality of Hispanic data in longitudinal and large-scale sample projects is indicative of the nescience of scholars and the consequent lack of research paradigms in this important area.

RESEARCH ON FINANCE

One area of Hispanic education on which significant attention has been focused, indirectly if not directly, is school finance research. As evidenced by the school finance litigation brought by Chicano litigants in *Serrano* and *Rodríguez* (*Serrano v. Priest,* 1971; *San Antonio Independent School District v. Rodríguez,* 1973), school finance equity considerations remain important to Hispanic educators and communities. The passage of Proposition 13 in California, however, has called into question the appropriateness of Senate Bill 90, the post-*Serrano* school finance mechanism, as have the more recent developments in the Los Angeles desegregation case.

In 1970, Coons, Clune, and Sugarman (1970, pp. 356–357) concluded that most minority children live in the wealthiest school districts, as measured by rankings of total assessed property value. However, a reanalysis of total-assessed-value data with assessed-value-per-pupil measures shows opposite results (Domínguez, 1977). In such a situation, it is necessary to establish ground rules in equity issues. The phrasing of fiscal inequities is extremely important; major efforts are required to review school finance decisions, summarize the equity implications, survey the technical considerations, and propose models of equitable school finance.

Another necessary K–12 finance initiative is bilingual education cost-index construction: Major data required include analyses of categorical programs, such as bilingual education, as well as more careful analyses of implementation of legal mandates. In California, for instance, bilingual programs include formula-based expenditures from the Educationally Disadvantaged Youth Program, Bilingual-Bicultural Programs (under A.B. 1329), Economic Impact Aid Program, and six additional state and federal programs. With proposed federal regulations for bilingual education meeting enormous resistance, it is urgent that realistic cost projections, personnel requirements, and assessment tools be developed. Additional federal initiatives to merge categorical programs into block grants will require better data on alleged cost savings and reduced overhead than those that exist at present.

There are four debates in higher-education finance that have major equity implications for Hispanics in higher education: two-year colleges, financial-aid packaging, financing graduate studies, and returns on schooling. While each of these is of obvious concern to majority students as well, the demographic condition and underrepresentation of Hispanics in higher education make these issues crucial for Hispanics. Although major technical and conceptual problems remain in analyzing these areas, more researchers have been investigating the problems, leading to greater clarity in these equity issues.

The resolution of the question "Do community colleges get their fair share of the funds?" is critical to Hispanic students because they are disproportionately enrolled in the two-year sector; in addition, there was a significant decline in Hispanic enrollment in the California community college system, due to the state's fiscal condition. Once again, the demographics of Hispanic enrollments make the study vital to an understanding of the underlying equity issues: If the distribution of Hispanic students throughout the postsecondary system is skewed into one sector, and that sector receives less than its "fair share" compared to the four-year sector, then there are serious questions of access and equity (Nelson, 1978, 1980). Two-year-college financing issues have two major dimensions: whether two-year institutions receive less money per student (or per student measure, as a full-time equivalent [FTE] formula), and whether students in two-year colleges receive less financial assistance than do their four-year counterparts. There are serious data deficiencies and major conceptual disagreements on both dimensions, and much work needs to be done in these areas.

Researchers employing different data sets or methodologies reach different conclusions in redistribution debates. The same is true in subsidy debates. Nelson and Breneman (1979) summarized the results of these arguments and categorized three intersectoral models: institutional spending per student, rates of state subsidies per sector, and comparisons of resources actually spent on a two-year student's education relative to those spent on a four-year-college student. In reviewing the conflicting results, the authors are persuaded that "community college students have approximately the same volume of resources spent on them and receive about as much subsidy as their counterparts at senior public institutions" (p. 33). They were particularly impressed by the arguments advanced by James, who reanalyzed 1966–67 data from a 1971 Carnegie Commission study—data that had shown only slight intersectoral disparities in favor of senior colleges. James measured subsidies (instructional costs minus tuition) and found evidence that two-year-college students "cost more and pay less" than do senior-college students (cited in Nelson, 1979). Hyde (1979) and Augenblick (1978) have concluded the opposite.

The short summary here of this complex debate obviously does not do justice to the topic. However, despite Nelson and Breneman's assertions that "the absence of serious expenditure differentials at least moves the burden of proof onto critics of the current funding patterns" (1979, p. 22), it is unclear whether the studies or the reanalyses of data warrant such an assertion. Several major issues have yet to be resolved; most important, the major studies have employed data that are not current. Indeed, the major data sets analyzed by Nelson and Breneman in 1979 dated back to 1964 and 1966–67. Since that time, the number of community colleges has increased considerably: The period between 1966 and 1974 saw more than one new public two-year college open each week, more than doubling the existing number of institutions—from 408 to 901. Even though the number of private two-year colleges declined, the total number of community colleges grew from 685 in 1966 to 1,151 in 1975. Further, agreement needs to be reached on how to account for capital expenditures. Two concerns should be paramount. First, capital expenditures are frequently administered by separate state agencies and bond authorities, so the construction costs and bond-repayment expenses vary even within state systems. Second, public two-year colleges rarely have dormitory facilities, in itself a measure of "opportunity" and a major consideration in any discussion of intersectoral equity.

FTE data are not an accurate measure for intersectoral comparisons because the two-year-college sector enrolls proportionately more part-time students than do senior colleges. For example, of the sixty largest colleges in the country, only one two-year college (Miami-Dade) enrolls more full-time than part-time students. Conversely, of the sixty, only six senior colleges enroll more part-time than full-time students. This difference, reflecting both comprehensive institutional missions and lack of residential facilities, means that an FTE measure in a two-year college is likely to be three or four students taking one course each (to equal twelve); the FTE measure in a senior college is likely to be one student taking twelve hours. The economies of scale become clear when the administrative costs (bursar, admission, financial aid, registrar, and so forth) are calculated to account for the increased number of registrants. Institutions are extraordinarily complex, with certain programs supporting other less popular or more expensive courses. This cross-subsidizing makes intersectoral comparisons difficult, particularly if technical or professional curricula are measured.

The debate on intersectoral subsidies has a counterpart in financial-aid awards: Do two-year colleges receive their "fair share" of student financial assistance? A study by Lawrence Gladieux (1975) answered "no" concerning campus-based programs—Supplemental Educational Opportunity Grants (SEOGs), National Direct Student Loans (NDSLs), and, to a lesser extent, the College Work Study Program (CWSP). He attributed this "underutilization" to a number of causes but found few systemic reasons for the pattern. He labeled the phenomenon an "enigma" and suggested that the community colleges themselves were not as entrepreneurial as senior colleges and that they were penalizing themselves by not placing more attention on the financial-aid function. Nelson, however, with more recent data, found less underutilization in the campus-based programs and found a "fair share" in Basic Educational Opportunity Grants (BEOGs). Further, she was critical of the "half-cost limitation," the differential treatment of veterans' benefits, and the data from which she drew her conclusions (Nelson, 1978). More attention by researchers to these intersectoral financial-aid patterns would enlighten the larger debates of distribution in the system and clarify our understanding of the effects of disproportionate Hispanic enrollments in the two-year sector.

Although both Gladieux and Nelson found a measure of underutilization in campus-based loan programs for two-year colleges, disaggregated packaging data for Hispanic freshmen tell a different story. In an analysis of 1972–73 financial-aid awards, Wagner and Rice (1977) found Hispanic students' packages to have a 10 percent higher proportion of loans—the only portion of packages that has to be repaid. In the first recent packaging study of Hispanic students, I found near-exclusive reliance upon grants by freshmen and concluded that need-based programs worked well but that the reliance upon grants portended problems. The data problems are particularly severe in this type of study, as are conceptual issues of "need" and appropriateness of packaging configurations. While there is no generally accepted "norm" for packaging financial assistance, Hispanics should have no more reimbursable aid in their packages than do majority students.

One possible reason for this finding may be the difficulty Hispanic families (and most low-income families) encounter in applying for assistance and in negotiating complex financial-aid applications. The financial-aid deadlines, for example, fall well before income tax returns are due, and poor families—who may or may not be required to file federal income tax forms—frequently miss deadlines for all nonreimbursable programs. Loans, however, can often be secured late in the admissions process, if students can negotiate the complex lending procedures. In this scenario, any first-come-first-served procedure would limit even the loan access for late filers. Moreover, poor families have to negotiate even more basic problems, such as whether financial aid will negatively affect public-assistance eligibility (it does, particularly for commuter students) or whether they can document their income, which frequently is paid in cash, with poor records (Mudrick, 1980).

These considerations, as well as the greater price elasticities of disadvantaged populations, should pose substantial questions for proponents of higher tuition/increased aid strategies. Even acknowledging the information barriers that all applicants (but particularly disadvantaged applicants) encounter, Nelson and Breneman (1979) conclude: "our analysis suggest that a higher tuition/higher aid strategy, the pricing policy traditionally supported by economists on efficiency grounds, is also the more equitable" (p. 33). Information theorists dispute this claim, as would those persons who saw rescissions across the board in BEOG payments for 1979–80. Concress disregarded the legislative reduction formula required by Title IV, initiating what became a series of trade-offs that disproportionately affected low-income students. The same is likely to happen again in Gramm-Rudman cutbacks.

A third consideration in Hispanic finance would be the manner in which Hispanic graduate students finance their studies. Data from the National Research Council (NRC) show that white and Hispanic students employ considerably different methods of financing this burden (NRC, 1980). The most evident disparity is the more obvious availability of teaching and research assistantships to white doctoral students. These patterns hold importance not only because of the basic issues of sustenance and living expenses but for informal and formal professional reasons. Assistantships are mainstream apprenticeship activities, involving graduate students in major teaching or research responsibilities with faculty mentors and departments.

Other data corroborate the need for further research on Hispanic graduate-education financing. NRC data for 1978 show that Hispanic doctoral students took an average of 10.2 years after the B.A. to complete the doctorate, with a total registered time of 6.3 years; for whites, it was 8.9 and 6.2 years, respectively (NRC, 1979). For Hispanics in 1979, the total time to the doctorate was 10 years, with a total registered time of 6.5 years; for whites it was 9.1 and 6.2 years, respectively (NRC, 1980). Thus, while the time in graduate school was similar, Hispanics took approximately one year longer, suggesting a longer time in the work force or a leave pattern different from that of whites.

Fellowship provisions are significant but largely unexplored. There is anecdotal evidence, for instance, that Title VII fellows become marginalized in elite universities and have difficulty securing intramural funding when the fellowships expire—usually during the dissertation-writing stage. The Ford Foundation doctoral fellowships were consolidated into a postdoctoral program, while the Graduate and Professional Opportunities Program (Title IX) fellowships to Hispanics have declined appreciably from 1978. There has not been any major change in Hispanic graduate enrollments or degrees since 1976, when the National Board on Graduate Education (1976) noted, "Mexican and Puerto Rican Americans appear to have the lowest [graduate] participation rates relative to other ethnic and minority groups" (p. 45).

A fourth area, returns on education to Hispanics, suggests itself in response to economists who argue that tangible benefits are more important than the less empirical "assumed-social-good" rationale advanced by many. Data in this area are particularly problematic. Refugee and immigration patterns, heterogeneity of the Hispanic work force, and historical exclusion from postsecondary education make research into educational returns difficult and cloud the equity issues. Therefore, studies have found unaccounted-for discrimination in pay differentials for Chicano workers, as well as higher returns on college investment to Chicano males than to Anglo males, even with lower absolute income for Chicanos. Although it is important for economists to sharpen these arguments, it is not clear whether Hispanics attempt to maximize their earning potential by attending college. Educational aspirations are a tangle of motivations, not all of them economic. Nonetheless, many Hispanic educators will need to address "returns on education" as a concern in increasing Hispanic participation in higher education.

GOVERNANCE RESEARCH

It is governance, particularly in the form of school boards or boards of trustees, that constitutes "the system" of education in the United States. State and local boards determine educational policy for school systems, while state coordinating or governing bodies and trustee boards determine higher education policy. Neither sector has been particularly responsive to the concerns of Hispanic parents or students, and the theoretical model of internal colonialism is premised largely upon such a system of unresponsiveness. While it is difficult to disentangle the electoral and political components of such a situation from the precise research questions posed by the condition, it is important to note that the history of Hispanic education has been one of struggle against insensitive government agencies and school boards, those organizations responsible for governing education systems. Whether this struggle has manifested itself in the form of litigation, political action, or legislation, the focus has continued to be upon sensitizing larger governance structures.

As on the institutional level, Hispanics have not historically had access to these structures: Few minorities are appointed or elected to school boards or to trustee boards. These boards and commissions are not "representative," however the norm may be defined. A 1978 study, for example, found only 1.1 percent (5 of 463) of state postsecondary commission members to be Hispanic, although the legislation requires the commissions to be "broadly and equitably representative of the general public" (Salazar & Martorana, 1978, table 2). Commission and board appointments constitute a major representative device in a democracy and are a significant policy arena, particularly as federal education policy shifts to a decentralized block-grant approach and as large amounts of federal financial aid are coordinated through states.

While a sense of history should inform all educational-governance research, in minority education most of the historical context has been a belated acknowledgment of racism and of slavery's effect upon the schooling of black children. Following the *Adams v. Califano* (1977) litigation, statewide boards have been involved in "desegregation" of public higher education. Because society tends to perceive desegregation solely in terms of black access into white institutions, the fate of historically black public colleges is uncertain. White and black colleges have been merged in order that the hybrid have no racial identity. While the lack of historically Hispanic colleges means that Hispanic students have little to fear from the *Adams* litigation, there is the danger of Hispanic student equity issues being ignored in *Adams* states with large black and Hispanic populations. This occurred in Texas, for instance, where the first Office for Civil Rights (OCR) study mandated by *Adams* did not examine Chicano access but instead concentrated upon the state's two public black colleges. No analysis of Chicano enrollment patterns, disproportionate community college attendance, or lack of Chicano faculty and staff was performed—although at the time, no Texas senior college had ever had a Chicano president. OCR has not exacted much from Texas institutions, and it is clear that little progress will result from the tepid plan (Martínez, 1983).

There has been little scholarly inquiry into the effects of racist immigration statutes on Asians, the systematic discrimination that continues against Native Americans, or exclusionary schooling policies affecting Hispanic children. The indicia of these practices are evident in minority educational achievement today, yet major historical analyses of minority schooling are rare. Nonetheless, legal decisions and administrative actions frequently turn upon the litigants' analyses of history, whether in quantifying school attendance zones, in measuring Hispanic children's historical access into bilingual educational programs, or even in arguing that Mexican Americans are to be included in desegregation plans.

These examples present persuasive evidence that Hispanics have not controlled the political or organizational structures of education but have been held in subordinate positions by school systems and postsecondary institutions. The victories of a few Hispanic parents or educators has not increased the quality of education for Hispanic students, and in several key indices, Hispanic educational conditions appear to have worsened. Moreover, the ascendancy of an Hispanic elite has been accomplished at great cost to these individuals, who frequently are ghettoized by majority policymakers and perceived pejoratively as compromisers by Hispanic communities. Although additional evidence of such structural discrimination is readily apparent, a theoretical explanation is essential for understanding how this condition could persist, even when major federal resources have been brought to bear upon school systems enrolling disadvantaged children. In fact, these resources have scarcely altered the patterns of governance, and a retreating federal commitment to education equity is evident.

HISPANIC EDUCATION AND INTERNAL COLONIALISM

In analyzing "academic colonialism," Arce (1978) noted that "the most prominent feature of the Chicano experience with higher education is its peripheralness relative to the overall academic enterprise." Arce developed a taxonomy of Chicano-Academe Contact Patterns within his framework of academic colonialism, modeled after Orlando Fals Borda's "colonialismo intelectual," a theory of marginalization in a South American context. In Arce's view, *academic colonialism* is

> the selective imposition of intellectual premises, concepts, methods, institutions, and related organizations on a subordinate group and/or the unselective and uncritical adoption and imitation of the intellectual premises, concepts, methods, institutions, and organizations of other groups, with the selection processes not being in the control of the subordinate group. Inherent in this definition is the monopolizing of the resources for academic enterprise (colleges and universities, foundation and government funding agency review boards, journals and other publishing outlets, etc.) by the dominant group and the provision of only limited and controlled access to these resources to the subordinate minority. (p. 77)

Within this scheme, there are six patterns that evolve from the subordinate Chicano role in higher education: structural accommodation and realignment, conscious assimilation, nationalist exhortative, affirmative action, independent transformational, and interdependent analytical. These patterns fall along axes of ideology and degree of infiltration within institutions, as shown in table I.1.

In the structural accommodation/realignment and conscious assimilation patterns, Hispanic students are docile and peripheral to the insti-

Table I.1:   Chicano-Academe Contact Patterns

	Institutional Relationship	
Ideology	Separated	Integrated
Marginal	Accommodation/realignment	Conscious assimilation
Co-optive	Nationalist exhortative	Affirmative action
Progressive	Independent transformational	Interdependent analytical

SOURCE: Adapted from Arce, 1978, p. 101.

tution. In the first typology, these students do not become involved in mainstream or ethnic activities on campus. They become marginalized, are likely to have high attrition rates, and if they do succeed in graduating, will in all likelihood have been average or below-average students in less demanding major fields of study. In the conscious assimilation pattern, Hispanic students are more likely to become involved in college activities but tend to shun ethnic identification or involvement. This Anglicization is a strong influence emanating from the college setting, and students who feel no sense of Hispanic community or whose families were not politicized are likely to be found in this category.

In the co-optive ideological categories, two major conservative practices prevail. Within the nationalist exhortative pattern, the singling out of outstanding Hispanics to serve as role models is combined with a tendency toward a romanticized reconstruction of history. The affirmative action pattern is more formal co-optation of Hispanic concerns manifested by specialized minority hiring to fill minority slots, which relieves the institutions of the need to integrate throughout their ranks. These responses to internal colonization are understandable, for curricula and instruction are sorely in need of Hispanic perspectives and revision, while existing job discrimination has excluded many Hispanics from any substantial employment in education. The danger, though, is clear when *Cinco de Mayo* festivities substitute for more extensive curriculum revision and when hiring is limited to affirmative action, bilingual education, or creating token positions.

The final two patterns exist primarily in theory, for they require an extraordinary combination of people, resources, and timing to exist and mature. As this model suggests, the system of structural discrimination present in American education makes progressive educational movements for minorities almost impossible. The independent transformational pattern is feasible only in a historically Hispanic institution, only three of which exist in the mainland United States, or in community-based organizations and alternative schools. Such alternatives to main-

stream institutions and school systems probably have their best ana-
logues in tribally controlled community colleges (which receive government funds) or in quasi-academic units such as research or training
divisions in Hispanic community-based organizations. The second progressive approach, the interdependent analytical pattern, links Hispanic
academics across institutional or disciplinary lines. Examples include the
National Chicano Council on Higher Education, the Special Interest
Group on Hispanic Research of the American Educational Research
Association, and similar collaborative intellectual exchange mechanisms.
The focus is on intellectual self-development and solidarity with other
Hispanic academics, which may be practiced through visiting appoint-
ments, professional meetings, caucuses, or other informal means.

As is evident in these patterns, marginalization is a major feature of
Hispanic participation in higher education, confirmed most notably in
attrition and underparticipation data. Those who do enter the system do
so in a peripheral, nonthreatening manner; more radical participation is
extremely rare and unlikely to generate its own resources or continuation. Observers on the scene of Hispanic education will recognize these
patterns not as rough approximations but as strikingly accurate portray-
als of the condition. While they are essentially pessimistic compared to
the Brazilian and Chilean experiences detailed in Paulo Freire's (1973)
notion of *conscientizacao,* these categories reflect an accurate ideological
and operational reality.

Arce's work complements the larger labor-market-segmentation
theory developed by Chicano scholar Mario Barrera. In particular,
Barrera's (1979) explication of an internal colonial model extends the
Arce thesis. Because the model has been most frequently employed to
explain labor discrimination, academic job discrimination against Hispanic educators is powerfully illuminated. Barrera uses University of
California hiring practices as evidence of structural discrimination,
concluding that in most organizations, structural discrimination against
Chicanos consists of labor repression, wage differentials, occupational
stratification, reserve labor pools, and peripheral buffer-role policies.
Bonilla and Campos (1981) have analyzed a similar colonial exploitation
of Puerto Ricans, noting that "the root problems of educational inequity
for Puerto Ricans remain unresolved and largely unaddressed" (p. 164).
These economic analyses suggest a circularity in defining Hispanic
educational inequality: Hispanics are undereducated because they have
been historically exploited, and their poverty precludes them from
further education. While this circle could conceivably surround many
discrete American groups, none except Native Americans can claim such
a long and misunderstood history of exclusion and underparticipation.

However defined or measured, Hispanics' participation in education is proportionate neither to their percentage of the U.S. population nor to their percentage of the school-age population. Although several scholars have questioned the validity of work within the internal colonialism framework (Muñoz, 1983), it has not been critically employed in the study of education, where it holds much promise.

While the foregoing discussion established the condition and described theories of Hispanic underparticipation, the measurement and understanding of root causes are crude and preliminary. The final section suggests a possible agenda for research on the condition of Hispanic education, focusing on structural, demographic, and historical means of inquiry, and introduces the articles that follow.

SUMMARY AND RESEARCH RECOMMENDATIONS: LATINOS IN HIGHER EDUCATION

At present, we can lay claim to only rudimentary knowledge about Hispanics in education and the socioeconomic and political forces that characterize the internal colonial status of Hispanics in American society. As Barrera (1979) has conceded, "for the foreseeable future, the politics of the Chicano community can be expected to revolve around both class and colonial divisions in a complex manner whose outlines we can only dimly perceive in the current period of confusion and redefinition" (p. 219). He might also have included Puerto Ricans and other Latinos, because population statistics aggregate Spanish-origin data; and even Cubans, perceived to be the least disadvantaged Hispanic group, find themselves victims of anti-Spanish-language and antirefugee hysteria. While popular hysteria and anti-immigration attitudes are the most extreme forms of negative behavior toward Hispanics, institutional practices that methodically exclude Hispanic participation present a far more serious and systemic barrier.

A research agenda for examining institutional attitudes requires two major foci: examination of *structural* phenomena and analysis of *individuals* within institutions. As detailed earlier, even when the data are inadequate and the methodologies frequently inappropriate, the condition of education for Hispanics remains poor relative to Anglo or other minority populations. This condition, manifested in several important, though indirect, indices, suggests an inquiry into organizational features. For instance, measuring Hispanic participation in school, despite its seeming simplicity, has not been done well: Schools are understandably reluctant to report their attrition rates accurately, particularly when funding formulas are based on attendance figures. Despite school finance litigation, complex appropriations and fiscal procedures often render school expenditure data incomparable. Sheer measurement difficulties, therefore, have presented researchers and policymakers with an incomplete picture of important school features. The debate concerning community college financing is a postsecondary example of the structural debate: How can intersectoral-equity arguments be mounted when there is no agreement on what an FTE expenditure represents in a two-year or senior college?

At the individual level, we know precious little about Hispanic students, in large part because survey methodologies have been inadequate in measuring Hispanic community characteristics. For instance, the National Assessment of Educational Progress (1977) has severe regional restrictions and poorly designed questions on language usage, while the Survey of Income and Education (1980) has the flaws of minority census data. Even the greatly improved minority information from the High School and Beyond data have been badly analyzed: A recent HSB study on minority students in private and Catholic secondary schools noted that "no distinction is possible in the present research between Cuban, Puerto Rican, and Mexican Hispanics" (Greeley, 1981, p. 8) when the data were able to be disaggregated. Indeed, the study indicated that 30 percent of Hispanic private school students were Cuban, a fact that would severely limit public policy implications for Mexican and Puerto Rican children.

This volume, a collaborative effort among colleagues trained in many disciplines, was an attempt to begin rectifying the nescience of the larger research community. Not unexpectedly, the condition of Hispanic data is poor. Nonetheless, even within the limitations of national data bases, the first four authors have found powerful evidence of Hispanic educational disadvantage in the transition from high school to college: Vilma Ortiz, using the National Longitudinal Surveys; Ernesto Ballesteros, using the Cooperative Institutional Research Program data; François Nielsen, using the High School and Beyond set; and Richard Santos, using the National Longitudinal Surveys. Each is a sophisticated user of the data, and these four papers give no evidence of the fallacy of "controlling for poverty." Rather, the four authors have shown, even with major data limitations, that Hispanics are demonstrably disadvantaged.

As in the use of data sets, so has theory been deficient in understanding Hispanic disadvantage. It is clear, however, that a cadre of

Hispanic psychologists and psychometricians is questioning old practical assumptions and proposing new directions for theory building on Hispanic achievement. The papers by Daniel Muñoz, José Mestre, Richard Durán, and Maria Pennock-Román critically examine the assumptions of widely accepted educational practices—admissions testing, counseling, measuring achievement—and find them wholly inadequate for Hispanic populations. Their careful research should begin to shift the burden of persuasion to those who would blindly apply old measures to new populations; each has suggested ways in which the merit of Hispanic students can be better measured and developed.

The third section forcefully presents analyses of major barriers to Hispanic access. My own research on financial-aid practices, based upon a particularly rich national data set, provides powerful evidence that government financial-aid programs, particularly need-based programs, are delivering major resources to Hispanic students. The essay does point to several troubling trends, however, particularly to the institutional practice of nearly exclusively employing federal aid for Hispanics while employing a more diversified portfolio of resources for non-Hispanic students. It warns that federal cutbacks in financial-aid programs will disproportionately affect Hispanic students and that information inequities may hurt efforts to distribute financial assistance. María Chacón, Elizabeth Cohen, and Sharon Strover have examined the barriers Chicanas encounter and find them to be substantially different from those encountered by either Chicanos or Anglo women. Not only do these findings corroborate earlier research by Muñoz and other contributors to this volume, but they pose larger questions about Hispanic access. Anglo and black women enroll at rates higher than those for white and black males, whereas Latinas enroll in substantially lower proportions. This paper, by focusing upon the time spent on domestic tasks, suggests reasons why the condition of Hispanic women's education is so poor and challenges Latinos and educators to improve this condition. The final essay, by Richard Verdugo, reviews stratification literature and adds to our understanding of the role played by racial ideology and colonialism in the condition of Hispanic education. All these papers remind readers that substantial educational reform will not be accomplished without more comprehensive social and economic reform.

NOTE
1. Data cited in this chapter, where not otherwise indicated, are from the National Center for Education Statstics special tabulations. I thank Samuel Peng and Jeffrey Owings from NCES for their assistance and support.

REFERENCES ON HISPANIC EDUCATION

Adams v. Califano, 430 F.Supp. 118 (D.D.C. 1977).

Aday, L. (1980). Methodological issues in health care surveys of the Spanish heritage population. *American Journal of Public Health, 70,* 367–374.

Admissions Testing Program. Unpublished 1979–80 SAT data.

Aguirre, A. (1979). The sociolinguistic situation of bilingual Chicano adolescents in a California border town. *Aztlán: International Journal of Chicano Studies Research, 10,* 55–67.

Allsup, C. (1977). Education is our freedom: The American GI forum and the Mexican American school segregation in Texas, 1948–1957. *Aztlán: International Journal of Chicano Studies Research, 8,* 27–50.

American Institutes for Research in the Behavioral Sciences. (1979). *Evaluation of the impact of ESEA Title VII Spanish/English bilingual education programs.* Palo Alto, CA: AIR.

Andes, J. (1974). *Developing trends in content of collective bargaining contracts in higher education.* Washington, DC: Academic Collective Bargaining Information Service.

Applied Management Sciences. (1980). *Study of the impact of the Middle Income Student Assistance Act (MISAA).* Silver Spring, MD: AMS.

Arce, C. (1978). Chicano participation in academe: A case of academic colonialism. *Grito del Sol: A Chicano Quarterly 3,* 75–104.

Arias, B. (1980). Issues in tri-ethnic desegregation. Paper presented at the meeting of the American Educational Research Association, Boston.

Aspira. (1976). *Social factors in educational attainment among Puerto Ricans in U.S. metropolitan areas, 1970.* New York: Aspira.

Astin, A. (1975). *The myth of equal access in public higher education.* Paper presented at the meeting of the Southern Education Foundation.

Augenblick, J. (1978). *Issues in financing community colleges.* Denver, CO: Educational Commission of the States.

Augenblick, J., & Hyde, W. (1979). *Patterns of funding, net price and financial need for postsecondary education students.* Denver: ECS.

Barrera, M. (1979). *Race and class in the Southwest.* Notre Dame, IN: University of Notre Dame Press.

Beck, M. (1976). *The analysis of Hispanic texts.* New York: Bilingual Press.

Berdahl, R. (1971). *Statewide coordination of higher education.* Washington, DC: American Council on Education.

Bonilla, F., & Campos, R. (1981, spring). A wealth of poor: Puerto Ricans in the new economic order. *Daedulus,* 133–176.

Boshier, R. (1972). The effect of academic failure on self-concept and maladjustment indices. *Journal of Educational Research, 65,* 347–351.

Breland, H. (1981). *Assessing student characteristics in admissions to higher education.* New York: College Entrance Examination Board.

Bridge, G. (1978). Information imperfections: The Achilles' heel of entitlement plans. *School Review, 86,* 504–529.

Brown, G., Rosen, N., Hill, S., & Olivas, M. (1980). *The condition of education for Hispanic Americans*. Washington, DC: National Center for Education Statistics.

Brunner, S., & Gladieux, L. (1979). *Student aid and tuition in Washington State*. Washington, DC: College Entrance Examination Board.

Burbules, N. (1979) *Equity, equal opportunity, and education*. Stanford, CA: Institute for Finance and Governance.

Burbules, N., & Sherman, A. (1979) *Equal educational opportunity: Ideal or ideology?* Stanford, CA: Institute for Finance and Governance.

Cárdenas, J. (1976). *Bilingual education cost analysis*. San Antonio, TX: Intercultural Development Research Associates.

Carter, T. (1970). *Mexican Americans in school*. New York: College Entrance Examination Board.

Carter, T., & Segura, R. (1979). *Mexican Americans in school: A decade of change*. New York: College Entrance Examination Board.

Catterall, J., & Thresher, T. (1979). *Proposition 13: The campaign, the vote, and the immediate aftereffects for California schools*. Stanford, CA: Institute for Finance and Governance.

Condition of Education, 1978, 1984. (1979, 1985). Washington, DC: National Center for Education Statistics.

Conlisk, J. (1977). A further look at the Hansen-Weisbrod-Pechman debate. *Journal of Human Resources, 10*, 147– 163.

Conrad, C., & Cosand, J. (1976). *The implications of federal higher education policy*. Washington, DC: American Association for Higher Education.

Coons, J., & Sugarman, S. (1978). *Education by choice*. Berkeley: University of California Press.

Coons, J., Clune, W., & Sugarman, S. (1970). *Private wealth and public education*. Cambridge: Harvard University Press.

Crain, R., & Mahard, R. (1978). *The influence of high school racial composition in Black college attendance and achievement test performance*. Santa Monica, CA: RAND

Cronbach, L., Yalow, E., & Schaeffer, G. (1979). *Setting cut scores in selection: A mathematical structure for examining policies*. Stanford, CA: Institute for Finance and Governance.

Dill, D. (1979). Teaching in the field of higher education: Politics of higher education courses. *Review of Higher Education, 2*, 30–33.

Domínguez, J. (1977). School finance: The issues of equity and efficiency. *Aztlán—International Journal of Chicano Studies Research, 8*, 175–199.

Drake, S. (1977). *A study of community and junior college boards of trustees*. Washington, DC: American Association of Community and Junior Colleges.

Durán, R. (1983). *Hispanics' education and background*. New York: College Entrance Examination Board.

Education Commission of the States. (1978). Summary of state regulations. *Higher Education in the States, 6*, 125–148.

Educational Testing Service. (1979). *Principles, policies, and procedural guidelines regarding ETS products and services*. Princeton, NJ: ETS.

Epstein, N. (1977). *Language, ethnicity, and the schools:* Washington, DC: Institute for Educational Leadership.

Estrada, L. (1979). A chronicle of the political, legislative and judicial advances in bilingual education in California. In R. Padilla (Ed.), *Bilingual education and public policy in the United States* (pp. 77–108). Ypsilanti, MI: Eastern Michigan University.

Fals Borda, O. (1970). *Ciencia propia y colonialismo intelectual.* Mexico City: Editorial Nuestro Tiempo.

Feldman, K., & Newman, T. (1973). *The impact of college on students.* San Francisco: Jossey-Bass.

Fernández, E. (1975). *Comparison of persons of Spanish surname and persons of Spanish origin in the United States.* Washington, DC: U.S. Bureau of the Census.

Finn, C. (1978). *Scholars, dollars and bureaucrats.* Washington, DC: Brookings Institution.

Fishman, J. (1966). *Language loyalty in the United States.* The Hague: Mouton.

Flores, F., et al. (1977). Right of undocumented children to attend public schools in Texas. *Chicano Law Review, 4,* 61–93.

Flores, R. (1978). *The economic returns of a college education to Mexican Americans.* Paper presented at the meeting of the Southwestern Social Science Association, San Diego.

Franssinetti, A. (1978). La marginalidad en América Latina: Una bibliografía comentada. *Revista Mexicana de Sociología, 15,* 221–331.

Freire, P. (1973). *Education for critical consciousness.* New York: Seabury Press.

García, J. (1979). Bilingual education program fiscal accountability. In R. Padilla (Ed.), *Bilingual education and public policy in the United States* (pp. 229–244). Ypsilanti, MI: Eastern Michigan University.

García, J. (1976). *Cost analysis of bilingual, special, and vocational public school programs in New Mexico.* Unpublished doctoral dissertation, University of New Mexico.

García, J. (1980). Ethnic identity and background traits: Explorations of Mexican-origin populations. *La Red/The Net, 29,* 2.

General Accounting Office. (1980). *The National Institute of Education should further increase minority and female participation in its activities.* Washington, DC: GAO.

Gladieux, L. (1975). *Distribution of federal student assistance: The enigma of two-year colleges.* Washington, DC: College Entrance Examination Board.

Gladieux, L., & Byce, C. (1980). *As middle-income student aid expands, are low-income students losing out?* Unpublished manuscript, College Entrance Examination Board.

Gladieux, L., & Wolanin, T. (1976). *Congress and the colleges.* Lexington, MA: Heath.

Golub, L. (1978). Evaluation design and implementation of a bilingual education program. *Education and Urban Society, 10,* 363–384.

Greeley, A. (1981). *Minority students in Catholic secondary schools.* Unpublished manuscript, National Opinion Research Center, Chicago.

Guerrero, M. (1979). Substantive due process for resident aliens. *Aztlán: International Journal of Chicano Studies Research, 10,* 31–54.

Gutierrez, F., et al. (1979). *Spanish-language radio in the southwestern United States.* Monograph Series. Austin: University of Texas.

Halstead, D. K. (1974). *Statewide Planning in Higher Education.* Washington, DC: U.S. Government Printing Office.

Hansen, J., & Gladieux, L. (1978). *Middle-income students: A new target for financial aid.* Washington, DC: College Entrance Examination Board.

Hanson, W., & Weisbrod, B. (1969). *Benefits, costs and finance of public higher education.* Chicago: Markham.

Haro, C. M. (1977). *Mexicano/Chicano concerns and school desegregation in Los Angeles.* Los Angeles: Chicano Studies Research Center Publications.

Hayes-Bautista, D. (1980). Identifying "Hispanic" populations: The influence of research methodology upon public policy. *American Journal of Public Health, 70,* 353–356.

Heffernan, J. (1973). The credibility of the credit hour. *Journal of Higher Education, 44,* 61–72.

Henderson, E., & Long, B. (1971). Personal-social correlates of academic success among disadvantaged school beginners. *Journal of School Psychology, 9,* 101–113.

Hernández, J. (1975). La migración Puertorriquena como factor demográfico: Solución y problema. *Revista Interamericana, 4,* 526–534.

Hernández, J., Alvirez, D., & Estrada, L. (1973). Census data and the problem of conceptually defining the Mexican American population. *Social Science Quarterly, 53,* 671–687.

Hernández, N. (1973). Variables affecting achievement of middle school Mexican-American students. *Review of Educational Research, 43,* 1–39.

Hyde, W. (1979). *The equity of the distribution of student financial aid.* Denver, CO: Education Commission of the States.

Jackson, G. (1979). *Community colleges and budget reduction.* Stanford, CA: Institute for Finance and Governance.

Johnson, J. (1979, April 12). Hispanic "label" protested. *Washington Post,* p. C4.

Katz, D., & Weiner, F. (1979). *Proposition 13 and the public schools: The first year.* Stanford, CA: Institute for Finance and Governance.

King, L. (1975). *The Washington lobbyists for higher education.* Lexington, MA: Heath.

Klees, S. (1974). *The role of information in the market for education services.* Occasional paper in the Economics and Politics of Education. Stanford, CA: Stanford University Press.

Korman, F., & Valenzuela, N. (1973). Patterns of mass media use and attitudes about mass media among selected Anglo and Chicano opinion leaders. *Aztlán: International Journal of Chicano Studies Research, 4,* 335–342.

Levin, B., et al. (1972). *Paying for public schools: Issues of school finance in California.* Washington, DC: Urban Institute.

Levin, H. (1979). *Educational vouchers and social policy.* Stanford, CA: Institute for Finance and Governance.

Levin, H. (1977). Postsecondary entitlements: An exploration. In N. Kurland (Ed.), *Entitlement studies* (pp. 1–51). Washington, DC: National Institute of Education.

Locks, N., Pletcher, B., & Reynolds, D. (1978). *Language assessment instruments for limited-English-speaking students, a needs analysis.* Washington, DC: National Institute of Education.

López, R. W., Madrid-Barela, A., & Macías, R. (1976). *Chicanos in higher education: status and issues.* Monograph No. 7. Los Angeles: Chicano Studies Center Publications, University of California, Los Angeles.

Lowry, I. (1980). *The science and politics of ethnic enumeration.* Paper presented at the meeting of the American Association for the Advancement of Science.

McGuinness, A. (1975). *The changing map of postsecondary education.* Denver, CO: Education Commission of the States.

McGuire, J. (1976). The distribution of subsidy to students in California public higher education. *Journal of Human Resources, 1,* 35–57.

Machlis, P. (1973). The distributional effects of public higher education in New York City. *Public Finance Quarterly,* 35–37.

Martínez, J. (1977). *Chicano psychology.* New York: Academic Press.

Martínez, O. (1978). Chicano oral history: Status and prospects. *Aztlán: International Journal of Chicano Studies Research, 9,* 119–131.

Martínez, R. (1983, December 2). Testimony before the U.S. House postsecondary subcommittee. Houston, Texas.

Martínez, V., & Lara, M. (1978). "Who gets in?" *Self-Determination Quarterly Journal, 2,* 17–25.

Martorana, S., & Nespoli, L. (1978). *Regionalism in American postsecondary education: Concepts and practices.* University Park: Pennsylvania State University.

Mexican American Legal Defense and Educational Fund. (1980). *Law school admissions study.* San Francisco: MALDEF.

Millard, R. (1976). *State boards of higher education.* Washington, DC: Higher Education.

Morris, L. (1979). *Elusive equality.* Washington, DC: Howard University Press.

Mudrick, N. (1980). *The interaction of public assistance and student financial aid.* Washington, DC: College Entrance Examination Board.

Muñoz, C. (1983). The quest for paradigm: The development of Chicano studies and intellectuals. In *History, Culture, and Society: Chicano Studies in the 1980s* (pp. 19–36). Ypsilanti, MI: Bilingual Press.

Muñoz, C., & Rodríguez, P. (1977). Origen, distribución y eficiencia del gasto educativo en México. *Revista del Centro de Estudios Educativos, 7,* 1–54.

Muñoz, D., & Garcia-Bahne, B. (1977). *A study of the Chicano experience in higher education.* Washington, DC: National Institute of Mental Health.

National Assessment of Educational Progress. (1977). *Hispanic student achievement in five learning areas.* Denver: NAEP.

National Board on Graduate Education. (1976). *Minority group participation in graduate education.* Washington, DC: NBGE.

National Institute of Education. (1979). *Survey of career information systems.* NIE Project 400-79-9920.

National Institute of Education. (1977). *Women and minorities in education R&D.* Washington, DC: NIE.

National Research Council. (1980). *Summary report 1979, doctorate recipients from United States universities.* Washington, DC: NRC.

National Research Council. (1979). *Summary report 1978, doctorate recipients from United States universities.* Washington, CD: NRC.

Navy BOOST. (1980). Washington, DC: NROTC.

Navy ROTC Bulletin, 1981. (1980). Washington, DC: NROTC.

Nelson, S. (1980). *Community colleges and their share of student financial assistance.* Washington, DC: College Entrance Examination Board.

Nelson, S. (1979). *Community college finance in California: Equity implications in the aftermath of Proposition 13.* Unpublished manuscript, Brookings Institution.

Nelson, S. (1978). *The equity of public subsidies for higher education: Some thoughts on the literature.* Denver, CO: Education Commission of the States.

Nelson, S., & Breneman, D. (1979, December). *An equity perspective on community college finance.* Paper presented at the meeting of the UK/US Conference on Collective Choice in Education.

Newman, M. (1978). A profile of Hispanics in the U.S. work force. *Monthly Labor Review, 101,* 3–14.

Nielsen, F., & Fernández, R. (1981). *Hispanics and the High School and Beyond data.* Unpublished manuscript, National Opinion Research Center, Chicago.

Ogbu, J. (1978). *Minority education and caste.* New York: Academic Press.

Olivas, M. (1979). *The dilemma of access.* Washington, DC: Howard University Press.

Olivas, M. (1981). *Financial aid: Access and packaging policies.* Stanford, CA: IFG.

Olivas, M. (1982). Hispanics in higher education: Status and issues. *Educational Evaluation and Policy Analysis, 4,* 301–310.

Olivas, M. (1982). Information inequities: A fatal flaw in parochiaid plans. In E. Gaffney (Ed.), *Government's role in non-public education* (pp. 133–152). Notre Dame, IN: University of Notre Dame Press.

Olivas, M. (1983). Research and theory on Hispanic education: Students, finance, and governance. *Aztlán: International Journal of Chicano Studies Research, 14,* 111–146.

Olivas, M., & Hill, S. (1980). Hispanic participation in postsecondary education. In Brown et al., (pp. 117–216).

Olmedo, E. (1977). Psychological testing and the Chicano: A reassessment. In J. Martínez (Ed.), *Chicano psychology.* New York: Academic Press.

Olmedo, E., & Padilla, A. (1978). An empirical and construct validation of a scale of acculturation for Mexican Americans. *Journal of Social Psychology, 105,* 781–790.

Pacheco, A. (1980). *Educational vouchers and their implications for equity.* Stanford, CA: Institute for Finance and Governance.

Padilla, A. (1979). Critical factors in the testing of Hispanic Americans: A review and some suggestions for the future. In *Testing, Teaching, and Learning.* Washington, DC: National Institute of Education.

Padilla, R. (1979). *Bilingual education and public policy in the United States.* Ypsilanti, MI: Eastern Michigan University.

Panel for the Review of Laboratory and Center Operations. (1978). *Report to NIE.* Washington, DC: National Institute of Education.

Pechman, J. (1970). The distributional effects of public higher education in California. *Journal of Human Resources,* 361–370.

Peñalosa, F. (1970). Toward an operational definition of the Mexican American. *Aztlán: International Journal of Chicano Studies Research, 1,* 1–12.

Peterson, G. (1972). *The regressivity of the residential property tax.* Washington, DC: Urban Institute.

Pfeffer, L. (1974). Aid to parochial schools: The verge and beyond. *Journal of Law and Education, 3,* 115–121.

Poston, D., & Alvírez, D. (1973). On the cost of being a Mexican American worker. *Social Science Quarterly, 53,* 697–709.

Roaden, A., & Worthen, B. (1976). Research assistantship experiences and subsequent research productivity. *Research in Higher Education, 5,* 141–158.

Salazar, J. L. (1977). *State 1202 commission member characteristics and positions on issues of importance to postsecondary education.* Unpublished doctoral dissertation, Pennsylvania State University.

Salazar, J. L., & Martorana, S. (1978). *State postsecondary education planning (1202) commissions: A first look.* University Park: Pennsylvania State University.

San Antonio Independent School District v. Rodríguez, 411 U.S. 1 (1973).

Serrano v. Priest, 487 P.2d 1241 (1971).

Siegel, J., & Passell, J. (1979). *Coverage of the Hispanic population of the United States in the 1970 census.* Washington, DC: U.S. Bureau of the Census.

Southern Regional Education Board. (1980). *Black and Hispanic enrollment in higher education, 1978.* Atlanta, GA: SREB.

Survey of Income and Education. (1980). *Characteristics of Hispanic postsecondary students.* Washington, DC: NCES.

Troike, R. (1978). *Research evidence for the effectiveness of bilingual education.* Rosslyn, VA: National Clearinghouse for Bilingual Education.

U.S. Bureau of the Census. (1980). *Conference on census undercount.* Washington, DC: U.S. Bureau of the Census.

U.S. Commission on Civil Rights. (1974). *Counting the forgotten.* Washington, DC: USCCR.

U.S. Commission on Civil Rights. (1978). *Improving Hispanic unemployment data.* Washington, DC: USCCR.

Valdez, A. (1979). The role of mass media in the public debate over bilingual education. In R. Padilla (Ed.), *Bilingual education and public policy in the United States* (pp. 175–188). Ypsilanti, MI: Eastern Michigan University.

Wagner, A., & Rice, L. (1977). *Student financial aid: Institutional packaging and family expenditure patterns.* Washington, DC: College Entrance Examination Board.

Windham, D. (1970). *Education, equality and income redistribution.* Lexington, MA: Heath.

Windham, D. (1980). *The benefits and financing of American higher education: Theory, research, and policy.* Stanford, CA: IFG.

Zimmerman, D. (1973). Expenditure-tax incidence studies, public higher education, and equity. *National Tax Journal, 26,* 65–70.

I | The Transition from High School to College

1 | Generational Status, Family Background, and Educational Attainment Among Hispanic Youth and Non-Hispanic White Youth

VILMA ORTIZ

The rapid growth of the Hispanic population in the United States during the past decade and the economically disadvantaged position of this population have led both policymakers and researchers to realize that there is much to be learned about our country's second largest minority group. One segment of the Hispanic population that merits special attention is its youth. Compared to majority white youth, Hispanic youth are disadvantaged in many respects but especially with regard to educational attainment (Brown, Rosen, Hill, & Olivas, 1980; Borus, Crowley, Rumberger, Santos, & Shapiro, 1980; U.S. Bureau of the Census, 1980). Hispanic youth not only are more likely to have acquired fewer years of schooling but are also disadvantaged along other indicators characterizing the educational process. Two important disparities in the education of Hispanic youth as compared to majority youth are that Hispanics are more likely to be delayed in school and to drop out of high school (Brown et al., 1980). Furthermore, while similar percentages of Hispanic high school graduates and non-Hispanic white high school graduates go on to college, Hispanics are further disadvantaged in that they are considerably more likely to attend two-year colleges and to not complete

This research was supported by a contract from the Department of Labor's Employment and Training Administration (No. 99-1-1588-33-3), to the National Council of La Raza. Institutional support was also provided by the Hispanic Research Center at Fordham University and the Institute for Social Research at the University of Michigan. I gratefully acknowledge comments made by Rosemary Santana Cooney, Douglas Gurak, and Carlos Arce.

29

their college education. Thus research on the educational attainment of Hispanics should focus not only on years of schooling acquired but on educational outcomes, such as the likelihood of dropping out of high school.

A considerable amount of sociological research has focused on factors that influence educational attainment. In the original model developed by Blau and Duncan (1967), the impact of father's education and occupation on son's education was examined. The model was later elaborated on to include number of siblings, the presence of two parents in the household, and characteristics of the mother (Duncan & Duncan, 1968; Duncan, Featherman, & Duncan, 1972; Featherman & Hauser, 1978; Sewell, Hauser, & Wolf, 1980). This research has shown that family background has a sizable impact on years of schooling acquired since it represents the mechanism by which achievement values, economic resources, and information about the world of work are transmitted intergenerationally.

The facts that Hispanics are more likely to come from disadvantaged families and to be recent immigrants have implications for their educational attainment. Recent immigrants are likely to be disadvantaged socioeconomically in comparison to later generations, and socioeconomic background has a strong impact on attainment. Featherman and Hauser (1978) provide evidence on the role of family background in explaining educational differences among generational groups. Foreign-born persons of different nationalities were found to have considerably fewer years of schooling in comparison to second and later generations, with the second and later generations not differing to a large extent. After controlling for family background, the first generation continued to be disadvantaged educationally, although less so, and the second generation was shown to have acquired more years of schooling than later generations. Thus the second generation achieved an educational level similar to or higher than that of later generations from similar backgrounds. Featherman and Hauser make these generational comparisons across national-origin groups as well as for Mexicans (the only national-origin group for which there was a sufficient number of respondents to analyze separately). The results for Mexicans were similar; the first generation had a significantly lower educational level than later generations, and the second generation a significantly higher level than later generations, after controlling for family background.

Featherman and Hauser (1978) also examined the impact of family background on educational attainment separately for generational groups across different national-origin groups. They found that family background was less influential in explaining variability in educational attainment among the second generation than among the first generation or later generations. This effect was due primarily to the weaker impact of father's education on attainment among the second generation. Thus the process by which family background affects achievement was found to vary by generational status.

These results are further supported by findings obtained by Cooney, Rogler, Correale, and Ortiz (1980) where the impact of family background on educational attainment among Puerto Rican immigrants was compared to that of their adult children, who were primarily second-generation or had arrived on the U.S. mainland during their preschool years. Father's characteristics had a significant impact on the educational attainment of the parents but not on the attainment of the children. In addition, Peñalosa and McDonagh's (1966) study of second-generation Mexicans in California found no relationship between parents' occupations and respondents' education, while Hirschman's (1978) study of first-generation Mexicans in Texas found significant relationships between fathers' education and occupational status and the respondents' education. In sum, these studies demonstrate that parental characteristics have a stronger impact on the achievements of the first generation and third generation than on the achievements of the second generation.

The results of these prior studies point to the unique experience of the second generation in the educational process and the intergenerational transmission of socioeconomic status. What implications does this have for the attainment of Hispanic youth? Because of the relatively recent immigration history of Hispanics to the United States, Hispanic youth are mostly first- and second-generation.[1] In addition, because of the socioeconomic position of Hispanics in this society, Hispanic youth are especially likely to come from disadvantaged backgrounds. Thus generational status and family background are certain to be important factors explaining the achievement of Hispanic youth. In this paper, the educational attainment of first-, second-, and third-generation Hispanic youth is compared to that of non-Hispanic white youth before and after controlling for family background. This analysis addresses the question of whether the achievement of second-generation Hispanic youth is greater than that of other Hispanic generational groups and greater than that of non-Hispanic white youth once family background is held constant. In addition, the impact of family-background characteristics on educational attainment is examined separately for Hispanic youth and non-Hispanic white youth and for generational groups within Hispanics, thus addressing the question of whether the *process* of achievement for Hispanic youth, and in particular the second-generation, differs from that of non-Hispanic white youth. Specifically, do parental

characteristics, especially parents' educational attainment, have less impact among second-generation Hispanic youth than among first- or
third-generation Hispanic youth or non-Hispanic white youth?

DATA AND METHODS

The analysis presented in this paper is based on the Youth Cohort of the
National Longitudinal Surveys of Labor Market Experiences conducted
by Ohio State University. The data used in this analysis are from the first-
year interviews collected in 1979 of a five-year longitudinal survey. This
cohort of approximately 12,700 youths was sampled to be nationally
representative of youths between the ages of fourteen and twenty-one.
In addition, Hispanics and blacks were oversampled; disadvantaged
non-Hispanic, nonblack youth were oversampled; and youth enlisted in
the military were oversampled.

The focus of this paper is on Hispanic youth and native-born non-
Hispanic white youth; therefore, blacks and other nonwhite groups were
excluded from the analysis. Race and ethnicity were obtained using a
self-identification measure in which respondents could identify with
more than one racial or ethnic group. Respondents who identified with a
group of Hispanic origin were classified as Hispanics even if they also
identified with another group. Respondents were classified as native-
born non-Hispanic white if they met the following criteria: identified
with a group of European descent or as American; did not identify with
a group of Hispanic origin; did not identify as black or with another
nonwhite group; were not racially coded as "black" or "other" by the
interviewer; and were born in the United States.

The dependent variables to be examined in this paper are highest
grade completed, delay in school, and dropping out of high school. The
operationalization of highest grade completed is straightforward. Delay
in school is the comparison of respondents who have fallen behind their
age cohort during their primary or secondary education to those who are
at the same level as their age cohort. Since the respondents in this sample
were not specifically asked about delays in school, this measure was
obtained by calculating the ideal grade the respondents should have
completed given their age cohort and comparing the ideal grade to the
actual grade enrolled in. Respondents who were two or more years
behind their age cohort were considered delayed.[2] High school completion is the comparison of respondents who have dropped out of high
school to those who have graduated from high school or are currently
enrolled in high school.

The analysis was restricted to respondents who were sixteen years of age or older. The fourteen- and fifteen-year-olds were omitted from the analysis because most are enrolled in high school. Among the remaining subsample, the sixteen- to twenty-one-year-olds, many have not completed their education. Thus the focus of this analysis is on educational outcomes that are especially relevant for this age group—delay in school and dropping out of high school. These measures may be considered indicative of early success in the educational process and serve as proxies for the respondents' eventual educational attainment.

Highest grade completed and age are highly correlated, that is, older respondents are farther along in school than younger respondents. For this reason, age is held constant in all the analysis to be presented.

DESCRIPTIVE ANALYSIS

Descriptive statistics of sex, age, and family-background characteristics for Hispanics and non-Hispanic whites are presented in table 1.1. Females slightly outnumber males among the Hispanic youth, while males slightly outnumber females among the non-Hispanic white youth. There is little difference between the two groups in terms of age. Both groups are, on the average, almost nineteen years old. As expected, Hispanics are disadvantaged relative to non-Hispanic whites in terms of family-background characteristics. For instance, the parents of Hispanic respondents have approximately eight to nine years of schooling on the average, while the parents of the non-Hispanic white respondents have approximately twelve years of schooling. Furthermore, the Hispanics

Table 1.1: Weighted Descriptive Statistics for Hispanics and Non-Hispanic Whites

	Hispanics		Whites	
	Mean	S.D.	Mean	S.D.
Female	.519	.500	.480	.500
Age	18.664	1.792	18.680	1.802
Father's education	8.847	5.100	12.485	3.258
Mother's education	8.383	4.377	12.174	2.310
Father's occ. status	44.706	26.483	62.086	22.138
Mother employed	.464	.499	.493	.500
Intact family	.764	.425	.893	.309
Number of siblings	4.542	2.952	3.032	1.924

are more likely to have fathers with lower-status occupations, mothers who did not work when the respondents were fourteen years old, only one parent in the household at the age of fourteen, and a greater number of siblings.[3]

Table 1.2 presents weighted means and proportions of the educational outcomes disaggregated by ethnicity, national origin, and generational status.[4] As can be seen from table 1.2, the Hispanic youth are considerably disadvantaged educationally in comparison to non-Hispanic white youth. The difference between the two groups in highest grade completed is an entire year; Hispanic youth are more than twice as likely to be delayed in school (20 percent vs. 9 percent) and to have dropped out of high school (30 percent vs. 12 percent). As can also be seen from table 1.2, the first generation is considerably more educationally disadvantaged than later generations, and there is little difference between the second and third generations. The first generation has completed one year less schooling than the second or third generation and is two times more likely than the second or third generation to be delayed and to have dropped out. Generational differences among the Mexicans,

Table 1.2: Weighted Means and Proportions of Educational Outcomes

	Highest Grade Completed	Delay in School	High School Dropout	(N)
Both groups	11.365	.100	.136	(6277)
Non-Hispanic whites	11.455	.086	.118	(4731)
Hispanics	10.515	.197	.305	(1546)
Generation 1	9.799	.312	.411	(536)
Generation 2	10.801	.170	.260	(461)
Generation 3	10.935	.115	.246	(549)
Mexicans	10.283	.212	.316	(955)
Generation 1	8.851	.401	.549	(266)
Generation 2	10.745	.178	.247	(244)
Generation 3	10.805	.131	.229	(445)
Puerto Ricans	10.410	.221	.386	(268)
Generation 1	9.815	.317	.504	(102)
Generation 2	10.761	.165	.247	(166)
Other Hispanics	11.134	.143	.226	(323)
Generation 1	10.965	.200	.194	(168)
Generation 2	11.311	.134	.141	(57)
Generation 3	11.298	.067	.306	(98)

Puerto Ricans, and other Hispanics are similar in that the first generation has the lowest attainment, followed by the second and third generation. Among the Mexicans, the difference between the first and second generation is greater (e.g., a two-year difference in highest grade completed) than among the Puerto Ricans (a one-year difference) or the other Hispanics (less than half a year's difference). Among the other Hispanics, the generational difference in terms of dropping out of school is reversed—the third generation has a higher rate (31 percent) than the first or second generation (19 percent and 15 percent respectively).[5]

When comparing the national-origin groups, we find that Mexican and Puerto Rican youth are similar to each other in highest grade completed (appropriately ten years of school) and being delayed (appropriately 20 percent are delayed). However, the dropout rate among Puerto Ricans is slightly higher than among Mexicans. Furthermore, Mexicans and Puerto Ricans are considerably more disadvantaged than other Hispanics in highest grade completed, delay in school, and dropping out of high school. Among the first generation, Mexicans are the most disadvantaged educationally, followed by Puerto Ricans, with the least disadvantage found among other Hispanics. The difference between Mexicans and Puerto Ricans and between Puerto Ricans and other Hispanics is approximately one year in highest grade completed and ten percentage points in delay in school. However, the difference between Mexicans and Puerto Ricans in dropping out of school is small, while other Hispanics have a considerably lower rate of dropping out. Among the second generation, Mexican and Puerto Rican youth are very similar in their levels of attainment, while the other Hispanic youth have a slightly higher level of attainment. Among the third generation, Mexicans are more disadvantaged than other Hispanics in highest grade completed and delay in school, but the other Hispanics have a higher rate of dropping out of school. Furthermore, the national-origin differences among the first generation are greater than the differences among the second or third generation. In sum, these figures demonstrate the disadvantaged educational profile of Hispanic youth, particularly among Mexican and Puerto Rican youth and among first-generation youth.

MULTIVARIATE ANALYSIS

As was clearly seen from the descriptive statistics presented in table 1.1, the Hispanic youth come from more disadvantaged family backgrounds than the non-Hispanic whites. What role do family background differences play in explaining educational differences between Hispanic youth and non-Hispanic white youth? Table 1.3 presents regression analysis for highest grade completed, delay in school, and dropping out of high school where Hispanic youth are compared to non-Hispanic white youth, controlling for (1) sex and age *without* controlling for family-background characteristics and (2) controlling for sex, age, and family-background characteristics. Comparisons are also made between first-, second-, and third-generation Hispanics and non-Hispanic whites *prior to* and *after* controlling for family-background characteristics.

The results presented in table 1.3 show that prior to controlling for family-background characteristics, the differences between Hispanic youth and non-Hispanic white youth are significant and that ethnicity accounts for a considerable amount of variance in educational attainment (ranging from 2 percent of the variance in dropping out of high school to 4 percent of the variance in highest grade completed). After controlling for family background, the difference between Hispanic youth and non-Hispanic white youth is reduced considerably. The difference in highest grade completed, although it continues to be significant, has decreased from almost a year's difference to approximately a tenth of a year's difference. The Hispanic-white difference in being delayed has decreased from an 11 percent difference to a 2 percent difference and is no longer significant. The ethnic difference in dropping out of high school has decreased from a 15 percent difference to no difference and is, also, no longer significant.

Next, first-, second-, and third-generation Hispanics are compared to non-Hispanic whites *prior to* and *after* controlling for family-background characteristics. As can be seen from table 1.3, all three generation groups differ significantly from non-Hispanic whites. The largest difference is between the first generation and non-Hispanic whites—the first generation has completed 1.7 fewer years of schooling and is approximately 20 percent higher in being delayed and in dropping out of school. The second and third generations are almost half a year behind non-Hispanic whites in highest grade completed, are respectively 9 percent and 5.5 percent more likely to be delayed, and are both 10 percent more likely to drop out of high school. After controlling for family background, we find that although the disadvantaged position of the first generation decreases, that generation continues to have significantly *lower* attainment—.8 fewer years of schooling, 6 percent more likelihood of being delayed, and 4.5 percent more likelihood of dropping out. In contrast, the second-generation Hispanic youth goes from significantly lower attainment before controlling for family background

Table 1.3: Regression Analysis of Educational Attainment on Ethnicity and Generational Status Without and With Family-Background Characteristics

	Highest Grade Completed[a]		Delay in School[b]		High School Dropout[b]	
	Without Background	With Background	Without Background	With Background	Without Background	With Background
Hispanic	-.890***	-.121**	.114***	.016	.150***	.001
Proportion of variance	.043***	.001**	.039***	.000	.024***	.000
Generation 1	-1.729***	-.763***	.174***	.060***	.228***	.045*
Generation 2	-.420***	.360***	.088***	-.010	.092***	-.070***
Generation 3	-.406***	.007	.055***	-.007	.108***	.012
Proportion of variance	.070***	.016***	.054***	.006	.031***	.003

*p<.05
**p<.01
***p<.001

[a] Ordinary least squares regression is used for the analysis of highest grade completed, and unstandardized regression coefficients are presented.

[b] Logit regression is used for the analysis of delay in school and dropping out of high school. This procedure uses an iterative maximum-likelihood solution to predict the logarithm of the probability of delay in school or dropping out of school. First-order partial derivatives are presented. These are computed as b_iP' $(1-P')$ where b_i is the coefficient of the relevant independent variable and P' is the proportion that is delayed or has dropped out. The sample proportion is chosen as a realistic representation of the probability of delay or dropping out (the derivatives would be different if computed at other points in the logistic curve). These derivatives are interpreted as the increment to the average probability of delay or dropping out associated with a one-unit increase in the independent variable.

to significantly *higher* attainment in highest grade completed and dropping out of high school after controlling for family background. And the difference between the second generation and non-Hispanic whites in being delayed in school is no longer significant after holding family background constant. The significant differences between the third generation and non-Hispanic whites prior to adjusting for family background decrease to nonsignificant, small differences after adjusting for family background.[6]

Table 1.4 presents the analysis for highest grade completed, delay in school, and dropping out of high school regressed on sex, age, and family-background characteristics separately for Hispanics and non-Hispanic whites. Among the non-Hispanic whites, females have significantly higher attainment than males on highest grade completed, delay in school, and dropping out of high school. This is consistent with U.S. population figures regarding the attainment of males and females (U.S. Bureau of the Census, 1980). Males have lower rates of high school completion and are more likely to drop out at younger ages. However, males are more likely to complete college and to attend graduate school. Therefore, females are advantaged at early points in the educational process while males are advantaged at later points; thus, across all age groups, the median educational attainment for males and females is similar. Among Hispanics, females have a lower rate of being delayed in school but do not differ from males in years of schooling acquired or likelihood of dropping out of high school. In sum, non-Hispanic white females are doing considerably better educationally than non-Hispanic white males, while there is a much smaller difference between Hispanic males and females.

The results presented in table 1.4 also show that age has a strong and significant impact on highest grade completed for both Hispanic youth and non-Hispanic white youth (this is the major reason for the large proportion of variance accounted for in highest grade completed, especially among the non-Hispanic white youth). This is understandable since older respondents are more likely to have acquired more years of schooling. Age does not have a significant impact on delay in school for either Hispanic youth or non-Hispanic white youth. Age does have a significant impact on dropping out of high school, but this effect is not as strong as it is for highest grade completed. In addition, the effect of age on dropping out of school is stronger among Hispanic youth than non-Hispanic white youth. Older Hispanic youth are more likely to drop out of high school than are younger Hispanic youth or non-Hispanic white youth.

What is the direct impact of family-background characteristics on educational attainment? Father's and mother's education have a signifi-

Table 1.4: Regression Analysis of Educational Attainment on Sex, Age, and Family Background for Hispanics and Non-Hispanic Whites

	Highest Grade Completed [a]		Delay in School [b]		High School Dropout [b]	
	Hispanics	Whites	Hispanics	Whites	Hispanics	Whites
Female	.018	.308***	−.052**	−.061***	−.025	−.053***
Age	.339***	.568***	.003	−.003	.048***	.009***
Father's education	.058***	.056***	−.009**	−.006***	−.009*	−.015***
Mother's education	.061***	.108***	−.007*	−.013***	−.006*	−.024***
Father's occ. status	.004	.005***	−.002***	−.001***	−.002*	−.002***
Mother employed	.239*	−.056	−.076***	.006	−.039	.002
Intact family	−.080	.242***	.025	−.016	−.039	−.094***
Number of siblings	−.132***	−.073***	.012***	.007***	.024***	.011
Constant	2.490	−1.590	−.112	.138	−.963	.207
Proportion of variance	.262***	.499***	.073***	.118***	.067***	.107***
Unweighted mean or proportion	10.390	11.415	.206	.073	.312	.151

*p<.05
**p<.01
***p<.001

[a] Ordinary least squares regression is used for the analysis of highest grade completed, and unstandardized regression coefficients are presented.
[b] Logit regression is used for the analysis of delay in school and dropping out of high school, and first-order partial derivatives are presented. These are interpreted as the increment to the average probability of delay or dropping out of school associated with a one-unit increase in the independent variable. See note b to table 1.3 for more detail.

cant impact on all three indicators of educational attainment among both Hispanic youth and non-Hispanic white youth. Father's occupational status affects highest grade completed, being delayed, and dropping out among Hispanic youth and non-Hispanic white youth, with the exception of highest grade completed among Hispanics. Mother's employment leads to higher grade completion and less delay among Hispanics but does not affect dropping out among Hispanics or any of the three achievement measures among non-Hispanic whites. Being in an intact family leads to higher grade completion and less dropping out among Hispanics but does not affect delay in school among Hispanics or any achievement measure among non-Hispanic whites. Number of siblings affects highest grade completed, being delayed, and dropping out among both Hispanics and non-Hispanic whites, with the exception of dropping out of school among non-Hispanic whites. In sum, family-background characteristics account for a significant proportion of variance in educational attainment.

To what extent do the relationships between family-background characteristics and educational attainment differ meaningfully between the groups? By meaningful differences, we mean that the relationship in one group is significantly stronger or weaker than in the other group. While these significance tests are not presented in the tables, the results of these comparisons are discussed in the following sections. Mother's education has a weaker impact on educational attainment among Hispanic youth than among non-Hispanic white youth. The differences between the groups are significant for all three indicators of attainment. One can see an example of this by examining the coefficients for highest grade completed regressed on mother's education. This coefficient among the non-Hispanic whites is almost twice the magnitude of the coefficient among the Hispanics. The impact of father's education differed between Hispanic and white youth only in dropping out of high school. And being in an intact family has a weaker impact on dropping out of school among Hispanic youth. The only instances of stronger relationships among Hispanics are those of mother's employment status to highest grade completed and delay in school and number of siblings to highest grade completed. The most consistent difference in these comparisons is the weaker impact of mother's education on the attainment of Hispanic youth.

If we make finer distinctions among Hispanics with respect to generational status, does the impact of family background vary by generational group? Specifically, is the weaker impact of mother's educational attainment, and to some extent father's, found among Hispanics in general particular to one generational group? Table 1.5 presents

Table 1.5: Regression Analysis of Educational Attainment on Sex, Age, and Family Background for Generational Groups Among Hispanics

	Highest Grade Completed[a]			Delay in School[b]			High School Dropout[b]		
	Gen. 1	Gen. 2	Gen. 3	Gen. 1	Gen. 2	Gen. 3	Gen. 1	Gen. 2	Gen. 3
Female	-.057	-.040	.085	-.025	-.055	-.079**	-.004	-.005	-.052
Age	.197***	.558***	.516***	.014	.003	-.001	.075***	.030**	.036**
Father's education	.098***	-.001	.051**	-.014*	-.000	-.010*	-.016**	-.002	-.011
Mother's education	.088**	.026	.039*	-.006	-.001	-.005	-.019**	.003	.005
Father's occ. status	-.001	.010**	.000	-.002	-.003**	-.001	.000	-.002	-.003*
Mother employed	.469*	-.089	.079	-.108*	-.034	-.046	-.097	.060	-.049
Intact family	-.209	-.162	.320	.123*	.005	-.038	-.056	-.061	-.001
Number of siblings	-.168***	-.060*	-.096***	.001	.015*	.017***	.026**	.019*	.024**
Constant	5.669	.453	.419	-.155	-.115	-.015	-1.322	-.822	-.782
Proportion of variance	.243***	.383***	.430***	.048***	.061***	.116***	.109***	.028*	.062***
Unweighted mean or proportion	9.646	10.761	10.807	.326	.167	.120	.435	.236	.255

*p<.05
**p<.01
***p<.001

[a] Ordinary least squares regression is used for the analysis of highest grade completed, and unstandardized regression coefficients are presented.
[b] Logit regression is used for the analysis of delay in school and dropping out of high school, and first-order partial derivatives are presented. These are interpreted as the increment to the average probability of delay or dropping out of school associated with a one-unit increase in the independent variable. See note b to table 1.3 for more detail.

regression analysis for highest grade completed, delay in school, and dropping out of high school by generational status. As can be seen from this table, the coefficients for both mother's and father's education are smaller among second-generation Hispanics than among first- or third-generation Hispanics. In addition, comparing the coefficients of the generational groups to those of non-Hispanic whites (presented in table 1.4), one can see that the weak relationships for parents' education among second-generation Hispanics are dramatically different from the relationships among non-Hispanic whites. The differences between the second generation and non-Hispanic whites are statistically significant in every instance, that is, for both mother's and father's education and for the three indicators of educational attainment. The comparisons between the first and second generation are also significant in almost every instance. The coefficients among the second generation are smaller than those among the third generation, although these differences are, for the most part, not statistically significant.

While the largest differences are between the second generation and non-Hispanic whites, to some extent the first and third generation also differ from non-Hispanic whites. The relationships between mother's education and the three indicators of achievement among the third generation are significantly weaker than among non-Hispanic whites. However, the impact of father's education on educational attainment does not differ between the third generation and non-Hispanic whites. Both mother's and father's education affect dropping out of school significantly less among the first generation than among non-Hispanic whites, while the effect of parents' education on highest grade completed and delay does not differ between the two groups. In sum, the impact of parents' education on education attainment is least strong among the second generation than any other generation or the non-Hispanic whites. Furthermore, the differences in the impact of parents' education are statistically significant when comparing the second generation to non-Hispanic whites and the first generation.

SUMMARY AND CONCLUSIONS

These findings show that Hispanic youth are considerably more educationally disadvantaged than non-Hispanic white youth. However, the differences between Hispanics and non-Hispanic whites can be partly explained by the disadvantaged family backgrounds of Hispanic youth. In addition, generational status was also found to be important for understanding the achievements of Hispanic youth. Even after controlling for family background, first-generation Hispanic youth are educationally disadvantaged. However, second-generation Hispanic youth have significantly *higher* achievements after controlling for family background, while third-generation youth do not differ significantly from non-Hispanic white youth.

These findings also demonstrate that the process of achievement differs for Hispanics and non-Hispanic whites. When non-Hispanic whites are compared to Hispanics as a group, mother's educational attainment has a weaker impact on educational attainment among Hispanic youth. When finer distinctions are made among Hispanics with respect to generational status, *both* mother's and father's educational attainment have a weaker impact among the second generation. Furthermore, the differences between the second generation and non-Hispanic whites and between the first and second generations are statistically significant in every comparison made, this is, for the three indicators of educational attainment regressed on both mother's and father's education. The relationships among the second generation are weaker than among the third generation, although these differences are largely not significant. Thus these findings are consistent in demonstrating that the impact of parents' education on educational attainment is less strong among the second generation than among other generational groups or non-Hispanic whites and that the largest differences are between the second generation, on the one hand, and non-Hispanic whites and the first generation, on the other hand.

What does it mean that second-generation Hispanics achieve as well as or better than the first or later generations, who are of similar socioeconomic background, although their achievements are less affected by family background than those of the first generation or later generations? To understand the unique educational process among the second generation, it seems one must consider both personal characteristics of the immigrant parents and structural characteristics of the immigration experience.

First, personal characteristics are important since immigrants are a select group in comparison to nonimmigrants. Immigrants choose to immigrate and are successful in immigrating. In addition, many immigrants move for economic goals, and even when these goals may not materialize for themselves, there is still the hope that the goals will be obtained by their children. In light of this, the relatively high achievements of the second generation are not surprising. It is probably true that immigrant parents provide more encouragement and hold higher expectations for their children than do nonimmigrant parents.

Second, structural characteristics are important for understanding why relatively higher status on the part of immigrant parents does not necessarily translate into greater achievement for their children. One characteristic of the immigrant parents' educational experience is that their education has been acquired in a different country. Since educational systems vary greatly from country to country, it may be that an educational advantage on the part of the parents in another country does not translate into an advantage for the child. An additional aspect of the immigrant parents' educational experience is that it is considerably lower than that of the non-Hispanic white parents. Variation in the educational attainment of the parents may be relevant only if this variation is around the educational norms present in that society. Thus differences at the lower end of the educational spectrum in a society where the norms and requirements are for a greater amount of schooling may have fewer implications for the attainment of the child. Therefore the combination of schooling acquired in a different country and schooling that is considerably lower than the U.S. norms may mean that differences in attainment on the part of immigrant parents do not translate into either an advantage or a disadvantage for their U.S.-born children, that is, the second generation. Third-generation youth, on the other hand, have parents who are U.S.-born and U.S.-educated; thus variation in their achievements may have greater relevance for the child. And among the first generation, to the extent that their education is acquired in the country of origin (which depends on their age of arrival), differences in their parents' achievements may be relevant to their achievement. Thus we see that the second generation holds a unique place in the transmission of class position from generation to generation. For the second generation, relatively higher achievement on the part of their parents does not necessarily translate into an advantage for them, yet they still acquire greater achievements than later generations who are of similar background.

NOTES

1. The two major national-origin groups included in the "Hispanic" category (both in this study and in the United States) are Mexicans and Puerto Ricans. Because of the commonwealth status of Puerto Rico, movement from Puerto Rico to the mainland is technically considered not immigration but migration. However, Puerto Rico is most similar to other Hispanic countries in terms of language and culture. Thus, in this discussion, island-born Puerto Ricans are considered immigrants.

2. In constructing this variable, the assumption is made that the oldest age a child will be when enrolling in school is seven years old, which is a fairly

conservative definition since other studies have assumed that children enter school at the age of six. A more conservative criterion is used because there are many instances of children not entering school until the age of seven. For example, in New York State, children may enroll in school in the year they turn six years old, but they are not legally required to enroll in school until the calendar year in which they turn seven.

3. Father's occupation, which was recoded to an occupational status measure of socioeconomic standing (Nam & Powers, 1968), was missing for approximately 20 percent of the sample. Therefore Cohen and Cohen's (1975) procedure for handling the instance where a substantial proportion of the sample has a missing value on an independent variable was employed. The missing value was recoded to the mean and a dummy variable signaling the presence of missing data for father's occupation was created and included in the analysis.

4. Among the Puerto Rican youth, only six respondents were third generation; therefore, the third-generation Puerto Ricans are combined with the second generation.

5. Generational differences among the other Hispanics are difficult to interpret because the generational groups are composed of different national-origin groups. The first generation consists primarily of recent immigrants such as Dominicans, Cubans, and Central and South Americans, while the third generation includes groups such as Hispanos in the Southwest.

6. The results presented in table 1.3 and the following tables are not disaggregated by national origin. Although there are national-origin-group differences in achievement (as demonstrated by table 1.2), there is no reason to believe that the hypothesized relationships regarding generational differences and the role of family background differ by national origin. To ensure that this was true, the results presented in tables 1.3 to 1.5 were redone for the Mexican youth and the Puerto Rican youth (the only national-origin groups where there were sufficient respondents to allow for separate analysis). Since the results for separate groups were similar to the results for combined groups of Hispanics, only the results for all Hispanics are presented.

REFERENCES

Blau, P., & Duncan, O. D. (1967). *The American occupational structure.* New York: Wiley.

Borus, M., Crowley, J., Rumberger, R., Santos, R., & Shapiro, D. (1980). *Pathways to the future: A longitudinal study of young Americans, Preliminary report: Youth and the labor market—1979.* Columbus, OH: Ohio State University Center for Human Resource Research.

Brown, G., Rosen, N., Hill, S., & Olivas, M. (1980). *The condition of education for Hispanic Americans.* Washington, DC: National Center for Educational Statistics, U.S. Government Printing Office.

Cohen, J., & Cohen, P. (1975). *Applied multiple regression/correlation analysis for the behavioral sciences.* Hillsdale, NJ: Erlbaum.

Cooney, R., Rogler, L., Correale, L., & Ortiz, V. (1980). *Intergenerational change in educational attainment among Puerto Ricans: A closer look at the migration experience.* Paper presented at the annual conference of the Population Association of America. Denver, CO.

Duncan, B., & Duncan, O. D. (1968). Minorities and the process of stratification. *American Sociological Review, 33,* 356–364.

Duncan, O. D., Featherman, D., & Duncan, B. (1972). *Socioeconomic background and achievement.* New York: Harcourt Brace Jovanovich.

Featherman, D., & Hauser, R. (1978). *Opportunity and change.* New York: Academic Press.

Hirschman, C. (1978). Prior U.S. residence among Mexican immigrants. *Social Forces, 56,* 1179–1181.

Nam, C., & Powers, M. (1968). Changes in the relative status level of workers in the United States, 1950–1960. *Social Forces, 47,* 635–657.

Peñalosa, F., & McDonagh, E. (1966). Social mobility in a Mexican-American community. *Social Forces, 44,* 498–505.

Sewell, W., Hauser, R., & W. Wolf. (1980). Sex, schooling, and occupational status. *American Journal of Sociology, 86,* 551–583.

U.S. Bureau of the Census. (1980). *Educational attainment in the United States, 1979.* Current population reports, Series P-20, No. 356. Washington, DC: U.S. Government Printing Office.

2 | Do Hispanics Receive an Equal Educational Opportunity? The Relationship of School Outcomes, Family Background, and High School Curriculum

ERNESTO BALLESTEROS

Issues of equal educational opportunity are always defined as issues of distribution. They arise from perceived inequities in the amounts of resources, access, or benefits available to different persons. That is, all views of equal education state who gets what, to what degree, and why it is just or unjust. If certain individuals are to receive a greater or a lesser amount of the distribution, there must be reasons for this entitlement. The differential distribution may be considered just, only if it is based on educationally relevant factors of distribution such as ability rather than sex, race, or wealth. For instance, some students in a school may have more access to educational opportunities or benefits than others. As a consequence, some groups of children may score higher on achievement tests, may be found in college-bound curricula more often, and may attain higher levels of education. Some schools may have more resources than other schools. This unequal access to resources would be considered unjust if it were a function of the socioeconomic characteristics of the community where those schools were located.

For the designers of the first public schools, mere exposure to a common school, curriculum, and resources constituted equality of educational opportunity. This view of equity further assumed that achievement and attainment were solely a function of these school inputs, regardless of differences in the values, communication abilities, and social behaviors that children brought to the school. It overlooked the influence of teachers' attitudes, values, and behaviors on school achievement. The child was expected to take full advantage of the school in order to achieve and attain; failure to do so was not the responsibility of the school.

47

A second stage in the evolution of the concept of equal educational opportunity challenged the premise that a common curriculum for all children would provide equal educational opportunities for all children to realize their potential through schooling. As a result of a 1918 report by the National Education Association, (Coleman, 1968), the school curriculum was diversified so that the high school could accommodate the greater influx of adolescents who were not college-bound. It was assumed that those who would not go on to college would be given a greater opportunity if they had a specially designed curriculum than if they had to take a program developed for the college-bound.

The problem with this way of thinking was that it assumed that a given child was going into a given postsecondary occupational or educational path. It further assumed that the decision to follow a certain curriculum was rationally made by the individual child or by the school system.

Although the development of separate curricula (college-preparatory and vocational-training) diversified the educational program, it may also have allowed certain groups to reap greater educational and non-educational social benefits, such as achievement, certificates, credentials, and entry into higher-status professions. In a sense, placement in a vocational or general secondary curriculum may have been unfair because it reduced freedom of choice of knowledge and culture; it reduced free access to careers and jobs, and it reduced the chances of obtaining higher levels of employment.

Although curriculum-placement criteria may have been based on previous school achievement, students from racial or ethnic minorities and low-income backgrounds were placed in vocational curricula more often than white, middle-class children, even though some of them had higher educational aspirations. They were denied equal educational opportunity or burdened by certain forms of discrimination that contributed to the differences in academic achievement.

> The purpose (or purposes) of the educational institution may be arbitrary and invidious. The institution may have been (consciously) designed to achieve a result that is unjust, such as the conservation of economic privilege for a favored class, the "legitimating" of arbitrary rationing of privilege, or the maintaining or racial segregation within society. (Ellett, 1977, p. 57)

The concept of equal educational opportunity later evolved from providing *equal access* to an education to assuring *equal effects* or outcomes. In the criteria of access, the fact that certain social groups (racial, ethnic, socioeconomic) might not benefit equally from the educational process provided by the educational system had nothing to do with equal educational opportunity. Green (1971) argues that the manner in which the educational system distributed its benefits (i.e., grades and certificates) among the population had nothing to do with equal opportunity and much to do with the children's choices and innate abilities as well as with their tenacity to exercise and further develop them.

While equal educational opportunity as an access issue had much to do with the distribution of inputs by the educational system, it had little or nothing to do with the outputs of schooling. After the Supreme Court's 1954 *Brown* reversal of its 1896 decision (Plessy v. Ferguson) on the constitutionality of "separate but equal," thinking evolved in the direction that equal educational opportunity should perhaps be evaluated according to the effects of schooling. A major factor in the *Brown* decision was the Court's belief that separate schools always affected school achievement negatively. This concern for the negative effect of separate schools and the perceived positive contribution that peers made to each other led to a third concept of equal educational opportunity, a concept that focused on the differential effects of schooling due to segregation.

However, even after the *Brown* decision, what desegregation took place did little to contribute to academic gains for minorities as a whole (Coleman, 1966; Jencks, 1972a; O'Reilly, 1970). There still exist predominantly black and predominantly Chicano schools. In racially mixed schools, these minorities are still more often found in non-college-preparatory high school curriculum tracks. Schafer, Olexa, and Polk (1973) suggest that tracking may be a means by which minorities are systematically denied equal educational opportunity. That is, because they do not experience the same educational environments as the white, middle-class majority group, minorities do not have the same chances for high attainment.

A fourth concept of equality of educational opportunity followed from the notion that the effects of schooling should be equal for individuals with unequal backgrounds and abilities and that equality of educational opportunity requires equality of results from schooling even when there are different individual inputs. The concern for equal effects of schooling implies that school outcomes ought to be equal after racial background is controlled. It is assumed that, if the effect of the school environment were the same for all students, then the difference in average achievement levels for racial majority and minority children would diminish, even though their initial abilities differed. That is, although not every child could be expected to achieve as much as every other child, not all high achievers would be found in any one racial group. A movement toward eliminating between-group differences in achievement would constitute progress toward the goal of equal educational opportunity.

The underlying assumption in this fourth concept is that other factors such as family and community environments are not as influential as the school environment in determining achievement. However, given the importance of the family in achievement, this concept would require the school to have a strong commitment to reducing the inequality among the racial and ethnic groups. Where the original concept of equal educational opportunity gave schools a passive role in student achievement, the new view gives them the responsibility for reducing unequal achievement levels between groups of children. It is assumed that the difference in achievement at grade 12 between the average Hispanic and the average white is, in effect, the degree of inequality of opportunity.

WHO IS ENTITLED TO WHAT EDUCATION?

Educational benefits such as skills and knowledge will not be distributed by the educational system equally among all children. Some will do better than others in obtaining these benefits or will reach the same achievement level at a faster rate. This unequal distribution of educational benefits is not objectionable unless children from a certain social class or racial group almost always achieve at the lowest or, conversely, at the highest level.

Even though members of a racial group or social class may want the best education obtainable, they may not get it if the educational system distributes its resources and benefits unequally among groups. Green (in Green, Erickson, & Seidman, 1980) argues that if we find that children who read poorly are almost always from a certain social class or of a certain sex or race, then we must wonder whether such a distributive result is acceptable. We should wonder on what basis the system distributes its benefits unequally. That they are unequally distributed is inevitable (because of innate ability differences), but that their unequal distribution should stem from irrelevant educational attributes such as sex, race, or social class does not seem inevitable or justified. These attributes are usually regarded as inappropriate grounds on which to justify unequal distribution of benefits.

Some researchers (Bowles & Gintis, 1976; Green et al., 1980) believe that the kind of education to which everyone is entitled by the equality principle is that which the wealthy provide for their children. To accomplish this goal would require not that the resources available to the wealthy be reduced but rather that the resources available to the poor be increased, at least to the level of those available to the rich. Leveling down resources would result in no one getting the best education possible.

The education that the rich provide for their children is generally one that bestows the greatest educational benefits (in terms of achievement, attainment, and credentials) and results in the greatest noneducational social rewards, such as higher-status jobs. By gaining access to a college-oriented curriculum in the high school and, consequently, by attaining higher levels of education, individuals from minorities and lower social classes could increase their freedom of choice of knowledge and culture, their freedom of job and career choices, and their chances of improving their socioeconomic situation. Unless it can be proved that only the white middle class and the rich can learn, then educational access and, consequently, achievement should be similarly distributed across all groups. The reaping of the highest levels of educational benefits by any one group would not constitute equality. Ability to learn must be related to factors other than sex, race, or social class.

Thus, everyone should be entitled to access to educational curricula that will develop abilities and interests and will enhance achievement and educational attainment. School systems that have special compensatory educational programs (for students with initially low school abilities) but still have an unequal racial distribution in the different high school curricula are not providing equality of educational opportunity. Thus, the best education available will have been provided when it is ascertained that graduates from the various curricula are equally distributed racially, sexually, and socioeconomically.

THE CONDITION OF MINORITIES IN EDUCATION

The causes of the underrepresentation of Hispanics in college-bound curricula are many, but it seems reasonable to assert that some are related directly to their preparation in elementary and middle school. Hispanics may, in part, choose occupational programs in the high school because of a lack of knowledge about the consequences of their choice. That is, Hispanics may not be aware that they are reducing their future occupational, cultural, and academic options. They may have been socialized to aspire only to low-status occupations, not to professional occupations. They may also come to realize that their education through the eighth grade has not prepared them adequately to pursue the more academic curricula.

Educational attrition among minority children in elementary and secondary schools may be attributable to factors that operate with the minority groups but do not affect majority, middle-class children. For example, minority families may still need the economic contributions of their children; some persons who have suffered socioeconomic instability may not see the advantages of delayed gratification; because they feel that the schools do not recognize the legitimacy of their cultural values and behaviors, minority students may have a low regard for learning, low self-esteem, and a lack of self-discipline; and minority students may be encouraged by their high school counselors and teachers to choose lower-status occupations.

The Hispanic child's capacity for learning, for doing schoolwork, and for choosing one curriculum over another is a result of the beliefs, values, and motivations developed in the home, among peers, and from interaction with schoolteachers and other school staff. Teachers and counselors who encourage minority children to choose a non-college-preparatory program because they feel that the minority child is not suited to, or cannot make a contribution in, a college-preparatory program may actually be violating the trust vested in them by the students and their parents. All too often, in advising minority children to enroll in a general education or vocational program, counselors and teachers may fail to recognize that these students have not been given a fair chance to develop adequate academic skills, that they have not been given the opportunity to explore all the educational opportunities and their consequent benefits, and that they, their families, and close peers may not be knowledgeable about how to reap the greatest benefits from schooling.

Amato (1980) found that the most important tracking distinction in the high school was between curricula. While ability rather than social class seems to be the major determinant of curriculum placement, the association of ability with socioeconomic status results in college-preparatory programs that enroll a disproportionate number of middle-class students and in general education programs that enroll a disproportionate number of lower-class students. Amato concludes that college preparation yields greater social benefits than other curricula. Thus, instead of operating to reduce social-class and educational inequality, schools operate to widen the attainment gap. Moreover, the negative consequences of placement in a vocational track are aggravated by the fact that upward mobility in the track system is limited: Once a student is placed in a low track, he or she tends to stay there.

Jencks (1972a) found that differences among racial or ethnic groups in measured knowledge and aptitude can be attributed both to cultural differences and (perhaps even more) to the prevailing system of tracking in elementary and secondary schools.

> Aside from differences in initial ability, the most obvious explanation for test score differences among students in the same school is that schools do not try to teach everyone the same things. At the elementary level, many schools put slow learners in slow classes and fast learners in fast classes. At the secondary level, they also put students in separate curriculums. If these differences do not affect students' test scores, nothing else is likely to do so. (Jencks, 1972a, p. 113)

Jencks states that curriculum assignment is susceptible to the same objections as school segregation: It is a denial of equal educational opportunity. Being placed in a non-college-preparatory school curriculum may limit the student's chances of attending college because most public high school students in vocational programs do not meet the admissions requirements of four-year colleges and universities.

Jencks also found that higher-scoring students are treated differently than lower-scoring individuals: Adolescents with high scores are more likely to be in a college-bound curriculum, more likely to get higher grades, and more likely to have ambitious educational and occupational plans. However, Jencks wonders to what extent higher-scoring students are more often found in a college-bound curriculum, get higher grades, talk more with teachers, have more ambitious friends, and develop more ambitious future plans because schools favor the abler student and to what extent abler students seek out favorable environments within a given school.

A survey of equality of educational opportunity (Coleman, 1966) was mandated in the Civil Rights Act of 1964. The act directed the commissioner of education to assess the "lack of equality of educational opportunity" among racial and other groups in the United States. The survey was designed to assess the condition of education given two sets of sharply different definitions of equality. The first three definitions of equality concerned *input* resources: those provided by the school system (facilities, curriculum, teachers); those brought to the school by other students in terms of background; and the intangible characteristics such as school morale that result from the interaction of school and student inputs.

The second set of definitions concerned the *effects* of schooling: the effect of the school for individuals with *equal background and abilities* (i.e., if individual inputs are equal, unequal school outcomes are a result of the school inputs or the racial composition or the other intangible inputs such as school morale) and the effect of school for individuals with *unequal backgrounds and abilities* (i.e., results should be equal even if student inputs are unequal; for example, children from Spanish-speaking homes as compared to English-background children would have an unequal English-language ability.)

The Coleman study (1966) found that the differences between schools attended by blacks and those attended by whites differed mainly in the educational backgrounds of fellow students. He found that teacher quality was not as important as the family backgrounds of fellow students and also that facilities and curriculum were the least correlated to the school differences between blacks and whites.

Coleman indicated that patterns of achievement in verbal skills at various grade levels varied by race and region of the country. He found that the period of school left average blacks in the Northeast at about the same level of achievement relative to whites as when they began school. The comparison of blacks with whites in the rural South showed an increasing difference over the first twelve years of schooling.

Given the importance of family background for achievement, Coleman argued that the differences between racial groups will diminish if the schools' influences are not only alike for blacks and whites but strong relative to divergent influences in the home and in the neighborhood. He believed that the intensity of the influences of the school versus that of the out-of-school influences determines the effectiveness of the educational system in providing equality of educational opportunity. He suggested that the concept of equality becomes one of degree of proximity to equality of opportunity since there will always be differences in existing divergent influences. He concluded that proximity to equality of opportunity is determined not merely by the equality of educational inputs but by the power of these resources in bringing about achievement.

The current literature on the status of Hispanics in higher education documents that they are underrepresented in institutions of higher education (University of California, 1975; Astin, 1975a; Haro, 1978; López, Madrid-Barela, & Macías, 1976; Olivas, 1978). Hispanics make up 4.0 percent of undergraduates enrolled in colleges and universities nationwide, whereas they make up 5.6 percent of the total U.S. population (Brown, Rosen, Hill, & Olivas, 1980). At the same time, their rates of attrition from college are very high: Hispanics receive only 2.8 percent of all the bachelor's degrees awarded in the United States (Olivas, 1978). Further, Hispanics are unevenly distributed among institutions of higher education, with comparatively large numbers enrolled in two-year colleges rather than in four-year colleges or universities (Astin, 1975a; Olivas, 1978). This maldistribution may be attributable to their lacking the high school credentials (grades, high school curriculum, and test scores) that would enable them to attend the more selective four-year institutions.

According to the California Postsecondary Education Commission

Report of 1977, Hispanics will probably be even more underrepresented among college students in the 1980s than they were in the 1970s. And even though declining enrollments may force many higher education institutions to lower their entrance requirements, the Hispanic students who are admitted to four-year colleges may still find it difficult to persist because of a lack of adequate support services and financial aid.

A STUDY ON THE EQUALITY
OF EDUCATIONAL OPPORTUNITY

The findings previously discussed indicate that race and wealth are major determinants of educational achievement and attainment. It was argued that unequal school outcomes may be a result of differential treatment based on socioeconomic factors, ethnicity, or language background. It was further suggested that placement in a non-college-bound curriculum may be a denial of equal educational opportunity at one or various grade levels, and that the disproportionate number of minority students in non-college-bound curricula precludes many of them from entering higher levels of education and from obtaining greater social benefits.

These findings led to a study (Ballesteros, 1982) of whether school outcomes (aptitude, high school achievement, educational aspirations, and college achievement) were equal for Chicano and white students. The premise of the study was that no differences should exist in educational outcomes if both groups received an equal educational opportunity. School-outcome variables were compared taking into account the effect of socioeconomic status, curriculum placement in the high school, and race and ethnicity.

The study used data collected through the Cooperative Institutional Research Program (CIRP), jointly sponsored by the American Council on Education and the University of California at Los Angeles.[1] The sample utilized was derived from all students who in the fall of 1975 enrolled as freshmen in the 325 institutions participating in the CIRP and who were followed up two years later, in the fall of 1977, when they had completed two years of college.

The study included all the sampled Chicano students who entered four-year colleges and universities as first-time freshmen in the fall of 1975 and who were followed up in 1977 ($N = 655$), as well as a subsample of the 9,448 white students. A random subsample of the white students, approximately the same size as the Chicano sample, was selected for purposes of comparison.

A structural-modeling approach (Joreskog, 1979; Bentler, 1980), whereby the observed variables were linked with relevant, theoretically constructed factors through a system of regression equations, was used (figure 2.1).[2] Six hypothetical factors were included in the postulated model: Socioeconomic status and high school curriculum made up the background latent factors, and aptitude, high school achievement, educational aspirations, and college achievement represented the hypothesized school outcomes. The four school-outcome factors are determined totally by the background and the residual factors included in the model.

The main concern of the study was the relationship between the latent factors. It was assumed that the relationship between latent factors would be equal for the two racial/ethnic groups if their high school experiences were equal. Thus, the structural parameters, the gammas and the betas, between the latent factors, were expected to be equal for the Chicano and white samples. Model H_1, described in figure 2.1, will be referred to as the "fully constrained" model. The model is constrained because all of the structural parameters were set to be equal in both groups. The hypothesized model (H_1) was evaluated in order to determine whether or not it was a plausible representation of the actual underlying interrelations among the observed variables. In order to determine the relationships between the latent factors, the postulated model was tested simultaneously over the two ethnic groups.

First, model H_1 was analyzed and maximum-likelihood parameter estimates were derived utilizing the LISREL IV computer program (Joreskog & Sorbom, 1978). The test yielded a chi-square of 126.66 with 71 degrees of freedom (table 2.1). The resulting chi-square statistic is large relative to the degrees of freedom; thus, the model cannot be judged a statistically plausible representation of the observed data.

A further review of the derived parameters of model H_1 indicates that the paths from socioeconomic status (SES) and high school curriculum to high school achievement were trivial. The critical values[3] for these paths did not reach the level of statistical significance.

Second, the postulated model was compared to a criterion model, the null model (H_0),[4] using the Bentler-Bonett index,[5] which represents the increment in fit obtained in evaluating any hierarchical comparison of two models. Although the model was not found to be an entirely accurate representation of the underlying causal structure that generated the data, it nevertheless explains a substantial proportion of the intercorrelation among the variables in the model. Looking at the right-hand side of table 2.1, one can see that even though the "fully constrained" model failed to fit statistically, it did explain a substantial

Figure 2.1: Structural Model of Student Background and School Variables

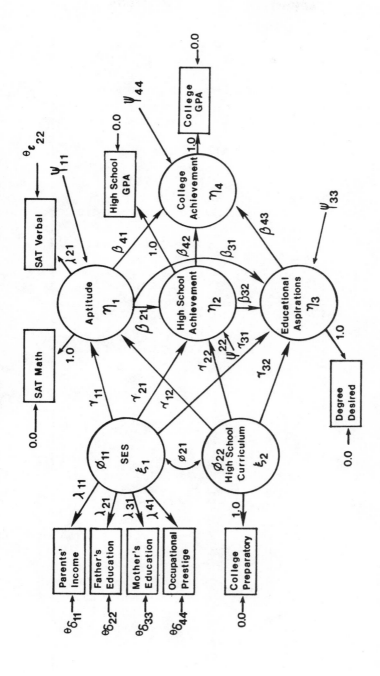

Table 2.1: Evaluation of Structural Models for School Outcomes

	Model Tests			Model Comparisons				
	χ^2	df	p	Comparison	χ^2	df	p	Δ^a
H_0: Null model	975.76	94	.0000	$H_0 - H_1$	849.10	23	.00	.870
H_1: Fully constrained	126.66	71	.0001	$H_1 - H_2$	-2.11	2	.40	.002
H_2: Fully constrained minus paths SES & H.S. Curr. to H.S. Ach.	128.77	73	.0001	$H_2 - H_3$	2.05	1	.20	.002
H_3: Relaxed path Aptitude to Col. Ach.	126.72	72	.0001	$H_3 - H_4$	0.00	1	.99	.000
H_4: Relaxed path H.S. Ach. to Col. Ach.	126.72	71	.0001	$H_4 - H_5$	1.25	1	.30	.001
H_5: Rexlaxed path Ed. Asp. to Col. Ach.	125.47	70	.0001	$H_5 - H_6$	0.57	1	.50	.001
H_6: Relaxed path Aptitude to Ed. Asp.	124.90	69	.0000	$H_6 - H_7$	2.77	1	.10	.003
H_7: Relaxed path Aptitude to H.S. Ach.	122.13	68	.0001	$H_7 - H_8$	0.12	1	.80	.000
H_8: Relaxed path H.S. Ach. to Ed. Asp.	122.01	67	.0000	$H_8 - H_9$	0.78	1	.50	.001
H_9: Relaxed path H.S. Curr. to Aptitude	121.23	66	.0000	$H_9 - H_{10}$	0.68	1	.50	.001
H_{10}: Relaxed path H.S. Curr. to Ed. Asp.	120.55	65	.0000	$H_{10} - H_{11}$	0.83	1	.50	.001
H_{11}: Relaxed path SES to Aptitude	119.72	64	.0000	$H_{11} - H_{12}$	2.18	1	.20	.002
H_{12}: Relaxed path SES to Ed. Asp.	117.54	63	.0000	$H_{12} - H_{13}$	0.52	1	.50	.001
H_{13}: Relaxed correlation SES to H.S. Curr.	117.02	62	.0000	$H_n - H_{13}$	858.74	32	.00	.880

^{a} Indicates the Bentler-Bonett Incremental Fit Index.

amount (87 percent) of the original variances and covariances relative to the null model.

Third, since the structural paths from socioeconomic status and high school curriculum to high school achievement were found not to be statistically significant, a second model (H_2) was developed by deleting these two paths from the postulated model H_1. In model H_2, as in the first model, all of the structural parameters were constrained to be equal in both the Chicano and the white student groups. This second model (H_2) was tested against the observed data and yielded a chi-square of 128.77 with 73 degrees of freedom. Again, this result indicated that model H_2, like model H_1, was a statistically inadequate representation of the observed data.

Finally, in an effort to determine whether the poor fit of model H_2 was partially attributable to the requirement that the model's structural parameters be equal across the two ethnic groups, alternate models were proposed and tested in which these constraints were relaxed. This was done on the assumption that structural paths may not be equal in both ethnic groups. Thus, each of the successive twelve models allowed the free estimation of one additional structural parameter in both racial/ethnic groups. The sequential loosening up of the model thus provided alternate hypotheses of structural relationships in the two groups. Comparisons of these hierarchically related models are also summarized in table 2.1.

The structural parameters were relaxed in a temporal order whereby the paths directed toward the last school outcome (college achievement) were the first to be loosened. Model H_3 represents the second of a series of twelve structural (hierarchical) models that are nested within the more restricted, "fully constrained" model (H_1) originally postulated in figure 2.1. The first alternative model (H_2) consisted of the original model less the structural paths from socioeconomic status and high school curriculum to high school achievement. Model H_2, however, did not propose the relaxation of any of the structural parameters.

Each of the successive models included the previously relaxed structural parameters in addition to a new one. Model H_3 proposed the relaxation of the structural path from aptitude to college achievement. In Model H_4, both the path from aptitude to college achievement and the path from high school achievement to college achievement were allowed to be estimated freely. The last model (H_{13}) was compared with the null model (H_0) in order to determine the degree of total improvement. However, the successive model-comparison tests did not substantially increase the Bentler-Bonett fit index (table 2.1).

Thus, the results indicate that allowing the structural effects to be different for Chicanos and whites did not yield substantially better models. For example, the degree of improvement from the first model (H_1) to the last model (H_{13}) was negligible (.87 vs. .88). Thus, the first, "fully constrained" model was just as accurate a representation of the data as those in which paths were freely estimated in both groups. However, the paths from SES and high school curriculum to high school achievement were found to be trivial; thus, structural paths were dropped from model H_1, forming model H_2. Consequently, model H_2 ("fully constrained," minus the two trivial paths from SES and high school curriculum to high school achievement) was used to evaluate the relationships among the hypothesized factors.

Free estimation of structural parameters in the two racial/ethnic groups did not statistically improve the "fully constrained" model H_2. Thus, it can be concluded that the interrelationships among the background factors and the high school outcomes of the Chicano sample were similar to those of the white sample. Chicanos who have completed two years of college at a four-year institution have patterns of aptitude, achievement, and aspirations that are similar to those of whites. Thus, the hypothesized model is not bound to either of the two groups sampled but rather has some generalizability. The implication is that these Chicanos either are being provided an equal educational opportunity or are working harder to achieve the same educational outcomes.

Figure 2.2 represents the final (standardized) LISREL solution. A review of the structural parameters (which can be interpreted analogously to standardized regression weights and correlations) indicates that there is a moderate correlation ($\phi = .253$) between SES and high school curriculum. SES and placement in a college-preparatory curriculum are also significantly related to the measurement of aptitude and to educational aspirations. Because the regression weight ($\gamma = .214$) between SES and aptitude is positive, a higher level of aptitude is associated with higher levels of socioeconomic status.

Since the coefficient between high school curriculum and aptitude is also positive ($\gamma = .134$), higher scores on aptitude tests can be expected from persons who were enrolled in college-preparatory curricula. Given that the magnitude of the regression weight from SES to aptitude is larger than the regression weight linking high school curriculum to aptitude, it can be concluded that socioeconomic status explains more of the variation in aptitude test scores than does the type of program in which the student was placed in the high school.

Placement in a college-preparatory curriculum also had a greater influence than SES on educational aspirations. SES may, however, carry much more weight on educational aspirations through other mediating

Figure 2.2: Final Standardized Solution of Student Background and School Variables Relationships

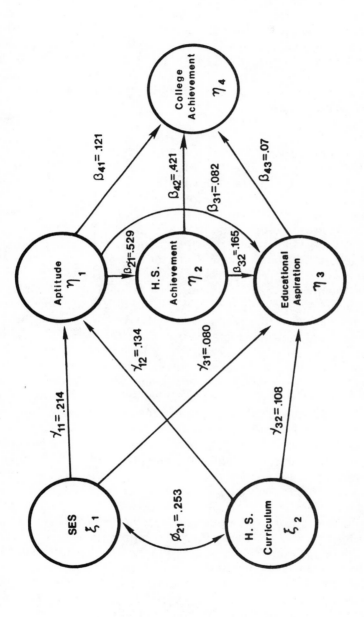

factors than is obvious from its direct relationship. Thus, social-class status and placement in a college-preparatory program seem to explain a significant proportion of the variation in school outcomes. For the two samples in the study, the final solution did not call for a direct path from socioeconomic status to college achievement. This finding is consistent with that reported by Astin (1971): He did not find any significant relationship between the income of the students' parents and freshman grade-point averages even after controlling for high school grade-point average and academic aptitude.

CONCLUSIONS AND POLICY IMPLICATIONS

Issues of equal educational opportunity are always defined as issues of distribution. They arise from perceived inequities in the resources or benefits available to different groups of people, in this case school-age children. However, even if resources were equally distributed among all children, it does not follow that they would achieve equal school outcomes. There will always be some interindividual variability in academic achievement.

In the introductory discussion it was pointed out that college-preparatory high school programs provide the student with greater educational benefits than other types of curricula. We saw that, historically, the development of multiple tracks or curricula at the secondary school level seemed to have created an inequitable situation in which those students enrolled in a college-preparatory curriculum were given an unfair advantage over those enrolled in other curricula (e.g., vocational) insofar as educational and noneducational social benefits are concerned. Because such curricula are not as academically rigorous as the college-preparatory curriculum, the students enrolled in them are not given adequate preparation to succeed in college or to pursue higher-status occupations. Thus, their aptitude and school achievement, as well as their self-concept and educational aspirations, could be negatively affected. Being placed in a vocational program could reduce the students' opportunity to acquire knowledge and culture and could limit their freedom in choosing among career options. The existence of one classical secondary school curriculum, as was originally the case, represented a more equitable situation, in that every child had access to the same resources and, therefore, had an equal opportunity to garner all the benefits of schooling.

Because disproportionate numbers of minority and lower-class children are enrolled in non-college-preparatory curricula, these groups generally do not experience the same educational environment as does the white, middle-class majority group. If equal educational opportunity were a reality, then the outcomes of schooling would be more equal, after social class, race, and ethnicity were controlled, and a smaller gap would exist between the average achievement levels of majority and of minority children. That is, even though not all children achieve at the same level, no one racial, ethnic, or socioeconomic group would have a disproportionately large share of high achievers. Unless it can be proven that only middle-class whites and the affluent are capable of learning, then educational attainment should be distributed equally across all racial/ethnic and income groups. Any progress toward eliminating between-group differences in achievement can be interpreted as progress toward the goal of equal educational opportunity.

This study investigated whether school outcomes were equal for Chicano and white students. In comparing the outcomes for the two ethnic groups, background factors (socioeconomic status and high school curriculum) were taken into account. The data showed that the school outcomes of the Chicano sample were similar to those of the white sample. That is, the interrelationships among the background factors and the high school outcomes of the Chicano sample were similar to those of the white sample. This suggests that Chicanos who have completed two years of college at a four-year institution have patterns of aptitude, achievement, and aspirations that are similar to those of whites. Thus, the hypothesized model of factor relationships is not bound to either of the two groups sampled but rather has some generalizability.

The results also indicate that socioeconomic status and high school curriculum placement have a statistically significant effect on aptitude and educational aspirations; and changes in aptitude directly affect school achievement. That is, those students from the higher social classes and those placed in a college-preparatory curriculum in the high school generally score higher on aptitude tests, make better grades in high school and college, and aspire to higher degrees than do students from lower socioeconomic classes and those placed in a vocational or general education curriculum in high school.

The results of this study have at least three important policy implications. The first deals with the method of curriculum placement; the second looks at "mastery learning" as a teaching methodology that may enhance academic achievement and attainment; and the third involves special college admission and support programs. First, since there is a significant correlation between socioeconomic status and high school curriculum, schools may have to look more closely at the criteria used for curriculum placement. The chief criteria for placing students in either college-preparatory or vocational curricula in high school are their earlier grades and their scores on achievement or aptitude tests; to a smaller degree, teachers' perceptions of their abilities may also play a role. Indeed, grades and test scores are ultimately the basis for many educational and career decisions, since they are generally assumed to be reliable estimates of the quality of learning as well as valid measures of the quality of the student. It should be recognized, however, that even though measurements of early school outcomes are highly predictive of future academic achievement, they do not adequately explain all the students' cognitive characteristics.

Second, given the finding that high school curriculum explains a significant amount of the differences in school outcomes, schools should ensure that all students receive an education that enables them to make sound and rational decisions about the kind and the amount of education they will pursue and about the careers they will enter. It is the responsibility of the schools to help all children develop their communication, thinking, and other academic skills. The schools' failure to meet this responsibility by treating the problem at the onset of the schooling experience may indeed result in racial, ethnic, and socioeconomic groups of students eventually being placed in non-college-preparatory programs. Such placement would constitute a form of tracking that is not permissible if our society is to achieve the goal of equality of educational opportunity.

Remediation may be required in the early school years to ensure that children acquire sound learning and communication skills. The goal should be to see to it that all children are sufficiently educated to qualify for placement in a college-preparatory program in high school if that is what they desire. Under the present educational system, students are rarely given an opportunity to remedy past deficiencies. Rather, they simply receive a grade based on their past academic performance and are moved on to the next level of learning without ever being given a chance to master the necessary learning prerequisites. In this way, students are "programmed" for failure.

The goal of equal educational opportunity cannot be met merely by exposing students to a given subject matter over a period of time. Alternate teaching methodologies should be considered to remedy educational inequalities. For example, mastery learning is a teaching methodology that ensures that the student has a grasp of the prerequisites for a higher level of learning. Through this approach, grades and test scores could be used to determine the students' level of mastery of the specific knowledge and skills needed to move to a higher level. Since much of the variation in learning is accounted for by differences in the cognitive-entry characteristics of different students, mastery learning would help ensure that each student reached an adequate level of competence in the prerequisites for each new learning task. Thus, there could be larger gains in learning, and variation in final achievement could be reduced. The possibility of "altering" cognitive-entry characteristics has profound policy implications for instruction, curriculum, and views of the learning potential of almost all students.

Policymakers and educators at all levels of education should recognize that special college admission and educational opportunity programs designed to give the disadvantaged access to higher education cannot by themselves solve the problem of unequal distribution of resources and unequal outcomes in the elementary and secondary schools. Lower-social-class and minority individuals may complete high school at a worse disadvantage than that with which they started. Even if they are admitted to college under special admission programs, their persistence and achievement are by no means assured. Steps must also be taken to provide them with the skills they need for success in college. Thus, remediation, tutoring, and counseling may also be required at the college level. Only if such efforts are made will the U.S. school system have any chance of reaching the goal of providing all students with equal opportunities to reap the full educational and social benefits to which national policy decrees they are entitled.

NOTES

1. The results of the survey are published annually in a national norms report. For a more detailed account of the CIRP, including procedures for weighting the data, the reader should refer to Astin and Cross (1979).

2. Observed or manifest variables are linked to the latent factors ksi (ξ) and eta (η) through regression equations. The causal paths between the latent factors and the manifest variables are depicted by the Greek letter lambda (λ); the lambdas represent factor loadings. Each manifest variable is also influenced by other variables not specifically defined but accounted for in the model: the Greek letter theta (θ) is used to depict this error term.

The hypothesized model consists of both explanatory and dependent factors. Each of the factors can be both explanatory and criterion "variables," in a regression-analytic sense, depending on the hypothesized relationships. A correlation between explanatory factors is indicated by the Greek letter phi (ϕ), and the regression paths between the explanatory and the dependent factors are depicted by the Greek letter gamma (γ). Structural relations among the criterion or dependent factors are indicated by the Greek letter beta (β). Dependent factors are also influenced by residual variables, which are represented by the Greek letter psi (ψ).

3. Critical values represent the ratio of the structural-parameter estimates to their respective standard errors, yielding large sample z-tests for significant departure of the parameter values from zero (Bentler, 1980; Joreskog & Sorbom, 1978). In general, the parameter estimate must be at least twice the value of its standard error to be significant at the .05 alpha probability level.

4. The relative fit of a model to the sample data can also be obtained by comparing it to the null model, which consists of the unique variances of each of the observed variables. The results of this comparison indicate how much of the original variance in the observed variables is explained by the hypothetical model.

5. Although the comparison of hierarchical models with the chi-square statistic provides information about the relative importance of each hypothesized model, it is also possible to determine the amount of information gained by each competing model. Each successive (hierarchical) model may provide an increment to the amount of variance explained by the preceding model. The Bentler-Bonett (1980) index represents the increment in fit obtained in evaluating any hierarchical step-up comparison of two models. The Bentler-Bonett index yields an estimate of the proportion of original variance and covariance among the observed variables that one model accounts for relative to another more restricted model. The normed Bentler-Bonett coefficient is bounded to lie between zero and unity, with greater values indicating a better fit.

REFERENCES

Aguirre, A., Jr. (1979). Intelligence testing and Chicanos: A quality of life issue. *Social Problems, 27*(2).

Amato, J. A. (1980). Social class discrimination in the schooling process: Myth and reality. *The Urban Review, 12* (3), 121–130.

Anderson, J. G., & Evans, F. B. (1976). Family socialization and educational achievement in two cultures: Mexican-American and Anglo-American. *(Sociometry, 39*(3), 209–222.

Arce, C. H. (1978). Chicano participation in academe: A case of academic colonialism. *Grito del Sol: A Chicano Quarterly, 3*(1), 75–104.

Arias, B. (1978). *Crawford, Mary Ellen v. Board of Education of City of L.A.* Unpublished paper (response to Judge Egly's request for expert witnesses' testimonies regarding Los Angeles Unified School Districts Desegregation Plan).

Asbury, A. (1975). Selected factors influencing over- and under-achievement in young-age children. *Review of Educational Research, 44*(4).

Assembly Permanent Subcommittee on Postsecondary Education. (1975). *Unequal access to college: Postsecondary opportunities and choices of high school graduates* (staff report). Sacramento, CA: California Legislature.

Astin, A. W. (1971). *Predicting academic performance in college.* New York: Free Press.

Astin, A. W. (1975a, July). *The myth of equal access in public higher education.* Keynote address for conference on equality of access in postsecondary education, Atlanta, GA.

Astin, A. W. (1975b). *Preventing students from dropping out.* San Francisco: Jossey-Bass.

Astin, A. W. (1977). *Four critical years.* San Francisco: Jossey-Bass.

Astin, A. W. (1979). Testing in postsecondary education: Some unresolved issues. *Educational Evaluation and Policy Analysis, 1*(6), 21–28.

Astin, A. W., Fuller, B., & Green, K. C. (1978). *Admitting and assisting students after Bakke.* San Francisco: Jossey-Bass.

Astin, H. S., & Cross, P. H. (1979). *Financial aid and persistence in college.* Los Angeles: Higher Education Research Institute.

Astin, H. S., Astin, A. W., Bisconti, A. S., & Frankel, H. H. (1972). *Higher education and the disadvantaged student.* Washington, DC: Human Service Press.

Ballesteros, E. J. (1982). *The Chicano and equal educational opportunity: The relationship between school outcomes, family background, and high school outcomes.* Unpublished doctoral dissertation, University of California, Los Angeles.

Barrera, M. (1977). Class segmentation and the political economy of the Chicano, 1900–1930. *The New Scholar, 6,* 167–181.

Bentler, P. M. (1980). Multivariate analysis with latent variables: Causal modeling. *Annual Review of Psychology, 31,* 419–456.

Bentler, P. M., & Bonett, D. G. (1980). Significance tests and goodness-of-fit in the analysis of covariance structures. *Psychological Bulletin, 88*(3), 588–606.

Bloom, B. S. (1981). *The new direction in educational research and measurement: Alterable variables.* Invited address at the American Educational Research Association Annual Meeting, Los Angeles.

Bowles, S., & Gintis, H. (1976). *Schooling in capitalist America.* New York: Basic Books.

Brown, G. H., Rosen, N. L., Hill, S. T., & Olivas, M. A. (1980). *The condition of education for Hispanic Americans.* Washington, DC: National Center for Education Statistics.

Brown v. Board of Education of Topeka, Kan., 347 U.S. 483 (1954).

Cheng, C. W., Brizendine, E., & Oakes, J. (1979). What is "An Equal Chance" for minority children? *Journal of Negro Education, 48*(3), 267–287.

Clark, M. (1976). Changing meanings of equal educational opportunity. *Theory Into Practice, 15*(1), 77–84.

Coleman, J. S. (1966) *Equality of educational opportunity.* Washington, DC: U.S. Office of Education, Department of Health, Education and Welfare.

Coleman, J. S. (1968). The concept of equality of educational opportunity. *Harvard Educational Review, 38*(1), 7–22.

Duncan, O. D. (1975). *Introduction to structural equations models.* New York: Academic Press.

Duncan, O. D., Featherman, D. L., & Duncan, B. (1972). *Socioeconomic background and achievement.* New York: Seminar Press.

Ellett, F. S., Jr. (1977). *Fairness of college admissions procedures: A criticism of certain views*. Unpublished doctoral dissertation, Cornell University, New York.

Espinoza, R., Fernández, C., & Dornbusch, R. (1977). Chicano perceptions of high school and Chicano performance. *Aztlán: International Journal of Chicano Studies, 8*.

García, J. (1977). Intelligence testing: Quotations, quotas, and quackery. In J. L. Martinez, Jr. (Ed.), *Chicano psychology*. New York: Academic Press.

García, J. (1977, November 21). The Bakke case: Reverse, or enforced discrimination? *La Gente*.

Gilmarten, K. J. (1980, April). *The status of women and minorities in education: A social indicator feasibility study*. Paper presented at the Annual Meeting of the American Educational Research Association, Boston.

Green, T. (1971). Equal educational opportunity: The durable justice. In R. D. Heslep (Ed.), *Proceedings of the Twenty-Seventh Annual Meeting of the Philosophy of Education Society* (pp. 121–143).

Green, T., Ericson, D. P., & Seidman, R. H. (1980). *Predicting the behavior of the educational system*. Syracuse, NY: Syracuse University Press.

Gutiérrez, F. (1978, August). *Through Anglo eyes: Chicanos as portrayed in the news media*. Paper presented to the Panel on Coverage of the Whole Community: Coverage of Non-elites of the History Division of the Association for Education in Journalism, Seattle, WA.

Harnquist, K. (1968). Relative changes in intelligence from 13 to 18. *Scandinavian Journal of Psychology, 9*, 50–82.

Haro, M. (1978). *Criticisms of traditional postsecondary school admission criteria: A search for alternatives*. Chicano Studies Research Center Publications (Vocational Paper No. 1), University of California, Los Angeles.

Jencks, C. (1972a). *Inequality: A reassessment of the effect of family and schooling in America*. New York: Basic Books.

Jencks, C. (1972b). *The effect of high schools on their students*. Cambridge, MA: Harvard Center for Policy Research.

Jencks, C. (1972c). *Who gets ahead*. New York: Basic Books.

Joreskog, K. G. (1979). *Longitudinal research in the study of behavior and development*. New York: Academic Press.

Joreskog, K. G., & Sorbom, D. (1978). *LISREL IV: Analysis of linear structural relationships by the method of maximum likelihood*. Chicago: National Educational Resources.

Karabel, J. (1972). Community colleges and social stratification. *Harvard Educational Review, 42*(4), 521–562.

Kerlinger, F. N. (1964). *Foundations of behavioral research* (2nd ed.). New York: Holt, Rinehart and Winston.

Levin, H. (1970). Educational reform: Its meaning. In *Educational Policy* (pp. 23–51). New York: Academic Press.

López, R., & Enos, D. (1972). *Chicanos and public higher education in California*. Sacramento, CA: Joint Committee on the Master Plan.

López, R. W., Madrid-Barela, A., & Macías, R. F. (1976). *Chicanos in higher education in California: Status and issues*. Chicano Studies Research Center Publications (Monograph No. 7), University of California, Los Angeles.

Mercer, J. (1973). *Labeling the mentally retarded.* Berkeley: University of California Press.

Muñoz, D. G., & García-Bahne, B. (1978). *A study of the Chicano experience in higher education.* Unpublished study funded by the Center for Minority Group Mental Health Programs of the National Institute for Mental Health, San Diego.

Nader, R., & Nairn, A. (1980). *The rating of the ETS: The corporation that makes up minds.* Washington, DC: The Ralph Nader Report on the Educational Testing Service, Learning Research Project.

Nesselroade, J. R., & Reese, H. W. (1973). *Life-span developmental psychology: Methodological issues.* New York: Academic Press.

Olivas, M. A. (1978, October). *Hispanics in higher education: Status and legal issues.* Paper presented to the National Association of College Admissions Counselors, Bal Harbour, Florida.

O'Reilly, R. C. (1970). Racially integrated schools and the future of public education. *Educational Leadership, 20*(8), 837–840.

Pantages, T. J., & Creedon, C. F. (1978). Studies of college attrition: 1950–1975. *Review in Educational Research, 48*(1), 49–101.

Pedrini, D. T., & Pedrini, B. C. (1976). Assessment and prediction of grade point and/or attrition/persistence for disadvantaged and regular college freshmen. *College Student Journal, 10*(3), 260–264.

Pedrini, D. T., & Pedrini, B. C. (1977). Multivariate prediction of attrition/persistence for disadvantaged and control collegians. *College Student Journal, 11*(3), 239–242.

Peng, S. S. (1976). *Some trends in the entry to higher education: A comparison between NLS and Project TALENT.* Paper presented at the annual meeting of the American Psychological Association, Washington, DC.

Peng, S. S., Ashburn, E. A., & Dunteman, G. H. (1977). *Withdrawal from institutions of higher education.* Chapel Hill, NC: Research Triangle Institute.

Peng, S. S., Dunteman, G. H., & Fetters, W. B. (1975). *Selected results from the base-year and the first follow-up surveys.* Paper presented at the annual meeting of the American Psychological Association, Washington, DC.

Peng, S. S., & Fetters, W. B. (1977). *College student withdrawal: A motivational problem.* Paper presented at the annual meeting of the American Educational Research Association, New York.

Plessy v. Ferguson, 163 U.S. 537, 16 Supreme Court 1138, 1896.

Rice, L. D. (1976, February). *Race, poverty and the colleges.* Paper prepared for the Conference on Racial and Ethnic Data of the Institute for the Study of Educational Policy, Howard University.

Rogosa, D. (1979). Causal models in longitudinal research: Rationale, formulation, and interpretation. In J. R. Nesselroade & P. B. Baltes (Eds.), *Longitudinal research in the study of behavior and development.* New York: Academic Press, pp. 263–302.

Schafer, W., Olexa, C., & Polk, K. (1973). Programmed for social class: Tracking in American high schools. In N. K. Denzin (Ed.), *Children and their caretakers.* (pp. 200–226). New Brunswick, NJ: Transaction Books.

Sewell, W. H., & Hauser, R. M. (1975). *Education, occupation, and earnings.* New York: Academic Press.

Thomas, G. E. (1975). *Race and sex effects in the process of educational achievement.* Unpublished doctoral dissertation, University of North Carolina.

Thomas, G. E., Alexander, K. L., & Eckland, B. K. (1979). Access to higher education: The importance of race, sex, social class, and academic credentials. *School Review, 87*(2), 133–156.

Thornton, C. H. (1977, March). The educational attainment process: Some important interaction effects. *The Black Sociologist.*

University of California. (1975). *Report of the President's Task Force on Chicanos and the University of California.* Berkeley: University of California, Berkeley.

U.S. Commission on Civil Rights. (1973–1974). *Mexican-American educational study* (Reports V and VI). Washington, DC: U.S. Government Printing Office.

U.S. Department of Commerce, Bureau of the Census. (1978). *Population characteristics: Persons of Spanish origin in the U.S., March 1977* (Series P-20, No. 329). Washington, DC: U.S. Government Printing Office.

Wilson, W. J. (1978). *The declining significance of race.* Chicago: University of Chicago Press.

Wingard, J. A. (1980). Measures of attitudes toward the elderly: A statistical reevaluation of comparability. *Experimental Aging Research, 6*(3), 299–313.

Wingard, J. A., Huba, G. J., & Bentler, P. M. (1980). *Psychosomatic symptomatology and substance use in adult women: A structural modeling analysis.* Unpublished manuscript, System Development Corporation and the University of California, Los Angeles.

Wolfe, L. M. (1978, March). *Strategies of path analysis.* Paper presented at the annual meeting of the American Educational Research Association, Toronto, Canada.

Wright, E. O. (1978). Race, class and income inequality. *American Journal of Sociology, 83*(6), 1368–97.

3 | Hispanics in High School and Beyond

FRANÇOIS NIELSEN

This paper is about High School and Beyond (HS&B), a national survey of students in the tenth and twelfth grades. The combination of a large national sample of Hispanics together with the wealth of information of special relevance for language minorities makes the HS&B data particularly useful for the study of many issues related to Hispanic education.[1] The main purpose of the paper is to discuss general substantive and methodological considerations that researchers are likely to face in using the HS&B data for the study of Hispanic education. In the first section, I emphasize the necessity of placing the HS&B data in a broad historical and demographic context. The core of the paper consists of a discussion of five examples of research concerns that illustrate the opportunities, difficulties, and pitfalls associated with data of this nature: school delay, school retention, the transition to higher education, and the effects of language skills and of bilingual education on school achievement. A major aspect of HS&B is its longitudinal design. Much of the substantive discussion that follows depends on the longitudinal structure of the HS&B study.

A DEMOGRAPHIC MODEL OF SCHOOLING AND A TYPOLOGY OF RESEARCH ISSUES

In order to organize policy and research issues concerning Hispanics in the U.S. school systems and to assess the import of HS&B with respect to these issues, it is necessary to emphasize the demographic and processual aspects of Hispanic education. The demographic view provides a very mechanistic picture of the schooling experience in which

Much of the research summarized in this paper was made possible by a grant from the Spencer Foundation, to which I wish to express my gratitude.

71

students with a variety of characteristics are processed by educational institutions over time and end up as adults in a variety of occupations, with different statuses, political influences, family situations, and so on.

The demographic focus as a starting point has several advantages. First, research issues concerning Hispanics can be naturally identified with a particular step, or set of steps, in this time-dependent model of the schooling process. This leads to a consistent typology of issues concerning Hispanic students or, for that matter, students in general. Second, basic demographic constraints are often forgotten in existing research on Hispanics. The model helps clarify the value of a wide array of empirical results and the potential importance of data sets with different structures. Third, the model helps in situating correctly historical aspects of the process, such as the effects of global political events. This should help prevent gross misperceptions resulting from a collapsed view of history. For example, two important events for the education of language minorities are Title VII in 1968 and the judicial mandate resulting from *Lau v. Nichols* in 1974. Students sampled in HS&B, who were in grades 10 or 12 in the spring of 1980, were in first grade during 1971 and 1969, respectively. These students would normally have started school well before *Lau v. Nichols*—at a time, especially for the seniors, when the full impact of Title VII on bilingual programs could not have been achieved. Since the availability of bilingual education is probably most crucial during the early years of schooling, the HS&B data capture the impact of these global events partially at best. Note, however, that, as I will discuss later, much bilingual education was already extant when these two cohorts were in the sensitive age brackets, either as informal arrangements or officially mandated, as for Cubans (see Pedraza-Bailey & Sullivan, 1979). To that extent, the data do provide information on these issues. (See the discussion of bilingual education below.)

The demographic model of schooling is summarized in figure 3.1. The figure is a particular implementation of a Lexis diagram used by demographers (see Pressat, 1972). Calendar time is represented on the horizontal axis, with intervals corresponding to the academic year. The vertical axis represents ideal steps in the life history of young men and women in the age brackets relevant for the HS&B target population. The educational careers of individuals can be represented as diagonal lines across the graph: As children become older, they go through the successive educational steps from kindergarten through primary and high school to college and university, ending up in the labor force. However, the regular progression of students through grades of the educational system as they grow older represents only a form of stan-

Figure 3.1: The Demographic Model of Schooling

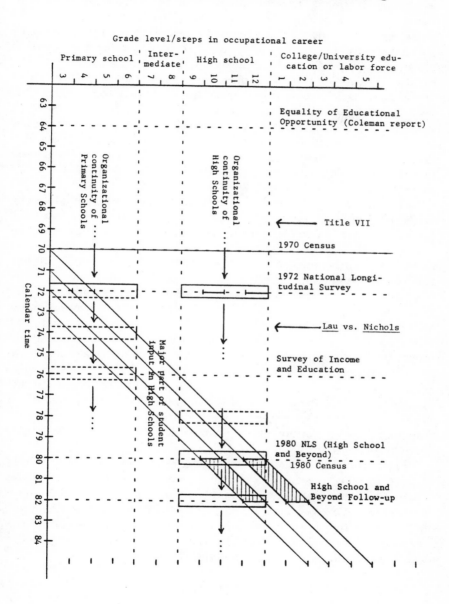

73

dard, or ideal, career profile. There are many ways in which the educational-occupational career of individual students may be nonstandard. Students may skip a grade, which would correspond to a vertical segment in the career profile. They can repeat a grade; this corresponds to a lateral shift (a horizontal segment) in the career trajectory. Students can also disappear from the educational-occupational ladder entirely, because of death or migration out of the system, or may drop out of school for a variety of reasons. Note, however, that the standard, or ideal, career assumes a crucial importance in most policy discussions of educational matters as a benchmark of comparisons between the fates of various subgroups of the population. The greater propensity of Hispanics to be left behind, to drop out of school, and to achieve generally lower levels of education than the general population are major topics for policy debate and research.

The fate of a group in the educational-occupational ladder can be represented by aggregating individual career trajectories. For example, the history of a particular age cohort would be represented as the diagonal surface with its base corresponding to the line segment between a minimum and maximum birth date. The diagonal surface, however, represents only the fate of those students who remain in the standard career. Individual deviations from the standard career for that cohort will result in a funnel-shaped graph as students deviate either vertically (grade skipping) or laterally (school delay) from the standard progression. Because the Lexis representation of age cohorts, with the appropriate details, provides a complete picture of the fate of a specific group of individuals, it can be used to compare the total effect of the social environment across groups defined by a variety of criteria. In this particular instance, the demographic model should be used to assess in a global way the progress of one or several culturally distinct groups (e.g., Hispanics from a variety of origins) within the entire educational-occupational ladder.

The demographic model above is a purely descriptive device. Most research issues revolve around the causal mechanisms that generate the fate of a particular group in the educational-occupational ladder. These more substantive aspects can be naturally associated with the demographic model of figure 3.1. To do this it is convenient to distinguish three broad categories of variables and relationships: those pertaining to the *input, process,* and *outcome* of education.

Input

A first category of variables relevant in the history of a cohort may be referred to as input variables. Input variables characterize the raw material schools have to deal with in the educational process. They may be measures of the language proficiency of students, of their socioeconomic background, or of other characteristics of the family—in general, measures of the result of the entire history of students prior to entry into the relevant educational and professional institution. Controlling for input characteristics upon entry into the educational-occupational organization of interest may be crucial for analytical purposes. For example, to assess the effect of high school practices on achievement, one must keep in mind that much of the achievement differences among students may be due to a heterogeneity already present upon entry, and that this heterogeneity may be the result in part of what happened in primary school or of experiences prior to that stage. Obviously, then, the impact of policy decisions directed at the secondary level, for example, cannot be properly assessed without controlling for input characteristics, the result of earlier events that cannot be controlled at this level of organization. In the logic of most research issues concerning Hispanics, input variables are not directly at stake but have the status of *controls* in the study of some other items of interest, such as the effectiveness of bilingual education or the effects of Hispanic concentration (or segregation).

Process

A second category of variables and causal relationships comprises all the elements that describe and explain the experience of students in high school. These elements pertain to the process of secondary education. Disentangling their effects on the fate of students is, of course, crucial for policymaking purposes. The process category is quite heterogeneous, so that further categorizations are useful. A first distinction is between those factors that pertain to the experience of students within the school setting, such as characteristics of the school environment or teaching practices, and the experience of students outside school. The distinction between *school* and *nonschool* variables is important simply because schools have control over only a limited fraction of the student's life. Within the school-variables subcategory, one might wish to distinguish further according to the relative degree of plasticity of various elements of the schooling process, between school *characteristics* and school *behavior*. Characteristics are relatively independent from school-level decisions; they can change only relatively slowly. The social and ethnic mix of the student body and the layout of the physical plant of the school are examples. *Behavior* refers to factors that are presumably more fluid, such as teaching practices. Within the category of nonschool variables, one might distinguish according to the level of analysis, or the degree to which a particular set of factors is idiosyncratic with respect to the student, between variables pertaining to the micro-, meso-, and macroenvironments. (See Nielsen, 1980, for further discussion of this classification.)

Outcomes

A third broad category of variables that are central for policy and research issues related to the education of Hispanics comprises various measures of the output of the system. Much of the policy debate with respect to the fate of a particular subgroup of the population in the educational system centers on comparisons of the outcomes of education for that group with the outcomes for a group identified as a suitable standard of comparison, such as the entire population or a subset assumed to be relatively privileged (e.g., white males not of Hispanic origin). One can distinguish two main categories of outcome variables: the *distributional* and *nondistributional* outcomes.

The distributional outcomes describe the distribution of members of the group within the general educational-occupational ladder introduced earlier. In view of the demographic model of schooling of figure 3.1, which represents the progression of a cohort through the educational-occupational ladder, these outcomes can be thought of as the result of a branching process by which members of a cohort are allocated to a variety of exits. Depending on emphasis, the distributional outcome may be measured at different stages of the process as school retention or holding power (the proportion taking the normal, or standard, exit at that stage), as dropout rates (the proportion leaving school), as the proportion continuing their education after high school (a variety of school retention), and, finally, as the distribution of members among occupational categories (characterized by their prestige, or the associated economic rewards) after the educational process is completed.

The nondistributional outcomes are measures of the accumulated effects of schooling and other factors on individual characteristics, skills, and attitudes that are conceptually independent of the position of an individual within the general educational-occupational ladder. These may be measures of the success of the school system in transmitting particular types of knowledge (cognitive skills) or of the effect of schooling on the psychological state of the individual (self-esteem, self-perception, aspirations). With respect to linguistic, cultural, and ethnic minorities such as Hispanics, an important set of nondistributional outcomes is the one related to the assimilationist effect of schooling. The latter comprises measures of language dissolution, language retention, ethnic identification, cultural (as opposed to linguistic) assimilation, and so on.

Table 3.1 provides a rough typology of research issues concerning the education of Hispanics and summarizes the previous discussion. The table may be viewed as the substantive counterpart to the demographic model of figure 3.1, inasmuch as it emphasizes the conceptual and causal aspects of the educational process. Most research issues pertain to the process and outcomes categories.

First, there are debates focusing on the *outcomes* of schooling for various Hispanic subgroups. These debates have the logical structure of a comparison of some outcome for Hispanics with the outcome for the population as a whole or for some other identifiable subgroup (such as "Anglos") chosen as a standard of comparison. The structure of such issues is often relatively simple because it emphasizes raw differences in outcomes without necessarily presuming anything with respect to the causal processes leading to the disadvantaged situation of the minority groups. The main research problem is one of measurement. However, some outcome issues can be quite controversial because there is political disagreement concerning the desired ends of the process. The desirability of maintaining the use of Spanish is a typical example.

Second, there are the *process* issues, which focus on some aspect of the technology or circumstances of the educational experience of Hispanics. These issues are intrinsically more complex than the outcome issues because they involve causal statements about the relationships between process variables and outcomes. Therefore, there may be disagreement with respect to both the desirability of the ends and the effectiveness of the means. Typical illustrations of the complexity of process issues are the discussions of effects of segregation-desegregation policies and of bilingual-bicultural programs. Insofar as process issues involve causal statements (at least implicitly) about the effect of some process variable on the outcome of interest, they typically generate problems of evaluation of the extent to which a modification of the educational technology (e.g., bilingual programs) produces the desired outcome. This is essentially an experimental problem. A central area of methodological concern with respect to High School and Beyond is the extent to which a data set with a quasi-experimental structure, insofar as many possibly confounding factors can be controlled for by covariance-control methods, can provide evaluation results relevant to these process issues. Examples of such concerns are discussed in the next section.

Table 3.1: Components of the Policy Debate with Respect to Hispanics in the Secondary School System

A. Input $\longrightarrow$	B. Process $\longrightarrow$	C. Output $\longrightarrow$

1. Group composition with respect to universalistic criteria (e.g., poverty, socioeconomic status of parents, living conditions)	1. School variables
	  a. School characteristics (e.g., segregation, physical plant)
	  b. School behavior; teaching practices (e.g., ways of dealing with language minority students)
		1. Distributional outcomes
		  a. School retention or holding power at various stages of schooling process; also what happens to those who quit
		  b. Distribution in the labor force

2. Group distinctiveness with respect to idiosyncratic criteria: (e.g., cultural and linguistic assimilation, historical differences among Hispanic subgroups)	2. Nonschool variables
	  a. Microenvironment (family circumstances during schooling)
	  b. Mesoenvironment (e.g., segregation in community, opportunities within local labor market)
		2. Nondistributional outcomes (e.g., cognitive achievement, self-esteem, aspirations, linguistic and cultural assimilation—keeping in mind dependent and independent status of these variables)

3. Experience of cohort prior to entry into high school system (e.g., primary school experience, recent immigration)	c. Macroenvironment (e.g., global economic trends, regional variations, state or federal policy decisions)	

NOTE: Arrows are drawn to emphasize the temporal ordering of various components of policy debates.

ANALYZING EDUCATIONAL ISSUES
WITH THE HS&B DATA

In this section, I discuss examples of educational issues that can be addressed, to varying extents, with the HS&B data: school delay, school retention, the transition to higher education, the effects of language skills on school achievement, and the role of bilingual education. Each discussion will either summarize analyses already done, suggest others that should be, or point out topics for research that can be fruitfully addressed when the follow-up data become available. The list of issues is by no means meant to be exhaustive. Rather, issues are chosen to illustrate typical possibilities, and limitations, of the HS&B data.

School Delay

From the demographic perspective advocated in the previous section, school delay, or the discrepancy between the educational level reached by students and the normal level corresponding to their age, is a typical distributional outcome of the educational process. Delay rates are substantially greater for Hispanics than for the general population (see, for example, U.S. Commission on Civil Rights, 1978, p. 6; Carter & Segura, 1979, p. 69; Aspira, 1976). Therefore, delay is justifiably viewed as an early symptom of the inherent disadvantage of Hispanic students in the school system.

School delay may be viewed as an undesirable condition in itself; more specifically, it measures the extra amount of time (and, presumably, also money and effort) that the delayed students and their families have to expend to reach the same educational credentials as students who follow a more typical career. But a more critical aspect of delay is that it often seems to constitute the first symptom of the malintegration of students within the school and the start of a cumulative process that ultimately results in the students leaving the school curriculum entirely. As students fall behind, they may become discouraged, be labeled by educators as low achievers, feel an increasing discrepancy between their normal physiological-psychological maturation and school conditions tailored for a younger group, be under greater pressures to earn a living, and so on, all of which lead to a decision to drop out. The relationship between delay and a greater propensity to drop out has been documented for Mexican Americans by Carter and Segura (1979) and for Puerto Ricans by Aspira (1976).

To give an idea of the magnitude of the disadvantage of Hispanics with respect to delay, table 3.2 gives the percentages, separately by sex,

Table 3.2:   Percentage Delayed at Least Two Years, By Sex

	Males		Females	
	%	*N*	*%*	*N*
Sophomores				
Mexican American	15.5	899	10.5	1026
Cuban	15.4	123	13.2	168
Puerto Rican	15.7	151	7.7	189
Other Latin American	10.4	308	8.3	342
Non-Hispanic black	16.8	388	10.0	487
Non-Hispanic white	6.3	467	3.4	495
Seniors				
Mexican American	10.7	863	9.0	940
Cuban	11.0	122	2.2	208
Puerto Rican	10.8	115	14.4	177
Other Latin American	6.9	285	11.2	301
Non-Hispanic black	9.4	376	5.2	528
Non-Hispanic white	3.8	471	1.4	503

SOURCE: Modified from Nielsen & Fernández (1982), appendix B.

of students in various groups whose age is at least two years above the modal age for the grade in the whole population (fifteen years for sophomores and seventeen years for seniors). Much could be said on the basis of the figures in table 3.2. Because of space limitation, I note only two of the patterns that emerge. First, Hispanics are delayed to a substantially greater extent than non-Hispanic whites. This only confirms the pattern found from other data sources. Second, the fact that delay rates are generally greater for sophomores than for seniors seems to confirm the suspicion that delayed students are more likely to drop out of school entirely. The relationship between delayed schooling and school leaving is discussed in the next section.

A natural research topic, one that can be addressed to some extent with the first wave of the HS&B data, is a search for the causes of delay. Several studies to date (Nielsen & Fernández, 1982; Nielsen & Lerner, 1982) have looked for causes of delay by regressing the age of the student on individual characteristics such as the socioeconomic status of the family, linguistic proficiency, or the history of residence in the United States. Salient findings from these studies are that greater English proficiency and higher socioeconomic status of the family reduce age (or delay). Conversely, more frequent use of Spanish at home increases the likelihood of delay. It should be noted that school delay is the only indicator of achievement for which the propensity to use

Spanish has a detrimental effect. As will be shown later, maintenance of the Spanish language has a beneficial effect on other aspects of achievement such as grade-point average and educational expectations.[2] The impact of the history of residence in the United States is complex. Nielsen and Lerner (1982) find that while age decreases the longer the *mother* has resided in the country, the length of residence of the *respondent* increases the likelihood that the student is left behind. Nielsen and Lerner discuss several interpretations of this puzzling result.

One pattern found in all the studies cited is that the predictive power of the regression equations is lower for age than for other measures of educational outcomes. While the R-square of an equation for grade-point average or educational expectations, for example, reaches about .3, the R-square for age is typically lower, on the order of .1. Two obvious reasons for this difference in the predictive power of a set of individual characteristics pertain to the peculiar nature of age as an indicator of achievement. First, it is largely cumulative over the entire school career of an individual since it is unusual for a student to skip a grade after repeating one. One would therefore expect current characteristics of the student to be less powerful in explaining delay than in explaining more current achievement measures, since grade repetition (or delay for another reason) may have occurred at an earlier age under different circumstances. Second, much of the age variation in the HS&B sample is probably due to the relationship between the respondent's birth date and the date of the survey in the spring of 1980, and largely random with respect to substantive explanatory factors. For this reason also, one would expect the fit of the explanatory model to be less.

However, there may be a more profound reason for the poor performance of models that emphasize individual characteristics as determinants of delay. Much age variation may be due to differences in the policies and practices of local school systems regarding grade repetition. Carter and Segura (1979) document the substantial variation in delay rates across states for Mexican Americans, and Aspira (1976) shows the variation across metropolitan areas for Puerto Ricans. Variations in school policies and practices *may* explain some of these differences. This possibility might be explored further with the data available by incorporating between-school or between-region variation in regression models for age. To my knowledge, no such research has been done so far. A finding of substantial heterogeneity across schools or regions (net of individual factors) would have interesting policy implications. It would suggest that reforming school policies could reduce the proportion of delayed students and minimize the harmful consequences of being left behind.[3]

Another natural avenue of research is to investigate the consequences of delay, especially on the propensity to drop out of school
before graduation. This possibility is discussed in the next section.
Two general limitations of the HS&B data with respect to the study of
school delay should be emphasized. First, and this is also a problem for
other research topics, students in the sample are selected, since those
who have dropped out before grade 10 (for sophomores) are not
included in the analysis. If delayed students tend to leave school disproportionately (as a comparison of sophomore and senior rates suggests),
HS&B figures underestimate the incidence of delay. This is true even
for sophomores. Estimates from the Survey of Income and Education of
1976 indicate that among Hispanic dropouts, 60 percent had left school
before grade 10 (NCES, 1976). Other methodological consequences of
selection will be discussed later. A second limitation is that the base-year
data do not provide information on the timing and circumstances of
grade repetition. It would be useful to know whether a student has had
to repeat a grade, and when. Grade repetition at a later age, for
example, would seem to constitute a more traumatic event for the
individual and to be more likely to precipitate a departure from school.
Information on grade repetition would also help clarify the meaning of
age as an indicator of delay, since students may be older than their peers
for a variety of reasons other than repeating a grade, such as having
started school at a later age, having experienced certification difficulties
in transferring to the U.S. school system from abroad, or having
dropped out of school for a period of time before reentering. Fortunate-
ly, information on grade repetition has been obtained in the 1982
follow-up and is now available for analysis, so that some of the ambiguities just mentioned can be investigated.

School Retention: Dropout, Pushout, Pullout

School retention or, conversely, school leaving constitutes another distributional outcome, since leaving school before graduation may be viewed
as a nonstandard exit from an educational career. In view of the
importance of educational credentials in modern society, and maybe
also the amount of learning these credentials represent, school
nonattendance is a crucial issue for Hispanics. The disadvantage of
Hispanics in the U.S. school system measured in various ways
(nonattendance in school for given age brackets, nongraduation from
high school) is documented by the U.S. Commission on Civil Rights
(1978, p. 10) and the NCES (1979, pp. 184–185). Although school
nonattendance for Hispanics has decreased since 1960, the rates are still

substantially greater than for the general population. Researchers have approached the problem of leaving school with very different assumptions about the appropriate category of explanations they seek. The initial assumptions are of three basic types and can be conveniently associated with the particular term a researcher uses to describe leaving school before graduation.

The term *dropout* is probably the traditional way of denoting a student who leaves the normal educational career. But the term seems to emphasize individual idiosyncratic reasons for the decision of a student to leave school, as in the sentence "He is a high school dropout." The responsibility for the regrettable event sounds as if it is located in some basic flaw of the individual. Those engaged in research or policy action who are sympathetic toward Hispanics or other minorities that are disadvantaged with respect to retention rates prefer the more recent term *pushout*. The expression implies that it is the behavior, and the failure, of the school that forces out students from a particular background disproportionately. Here organizational causes, such as the inadequacy of the school, are emphasized. However, a third conceptual approach emphasizes neither individual attributes nor the responsibility of the school system. Rather, the emphasis is on environmental causes of the decision to quit. These environmental factors might be the structure of economic opportunities, peer pressures, or other causes. In an early article, for example, Beverly Duncan (1965) shows convincingly that historical changes in continuation rates, which is one possible measure of school retention, have regularly covaried with changes in job opportunities for the general population: "When jobs are scarce, young men seem to defer leaving school; when jobs are plentiful, the dropout rate accelerates" (p. 134). To express this focus on the environmental context and keep the terminology symmetrical, I propose the term *pullout* to describe the process by which a student leaves school because of the greater attraction of opportunities outside.

With respect to Hispanics, it seems both that the pullout mechanisms of school retention are crucial and have not received enough systematic attention, and that it is theoretically useful to adopt a definition of "economic opportunities" broader than the one most social scientists would normally assume. For example, Moore, García, García, Cerda, & Valencia (1978, pp. 27–34) argue that the labor market of the barrio is composed of three sectors. Besides the normal wage-labor market, two major alternative sources of income for residents are welfare (food stamps, Aid to Families with Dependent Children, and other benefits) and the illegal economy. The illegal sector, which may include drug dealing, fencing, illegal gambling, and other gang activities, should be viewed as an integral part of the structure of economic opportunities, insofar as it may provide sources of income sufficiently attractive to induce a student to leave school, even though its importance may be hard to estimate. The main point here is that a researcher analyzing pullout mechanisms should look beyond "the type of jobs always described in the American dream of normalcy . . . with security, good pay, and a career ladder" (Moore et al., 1978, p. 27), since such jobs are typically scarce in communities where many Hispanics live.

The dropout, pushout, and pullout contrast has definite research implications. It points to the necessity of distinguishing individual, organizational, and nonschool environmental reasons for leaving school. There is little conclusive evidence at present on the relative importance of the three categories of causes for Hispanics. (See, however, Lucas, 1971; Takesian, 1967; Alicia & Mathis, 1975.) The HS&B data provide a comprehensive set of variables at both the individual and the school level (from a special questionnaire completed by a school administrator). Other school variables could be constructed by aggregating individual data within the school. Researchers may therefore be able to distinguish between the dropout and the pushout aspects of school retention. Controlling for pullout mechanisms seems inherently more difficult, although when the 1980 Census data at the requisite level become available, it may be possible to measure directly relevant aspects of the social context.

Whatever the analytical approach, the more meaningful research on school leaving will have to use the follow-up data on sophomores. It will then be possible to investigate the reasons Hispanic students drop out of school. The base-year data are not very useful for this purpose. While one might think that the question on educational expectations ("how far in school do you think you will get?"), which includes a "less than high school graduation" answer category, might serve as a proxy for the intention to leave school, the percentages of respondents who do not expect to graduate are so small (see table 3.3) that the question cannot be considered a realistic indicator. The decision to leave school, it seems, is typically not planned in advance by students. They leave school when faced with adverse circumstances associated with remaining in school and acceptable alternatives to school. These circumstances temporarily combine to make continuation undesirable or impossible. The convergence of bad luck is probably rarely foreseen.

While the follow-up data will certainly permit illuminating analyses, it should be kept in mind that the generality of the findings will be inherently limited. Only students who dropped out after the spring of their sophomore year are included in the sample. Those who left school

Table 3.3: Percent Distribution of Years of Schooling Respondents Expect to Complete by Population Subgroup, Spring 1980

Subgroup	Sample Size	Total	Less Than High School Completion	At Least High School but Less Than 4 Years College	4-year College Degree	Master's Degree	Ph.D., M.D., or Other Advanced Degree	Total College[a]
Sophomores								
Mexican American	2,031	100.0	2.5	69.5	14.0	6.6	7.3	27.9
Cuban	292	100.0	1.7	48.3	22.6	6.6	20.9	50.1
Puerto Rican	354	100.0	2.1	62.0	17.4	8.0	10.5	35.9
Other Latin American	691	100.0	1.6	61.5	21.5	6.1	9.2	36.8
Non-Hispanic black	939	100.0	1.7	56.5	23.1	6.9	11.7	41.7
Non-Hispanic white	971	100.0	1.0	55.6	25.0	8.7	9.7	43.4
Seniors								
Mexican American	1,857	100.0	1.1	65.3	19.0	8.6	6.0	33.6
Cuban	327	100.0	0.7	44.4	22.1	17.2	15.6	54.9
Puerto Rican	302	100.0	1.0	64.4	15.8	11.2	7.5	34.5
Other Latin American	631	100.0	1.0	62.2	20.0	7.2	9.5	36.7
Non-Hispanic black	963	100.0	0.9	53.6	24.3	11.2	9.9	45.4
Non-Hispanic white	977	100.0	0.2	56.2	23.9	10.7	9.0	43.6

Source: Nielsen & Fernández (1982), table 2.2

Note: Percentages are weighted.

[a] This column is not included in the percentage distribution.

before that time did not participate in the survey. The value of the research therefore depends on how different the causal mechanisms that determine school leaving early or late are. Only research using different data, from a different angle, can settle such issues.

Transition to Higher Education: A Race for the Handicapped

The transition from high school to college, obviously a crucial issue for Hispanics, can be studied in great detail when the follow-up data for seniors become available. It will then be possible to know exactly the educational status of the respondents roughly one and a half years after the normal time of graduation and to look for factors that differentiate between those who do or do not accede to higher education. I will argue in this section that a correct interpretation of these data necessitates, more than ever, placing the HS&B study within the larger demographic and historical framework.

Prior to the availability of the follow-up data, the base-year survey already provides information on Hispanic access to higher education. Students were asked both how far in school they "would like to get" and how far they "thought" they would get. Table 3.3 reproduces figures on the answers to the second question, which contains an element of realism. Salient features of the table, considering only the "total college" category, are the relatively lower levels of educational expectations of Hispanics compared to both whites and blacks, with the exception of Cubans, who have expectations *higher* than any other group. Note that the advantage of Cubans appears also in the greater percentage expecting more advanced degrees (Ph.D., M.D., and so forth). The small percentages of those who do not expect to complete high school have been discussed in the previous section.

Since educational expectations have been shown to be among the best predictors of actual achievement (Otto & Haller, 1979), the results of causal analyses with expectations as the dependent variable have considerable interest. Such analyses can be found in Nielsen and Fernández (1982), Fernández and Nielsen (1986), and Nielsen and Lerner (1982). Nielsen and Lerner (1982) find, for example, that for a sample of Hispanic seniors with Spanish-language background the two major determinants of expectations are ability and the socioeconomic status of the family. More intriguing findings are that while English proficiency has no effect on expectations, the extent to which a student knows Spanish and uses it at home has a substantial *positive* effect. In other words, the better students maintain the Spanish language, the higher their educational expectations. The positive effect of Spanish-language maintenance on educational expectations should be contrasted with the finding discussed above that Spanish maintenance increases the likelihood of delay. In the case of expectations, this variable has a positive effect on achievement. Finally, the relative advantage of Cubans disappears entirely when other variables are controlled for. These results and others are fully discussed in the work cited.

It will be possible to verify such causal patterns by replicating the analyses using "harder" data on actual educational achievement from successive waves of the HS&B project. However, it is important to discuss beforehand the meaning of further results on access to higher education for Hispanic education as a whole. In the demographic perspective, such as the one proposed by Duncan (1965) and elaborated in a previous section, schooling consists of a series of transitions, such as going from one grade to the next or from high school to college. A certain mortality rate is attached to each transition. The mortality rate here is defined as the proportion of students who leave the educational system at a particular transition point. Duncan defines "educational barriers" as the transitions with the highest mortality rates.[4] Educational barriers have been changing historically for the general population, which is the topic of Duncan's article. The most serious barrier used to be the one between elementary (junior high school) and high school, in the sense that most students left school after graduating from junior high. Around World War I, this transition became less important, and the transition from high school to college became the most serious obstacle.

The displacement of the major educational barrier from one educational level to a higher one has historically been accompanied for the general population both by an increase in overall attainment (measured in years of schooling) and, counterintuitively, by a *higher* mortality (dropout) rate at the new educational barrier. These dual consequences of a shift in barriers should be kept in mind in interpreting the historical-demographic evolution of Hispanic education, since there is evidence that the aggregate evolution of school attainment of Hispanics has followed the same path, with a considerable time lag, as for the general population. Figures presented by the U.S. Commission on Civil Rights (1978, p. 10) suggest that school nonattendance of Hispanics in the younger (fifteen-to seventeen-year-old) age group has declined regularly during the last two decades. However, as the NCES (1979, p. 114) shows, rates of nongraduation have not declined to the same extent; in 1977, for example, the percentage of Hispanic high school graduates in the eighteen-to thirty-four-year old population was only 56 percent, as compared to 84 percent for non-Hispanic whites.[5] These trends are consistent with the hypothesis of an upward shift in the main educational barrier for Hispanics from earlier grades to actually finishing high school. As would be expected from the demographic model, the higher overall attainment of Hispanics has meant increased attrition just prior to graduation.

A clear understanding of these demographic aspects of education is necessary to interpret correctly the information on transition to college that HS&B, especially the follow-up surveys, will provide. Clearly, going to college constitutes a crucial step in the educational career, since this particular transition often represents a major disruption in the life of the students concerned. Continuing from grade to grade in the same school system only involves, in principle, resuming day after day the same routine of getting up in the morning, traveling to familiar buildings, recognizing known faces, and so on. If there is a propensity to exit at this stage, it may be somehow dampened by the force and security of habit and investment in a known social network.

On the other hand, the transition from high school to college seems to imply a much more brutal experience for the student. First, the transition implies switching from one organization to another. This is always costly because of the necessity of establishing credentials (filling out application forms, etc.), adapting to a new environment that may be psychologically difficult, and often moving to a different geographical area. All these constitute personal costs in terms of money, time, and energy. Second, there is the generally higher cost of college education itself. Many simply cannot afford it. Third, going to college implies that individuals cannot "cash in" their newly acquired credentials. The cost of forgone opportunities becomes suddenly greater after graduation from high school, since employers tend to view education as a categorical variable measured in certificates, rather than a continuous one measured in years of schooling. Finally, this is the point at which students may have a greater burden of confronting the disapproval of parents and others who do not think going to college is the right thing to do. Any cultural difference in values would appear strongly at this point. While all these costs and difficulties would apply to some extent to all students, it seems natural to argue that they would constitute a greater obstacle for members of a relatively underprivileged minority and that this group would suffer major casualties at this transition point.

There is evidence, however, that the transition from high school to college does not (or did not until recently) constitute a major "barrier," in Duncan's technical sense of a transition with the highest mortality rate, in the education of Hispanics compared to the rest of the population. This rather startling statement can be appreciated by examining the enrollment figures for Hispanics, blacks, and whites in the eighteen- to thirty-four-year-old age group compiled by the NCES (1979, p. 114) from 1972 to 1977. The figures show that during that period, enrollment of Hispanic high school *graduates* in college has been similar to, or slightly higher than, enrollment of white graduates. In 1977, for example, the percentage of Hispanic graduates enrolled was 21 percent, as contrasted with 20 percent for non-Hispanic whites. As discussed earlier, the major disadvantage of Hispanics pertained to the percentage of high school graduates, which was much lower than for whites. These figures suggest that the major educational barrier for Hispanics has been (and maybe still is) not the transition from high school to college but high school graduation. Once Hispanic students have graduated, they have had the same or a better chance to go on to college.

Further evidence of this pattern is provided by an analysis of the 1972 National Longitudinal Survey (NLS) data by Peng (1977). His analysis, based on a longitudinal survey of which HS&B is partly a replication, shows that the overall college-going rate for Hispanic high school *graduates* is superior to that of whites but inferior to that of blacks, who have the highest rate. Peng attributes this finding to the success of affirmative action, but I believe that much more powerful mechanisms, having to do with differential selection or a "creaming effect," are at work. This point is made most clearly by the use of a parable, which I call "A Race for the Handicapped."

Suppose that a foot race is organized and there are two hundred entrants. When the participants arrive at the track, half of them are randomly selected to be "handicapped": They have to run the race holding their right foot in their hand. The race is started, and those who make it to the finish line are counted. Given the length and difficulty of the race, it is found that only fifty of the one hundred handicapped runners finish the race, as opposed to eighty of the nonhandicapped. Another finding is that the handicapped also take longer than the nonhandicapped, on the average, to complete the race. After an appropriate resting period, a second race is run involving only those who have finished the first race: the fifty survivors from the handicapped group, and the eighty from the nonhandicapped. Only this time, nobody will have to run with right foot in hand. Everybody is allowed to run with two legs. At the finish line, there is another intriguing finding: 95 percent of those who had been handicapped in the first race finished the second, but only 75 percent of the nonhandicapped did. The average time for the formerly handicapped is also lower. After some thinking, the organizers of the race find the most plausible explanation for this discrepancy: Obviously, the first race had exerted the greatest selective pressure on the handicapped. Those who made it to the finish had, on the average, greater stamina, physical strength, and energy than the nonhandicapped who succeeded. When the second race is run, literally, on equal footing, these stronger qualities will show up, and the previously handicapped, the selected group, will perform better.

In the analogy, the finish line of the first race is high school graduation. For the second race, it is college entrance. Hispanics (and other minorities) are handicapped with respect to high school completion for all the reasons that I have classified into the dropout, pushout, and pullout categories discussed in the previous section. This means that the handicap for the first race in the educational system may be a compound of individual, organizational (school), and environmental factors. But then, one would expect those who succeed among the disadvantaged group to have been more rigorously selected with respect to whatever qualities ensure success in the educational curriculum. Therefore, there *should* be a higher rate of success in the second race, the one from high school to college, for that selected group.

However, the race parable is only a simplified one. There is no guarantee in the real segment of the analogy that runners in the second race enter with no handicap: There can still be discrimination in acceptance in college and other reasons that amount to a partial handicap for the minority students. The opposite effects of greater selection and continuing handicap may well cancel out to produce enrollment figures for Hispanic graduates that are similar to those for whites. The race analogy is further simplified by assuming that finishing the race is an homogeneous outcome. In reality, the college experience is extremely variable. Institutions of higher learning differ in their prestige, the intellectual content of the education they provide, the social networks to which they give access, and other components of the quality of education. A student may also be enrolled in college full time or part time. There is definite evidence that Hispanics who do accede to higher education are more likely than whites to attend two-year colleges (Brown, Rosen, Hill, & Olivas, 1980, table 3.13) and that those in four-year institutions are concentrated in a few less prestigious schools (see Olivas, 1982, 1983, for additional clues to the lower quality of Hispanic higher education). These differences in quality are confounded in raw enrollment figures. Some of these issues, which I will not discuss further here, may be addressed with the HS&B data.

The parable is but a restatement, with emphasis on substantive aspects, of the demographic perspective used by Duncan (1965). The demographic perspective is indispensable for interpreting potentially counterintuitive results on college access. It is quite possible, for example, that the first follow-up data of 1982 will reveal relatively lower percentages of college enrollment for Hispanic graduates compared to non-Hispanic whites than for the 1972 NLS. Such figures may not indicate a general worsening of the fate of Hispanics in the educational system. An alternative possibility is that there has been a gradual improvement in the educational condition of Hispanics, resulting in a higher rate of graduation from high school. As Duncan (1965) shows, such an improvement has historically resulted in both a higher average educational achievement *and* a greater mortality rate in front of the new barrier, in this case college access. Paradoxically, lower rates of college enrollments for Hispanic graduates compared to earlier periods might be the direct symptom of further overall improvement in educational attainment, that is, higher graduation rates. Lower continuation rates would simply mean that the effects of selection, and the mortality rate, are now strongest at the higher barrier, the transition to college. To evaluate Hispanic access to higher education, it is therefore essential to consider jointly the two major transitions involved: high school graduation *and* college entrance.

Language Skills and School Achievement

All aspects of language are obviously central in policy controversies concerning Hispanic education. These issues can be approached from a variety of perspectives. A major distinction applicable to these perspectives is whether language skills are viewed as an *outcome* of or as a *factor* in the educational process. As an example of the emphasis on language as outcome, a researcher may be concerned with the effects of schooling on language skills and in particular with the extent to which schooling contributes to or undermines the maintenance of the Spanish language. Linguistic outcomes of a career in the U.S. school system have considerable social, political, and commercial implications for society as a whole (President's Commission on Foreign Language and International Studies, 1979). Another avenue of research treats language mostly as a factor, or independent variable. One may wonder, for example, about the effects of speaking Spanish at home on school achievement. Since education is a precondition for access to so many lucrative, prestigious, or otherwise desirable occupations, these effects concern anyone interested in improving the fate of Hispanics in this country. Later in this section, I will summarize results already obtained from the HS&B data on the effects of language skills on educational achievement. Space limitations prevent me from treating the first category of issues, language skills as an outcome, in sufficient detail (see Nielsen & Lerner, 1982). Before discussing substantive issues, it is necessary to describe briefly the linguistic indicators available in HS&B.[6]

Respondents with a non-English-language background were determined by a skip pattern based on a series of five questions:

1. Mother tongue—"What was the first language you spoke when you were a child?" (List of possible languages)
2. Second mother tongue—"What *other* language did you speak when you were a child before you started school?" (List including languages, and "I spoke no other language.")
3. Current language—"What language do you *usually* speak *now*?" (List of languages)
4. Usual home language—"What language do the people in your home *usually* speak?" (List of languages)
5. Second home language—"What *other* language is spoken in your home?" (List including languages, and "No other language is spoken.")

The skipping instructions specified that a respondent who had answered "English" or "No other language" to all of these five questions had completed the questionnaire. Others were instructed to continue answering the more detailed questions, having been told that the language other than English would be called "that language" in further questions. Respondents answering "Spanish" to any of the five filter questions were deemed to be of Spanish-language background.[7]

Table 3.4 shows the percentages of respondents with Spanish background for various Hispanic groups. The table reveals the substantial variation in Spanish-language background across groups: for seniors, from about 80 percent for Cubans and Puerto Ricans to 38 percent for other Latin Americans, a group that appears mostly English monolingual in background.

Respondents who had "passed" the filter were instructed to answer three additional sets of questions. The first set concerns proficiency in the language other than English: "How well do you . . . Understand that language when people speak it . . . Speak . . . Read . . . Write that language?" The four possible answers ranged from "Very well" to "Not at all." The second set inquires about the frequency of use of the non-English language in various contexts with questions of the form "How often do you speak that language to . . . ?" or "How often does . . . speak that language to you?" The five answer categories vary from "Always or almost always" to "Never." The ten questions involve the frequency of

Table 3.4: Percent Distribution of Language Background by Population Subgroups, Spring 1980

Subgroup	Sample Size	Total	Spanish Background [a]	No Spanish Background
Sophomores				
Mexican American	2,123	100.0	66.6	33.4
Cuban	306	100.0	75.0	25.0
Puerto Rican	369	100.0	72.9	27.1
Other Latin American	723	100.0	31.5	68.5
Seniors				
Mexican American	1,893	100.0	72.0	28.0
Cuban	334	100.0	79.6	20.4
Puerto Rican	308	100.0	79.6	20.4
Other Latin American	642	100.0	37.5	62.5

SOURCE: Nielsen & Fernández (1982), table 1.2

NOTE: Percentages are weighted.

[a] Respondent answered "Spanish" on at least one of five language questions concerning first language spoken; other preschool language usage; usual language spoken at home; other language spoken at home; and usual language of respondent.

use of Spanish (in this case) with the mother and the father; the parents with each other; the respondent with other relatives, best friends, and other students in school; in stores, and at work. The third set of four questions concerns proficiency in English; these questions are phrased in the same way as the Spanish-proficiency questions: "How well do you . . . English?"[8]

One objection often voiced by researchers to the HS&B language data, especially those on proficiency and use, is that they are based on self-reports. It is felt that more objective tests of language proficiency and use would be preferable. However, besides the practical difficulty of administering such tests in various non-English languages in the context of a survey such as HS&B, there are empirical reasons to take self-reported indicators seriously. Previous research (Fishman & Cooper, 1969; Fishman & Terry, 1969) has shown that this type of data is quite valid and reliable compared to many "objective" indicators of the linguistic profile. Fishman and his colleagues attribute the quality of self-reports on language to the fact that respondents are forced to perform a global assessment of their linguistic skills and habits. Most "objective" measures, such as accentedness as assessed from phonological analysis, capture more fragmentary aspects of language usage and have correspondingly lower validity.[9]

Much insight into the meaning of linguistic indicators in HS&B may be obtained from existing data. To illustrate this possibility, I summarize briefly some of the research that has been done on the effects of language skills and habits on educational achievement of bilingual Hispanics. Nielsen and Fernández (1982), for example, presented equations regressing indicators of achievement (educational aspirations, test scores, age) on a set of independent variables that included simple scales of Spanish proficiency, English proficiency, and Spanish use. One curious pattern that emerges is that, while Spanish proficiency and Spanish use are highly correlated, they have effects in opposite directions on achievement. Spanish proficiency (i.e, how *well* a student *knows* Spanish) has a positive effect on achievement, but Spanish use (i.e., how *often* a student *speaks* Spanish) has a negative effect. Such results are difficult to interpret theoretically, and the policy implications one might be tempted to draw are rather peculiar: "To improve educational achievement, Hispanics should know Spanish very well but not speak it."

Nielsen and Fernández speculate that, besides statistical artifacts, this strange result may be due to the fact that the Spanish-proficiency questions (and also those concerning English proficiency) are not pure indicators of linguistic skills. Proficiency questions ask "how well" the respondent performs a variety of verbal tasks. Even in a purely monolingual population, answers to these questions would vary, and much of this variation would represent different assessments by respondents of their general verbal ability. In other words, answers to these questions reflect a self-assessed ability component. In a bilingual population, the variation in answers might still reflect the ability component, in addition to a purely linguistic one such as the degree of Spanish dominance. Then, the positive effect of Spanish proficiency on achievement might be due to the fact that it is in part a measure of ability.

Nielsen and Lerner (1982) pursue this line of reasoning further with the use of a more complex measurement model in which ability is controlled for. Indicators of Spanish use and proficiency are viewed as multiple indicators of an underlying factor (called "Hispanicity") that represents a general propensity to know Spanish well and to speak the language frequently. It is found that the composite Hispanicity indicator has *positive* effects on achievement except for age (which is the measure of delayed schooling), after controlling for a set of background variables. These findings (and others discussed in the work cited) suggest that the structure of the language indicators in HS&B may be quite complex but that at least some of the ambiguity may be unraveled by careful analysis of the data available.

A Process Issue:
The Role of Bilingual Education

The role of bilingual education, as a research and policy issue, is central for Hispanics. A full discussion of the topic is certainly beyond the scope of this chapter. In this section I will describe briefly the HS&B data directly related to the exposure of a student to bilingual education and discuss general methodological considerations relevant to their use for research.

The indicators of exposure to bilingual education available are the following:

- Participation in a bilingual-bicultural program (in the main questionnaire)
- Whether a respondent has taken an English course designed for persons who are not native English speakers
- Whether they were taught reading and writing in a language other than English
- Whether they had had a course about the history and culture of their ancestors
- The amount of teaching done in the non-English language.

All the bilingual education questions, except the first one, were in the ID pages of the questionnaire, after the language questions, and were asked separately for grade brackets 1–6, 7–9, and 10–12.

Several considerations are important in approaching these indicators either as providing aggregate measures of the extent to which Hispanic students have been exposed to this form of education or in research on the effects of bilingual schooling on a variety of outcomes. I have already pointed out one of these considerations in a previous section: Many of the respondents in the HS&B sample may have started school before the full impact of major legislative and judicial events on the implementation of bilingual programs was felt. Therefore, aggregate measures from the HS&B data would probably underestimate the amount of bilingual education taking place in U.S. schools *now*, assuming that these events have increased the availability of bilingual programs.

Second, one should not underestimate the difficulty of measuring exposure to bilingual education, in a retrospective way, in a non-experimental setting such as the HS&B survey. These difficulties largely guided the phrasing of the questions. For example, the first question above asks whether a respondent has participated in "a bilingual-bicultural" program. Using this administrative-legal terminology is obviously insufficient to capture the full extent of the bilingual experience of a student, since students in a program may never have been informed in these words of their placement. It is also clear to those familiar with school practices that much informal bilingual education may take place in the classroom without the official existence of a "program"; this was especially so in the past. The additional bilingual education questions, which attempt to measure exposure to various ingredients of such an education, are therefore necessary for a closer approximation of the reality of school experience. One finding from preliminary analyses that corroborates these suspicions is that answers to the question using the "official" terminology are only weakly correlated with the "substantive" questions. Obviously, much more work remains to be done to clarify the meaning of these indicators.

A third category of problems has to do with the use of the HS&B bilingual education data for evaluation purposes, for example, to measure the effect of exposure to bilingual education on some outcomes (e.g., achievement) after controlling for background factors. There may be problems with this type of analysis in a nonexperimental context because of the possibility of preselection bias. The difficulty arises because assignment to a bilingual-bicultural program is rarely random: It is impossible to force parents and pupils to participate in the program if they do not want to. Presumably also assignment to, or choice of, the program is not independent of certain characteristics of the child, especially the degree of English fluency. If this is the case, it is possible to gravely misestimate the real effect of participation on later outcomes. This problem has plagued much evaluation research in bilingual education (Zappert & Cruz, 1977).

Figure 3.2 illustrates the problem. It assumes that, in the true process, participation in a program has a beneficial (positive) effect on achievement. However, proficiency in English has a negative effect on the probability of participation in the program, since the most linguistically assimilated students are more likely to choose the regular curriculum, and also the early linguistic proficiency may continue to operate at later periods and therefore have a direct positive effect on later achievement. Given the signs of the effects, if the cultural factors are not controlled, the estimated effect of participation on achievement will be biased downward. In other words, participation in the program will appear less beneficial than it actually is, or even detrimental. This is a troublesome possibility given the emotional atmosphere in which bilingual education research often takes place. While one is never absolutely

**Figure 3.2: Assessing the Effectiveness of Bilingual Education:
The Evaluation Problem**

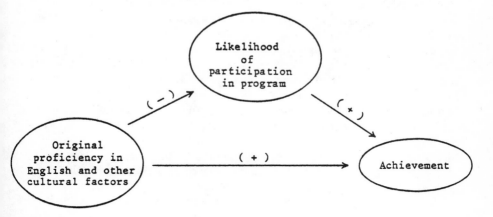

sure that one has controlled for all the relevant factors, inclusion as controls of the detailed linguistic and immigration-history variables should reduce the severity of this particular type of bias.

While the linguistic factors may be controlled to a considerable extent with the data available, there is a fourth potential difficulty that seems less easy to deal with internally. It is also related to the mechanisms by which pupils are selected for bilingual programs, and it has considerable substantive research and policy implications in addition to methodological ones. Pupils may be recruited into bilingual programs not purely on the basis of their linguistic skills but also, in part, because of their general mental abilities. Several scenarios may lead to this occurrence. A common one may start with a child doing poor work or being otherwise maladjusted in the regular curriculum. If the child is not a native English speaker, the poor performance may be attributed to linguistic difficulties when it is in fact the result of a more general intellectual deficiency. The child may be steered toward a bilingual program, which then assumes, in part, the role of a remedial device. In other cases the mechanism is more naked, when students from a non-English background who fail to reach a certain score on a standard IQ test are automatically assigned to the program. Such procedures are quite widespread. These scenarios would tend to produce a negative correlation between mental ability and the likelihood of exposure to bilingual education and to confound intellectual and linguistic factors. (See Hakuta & Díaz, 1983, for a perceptive discussion of the relationship between bilingualism and cognitive abilities.)

The empirical consequences of this type of selection process are predictable. They are but instances of the general problem of specification bias (see, e.g., Hanushek & Jackson, 1977; Heckman, 1979) and are due to causal mechanisms that are formally identical with those depicted in figure 3.2 for linguistic factors. If mental ability is negatively related to the exposure to bilingual education because of the selection procedures discussed above and is even partially stable over time, so that it is positively associated with later achievement, the effect of exposure to bilingual education on achievement may appear negative even if it is beneficial in the "true" state of affairs. Analyses attempting to evaluate effects of bilingual schooling on educational achievement are likely to produce such dismal results if the circumstances of selection into a bilingual program are not properly modeled and controlled for.

With the HS&B data, it is impossible to control directly for this type of bias in estimating the effect of bilingual education because the students in the sample were not tested for mental aptitude ten or twelve years ago before assignment to a program. The unavailability of a pretest cannot be completely compensated for, but there are analytical strategies that may correct in part the likelihood of bias. First, if a researcher is willing to make the strong assumptions that scores on tests administered in conjunction with the HS&B questionnaire are largely measures of ability as opposed to achievement (see Heyns & Hilton, 1982) and that the ability of individuals is largely stable over time, then current test scores may be used as a proxy for "native" ability and included as controls in models (e.g., regression equations) predicting achievement on the basis of exposure to bilingual education. Another, more expensive strategy would be to conduct a separate study of the relative impact of intellectual and linguistic factors in the assignment of pupils to bilingual programs. With this information, and the use of special statistical techniques for controlling selection bias (e.g., Heckman, 1979; Berk & Ray, 1982), it would be possible to obtain clearer estimates of the effect of bilingual education on achievement. There is, however, no guarantee that the selection process as it operates now is the same as the one students in the HS&B sample underwent.

CONCLUSION:
HS&B AND THE TRIANGULATION STRATEGY

As Jean-Paul Sartre argues in *Qu'est-ce que la littérature?* (*What is Literature?*), any attempt to describe reality both reveals and conceals parts of it. While Sartre has in mind mostly the literary discourse, the same principle is stated more formally by Webb, Campbell, Schwartz, & Sechrist (1966) with respect to social science research: data sets with different structures (e.g., time-series, cross-sectional, panel) reveal at best part of a process and conceal another. In particular, different data sets are likely to have different structures of the error term, or unmeasured aspects of the process. This points to a research strategy that combines several data sets that describe the phenomena under different and complementary angles. I argued above that the study of the High School and Beyond data, despite their powerful longitudinal structure, would benefit in several instances of such a triangulation strategy.

The need to supplement the High School and Beyond data with other sources is most clearly illustrated with respect to the problem of school retention for Hispanics discussed earlier. Hispanics typically have much higher dropout rates than the rest of the population. Furthermore, many students drop out of school before reaching grade 10. These students are excluded from the High School and Beyond study by definition, and one would expect the samples of Hispanics from grades 10 and 12 to be selected to a larger extent than the rest of the population because of the higher dropout rate prior to the survey. Then, the sample of Hispanics generated by the survey cannot be expected to be representative of, say, the "population of Hispanics in age groups such that they normally would be in school in the tenth and twelfth grades." Therefore, a more representative picture of the situation must be obtained, for example, from general household surveys (such as the Census or the Survey of Income and Education) that do not make inclusion in the sample dependent on school attendance.

On the other hand, the longitudinal structure of High School and Beyond can help clarify aspects of school retention that cannot be investigated with other forms of analysis. Dropout rates, for example, are often estimated from figures provided by internal school accounts. Schools distinguish between a student who has dropped out and one who has transferred to another school on the basis of a request by the other school for the record of the student. It is not difficult to imagine many scenarios that make this method of accounting suspect. With longitudinal data, it will be possible to find out exactly where students who leave a particular school go, at least for those students who drop out between their sophomore and senior years. In addition, as I have emphasized above, the HS&B data contain a wealth of information of special relevance for Hispanics (such as the detailed linguistic questions and measures of exposure to bilingual education) that is rarely, if ever, available from other studies. (The Survey of Income and Education conducted in 1976 is a partial exception.)

A systematic research strategy based on the triangulation principle would consist in identifying weaknesses of the HS&B study (some of which were illustrated in this chapter) and would set research priorities in such a way as to "fill in" the missing information or unravel possible causes of bias. For example, I have suggested above the potential usefulness of a systematic study of the demographics of school retention for Hispanics, of the selection mechanisms involved in participation in a bilingual program, and of the quality of language indicators based on self-reports, among others. While the potential rewards of such a coordinated research agenda are clear, I am not very hopeful that it will ever be implemented. Unfortunately, the autonomous dynamics of personal research interests and the structure of funding are obstacles that are often difficult to overcome.

NOTES

1. The HS&B survey is conducted for the National Center for Education Statistics (NCES) by the National Opinion Research Center (NORC) at the University of Chicago. The first wave of the survey, which took place in the spring of 1980, involved a two-stage stratified probability sample of 1,015 schools in the continental United States. Once a school was selected, up to 36 sophomores and 36 seniors were drawn randomly from the students enrolled in the school. Because the target numbers of students could not be reached in all schools for a variety of reasons, the total number of students interviewed in the first wave was 58,270. Hispanic students were oversampled to produce a sufficient number of cases. This was done by selecting, disproportionately, schools with high percentages of Hispanics in the first stage of sample selection. Schools with high proportions of Cubans were selected with even greater probability to secure enough members of that small group. This strategy produced a total of 6,698 Hispanic students, either sophomores or seniors. The questionnaire incorporated detailed questions on language usage and skills, immigration history, and exposure to bilingual education. The base-year survey of 1980 has already been complemented by the first follow-up, conducted in the spring of 1982. Follow-up data were made available to researchers in the summer of 1983. However, results summarized later in this chapter correspond to the base-year data, because the follow-up data were not available at the time of this writing. Complete documentation on the sample design and the data themselves are available from the NCES (Statistical Information Office, NCES, 1001 Presidential Building, 400 Maryland Avenue, S.W., Washington, DC 20202; Phone 202-436-7900). The oversampling of Hispanics and additions to the questionnaire were made possible by funds provided by the Office of Bilingual Education and Minority Language Affairs (OBEMLA) and the Office for Civil Rights (OCR). Detailed descriptive information on Hispanics in HS&B may be found in Nielsen and Fernández 1982.

2. The positive relationship between Spanish use and delay appears in the three studies cited, even though the analytical models used differ. However, the relationship between linguistic practices and school achievement is more complex than this brief summary indicates. Fernández & Nielsen (1986), for example, finds that while Spanish use (how often a student speaks Spanish) increases delay, Spanish proficiency (how well a student knows Spanish) does not. Such contradictory patterns are discussed below in the paragraph on linguistic skills.

3. It would *not* follow from such a finding, however, that automatic promotion to the next grade of students experiencing difficulties in school is desirable educational policy, as much current disappointment with "social promotion" and the failure of high school graduates to reach minimum levels of competency suggests. The pedagogical consequences of alternative policies concerning grade repetition would have to be thoroughly explored before practical recommendations were made.

4. Note that Duncan's technical definition of an educational barrier may differ somewhat from an intuitive understanding of "barriers" to Hispanic educational achievement. I use Duncan's definition in the remainder of this discussion.

5. The interpretation of these trends is discussed more thoroughly in Nielsen (1980).

6. The linguistic questions, in a strict sense, were contained in a separate part of the HS&B questionnaire called the "identification pages" (ID pages), the main purpose of which was to help locate the respondent in future follow-ups. Other "paralinguistic" questions, such as the indicators of exposure to bilingual education discussed in the next section, were also in the ID pages. Several questions of closely related interest, such as nativity; length of residence in the United States of respondent, mother, and father; and ethnic identification, were dispersed in the main part of the instrument. The linguistic questions were phrased in general terms such as "the language other than English" so that information was obtained on members of language minorities other than Hispanics. See Nielsen (1980) for details.

7. It should be noted that, from the linguistic point of view, this is a rather broad (inclusive) definition of "Spanish-language background."

8. The proficiency and frequency-of-use questions incorporate several central theoretical concerns of sociolinguistics: the *medium* of language use (spoken/written), the *passive* versus *active* use of the language (e.g., understand/speak), and various "spheres" or "domains" of language use (e.g., home/school). See Fishman (1966).

9. The samples on which these researchers base their conclusion are quite different from the HS&B sample (e.g., they are much more heterogeneous with respect to age and education). Therefore, it would be worthwhile to investigate the quality of the language indicators in populations comparable to those surveyed in HS&B. Such a validation study, which to my knowledge no one contemplates at present, would of course require a substantial amount of new data collection. A parallel study of that nature would be an implementation of the strategy of triangulation that I propose in the conclusion to this paper.

REFERENCES

Alicia, V. G., & Mathis, J. (1975). *Determinants of educational attainment among Puerto Rican youth in the U.S.* Washington, DC: Universidad Boricua.

Aspira. (1976). *Social factors in educational attainment among Puerto Ricans in U.S. metropolitan areas, 1970.* New York: Aspira.

Berk, R. A., & Ray, S. C. (1982). Selection biases in sociological data. *Social Science Research, 11,* 352–398.

Brown, G. H., Rosen, N. L., Hill, S. T., & Olivas, M. A. (1980). *The condition of education for Hispanic Americans.* Washington, DC: National Center for Education Statistics.

Carter, T. P., & Segura, R. D. (1970). *Mexican Americans in school: A decade of change.* New York: College Entrance Examination Board.

Duncan, B. (1965). Dropouts and the unemployed. *Journal of Political Economy, 73*(2), 121–134.

Fernández, R. M., & Nielsen, F. (1986). Bilingualism and Hispanic scholastic achievement: Some baseline results. *Social Science Research, 15*(1).

Fishman, J. A. (Ed.). (1966). *Language loyalty in the United States.* The Hague: Mouton.

Fishman, J. A., & Cooper, R. C. (1969). Alternative measures of bilingualism. *Journal of Verbal Learning and Verbal Behavior, 8,* 276–282.

Fishman, J. A. & Terry, C. (1969). The validity of census data on bilingualism in a Puerto Rican neighborhood. *American Sociological Review, 34,* 636–650.

Hakuta, K., & Díaz, R. M. (1983). The relationship between degree of bilingualism and cognitive ability: A critical discussion and some new longitudinal data. In K. E. Nelson (Ed.), *Children's language, Vol. 5.* Hillsdale, NJ: Erlbaum.

Hanushek, E. A., & Jackson, J. E. (1977). *Statistical methods for social scientists.* New York: Academic Press.

Heckman, J. J. (1979). Sample selection bias as a specification error. *Econometrica, 47,* 153–162.

Heyns, B., & Hilton, T. L. (1982). The cognitive tests for high school and beyond: An assessment. *Sociology of Education, 55* (2/3), 89–102.

Lau v. Nichols, 414 U.S. 563 (1974).

Lucas, I. (1971). *Puerto Rican dropouts in Chicago: Numbers and motivations.* Final report to the Office of Education, Project No. O-E-108.

Moore, J. W., García, R., García, C., Cerda, L., & Valencia, F. (1978). *Homeboys: Gangs, drugs and prison in the barrios of Los Angeles.* Philadelphia: Temple University Press.

National Center for Education Statistics. (1976). [Grade completion of persons 14 to 25 years old . . .]. Unpublished table based on SIE.

National Center for Education Statistics. (1979). *The condition of education: A statistical report.* Washington, DC: U.S. Government Printing Office.

Nielsen, F. (1980). *Hispanic youth in U.S. schools: A design for analysis.* Report to the National Center for Education Statistics. Chicago: National Opinion Research Center.

Nielsen, F., & Fernández, R. M. (1982). *Achievement of Hispanic students in American high schools: Background characteristics and achievement.* Washington, DC: U.S. Government Printing Office.

Nielsen, F., & Lerner, S. J. (1982). *Language skills and school achievement of bilingual Hispanics.* Unpublished report to the Spencer Foundation. Chapel Hill, NC: Department of Sociology, University of North Carolina at Chapel Hill.

Olivas, M. A. (1982). Federal higher education policy: The case of Hispanics. *Educational Evaluation and Policy Analysis, 4*(3), 301–310.

Olivas, M. A. (1983). Research and theory on Hispanic education: Students, finance and governance. *Aztlán: International Journal of Chicano Studies Research 14*(1), 111–146.

Otto, L. B., & Haller, A. O. (1979). Evidence for a social psychological view of the status attainment process: Four studies compared. *Social Forces, 57,* 887–914.

Pedraza-Bailey, S., & Sullivan, T.A. (1979). Bilingual education in the reception of political immigrants: The case of Cubans in Miami, Florida. In R. V. Padilla (Ed.), *Bilingual education and public policy in the United States* (pp. 376–394). Ypsilanti, MI: Department of Foreign Languages and Bilingual Studies, Eastern Michigan University.

Peng, S. S. (1977). Trends in the entry to higher education: 1961–72. *Educational Researcher, 6*(1), 15–19.

President's Commission on Foreign Language and International Studies. (1979). *Strength through wisdom: A critique of U.S. capability.* Report to the President. Washington, DC: U.S. Government Printing Office.

Pressat, R. (1972). *Demographic analysis: Methods, results, applications.* (J. Matras, Trans.). Chicago: Aldine.

Takesian, S. A. (1967). A comparative study of the Mexican American graduate and dropout. Unpublished doctoral dissertation, University of Southern California, Los Angeles.

U.S. Commission on Civil Rights. (1978). *Social indicators of equality for minorities and women.* Washington, DC: U.S. Government Printing Office.

Webb, E. J., Campbell, D. T., Schwartz, R., & Sechrist, L. (1966). *Unobtrusive measures: Nonreactive research in the social sciences.* Chicago: Rand McNally.

Zappert, L. T., & Cruz, B. R. (1977). *Bilingual education: An appraisal of empirical research.* Berkeley, CA: Bahia Press.

4 | Hispanic High School Graduates: Making Choices

RICHARD SANTOS

High school completion represents a formidable educational hurdle for Hispanics; two-fifths of Hispanics aged twenty-five and older have completed four years of high school or more as compared to two-thirds of the non-Hispanic population (U.S. Bureau of the Census, 1979, table E). The high school dropout rate is especially acute for young Hispanic adults; over one-third of Hispanics aged eighteen to twenty-one are high school dropouts (Borus, 1983, p. 108). For young Hispanics, certain career choices—attending college, obtaining further vocational training, finding work, or entering the military—that are accessible to high school graduates will not readily be available for those who fail to complete school. Hispanic high school dropouts are simply not likely to succeed in a labor market that will require an educated as well as a computer-literate work force.

Arresting the high school dropout rate among youth thus remains a paramount concern for both the Hispanic community and educators. To be sure, attention should be given to increasing the proportion of youth who complete high school. The experiences beyond high school should, however, merit study for those youth who are able to complete high school. In particular, it is important to ask, How accessible are the alter-

Research support for this study was provided by The Ohio State University Center for Human Resource Research. Funding for the National Longitudinal Surveys of Youth Labor Market Experience is provided by the U.S. Department of Labor. Researchers undertaking such projects under government sponsorship are encouraged to express their own judgments. Interpretations on viewpoints contained in this study do not necessarily reflect the official position or policy of the sponsoring agencies. I would like to thank Linda Tyner for her research assistance on this study and Professor John García for his suggestions and comments.

natives available to Hispanic high school graduates? For example, are Hispanic graduates equally likely as other youth to attend college? Furthermore, are Hispanic graduates more likely than other youth to explore other alternatives to attending college—entering the military, going to work, or obtaining vocational or skill training in a noncollege setting?

A cursory overview of career-related choices available to high school graduates shows how Hispanic youth are limited by non-school-completion rates. As one would expect, college entrance is dependent upon graduation from high school or a demonstrated school equivalency. A high proportion of school dropouts helps explain why less than one-tenth of Hispanics twenty-five and older have completed four years or more of college. For non-Hispanics, the proportion of college graduates is nearly one-fifth (U.S. Bureau of the Census, 1979, table E).

In addition, military enlistment favors youth who graduate from high school; among Hispanic males, the proportion of graduates in the armed forces was twice that of school dropouts. For white males, the participation rate in the armed forces did not vary between graduates or school dropouts (Kim, Nestel, Phillips, & Borus, 1980, table 2.1). Finally, employment prospects increase for Hispanic youth who graduate from high school; the unemployment rate of school dropouts in 1979 was three times that of graduates (Santos, 1982a, table 4).

Several studies have analyzed the choices available to high school graduates (Nolfi et al., 1978; Rumberger, 1982; Borus & Carpenter, 1982; Kim, 1982; Campbell, Gardner, & Winterstein, 1984). Further work is needed, however, to analyze the factors that could influence the choices available specifically for Hispanic high school graduates. Are there differences, for example, among Hispanic groups in deciding which career-related alternatives beyond high school to choose? The effects of limited English and foreign birthplace on the choices available to Hispanic youth also require study.

Using data available from the National Longitudinal Surveys of Youth Labor Market Experiences, a preliminary inquiry can be made into the factors that influence career-related decisions by Hispanic youth who graduate from high school. As will be shown in the data to be presented, the proportion of youth who decide to attend college varies only slightly by race and sex. Differences by race and sex are, however, readily apparent on whether one attends a four-year or two-year college, as well as the alternatives to college available to high school graduates. Attention will be given specifically to factors that contribute to the likelihood of college attendance and military service. The proportion of high school graduates who take additional government training as well as their work experience is also reviewed.

THE NATIONAL LONGITUDINAL SURVEYS OF YOUTH LABOR MARKET EXPERIENCES

Information on 1975–1979 high school graduates is obtained from the National Longitudinal Surveys of Youth Labor Market Experiences. In 1979, the NLS initially interviewed a nationally representative sample of 12,686 young people aged fourteen to twenty-one. The NLS is scheduled to interview the youth sample annually through 1985. For the purposes of this study, youth in the 1981 NLS who reported graduating from high school between 1975 and 1979 are the major reference group.[1] A total of 5,771 youths had graduated from high school between 1975 and 1979 in the NLS. Included in the 1975–1979 graduating classes were 469 Hispanics.

For comparison, youth who by age should have graduated in 1975 through 1979 but were not enrolled in school in 1981 and were without a high school degree were selected for study. A total of 1,506 youths aged nineteen to twenty-four, including 377 Hispanics who should have graduated in 1975 through 1979, constituted the school-dropout comparison group. In the case of Hispanic youth, a comparison group of high school dropouts is needed to adequately analyze the options available to high school graduates. Since many of the Hispanic youth are likely to be dropouts, a selective bias, or "creaming effect," may result in comparing the alternatives of graduates by race. In other words, the experiences of Hispanic graduates may be overstated relative to blacks and whites.

CAREER-RELATED CHOICES OF HIGH SCHOOL GRADUATES, 1975–1979

Among the choices available to high school graduates that will be examined in this section are the proportion of youth by race and sex who have attended college, entered the military service, sought additional training, or engaged in work activity. These career-related choices are not mutually exclusive; a young person can attend college, enter the military, and also gain work experience and training. Since the purpose of this section is to obtain a preliminary analysis of the choices available to Hispanic graduates, each career-related choice or alternative will be examined separately.

College Attendance

Hispanics represented only 4 percent of undergraduate students in 1978; the low proportion of Hispanic college students can partially be attributed to a lack of high school graduates (Olivas, 1983, p. 114). As table 4.1 shows, however, once Hispanics graduate from high school, they are as likely as other graduates to attend college; half of the graduates have attended college, and with the exception of black males, no differences by race and sex are evident. Although college attendance is uniform for white and Hispanic graduates, the type of college attended is not. Among graduates who have attended college, Hispanics are the group least likely to enroll in four-year colleges; close to half of the Hispanics attended two-year colleges, as compared to one-third of other graduates.

Other differences in college experience were also apparent among

Table 4.1: Decision to Attend College of High School Graduates 1975–1979 by Race and Sex (Percent Distribution)

	Female			Male			
	Black	Hispanic	White	Black	Hispanic	White	TOTAL
Ever attended college[a]							
Yes	53	50	51	40	51	50	50
No	47	50	49	60	49	50	50
Ever attended four-year college[b]							
Yes	64	52	65	71	56	70	67
No	36	48	35	29	44	30	33
Full-time student[b]							
Yes	90	79	88	85	83	87	87
No	10	21	12	15	17	13	13
Ever received loan for college[b]							
Yes	34	26	25	30	25	24	25
No	66	74	75	70	75	76	75
Received any other financial aid[c]							
Yes	77	56	40	66	54	39	44
No	23	44	60	34	36	61	56

[a] Universe: high school graduates, 1975–1979.
[b] Asked only of youth who have graduated since September 1, 1978.
[c] Asked only of youth who were enrolled in college in 1979.

the graduates by race and sex (table 4.1). Although most college students attended full time, Hispanic females reported the lowest proportion. Furthermore, about one-fourth of whites and Hispanics received loans to attend college, in comparison to about a third of blacks. Black graduates also ranked as the group more likely to receive other forms of financial aid.[2] Whites received the lowest proportion of other financial aid, and Hispanic graduates were intermediate. The uneven distribution of financial aid by race suggests that close attention be given to variations in family income by Hispanic groups. Family income among Cubans, for example, resembles that of whites, whereas income of Puerto Ricans is similar to that of blacks (Santos, 1982b).

Military Service

The U.S. Armed Forces provides employment and training for its personnel; in fiscal 1982, about 350,000 recruits enlisted and over $10 billion was spent on training by the military (Cooper & Huerta, 1982, p. 39). Not everyone is eligible for military service, however; potential recruits must meet mental, physical, and moral standards. Although high school dropouts are not ineligible, the likelihood of satisfying the mental-ability criteria set by the Armed Services Vocational Aptitude Battery (ASVAB) decreases for school dropouts (Cooper & Huerta, 1982, p. 46).

Table 4.2 shows that the military is more of an option for high school graduates who have not attended college than for either graduates with college experience or high school dropouts. Furthermore, the decision to enlist varies by race and sex. Although the number of women in the armed forces is increasing, few of the females, irrespective of educational experience, have served in the military. Among male graduates who have attended college, the proportion of Hispanics and whites who have served in the military are similar; black graduates were twice as likely to serve than either whites or Hispanics, 13 percent versus 7 percent. For graduates without college experience, especially blacks and Hispanics, the prospect of military service increases: one-third of the blacks have served in the armed forces, one-fifth of the Hispanics, and under one-seventh of the whites.

As in the case of graduates with college experience, but for obviously different reasons, the military does not appear to be an alternative used by the high-school-dropout comparison group. Less than 6 percent of the black or Hispanic male dropouts have served in the armed forces. White male dropouts, however, had twice the rate of minority dropouts.

Table 4.2: Choices Among Youth by Educational Attainment, Race and Sex (Participation Rate per 100)

	Served in Military	Took Gov't-Sponsored Training[d]	Took Other Training[d]	Worked in 1980
Graduates Who Attended College[a]	4	2	18	90
Males				
Black	13	3	16	86
Hispanic	6	2	21	89
White	7	3	16	91
Females				
Black	2	6	23	83
Hispanic	1	3	18	89
White	1	1	19	92
Graduates Who Did Not Attend College[b]	10	3	25	84
Males				
Black	33	4	14	72
Hispanic	20	4	23	84
White	15	2	27	87
Females				
Black	5	9	25	71
Hispanic	1	6	22	78
White	2	2	26	86
High School Dropouts[c]	5	7	12	69
Males				
Black	6	16	15	63
Hispanic	5	7	8	84
White	11	5	14	88
Females				
Black	0	8	8	40
Hispanic	1	8	7	49
White	1	5	11	58

[a] Universe: High school graduates 1975–1979 who have attended college.
[b] Universe: High school graduates 1975–1979 who have not attended college.
[c] Universe: High school dropouts who by age should have graduated 1975–1979.
[d] Training taken since year of graduation or last year of school.

For high school male dropouts, the military is not a readily available option, but whites are more likely to enlist than minorities.

Training Experience

Post-high-school vocational training represents another career-related choice for graduates (Borus, 1983). Youth in the NLS sample were asked if they had participated in government-sponsored skill training programs such as those under the Comprehensive Employment and Training Program (CETA) or the Job Corps. In addition, youth were asked if they had participated in other training programs such as a business college, vocational institute, barber school, or company training program. Table 4.2 presents the proportion of youth who have participated since leaving school in government-sponsored training programs and other training programs. Few youth irrespective of educational attainment have ever participated in government-sponsored training since leaving school. Most of the government-sponsored programs for youth are designed for students, and this may account for the low proportion of participation among out-of-school youth.

Participation in other training programs since leaving school was, however, reported more frequently for graduates but less for the dropout comparison group: Over one-fifth of the graduates in comparison to about a tenth of the school dropouts participated. Hispanic graduates were equally likely as other youth to participate in other training programs. Few of the dropouts had been involved in training since last leaving school; among male school dropouts, blacks and whites were, however, twice as likely as Hispanics to have participated in other training programs.

Work Experience

Entry into the work force is another choice for high school graduates. Table 4.2 shows the proportion of youth by educational attainment who worked in 1980. Most high school graduates in 1975–1979 worked in 1980; those who attended college had a slightly greater proportion than those not attending. Among high school graduates, Hispanics and whites had similar proportions who worked in 1980, but blacks less so; male and female graduates within respective racial groups were equally likely to have worked in 1980.

The transition from school to work does not favor school dropouts: The high-school-dropout comparison group had the lowest proportion with work experience—69 percent. Obtaining work experience was, however, more realistic for white and Hispanic male dropouts—they were equally likely to work in 1980 as those who completed high school but did not attend college. By comparison, female dropouts and black male dropouts had the least work experience; less than half of black and Hispanic female dropouts for example worked in 1980. For minority female school dropouts, early family responsibilities such as child care are frequently cited as reasons for not being in the work force (Borus, 1983, p. 17).

ANALYSIS OF COLLEGE ATTENDANCE AND MILITARY ENLISTMENT

College attendance and military enlistment are two choices available to high school graduates that merit additional attention. Attending college is generally viewed as economically advantageous, and the military is considered a vehicle for obtaining additional training. Regression analysis is used to identify the factors that are associated with affecting the decision among high school graduates to attend college and the military-enlistment decision among male graduates who have never attended college.[3] In the decision to attend college, ability, costs, and socioeconomic status of parents have been identified as factors that may influence the college decision (Christensen, Melder, & Weisbrod, 1975, p. 174). Positive intentions to serve in the military have been associated with minority status, low income, married youth, unemployment, and non-college-bound youth (Kim et al., 1980, p. viii). Similar types of variables are used in the regression analysis to examine the effects on college attendance and military enlistments. In addition, language problems, nativity, and Hispanic-origin group are examined for their effects on the decision by Hispanics to attend college or enlist.

The College Decision

Table 4.3 presents the means and standard deviations of the selected variables that were examined for their influence on the decision to attend college among high school graduates. Overall, major variables that were found to significantly affect the decision to attend college included gender, enrollment in a college-preparatory program, knowledge of the world of work (KWW), educational aspirations, and the educational aspirations of friends (table 4.4). Black and white males were less likely than females to attend college, but the gender coefficient was not statistically significant for Hispanics. Graduates who had been enrolled in a college-

Table 4.3: Means and Standard Deviations of Variables Used in the College-Attendance Equation of High School Graduates, 1975–1979

Variable	Black Mean	S.D.	Hispanic Mean	S.D.	White Mean	S.D.
Percentage of youth who were in a college-preparatory program	0.36	0.48	0.35	.48	0.40	0.49
Percentage who graduated with a GED	0.06	0.23	0.05	0.22	0.05	0.21
Percentage whose family income was classified as						
Poor	0.23	0.42	0.18	0.38	0.06	0.23
Nonpoor	0.50	0.50	0.63	0.48	0.71	0.45
Not available	0.27	0.44	0.19	0.39	0.23	0.42
Knowledge of the World of Work	5.75	1.95	6.25	1.90	7.21	1.60
Percentage of Hispanic youth by group						
Chicano	—	—	0.52	0.50	—	—
Cuban	—	—	0.09	0.28	—	—
Puerto Rican	—	—	0.13	0.33	—	—
Others	—	—	0.26	0.44	—	—
Reading materials index—values range from 0 to 3 (one point for each positive response to having newspaper, magazine or library card in home at age 14)	1.97	0.99	1.95	0.99	2.51	0.72
Educational aspirations of youth in 1979, grade level	15.30	1.98	15.25	1.95	14.95	2.12
Educational aspirations of freinds in 1979, grade level	14.80	2.08	14.80	2.13	14.61	2.19
Percentage responding that a problem with English caused difficulties in getting a good job	0.03	0.17	0.09	0.28	0.01	0.12
Percentage born in the United States	0.96	0.19	0.77	0.42	0.97	0.17
Percentage responding that language other than English was spoken in household as a child	0.04	0.19	0.88	0.33	0.10	0.31
Percent male	0.46	0.50	0.48	0.50	0.50	0.50

Table 4.4: The Decision-to-Attend-College Equations of High School Graduates, 1975–1979, by Race

Independent Variables	Black Coefficient (t-value)	Hispanic Coefficient (t-value)	White Coefficient (t-value)
College prep	.117 (4.47)**	.070 (1.79)†	.191 (13.30)**
GED	−.200 (−3.81)**	−.195 (−2.46)*	−.120 (−4.15)**
Poor (comparison group)	—	—	—
Nonpoor	.016 (0.51)	.045 (0.95)	−.060 (−2.27)*
Poverty status not available	−.084 (−2.44)*	−.055 (−0.94)	−1.09 (−3.87)**
KWW	.021 (3.14)**	.036 (3.66)**	.016 (4.08)**
Chicano (comparison group)	—	—	—
Cuban	— —	.245 (3.59)**	— —
Puerto Rican	—	−.029 (−0.54)	—
Others	—	.019 (0.43)	—
Reading materials index	.008 (0.64)	−.0003 (−0.02)	.042 (4.79)**
Educational aspirations	.099 (13.29)**	.079 (7.47)**	.106 (28.75)**
Friends' educational aspirations	.014 (2.08)*	.042 (4.45)**	.027 (7.99)**
English problem	−.099 (−1.40)	.077 (1.16)	−.073 (−1.41)
Born U.S.	−.019 (−0.30)	.010 (0.21)	−.022 (−0.58)

(Continued)

Table 4.4   *(Continued)*

Independent Variables	Black Coefficient (t-value)	Hispanic Coefficient (t-value)	White Coefficient (t-value)
Other language	.001 (0.01)	−.028 (−0.50)	.007 (0.33)
Male	−.137 (−5.68)**	−.037 (−1.08)	−.046 (−3.84)**
Constant	−1.319 (−10.59)	−1.584 (−8.67)	−1.645 (−23.24)
R²	.303	.280	.468
N	1237	621	3682
F	45.88	17.08	271.16

† Significant at the 10 percent level.
* Significant at the 5 percent level.
** Significant at the 1 percent level.

preparatory program in high school, as compared to other programs, increased their likelihood of attending college. Scores on the KWW, a test to ascertain one's knowledge of occupations, were correlated positively with the decision to attend college. The KWW scores could be viewed as a proxy for ability. As one would expect, the higher levels of educational aspirations held by students and by close friends were both likely to increase the prospects of college attendance.

For Hispanics, the regression results reveal that Cubans were more likely to attend college than Chicanos. Puerto Ricans and other Hispanics did not significantly differ from Chicanos in the decision to attend college. Other Hispanic-related variables such as nativity or language did not significantly affect the decision to attend college. The presence of magazines, newspapers, or a library card in the youth's household at age fourteen (reading materials index variable) did not significantly affect the probability of college attendance for Hispanics or blacks, but it did for whites.

Finally, family income as measured by poverty status produced a mixed result on the decision to attend college. For black and Hispanic graduates, the poor and nonpoor did not significantly differ in their college decision; but white graduates living in poverty are more likely to attend college. The effect of poverty status on the college decision remains puzzling. In comparison to other socioeconomic factors such as

Table 4.5: Means and Standard Deviations of Variables Used in the Military Enlistment Equation of Male High School Graduates, 1975–1979, Who Have Never Attended College

Variable	Black Mean	Black S.D.	Hispanic Mean	Hispanic S.D.	White Mean	White S.D.
Percentage who were in a college-preparatory program	0.27	0.44	0.20	0.40	0.15	0.36
Percentage who graduated with a GED	0.10	0.30	0.07	0.26	0.09	0.28
Percentage whose family income was classified as						
Poor	0.19	0.39	0.18	0.39	0.04	0.20
Nonpoor	0.44	0.50	0.52	0.50	0.71	0.46
Not available	0.37	0.48	0.29	0.46	0.25	0.43
Knowledge of the World of Work	5.31	1.89	6.03	1.93	6.94	1.65
Percentage of Hispanic youth by group						
Chicano	—	—	0.57	0.50	—	—
Cuban	—	—	0.03	0.17	—	—
Puerto Rican	—	—	0.12	0.33	—	—
Others	—	—	0.28	0.45	—	—
Educational aspirations of youth in 1979, grade level	14.60	2.14	14.47	2.12	13.65	1.96
Percentage responding that a problem with English caused difficulties in getting a good job	0.04	0.21	0.07	0.25	0.02	0.15
Percentage born in the United States	0.97	0.18	0.81	0.40	0.97	0.18
Percentage responding that language other than English was spoken in household as a child	0.05	0.22	0.85	0.36	0.09	0.30
Percentage desiring additional job training beyond regular schooling	0.87	0.34	0.78	0.42	0.76	0.43

parents' education or occupation, however, family income has been found to be the least important influence on college attendance (Christensen et al., 1975, p. 175; Borus & Carpenter, 1982, p. 127). In addition, the poverty variable used may not be valid; over one-fourth of the graduates did not report any family income. Furthermore, students who are attending college and living away from home are considered separate households, and their incomes rather than their parents' are used to determine poverty status.

The Enlistment Decision

Male high school graduates who do not attend college were earlier identified as the group most likely to enlist in the military. Table 4.5 presents the means and standard deviations of the selected variables used in the regression analysis to analyze the enlistment decision among non-college-bound high school graduates. Two variables significantly affected the enlistment equations for all the racial groups under study (table 4.6). Youth who graduated with a General Equivalency Degree (GED) were more likely than other graduates to enlist. Among the graduates not going to college, those with higher aspirations increased the likelihood of enlistment. Enrollment in a college-preparatory program, as one would expect, reduced the enrollment possibility; it was, however, not a significant effect, possibly because these are graduates who have not attended college.

Other variables produced mixed effects in the enlistment decision. For example, being nonpoor as compared to poor decreased the probability of enlistment for Hispanics, but nonpoor status did not significantly affect the decision for blacks or whites. For blacks and Hispanics, an expressed desire for additional job training did not significantly affect the enlistment decision, but it increased the chances for whites. Other Hispanic-related variables such as language or nativity were found not to be significant. Puerto Ricans and Cubans did not differ in the enlistment decision in comparison to Chicanos, but other Hispanics were more likely to enlist than Chicanos.

WORK EXPERIENCE IN 1980

Entry into the work force is an option for high school graduates as well as school dropouts. The work experience of youth who worked in 1980 is examined by educational attainment in this section. Attention will be directed toward differences by educational attainment in weeks worked, hourly wages, and employment by occupation and industry.

Weeks Worked

By educational attainment, high school graduates who have not attended college worked in 1980 on average the most weeks (table 4.7). For male

Table 4.6: Decision-to-Enlist-in-the-Military Equations of Male High School Graduates, 1975–1979, Who Have Never Attended College

Independent Variables	Black Coefficient (t-value)	Hispanic Coefficient (t-value)	White Coefficient (t-value)
College prep	−.016 (−0.32)	−.037 (−0.50)	−.012 (−0.39)
GED	.152 (1.98)*	.256 (2.35)*	.203 (5.54)**
Poor	—	—	—
Nonpoor	−.085 (−1.36)	−.163 (−2.15)*	−.014 (0.28)
Poverty status not available	.312 (4.88)**	.116 (1.31)	.294 (5.48)**
KWW	.008 (0.66)	.016 (1.03)	−.013 (−2.13)*
Chicano	—	—	—
Cuban	—	.032 (0.19)	—
Puerto Rican	—	0.31 (0.35)	—
Others	—	.269 (3.81)**	—
Educational aspirations	.033 (3.00)**	.043 (3.14)**	.040 (7.16)**
English problem	.190 (1.73)†	.115 (1.02)	−.049 (−0.72)
Born U.S.	−.148 (−1.06)	.079 (1.07)	−.073 (−1.22)
Other languge	−.068 (−0.60)	.057 (0.68)	.036 (0.99)
Additional job training	.071 (1.06)	−.015 (−0.22)	.083 (3.51)***
Constant	−.200 (−0.91)	−.657 (−3.05)	−.391 (−3.64)**
R²	.186	.338	.208
N	370	159	1010
F	9.41	7.21	27.51

† Significant at the 10 percent level.
* Significant at the 5 percent level.
** Significant at the 1 percent level.

Table 4.7:   Employment-Related Characteristics of Youth Who Worked in 1980 by Educational Attainment, Race, and Sex

	Mean Weeks Worked	Mean Hourly Rate of Pay
Graduates Who Attended College [a]	37.5	4.85
Males		
Black	35.8	4.76
Hispanic	39.6	5.23
White	36.9	5.16
Females		
Black	37.1	4.27
Hispanic	40.1	4.76
White	38.0	4.63
Graduates Who Did Not Attend College [b]	43.5	5.01
Males		
Black	39.9	5.15
Hispanic	44.3	5.26
White	45.3	5.81
Females		
Black	39.3	4.05
Hispanic	40.7	4.60
White	42.7	4.30
High School Dropouts [c]	36.5	4.63
Males		
Black	36.2	4.41
Hispanic	38.7	5.16
White	39.2	5.20
Females		
Black	24.7	3.76
Hispanic	35.2	3.99
White	33.5	3.67

[a] Universe: see table 4.2.
[b] Universe: see table 4.2.
[c] Universe: see table 4.2.

graduates without college experience, whites and Hispanics worked the same number of weeks on average; blacks, however, worked fewer weeks. Both black and Hispanic female graduates without college experience trailed slightly the average annual weeks worked by white females. Since some of the high school graduates with college experience are still attending school, it is not surprising that the annual average weeks worked for male dropouts was similar to the work experience of male graduates who have attended college. Among the graduates with college experience who worked in 1980, Hispanic males and females led the groups in average weeks worked. Female dropouts had the lowest mean number of weeks worked, ranging from twenty-five weeks for blacks to thirty-five weeks for Hispanics.

Hourly Rate of Pay

Irrespective of educational attainment, males earned higher average hourly wages than females in the current or last job held in 1980 (table 4.7). In general, graduates without college experience averaged a higher hourly rate of pay than those with college experience or the high-school-dropout group. Among the graduates with college experience, Hispanic males and females led in average wages in their respective groups. For male graduates without college experience, average wages of blacks and Hispanics trailed those of whites; but among females, Hispanics ranked foremost in wages. Among the male high school dropouts, average hourly wages of Hispanics and whites were similar and above those of blacks. In the case of female dropouts, the average wages of whites were below those of blacks or Hispanics.

Occupation

Among males, high school graduates who had attended college engaged in a variety of occupations—service, clerical, professional/technical, and labor (table 4.8). The wide range of occupations including a relatively large proportion of clerical work held by males with college experience can probably be accounted for by those graduates still attending school, that is, working in school-related clerical jobs. Among male graduates with no college experience, the type of work performed was concentrated in relatively fewer occupations; craftspersons and operatives accounted for half of the work for whites and about two-fifths for blacks and Hispanics. Blacks were three times and Hispanics two times more likely than whites to work in service occupations. For males who dropped out of high school, the craftsperson and operative occupations provided the bulk of work; over a third of the Hispanic dropouts worked as operatives. Black and Hispanic dropouts were more likely than whites to work in service occupations, but Hispanics were the least likely to work as laborers.

For female high school graduates irrespective of college experience, table 4.9 shows that clerical work ranked as the foremost occupation; among Hispanic graduates, the majority of employment was clerical. Hispanic graduates, however, had the lowest proportion by race in ser-

(Continued on page 123)

Table 4.8: Occupational Distribution of Employed Male Youth in 1980 by Educational Attainment and Race (Percent Distribution)

Occupation	Graduates—Attended College[a]			Graduates—No College Attendance[b]			High School Dropouts[c]		
	Black	Hispanic	White	Black	Hispanic	White	Black	Hispanic	White
Professional, technical	16	14	18	2	2	3	2	3	2
Managers, administrators	7	10	7	4	2	5	1	0	1
Sales	4	6	8	1	2	5	2	3	2
Clerical	19	20	14	11	8	9	4	3	3
Craftsmen	6	14	13	15	25	28	21	21	29
Operatives	7	7	5	25	19	22	19	35	23
Transport	5	2	5	10	11	7	7	5	7
Laborers	12	10	10	11	13	12	20	13	22
Farmers	0	0	0	0	0	*	0	0	0
Farm laborers and foremen	0	3	1	1	3	2	6	2	3
Service workers	23	14	20	21	15	7	19	16	8
Private household workers	0	0	0	0	0	0	0	0	0
TOTAL PERCENTAGE	100	100	100	100	100	100	100	100	100

[a] Universe: see table 4.2.
[b] Universe: see table 4.2.
[c] Universe: see table 4.2.
* Percentage is between 0.1 and 0.5.

Table 4.9: Occupational Distribution of Employed Female Youth in 1980 by Educational Attainment and Race (Percent Distribution)

Occupational	Graduates—Attended College[a]			Graduates—No College Attendance[b]			High School Dropouts[c]		
	Black	Hispanic	White	Black	Hispanic	White	Black	Hispanic	White
Professional, technical	13	20	21	5	4	3	0	0	1
Managers, administrators	2	3	4	4	2	4	0	0	2
Sales	4	6	8	2	7	7	6	6	3
Clerical	51	52	37	34	55	48	16	26	24
Craftsmen	2	2	2	2	3	3	4	4	1
Operatives	3	2	4	18	11	11	23	37	21
Transport	*	0	*	2	0	*	0	0	1
Laborers	1	1	1	3	2	2	1	6	1
Farmers	0	0	0	0	0	0	0	0	0
Farm laborers and foremen	0	0	0	0	0	*	2	3	3
Service workers	22	14	22	29	14	20	44	17	33
Private household workers	1	0	1	1	3	2	5	2	10
TOTAL PERCENTAGE	100	100	100	100	100	100	100	100	100

[a] Universe: see table 4.2.
[b] Universe: see table 4.2.
[c] Universe: see table 4.2
* Percentage is between 0.1 and 0.5.

Table 4.10: Industrial Distribution of Employed Male Youth by Educational Attainment and Race (Percent Distribution)

Industry	Graduates Attended College[a]			Graduates No College Attendance[b]			High School Dropouts[c]		
	Black	Hispanic	White	Black	Hispanic	White	Black	Hispanic	White
Agriculture, forestry, fisheries	1	5	3	2	6	3	10	3	6
Mining	1	0	1	3	3	2	0	5	4
Construction	5	3	8	6	6	15	17	11	20
Manufacturing	10	16	13	32	29	30	22	32	32
Transportation, communications, public utilities	8	5	5	10	6	6	6	2	5
Wholesale and retail trade	19	27	31	19	28	25	20	22	21
Finance, insurance, real estate	10	6	3	3	3	3	*	2	1
Business and repair	3	5	6	9	9	8	7	12	5
Personal services	6	3	3	3	2	2	6	4	1
Entertainment and recreation	2	4	3	1	0	1	1	1	3
Professional	29	20	19	6	2	4	10	4	2
Public administration	7	6	5	6	7	2	2	2	1
TOTAL PERCENTAGE	100	100	100	100	100	100	100	100	100

[a] Universe: see table 4.2
[b] Universe: see table 4.2
[c] Universe: see table 4.2

* Percentage is between 0.1 and 0.5.

vice work. As one would expect, operative work is more frequent for graduates without college experience than for those who have attended college.

Among female dropouts, the lack of a high school education reduced the proportion employed in clerical work; only one-fourth of whites and Hispanics and less than one-seventh of the blacks are clerical workers. Service work becomes the foremost occupation for black and white dropouts, but operative work is the model occupation for Hispanic dropouts.

Industry

Among males, professional employment provided more jobs for high school graduates with college experience, while manufacturing provided more work for graduates not going to college (table 4.10). For graduates who have not attended college, whites are twice as likely as blacks or Hispanics to work in construction. Construction, however, becomes a leading employer among black and white dropouts, but less so among Hispanics.

Female employment by industry was similar to those of males; professional-related employment provided most of the jobs for graduates with college experience (table 4.11). Among graduates with no college experience, the role of professional-related employment declines, and the importance of manufacturing increases. Hispanic graduates without college attendance were equally likely as other women to work in manufacturing, but more so in finance/insurance/real estate.

Among female high school dropouts, the industrial distribution differs from that of graduates in more personal-service-related employment; one-fifth of the jobs for whites, one-seventh for blacks, but few jobs for Hispanics. Manufacturing, however, accounted for half of the work for hispanic female dropouts as compared to one-fifth for blacks and one-fourth for whites.

CONCLUSIONS

Attending college, entering the military, obtaining additional training, and working are some of the major career-related choices available to high school graduates. These choices are not necessarily mutually exclusive, and some youth undertake a variety of activities upon graduation. Many of the choices available to graduates and reviewed in this study are also dependent upon each other. Youth who are in college are less likely,

Table 4.11 Industrial Distribution of Employed Female Youth by Educational Attainment and Race (Percent Distribution)

Industry	Graduates Attended College[a]			Graduates No College Attendance[b]			High School Dropouts[c]		
	Black	Hispanic	White	Black	Hispanic	White	Black	Hispanic	White
Agriculture, forestry, fisheries	0	0	*	*	0	*	4	8	3
Mining	0	1	*	0	1	*	0	0	0
Construction	1	0	*	1	2	1	0	0	1
Manufacturing	8	8	9	21	18	20	18	46	28
Transportation, communications, public utilties	4	4	4	3	2	3	0	0	2
Wholesale and retail trade	19	23	32	22	23	28	19	17	32
Finance, insurance, real estate	8	14	9	12	21	14	2	8	0
Business and repair	1	6	3	3	3	3	6	3	3
Personal services	4	3	3	4	6	8	20	3	14
Entertainment and recreation	2	0	2	1	2	*	0	0	2
Professional	45	33	35	27	15	19	19	9	13
Public administration	8	5	3	6	6	4	12	5	1
TOTAL PERCENTAGE	100	100	100	100	100	100	100	100	100

* Percentage is between 0.1 and 0.5.

[a] Universe: see table 4.2
[b] Universe: see table 4.2
[c] Universe: see table 4.2
[a] Universe: see table 4.2

for example, to enter the military or obtain additional training. Some choices are also more readily available to youth who complete high school. In examining socioeconomic factors that affect the decision to attend college or the military, the impact of these variables may be less on these decisions than on high school graduation. It is, therefore, understandable why attention has been given to factors that affect the school-dropout decision (Fligstein & Fernández, 1982).

A preliminary analysis of career-related alternatives among high school graduates nevertheless revealed that some choices are more readily available to some youth than others. Half of the graduates between 1975 and 1979, for example, attended college, and with the exception of black males the proportion attending college was uniform by race and sex. Among Hispanics, Cubans were more likely than Chicanos to attend college, and no significant difference was noted between Chicanos and Puerto Ricans in the proportion going to college. Other Hispanic-related variables such as nativity or language did not significantly affect the probability of college attendance for Hispanic graduates. As with other high school graduates, the decision among Hispanic graduates to attend college was influenced by type of school curriculum (college-preparatory program), ability, and educational aspirations.

Although Hispanic graduates do not appear to differ from other groups in many of the basic considerations to attending college, they do differ in the types of colleges attended. Two-year colleges are the mode for Hispanics in comparison to four-year colleges among other youth. Hispanics are equally likely to receive college loans as whites but less so than blacks. Attention should be given to the reasons as well as the implications of the greater proportion of Hispanics attending two-year colleges as opposed to four-year colleges.

The military emerged as an alternative more for male high school graduates not going to college than for those attending college. The foremost group of graduates not attending college to choose the military were minority males; one-third of the blacks and one-fifth of the Hispanics compared to under one-seventh of the whites. For high school dropouts, and especially the minorities, the military is not a readily available alternative; although Hispanics have the highest dropout rate, only one out of every twenty dropouts has served in the military in comparison to one out of ten white dropouts.

Similar to other high school graduates, about a fifth of the Hispanic graduates have participated in post-high-school vocational training programs. Few graduates have participated in government-sponsored training since leaving school. More disturbing is the low proportion (about one-tenth) of dropouts who reported undertaking training since leaving school. Among male dropouts, blacks and whites were however twice as likely as Hispanics to have received non-government-sponsored training. Training beyond high school is an area that merits further study.

Work is an activity undertaken extensively by high school graduates, irrespective of college attendance. For females and black males, dropping out of school substantially reduces work activity; only half of the Hispanic female school dropouts, for example, worked in 1980. Early family responsibilities and lack of child care could contribute to withdrawal from school as well as the labor force. Leaving school before graduation also restricts career-related choices. For Hispanics, the work experience and career choices of dropouts are especially important because of the high proportion failing to complete high school. The results show that Hispanic high school dropouts do not have alternatives— military service or other forms of training—available to them. Operative work is an option for female and male dropouts but one whose long-run economic rewards are very likely to be limited. In examining the choices of Hispanic high school graduates, it is worthwhile remembering the high proportion of youth who are not in a position to make these choices.

NOTES

1. The observation period is not uniform for high school students who graduated between 1975 and 1979. Graduates had between graduation date and the 1981 interview date to decide on the career-related choices under study. The decision to pool high school graduates between 1975 and 1979 was made because of the small Hispanic sample within each graduation-year class.

2. Other forms of financial aid could include scholarships, grants, fellowships, assistantships, tuition waivers, veteran's benefits, and related forms of financial aid.

3. Ordinary least squares were used in the regression instead of logit or probit because of ease of interpretation.

REFERENCES

Borus, M. E. (Ed.). (1983). *Tomorrow's workers.* Lexington, MA: Lexington Books.

Borus, M. E., & Carpenter, S. (1982). Choices in education. In M. E. Borus (Ed.), *Pathways to the future, Vol. 2* (pp. 97–130). Columbus: Center for Human Resource Research, Ohio State University.

Campbell, P. B., Gardner, J. A., & Winterstein, P. (1984). *Transition patterns between education and work.* Columbus: National Center for Research in Vocational Education, Ohio State University.

Center for Human Resource Research. (1981). *The national longitudinal survey handbook*. Columbus: Ohio State University.

Christensen, S., Melder, J., & Weisbrod, B. A. (1975). Factors affecting college attendance. *Journal of Human Resources, 2*, 174–188.

Cooper, R. V. L., & Huerta, M. P. (1982). Military training and youth employment: A descriptive survey. In R. E. Taylor (Ed.), *Job training for youth*. Columbus: National Center for Research in Vocational Education, Ohio State University.

Fligstein, N., & Fernández, R. N. (1982). *The causes of Hispanic educational attainment*. Final Report to the National Commission for Employment Policy. Chicago: National Opinion Research Center.

Kim, C. (1982). *The all-volunteer force: 1979 NSL studies of enlistment, intentions to serve, and intentions to reenlist*. Columbus: Center for Human Resource Research, Ohio State University.

Kim, C., Nestel, G., Phillips, R. L., & Borus, M. E. (1980). *The all-volunteer force: An Analysis of youth participation, attrition, and reenlistment*. Columbus: Center for Human Resource Research, Ohio State University.

Nolfi, G. J., Fuller, W. C., Lorazzini, A. J., Epstein, W. H., Freeman, R. B., Manski, C. F., Nelson, V. I., & Wise, D. A. (1978). *Experiences of recent high school graduates*. Lexington, MA: Lexington Books.

Olivas, M. A. (1983). Research and theory on Hispanic education: Students, finance, and governance. *Aztlán: International Journal of Chicano Studies Research. 1*, 111–146.

Rumberger, R. W. (1982). Recent high school and college experiences of youth. *Youth and Society, 4*, 449–470.

Santos, R. (1982a). Estimating youth employment and unemployment: The national longitudinal surveys of youth labor market experience. *Review of Public.Data Use, 10*, 127–135.

Santos, R. (1982b, May). Hispanic youth. *Le Red/The Net*, No. 53. Newsletter for the National Chicano Council on Higher Education.

U.S. Bureau of the Census. (1979). *Persons of Spanish origin in the United States: March 1979*. Advance Report, Series P-20, No. 354. Washington, DC: U.S. Government Printing Office.

II | Hispanic Student Achievement

5 | Identifying Areas of Stress for Chicano Undergraduates

DANIEL G. MUÑOZ

Chicana undergraduates report significantly more stress than do their male counterparts, and for both groups the principal sources of concern are financial. These are among the chief results of a 1974–1977 study on the Chicano experience in higher education I conducted, as principal investigator, with Betty García-Bahne as co-investigator (Muñoz & García-Bahne, 1978). We also found that Chicano undergraduates of both sexes reported much greater stress than did Anglo students. Casso (1975) reported that college students who were not from the white middle to upper class experienced greater degrees of stress in pursuing a college degree. Thus, our primary hypothesis was that Chicano undergraduates experience more stress than do Anglo students since fewer Chicanos are middle- or upper-class in income. We suggest that this added stress directly or indirectly impairs students' ability to persevere toward graduation and thus would help to explain the higher dropout rate of Chicano undergraduate students as compared to Anglo students. It is extremely difficult to obtain precise information from colleges and universities on the attrition rate of any minority group. But López, Madrid-Barela, and Macías (1976) estimated that only 19.6 percent of Chicano students who start a four-year undergraduate program graduate, compared to 37.7 percent of nonminority students.

For purposes of this research, Coleman's (1973) definition of stress was used: "Essentially stress refers to the adjustive demands made upon the individual . . . to the problems in living with which he must cope if he is to meet his needs" (p. 170). According to Coleman, there are three types of stress: frustration, conflict, and pressure. Frustration may occur when the ability to achieve a desired goal is impeded or blocked (as in the case of a student who must leave school because of financial problems). Conflict may occur when a choice must be made between two or more goals (for example, when a student wants to pursue one course of study while his or her parents are pressing for a different career). Pressure involves demands that force one to speed up or intensify one's efforts (for instance, those Chicano students who have received an inferior elementary and secondary education face enormous pressure when they must compete with students from wealthier families and highly rated schools). Coleman adds that adjustive demands such as frustration, conflict, and pressure "are closely interrelated and form part of the total stress pattern which every individual faces" (p. 177). Therefore, this study attempted to consider the total adjustive demands confronting Chicano undergraduates. It further identified and measured specific stress-inducing aspects of the Chicano experience in higher education.

REVIEW OF RESEARCH ON STRESS

The concept of psychological stress has been elusive for researchers. In evaluating literature on this subject, it is apparent that *stress* has come to describe more than the reaction of individuals to extreme environmental or psychosocial conditions; it has in fact become virtually synonymous with such terms as *anxiety, conflict, emotional distress, ego threat, frustration, threat to security, tension,* and *arousal.* Early research on stress had a heavy medical and biological emphasis. Cannon (1929) made detailed observations of bodily changes related to pain, hunger, and the major emotions. He referred to the body's condition of arousal as the "fight or flight" syndrome. Cannon's work was elaborated by Meyer (1951), who advocated a "life chart" as a tool in medical diagnosis. The life chart was to provide a method for organizing medical data as a dynamic biography involving biological, psychological, and sociological phenomena in relationship to human health and disease.

Stress Versus Distress

Perhaps one of the most prolific (and still prominent) researchers in the area of stress is Hans Selye, who was the first to use the term *stress response.* He was also the first theorist to clarify the primary glandular secretions and interactions that constitute the stress response and to identify the key organs and hormones involved. Selye (1956) defined stress as "the nonspecific response of the body to any demand made upon it" (p. 47). What Selye meant by "nonspecific response" is clarified in *Stress Without Distress* (1974) as follows:

> From the point of view of its stress-producing or stressor activity, it is immaterial whether the agent or situation we face is pleasant or unpleasant. . . . It is difficult to see how such essentially different things as cold,

heat, drugs, hormones, sorrow, and joy could provoke an identical bio-chemical reaction in the body. Nevertheless, this is the case. (P. 16).

Selye was suggesting that the agents (or situations) that create stress can be positive or negative; he also maintained that stress itself can lead to positive or negative results. Positive stress (or *eustress*) is the stress of achievement, triumph, and exhilaration. This form of stress can be part of the athlete's physical and mental effort to win, the professional's determination to do a good job, or the student's attempt to study hard. The eustress within us brings us to accept challenges and to have the ambition to succeed. All of us to some extent welcome the various challenges in our lives, for it is our commitment to accomplish those things that are important to us that gives us positive feelings. That is, it is our application of eustress that provides life with meaning and satisfaction. On the other hand, according to Selye, stress becomes negative (*distress*) when for any reason we begin to lose our feelings of security and adequacy. The fear of failure, helplessness, and disappointment turns stress into distress. Depression and negative self-feelings are the emotions that often accompany ongoing distress. Moreover, prolonged distress can lead to illness.

Nonetheless, as conceived by Selye, the results of stress need not be bad. According to him, people should attempt to deal more effectively with the stress in their lives so that they can meet, challenge, and enjoy the positive feelings of being productive. They should take advantage of opportunities to succeed rather than avoid them. Learning to cope with stress thus becomes an important dimension in reducing unpleasant pressures in life. Though he describes stress as "the spice of life," he suggests that people don't actually die of old age, but rather of stress. In fact, his definition of stress includes "the rate of wear and tear on the body caused by living" (1956, p. 274).

Attitudinal Measurement of Stress

The work of Holmes and Raye (1967), Dohrenwend and Dohrenwend (1974), Meyer (1951), and Paykel, Myers, & Dienelt (1969) began to quantify the stress generated by specific life events (that is, by change). Holmes and Raye developed a list of life changes and used it to predict health breakdown as a consequence of stress overload. They wanted to determine whether the relative amount of change in a person's life (positive or negative; getting married or losing a job) could be used to predict the likelihood of serious illness. The hypothesis that change (and therefore stress) and illness could be related has been tested by a number of researchers. Dohrenwend and Dohrenwend (1970) studied the relationship between stressful occurrences, such as the death of a relative or friend, personal illness, or an economic setback, and found that they induced temporary symptoms of psychological disturbance. Even President Kennedy's assassination was found (Sheatsley & Feldman, 1964) to have a large psychological impact on the nation. Holmes and Rahe (1967) studied the case histories of 2,500 Navy men on three cruisers. He found that those men who reported the highest life-change scores became sick during the first month of a new cruise at vastly higher rates than did those with the lowest scores. Holmes and Rahe (1967) subsequently developed a Life Stress Inventory consisting of forty-three events, for example, death of a spouse, divorce, marital separation, and detention in jail. Rahe (1975) later expanded the list to include seventy-six items.

Difficulties in Defining Stress

In his review of the field, Howard (1960) commented on the difficulties encountered by many researchers regarding the conceptual confusion surrounding *stress*. His analysis of the controversy pointed out that the word is used in the literature in at least four ways:

> Sometimes it is the stimulus, as implied by the phrase "stress-evoked behavior," other times it may be the response, as when reference is made to "stress-inducing stimuli." Sometimes, it is a combination of both. . . . Yet another usage of the word describes stress as a total situation possessing a certain quality—a kind of dynamic matrix in which the subject himself is the only variable. . . . Lastly, it is defined as a class of conditions productive of disturbance within the individual, and envisaged as a continuum of stimuli. . . . Like the engineer, the psychologist sees stress in a variety of forms, which range from the subtly psychological, through the biochemical to the crudely physical. (Pp. 186–187)

As has been noted, the research in this chapter is based on the definition of stress offered by Coleman (1973) as the "adjustive demands made upon the individual . . . to the problems in living with which he must cope if he is to meet his needs."

STRESS AND
THE CHICANO AND THE CHICANA

What then are the "adjustment demands" made upon the Chicano college student—the problems with which he must cope if he is to persevere through graduation? Being male or female has a significant impact upon graduation. The U.S. Commission on Civil Rights (1978) reported that while 32 percent of all Mexican American men who entered college completed a degree, only 15 percent of all Mexican American women did so. Mexican American women often experience intense role conflict when aspiring to education and career rather than the traditional stereotypic roles of wife and mother (Keefe, Padilla, & Carlos, 1978). Hence it is not enough to report the data regarding the Chicano experience in higher education without delineating the Chicana experience from the Chicano experience.

Socioeconomic Background

The Chicano students sampled in this study were reflective of the socioeconomic status that people of Mexican background occupy in the state of California. The vast majority were from the lowest fourth and fifth SES levels using Hollingshead formula combining parents' highest level of education and highest level of occupational functioning. In other words, the typical Chicano student came from a family in which the highest educational level of either parent was six to nine years of formal schooling. Most parents of the students interviewed were born and educated in Mexico. In addition, the highest level of occupational functioning using the classification system of the U.S. Department of Labor was generally at an unskilled labor level.

The literature (Astin, 1971, 1975; Vásquez, 1978) is uniform in indicating that students from higher SES backgrounds tend to obtain better grades and have a higher likelihood of persisting through graduation. Furthermore, the findings (Astin, 1975) indicate that students whose parents are the primary source of support for their education have a higher likelihood of graduating than students who come from a lower SES and rely primarily upon financial aids for their educational support. Other researchers (Cope & Hannah, 1975) comment upon the process of socialization in which lower-SES children incorporate the frustrated hopes and expectations of their parents; they also acquire verbal and auditory skills that have an impact upon their ability to respond to the demands of college. With the strong importance of the family to the Chicano, it is not surprising that researchers state that in the lower-SES families, poverty causes stress (Cuéllar & Moore, 1970). Furthermore, poor people most often are the victims of discrimination and of segregated and inferior schools. Thus academic achievement produces intense stress for the Chicano student, who must overcome the obstacles of poverty and discrimination in developing positive predispositions, habits, knowledge, and experiences to succeed in higher education (Hernández, 1973). Finance, or the lack of money, remains the greatest concern for Chicano undergraduates (Muñoz & García-Bahne, 1978).

Methodology of the Study

This research was conducted in California with samples consisting of 342 Chicano students and 120 Anglo students enrolled in two different campuses of the University of California system (Berkeley and San Diego) and two different campuses of the California State University system (Northridge and San Diego). Because of the limited resources of the study, the focus was directed toward studying the Chicano experience in public four-year institutions of higher education. Other factors considered for selecting the above campuses were comparison of university systems, geographical differences (two campuses were within sixty miles of the Mexican border while the other two campuses were three hundred and six hundred miles from the border), and rural versus urban. Traditional random-sampling selection techniques were not employed for two reasons. Chicano students made up less than 5 percent of the total campus population, and we wanted to be sure to include as many students as we could rather than risk excluding students by using a random-selection procedure. Second, neither of the campuses had a reliable list of all Mexican American students attending. Therefore, a random-selection technique would be invalid from the beginning. One week prior to interviewing students, the following procedure was instituted to recruit participants for the study. Individual letters were written to all Spanish-surnamed Equal Opportunity Program (EOP) students introducing ourselves and explaining the objectives of our study. We advertised in the campus newspapers and met with the Chicano faculty and Chicano student organizations such as Moviemento Estudiantil Chicano de Aztlán (MECHA). Time, location, and phone numbers were provided for interested students who wanted to make appointments. At the time of the interviews, we reiterated that at least one of their respective parents was to be of Mexican background. At the end of the approximately two-hour interview, students were paid twelve dollars for their time.

The structured interviews were performed by a team of five men and women, all of Mexican background. Three of the interviewers were recent University of California, San Diego graduates, while the remaining two interviewers were a social worker and a psychologist who were also on the Counseling Psychological Services staff at the University of California, San Diego. Interviewer training and pilot runs were conducted prior to the actual data collection.

The interview format included one hour of one-to-one, structured questions (e.g., "When did you first think of going to college?" "What were the factors that led you to choose this campus?" "How do you refer to yourself with respect to your ethnic identity?"). The interview focused on students' attitudes, perceptions, and descriptions of coping styles. The second portion included a paper-and-pencil demographic questionnaire (e.g., age, place of birth, parental education, number of siblings, language spoken at home). The third phase consisted of the administration of the College Environmental Stress Index (CESI; see Appendix A).[1] The results of the CESI form the primary topic of this paper. The CESI was devised to gain a quantitative expression of the stresses experienced. Thus, students were asked to rate various events ranging from "taking a test" to "having health problems" on a scale from 1 to 20, with 1 being "not stressful" and 20 being "most stressful."

A t-test for differences between the mean scores for each item was run using the Statistical Package for the Social Sciences (SPSS) computer program (see Appendix B). The tables in Appendix B also indicate the mean differences between groups that were significant at the .001 and .05 level. The 1-to-20 scaling was devised to provide a mean score for each CESI item and to indicate a rank ordering for each subgroup of most to least stressful on all thirty-nine CESI items. A Pearson Rank Order Correlation was reported (see table 5.1) for each of the subgroup comparisons. The subgroup correlations were then compared for significant differences. A chi-square analysis was done to test the significance between CESI items and SES level, high school grade-point average, college grade-point average, year in college, college enrolled in, number of siblings in family, and primary language spoken at home.

The items listed on the CESI were subdivided for analysis into four areas—financial, academic, familial, and personal—while a series of comparisons were made between student responses. Appendix C provides a breakdown of CESI items by categories. In some cases, a particular item may overlap different categories; for instance, "contributing money to help support the immediate family" overlaps with the categories of financial and family. For purposes of the statistical analysis each CESI item was assigned to one specific area.

Results of the Study

The following report of our findings begins with an overall comparison of Chicano and Anglo responses to the CESI. Next the scores of males and groups are compared. Then data on differences within the Chicano population are examined, especially gender differences. Finally, we compare Chicano males and Anglo females and Chicanas and Anglo males, and offer a brief review of other factors influencing stress among Chicanos. Tables 5.1 and 5.2 present a summary of the CESI results and will be referred to throughout this discussion.

According to table 5.1, there was a moderate similarity between Chicanos and Anglos ($r = .84$) in ranking items from most to least stressful. Table 5.3 provides a rank-order breakdown for each group by each of the CESI items. The lack of money and the uncertainty of obtaining it are the two highest sources of stress for Chicano students. Not meeting personal expectations for academic achievement and having personal problems are the two highest rankings for Anglo students. Although there is a similarity in rankings between the groups, there are notable differences both with respect to items ranked as most stressful and in the intensity of perceived stress.

Table 5.1 also indicates that of the twenty-one significantly different items, Chicanos rated seventeen more stressful than did Anglos. Table 5.2 includes a breakdown by area for both Chicanos and Anglos. The greatest stresses for Chicanos occurred in the following order: financial, academic, familial, and personal. Anglo students reported greater stress levels on only four items, of which three fell in the personal area.

There was a significant difference between Chicanos and Anglos on

Table 5.1: A Comparison of Subgroups Based Upon Rank Correlations and Mean Differences of the College Environmental Stress Index

	Rank Correlations	Number of Items with Significant Differences	Number of Items Reported as More Stressful for Each Group	
Chicano/Anglo	.84	21	Chicano: 18	Anglo: 3
Chicana/Chicano	.96	28	Chicana: 28	Chicano: 0
Anglo male/ Anglo female	.87	6	Anglo male: 3	Anglo female: 3
Chicano/Anglo male	.79	12	Chicano: 7	Anglo male: 5
Chicana/Anglo female	.83	15	Chicana: 14	Anglo female: 1
Chicano male/ Anglo female	.76	9	Chicano male: 3	Anglo female: 6
Chicana/Anglo male	.79	29	Chicana: 25	Anglo male: 4

all seven of the financial situations included on the CESI. Chicanos had higher stress scores on six of the seven items. "Not having money for bills," "the uncertainty of receiving financial aid," and "finding employment while going to school that would not jeopardize academics" were the dominant concerns of Chicano students. "Contributing money to help support one's family," "being obligated to repay student loans," and worry over "parents' willingness to provide personal income information for financial-aid applications" were three other financial events that generated more stress for Chicano students than for their Anglo counterparts.[2]

Anglos reported greater stress than did Chicanos over "lack of parents' contribution for financial assistance and support." This item might well be less distressing to Chicano than to Anglo students, since most Chicano students have little expectation of financial help from their parents, whereas for Anglo students, parental support is a major source of funds. Because parental support is not something most Chicano students depend on to get through college, they must rely on institutional or governmental support, such as grants, scholarships, loans, and employment.[3]

Table 5.2: Number of Stress Items with Significant Differences by Subgroup and CESI Area

Subgroups	CESI Areas			
	Financial	Academic	Familial	Personal
Chicano	6	7	2	2
Anglo	1	0	0	3
Chicana	6	11	5	6
Chicano	0	0	0	0
Anglo male	0	0	0	3
Anglo female	2	0	1	0
Chicano	5	2	0	0
Anglo male	1	0	1	3
Chicana	3	7	3	1
Anglo female	1	0	0	0
Chicano male	2	1	0	0
Anglo female	0	0	2	4
Chicana	6	11	5	2
Anglo male	1	0	0	4

Table 5.3: A Comparison Between Anglo and Chicano Rankings and Mean Scores by Each of the CESI Items

Stress Items	Chicano Rank Order Highest to Lowest	Anglo Rank Order	Chicano $\overline{M}$ Scores	Anglo $\overline{M}$ Scores	t-Test Between Groups
STR001	1	3	16,544	14,330	$p<.001$
STR003	2	11	15,508	12,070	$p<.001$
STR012	3	1	14,938	15,165	N.S.
STR023	4	9	14,671	12,346	$p<.001$
STR027	5	4	14,442	13,236	$p<.05$
STR028	6	7	13,991	12,559	$p<.05$
STR026	7	2	13,761	14,779	$p<.05$
STR021	8	16	13,287	11,307	$p<.001$
STR004	9	19	13,255	10,897	$p<.001$
STR022	10	20	12,958	10,362	$p<.001$
STR020	11	6	12,956	11,892	N.S.
STR024	12	8	12,700	12,527	N.S.
STR039	13	13	12,526	11,892	N.S.
STR009	14	5	12,334	12,645	N.S.
STR010	15	18	12,318	11,181	N.S.
STR018	16	30	12,044	8,645	$p<.001$
STR030	17	14	11,838	11,873	N.S.
STR005	18	22	11,811	10,145	$p<.01$
STR011	19	10	11,716	12,134	N.S.
STR016	20	21	11,383	10,307	N.S.
STR025	21	12	11,279	11,952	N.S.
STR002	22	28	11,152	9,424	$p<.01$
STR031	23	26	10,914	9,724	$p<.05$
STR013	24	15	10,380	11,330	N.S.
STR015	25	29	10,109	9,408	N.S.
STR035	26	31	9,894	8,611	$p<.05$
STR029	27	24	9,820	10,070	N.S.
STR014	28	34	9,627	7,420	$p<.001$
STR019	29	32	9,483	8,126	$p<.05$
STR017	30	23	8,997	10,013	N.S.
STR008	31	33	8,005	7,559	N.S.
STR036	32	25	7,498	10,058	$p<.001$
STR007	33	17	7,458	11,211	$p<.001$
STR032	34	35	7,275	6,574	N.S.
STR037	35	27	6,967	9,716	$p<.001$
STR006	36	37	6,900	5,422	$p<.05$
STR038	37	36	6,894	6,166	N.S.
STR034	38	39	6,167	4,358	$p<.001$
STR033	39	38	5,276	5,141	N.S.

Ironically, receiving financial aid does not appear to reduce stress for Chicano students. On the contrary, they reported more financial stress than did Anglo students regardless of the campus attended or the financial-aid package they received. Students in our sample often claimed that being on financial aid was uncomfortable because from year to year there were no guarantees of continued aid. Also, they pointed out that, given the growing expenses of attending even a public university, as well as the general rising cost of living, they had no assurance of receiving adequate assistance.

The most pressing factor, though, was the burden of debt incurred by students who take out loans. During the interview, we determined that almost twice as many Chicanos as Anglo students expected to be in debt when they graduated. The thought of a sizable debt looming just beyond graduation is undoubtedly highly stressful and was something most of the Chicano students in the sample had to live with. To offset the magnitude of the loans they had to take out in order to attend college, many students opted for employment on or off campus. In interviewing our samples, we found that more Chicanos (83 percent) than Anglos (57 percent) had been employed at some time while enrolled, and that 52 percent of the Chicano sample were employed at the time of the survey, compared to 33 percent of the Anglos.

Astin (1975) has suggested that persistence in college correlated with the type of financial aid received. Loans, work study, grants, and parental support have a varying impact on persistence. He speculated that some forms of financial assistance (for example, loans) may increase the likelihood of a student's dropping out. He also concluded that students who receive support for college expenses from their parents are more likely to complete their education than those who do not. The Chicano students' high financial-stress scores tend to corroborate Astin's findings regarding persistence and attrition. Most did not receive financial support from their parents. In addition, many Chicano students voiced strong concern for their families' economic welfare. "Contributing money to help support the immediate family" was one of the concerns of greatest importance to them.

Academic work itself generates stress that affects scholastic performance. The CESI listed fifteen potentially stressful academic events that all students eventually confront. Of these, significant differences were obtained on seven items, with Chicano students scoring higher than Anglos on all of them. "Uncertainty of being accepted by a college or graduate school," "writing a paper," "taking a test," "taking unmeaningful, irrelevant courses," "adjusting to a new school environment," "seeking help with academic problems," "not meeting teachers' expectations," "finding employment that will not jeopardize academics while attending college," and "approaching a staff or faculty member for assistance"—all of these were seen as greater scources of stress by Chicanos than by their Anglo counterparts.

It appears that the whole of the academic experience is more stressful to the Chicano student than to the Anglo student. From the initial "uncertainty of being accepted by a university" through anxiety about "adjusting to a new school environment," a general theme of insecurity is prevalent in Chicano students' responses. This same theme was expressed in the interview section of the study, in which alienation—a feeling of not belonging—was referred to again and again as an important personal problem. The feeling of alienation seems to relate to the entire institutional setup: the enormous size of the university, the physical plant, the bureaucracy. Chicanos also report extremely high stress in asking for academic assistance. "Seeking help with academic problems," "not meeting teachers' expectations," and "approaching a faculty or staff member for academic assistance" all generated high scores. From the interviews, we became aware of the generally low use of academic support services by Chicano students, despite the fact that most rated their precollege educational preparation as fair to poor.

Five items relating to family life were included in the CESI, for family concerns can be a definite source of stress for college students. Chicano students scored significantly higher than did Anglo students on two of the five items: "family members having health problems" and "family members having personal problems." No significant differences in scores between Chicanos and Anglos occurred on the other items. An additional two items that were family-oriented overlapped with the financial scores; on both, Chicanos' scores were higher than Anglos' scores. These items were "contributing money to help support the immediate family" and "parents' willingness to provide personal income information for financial-aid applications."

The Anglo students in our sample, for the most part, were from families that enjoyed a comparatively high socioeconomic status, which ensured that most family financial needs could be met. Most of the Chicano students in the sample came from much lower socioeconomic levels; their families' financial situation and cultural and language differences intensified the reliance of Chicano family members on each other. This reliance is perhaps one of the reasons that for Chicano students, the personal, health, and financial needs of their families are concerns they bring with them to the university. Many of the students in our sample voiced a deep sense of responsibility for alleviating the hardships their families experience daily. Their role as college students accentuated their value as a resource to their families; for the most part, they were the most educated members of their families, the most articulate at representing family concerns when dealing with an English-speaking, Anglo society, and potential wage earners for their families. These factors, though a source of personal and family pride, likewise add to the pressures that bear on them while they attend the university. Thus, our study supports Murillo's claim (1971) that responding to family needs is an ultimate priority for the Chicano: "if his help is required by the family, he may temporarily forego job, school, or any other activity that might prevent him from meeting his family obligations" (p. 105).

Personal stress, although often less visible and less discussed, and usually more difficult to describe, can be a great drain on students' mental energy. Of twelve personal-stress events listed on the CESI, significant differences occurred on five. Chicanos reported greater stress than did Anglos on "seeking help with your personal and academic problems" and "meeting parents of friends from other ethnic or social groups." Anglos perceived greater stress on three items: "asking for a date," "difficulty in getting a date," and "having personal problems." It is noteworthy that of the twenty-one items on which Chicanos and Anglos had significant differences, Anglos scored higher (that is, perceived more stress) on only five. And, as mentioned, three of these related to personal stress. It is possible that Chicanos view "personal problems" as a luxury they cannot afford given their concern over bills, family, and the demands of academic life.

A comparison of the CESI scores of Chicano and Anglo males revealed that they differed significantly on twelve items; on seven of these, Chicanos scored higher than Anglo males; Anglos scored higher on five (see table 5.2). Financial stress is the primary area of difference between the two groups. Of the seven financial items, Chicanos reported greater stress on five: "not having money for bills," "contributing money to help support the family," "uncertainty of receiving financial aid," "finding employment that will not jeopardize academics," and "parents' willingness to provide personal income information for financial-aid applications." Anglo males reported greater stress than did Chicanos regarding "parents' contribution for financial support."

The dominant stress themes for Anglo males were oriented more toward personal-social and parent-relationship issues. Thus, the four other items that were more distressing to Anglo males than to Chicanos were "having personal problems," "being told by parents to attend or not to attend school," "asking for a date," and "difficulty in getting a date." Economic survival and concern for family welfare, on the other hand, were predominant stresses for Chicanos. In addition, academics were another primary concern for them. Chicanos reported higher stress on two academic items: "taking unmeaningful and irrelevant courses," and "not meeting teachers' expectations for academic achievement."

Overall, Chicanas reported significantly higher stress scores than did Anglo women. Of the thirty-nine items on the CESI, significant differences occurred on fifteen, and Chicanas perceived greater stress on fourteen of them. Chicanas indicated higher stress on four of the seven financial scales—their responses corroborate our findings that finances are the dominant source of stress for Chicano students in higher education. Chicanas identified the following financial items as more stressful: "not having money for bills, social events, and so on," "uncertainty of receiving financial aid," "finding employment that will not jeopardize academics," "repaying student loans." Anglo women perceived one item as more stressful: "lack of parents' contribution for financial support." In the academic area, Chicanas perceived greater stress than did Anglo women on seven of the fifteen items: "uncertainty of being accepted into college or graduate school," "writing a paper," "going through the process of applying to college or graduate school," "taking unmeaningful or irrelevant courses," "seeking help with academic problems," "not meeting teachers' expectations for academic achievement," and "approaching a staff or faculty member for assistance."

Chicanas scored higher than did Anglo women on the following family-stress items: "family members having personal problems," "family members having health problems," and "not meeting parents' expectations for academic achievement." In the personal area, only one significant difference was noted: Chicanas scored higher than did Anglo women regarding "meeting parents of friends from other ethnic or social groups." Anglo women were significantly higher than Chicanas on one item: "lack of parents' contribution for financial support." The marked difference in total stress scores as well as only a moderate rank-order correlation between Chicanas and Anglo women indicate no strong similarity between the two groups in their perception of the stress intensity of particular events or in their ranking of stress events.

We were not surprised to find that Chicanos' and Chicanas' ranking of the stress events yielded more similar results than did any other comparison we made ($p<.001$); that is, the Chicanos and Chicanas in our sample agreed most in placing the thirty-nine events in a stress hierarchy. Although Anglo men and women had a moderate to strong similarity in ranking the stress items, Chicano men and women were significantly more similar. The results of the comparison between Chicanos and Chicanas are surprising in their stress intensity. Despite their common language, SES, and cultural background, there were major differences between Chicanos and Chicanas in their perception of the degree of stress in every area. Chicanas' stress scores were significantly higher than were the scores of Chicanos on twenty-eight of the thirty-nine items.

Chicanas perceived greater stress on six of the seven financial items: "not having money for bills," "contributing money to help support the family," "uncertainty of receiving financial aid," "finding employment that will not jeopardize academics," "being obligated to repay loans," and "lack of parents' contribution for financial support." They scored higher on eleven of the academic items: "uncertainty of being accepted into college or graduate school," "writing a paper," "applying to college or graduate school," "taking unmeaningful or irrelevant courses," "seeking help with personal or academic problems," "not meeting teachers' expectations for academic achievement," "approaching a staff or faculty member for assistance," "being asked to verbally participate in class," "taking a test," "adjusting to a new school environment," and "adjusting to a new school environment." Their scores were higher on five of the familial items: "being told to attend or not to attend school," "having conflict with family members," "family members having health problems," "family members having personal problems," and "family disapproval of social life style." They also scored higher on these personal items: "not meeting personal academic expectations," "having conflict with personal values," "letting someone know you disagree with them," "presenting friends of different ethnic or social groups to your immediate family," "having health problems," and "having personal problems."

The differences between Chicanos and Chicanas were significantly greater than the differences we found between the total Chicano and total Anglo groups, as well as between Anglo males and Chicanos and between Anglo females and Chicanas. Male-female differences in the Anglo sample were almost inconsequential: Anglo men's and women's perceived-stress differences were minimal—only six out of the thirty-nine items—and of these six items, Anglo men scored higher in stress than did women on half of them. Chicanas as a group consistently reported greater stress than any other group. These findings suggest that cultural background, specifically sex-role socialization, provides significant discontinuity for the Chicana in higher education. A comparison between Chicano males and Anglo females yielded significance on nine items, and on three of these, Chicano men scored higher than Anglo women; Anglo women scored higher on six. Differences occurred in all four areas: financial, academic, personal, and familial. In addition, the two groups obtained the lowest rank-order correlation of any of the groups. Though both groups indicated anxieties in securing financial assistance, the Chicanos indicated concern regarding the "uncertainty of receiving financial aid," whereas the Anglo women were concerned about the "lack of parents' contribution for financial support." Anglo women were more distressed than were Chicano males regarding parental pressures—specifically "being told by parents to attend or not to attend college" and "family disapproval of social life style." Chicano males were more concerned at a broader social level, indicating anxiety about "meeting parents of friends from other backgrounds." Anglo women listed more introspective personal issues including "having health problems" and "being in conflict over changing personal values."

Aside from the comparison between Anglo males and females, the comparison between Chicano men and Anglo women obtained the least number of significantly different items (nine). However, the least number of significant differences in the intensity of stress perceived does not necessarily indicate a strong similarity between these two groups. The Chicano males' and Anglo females' rank-order correlation (.76) differed significantly ($p<.001$) from the Chicano-Chicana ranking (.96).That is, Chicanas and Chicanos shared an extremely high agreement as to what specific events generate the most stress, whereas Chicano males and Anglo females indicated the lowest agreement in ranking stressful events. There was as remarkable a dissimilarity between Chicanas and Anglo men (twenty-nine significantly different items) as there was between Chicana and Chicano students (twenty-eight items). Of the twenty-nine significantly different items reported by Chicanas and Anglo men, Chicana scores were higher than those of Anglo men on twenty-four. Financial, academic, and familial concerns were the most frequently noted stressful items for Chicanas in comparison to Anglo men, whereas Anglo men most notably reported higher stress scores than Chicanas on personal items.

The study also looked at demographic variables that could influence the stress levels perceived by Chicano students. The data supported the following conclusions: The Chicano whose background is primarily Spanish-speaking tends to be more highly stressed than the Chicano whose background is bilingual or primarily English-speaking on the following five items: "meeting parental academic expectations" ($p<.05$), "taking tests" ($p<.05$), "taking irrelevant courses," "having adequate English-speaking skills" ($p<.01$), and "making friends with people of different backgrounds ($p<.05$); Chicanos of lower family incomes indicated slightly more concerns than did Chicano students of higher family incomes on academic, familial, and personal issues. High school grade-point average (GPA) did not correlate significantly with any of the thirty-nine stress items. College GPA correlates significantly with only two of the thirty-nine items. Students with lower GPAs reported more stress than students with average to high GPAs regarding "taking a test" (*p*<.01) or "approaching a teacher for assistance" (*p*<.01). Freshmen were more concerned than upper-class students (on five of the thirty-nine items) about "adequate English skills," "peer discrimination" (*p*<.05), "parental academic expectations" (*p*<.01), "family disapproval of life style" (*p*<.01), and "adjusting to a new school environment" (*p*<.05). The size of the family that a student came from correlated significantly with only one of the thirty-nine items. Chicano students from larger families reported higher stress regarding feelings of alienation in college.[4]

CONCLUSIONS

The university must know the needs of its students: where they come from, who they are, what they need. Problems must be viewed not only as individual issues but as social and institutional ones as well. While all students face some stress-provoking situations upon entering higher education, this research has demonstrated that the stress produced is higher for Chicano students than for Anglo students; for Chicanas it is higher still. The primary source of strain for Chicano students relates to finances. This results from that fact that Chicano students come from lower socioeconomic levels than Anglo students and therefore receive less parental aid. Thus, they are required to take on greater debt, to work outside of school, and to rely more on increasingly undependable sources of institutional aid. Further, they perceive themselves to be not as well prepared academically as their Anglo counterparts. Family stress arises from the fact that Chicano students often have more family responsibilities than do Anglo students. Their families are, in general, larger, less well educated and in more precarious economic condition. They are also frequently in the midst of adjusting to a totally new culture with new values and expectations.

The psychological ramifications of these high stress levels—the frustrations, the conflicts, the pressures—are unknown. How do those Chicano students who continue their education into college cope with the financial, academic, and personal demands placed upon them? In comparison with Anglo students, what is the incidence of depression, anxiety, poor self-concept, and alcohol or substance abuse? Do they experience more stress-related physical problems—headaches, ulcers, insomnia? At what point do they drop out? Chicano students clearly need more reliable financial support. They need more encouragement to use academic support systems and personal support groups. Researchers and educators need greater awareness of their problems.

Chicano students are often unaware of the sources of their anxiety, unhappiness, or guilt or of the effects that these can have on academic performance. Not having money to pay the rent can interfere with one's ability to study chemistry. Guilt over doing poorly on a test can get mixed up with suppressed guilt over living better in a college dormitory than one's family is living at home. I counseled one Chicana, seemingly in tears over bad grades, whose brother had been killed in a gang slaying the previous week. And another student with a 3.6 grade-point average in the arts felt only failure because the arts were held in disdain by his mother. Students must understand that it is stressful to share a dorm with students from more economically secure, more well-to-do families; to share classrooms with students who are culturally different; to have friends with better clothes, cars, and academic preparation—and perhaps a surer sense of the future.

University staff must look under the surface to see what problems students are facing. Student personnel staff are often surprised to find that a Chicano student who had initially been doing quite well was ultimately dismissed by the university for poor grades. To the end, the student continued to function well socially, and no one—not friends, not professors, not administrators—suspected that the student was in very deep trouble. The importance of being able to say "I have a problem" cannot be minimized. Professionals from similar cultural backgrounds can help here by shedding facades of invulnerability and sharing with students the problems they have had. They can also help by pointing out that some stress, if understood and channeled constructively, can lead to highly positive results.

Researchers must address the reality of what is happening to the Chicano consumer as he or she attempts to succeed in the institutions of education. We are all too familiar with the outcome statistics pointing to underrepresentation and institutional racism. If we are to effectively intervene in the process, we must understand the educational/life experience for the Chicano and the Chicana alike. What impact do marriage, age, language, role models, motivation, acculturation, and assimilation have on persisting through college graduation? Can we isolate the two, three, or four factors that are important in influencing the process and modify them toward the goal of encouraging more students of Mexican background toward graduation?

APPENDIX A: STRESS SCALE

Definition. Stressful events are defined as situations that are upsetting to you.

On the following pages is a list of events that may occur to college students. We would like you to think about each event and decide how upsetting it is. Use your own experience to make your decision. A particular event might be more stressful to some people than to others. Try to think how stressful the event would be for you.

Below is a row of numbers (scale) to show how stressful the event is. In the blank next to each event, write the number that shows how stressful that event is.

For each event, think about how stressful it is for you. If you personally have not experienced an event, evaluate how stressful it would be for you if it had occurred.

Scale. 1 2 3 4 5 6 7 8 9 10 11 12 13 14 15 16 17 18 19 20
Not   Most
stressful   stressful

1. Not having money for bills, social activities, living expenses. _____
2. Contributing money to help support the immediate family. _____
3. Uncertainty of receiving financial aid, i.e., grants, loans, work-study. _____
4. Finding employment that will not jeopardize academics, i.e., part-time, summer. _____
5. Being obligated to repay student loans. _____
6. Parents' willingness to provide personal income information for financial-aid applications. _____
7. Lack of parents' contribution for financial support. _____
8. Being asked to verbally participate in class. _____
9. Enrolling in school and not having adequate English reading, writing, and speaking skills. _____
10. Teachers treating you differently than other students. _____
11. Peers treating you differently than other students. _____
12. Not meeting personal expectations for academic achievement. _____
13. Not meeting parents'* expectations for academic achievement. *("Parents" implies any adults that might have raised you.) _____
14. Not meeting teachers' expectations for academic achievement. _____

15. Attempting to get higher GPA than peers.   _____
16. Receiving lower GPA than peers.   _____
17. Being told by parents to attend or not to attend school.   _____
18. Taking "unmeaningful/irrelevant" courses.   _____
19. Approaching a teacher, staff member, or administrator to resolve an issue, conflict, get assistance, etc.   _____
20. Taking a test.   _____
21. Writing a paper.   _____
22. Going through the process of applying to college or graduate school.   _____
23. Uncertainty of being accepted into college or graduate school.   _____
24. Having a conflict with family members.   _____
25. Having health problems.   _____
26. Having personal problems.   _____
27. Family members having health problems.   _____
28. Family members having personal problems.   _____
29. Family disapproval of social life style.   _____
30. Conflicts with changing personal values.   _____
31. Adjusting to a new school environment.   _____
32. Making friends with people from different backgrounds and/or values.   _____
33. Presenting friends of different ethnic or social groups to your immediate family.   _____
34. Meeting parents of friends from other ethnic or social groups.   _____
35. Seeking help with your personal or academic problems.
36. Asking for a date.
37. Difficulty getting a date.   _____
38. Letting someone know you disagree with them.   _____
39. Enrolling in school and feeling different (isolated, alienated, not belonging.)   _____

Table 5.4: A Comparison Between Anglo Female and Chicana Rankings and Mean Scores by Each of the CESI Items

Stress Items	Chicana Rank Order	Anglo Female Rank Order	Chicana $\overline{M}$ Scores	Anglo Female $\overline{M}$ Scores	t-Test Between Groups
STR001	1	2	17,507	15,600	$p<.01$
STR003	2	9	16,682	12,780	$p<.001$
STR012	3	3	16,204	15,480	N.S.
STR027	4	4	16,068	14,000	$p<.05$
STR028	5	7	15,980	13,080	$p<.001$
STR023	6	13	15,837	12,280	$p<.001$
STR026	7	1	15,551	15,720	N.S.
STR021	8	22	14,476	10,940	$p<.001$
STR022	9	25	14,370	9,980	$p<.001$
STR004	10	20	14,189	11,200	$p<.001$
STR024	11	5	14,102	13,640	N.S.
STR030	12	14	14,054	13,020	N.S.
STR020	13	10	13,891	12,680	N.S.
STR039	14	15	13,649	11,857	N.S.
STR009	15	11	13,115	12,531	N.S.
STR018	16	27	13,041	9,740	$p<.01$
STR010	17	16	13,000	11,680	N.S.
STR005	18	24	12,784	10,020	$p<.01$
STR025	19	6	12,646	13,360	N.S.
STR011	20	14	12,405	12,260	N.S.
STR029	21	12	12,326	12,460	N.S.
STR002	22	19	12,270	11,224	N.S.
STR016	23	23	11,986	10,260	N.S.
STR031	24	26	11,769	9,960	N.S.
STR013	25	17	11,116	11,660	N.S.
STR035	26	31	11,075	8,122	$p<.001$
STR014	27	34	10,939	7,640	$p<.001$
STR017	28	21	10,939	11,020	N.S.
STR015	29	28	10,769	9,204	N.S.
STR019	30	29	10,537	8,580	$p<.05$
STR008	31	32	9,520	8,080	N.S.
STR007	32	18	8,730	11,604	$p<.05$
STR036	33	30	8,007	8,574	N.S.
STR038	34	36	8,000	6,479	N.S.
STR032	35	35	7,592	6,560	N.S.
STR006	36	37	7,507	7,816	N.S.
STR037	37	33	6,919	7,816	N.S.
STR034	38	39	6,442	3,673	$p<.001$
STR033	39	38	5,952	5,531	N.S.

Table 5.5: A Comparison Between Anglo Male and Chicano Male Rankings and Mean Scores by Each of the CESI Items

Stress Items	Chicano Rank Order	Anglo Rank Order	Chicano Mean Scores	Anglo Mean Scores	t-Test Between Groups
STR001	1	3	15.804	13.506	$p<.001$
STR003	2	12	14.613	11.610	$p<.001$
STR012	3	1	13.979	14.961	N.S.
STR023	4	7	13.789	12.390	N.S.
STR027	5	4	13.198	12.740	N.S.
STR004	6	21	12.539	10.701	$p<.05$
STR028	7	8	12.469	12.221	N.S.
STR026	8	2	12.399	14.169	$p<.05$
STR021	9	13	12.387	11.545	N.S.
STR020	10	6	12.247	12.507	N.S.
STR022	11	22	11.897	10.610	N.S.
STR010	12	20	11.799	10.857	N.S.
STR009	13	5	11.736	12.720	N.S.
STR039	14	10	11.670	11.917	N.S.
STR024	15	11	11.632	11.805	N.S.
STR018	16	31	11.286	7.935	$p<.001$
STR011	17	9	11.191	12.053	N.S.
STR005	18	24	11.062	10.230	N.S.
STR016	19	23	10.922	10.338	N.S.
STR002	20	30	10.299	8.263	$p<.05$
STR031	21	25	10.264	9.571	N.S.
STR025	22	16	10.238	11.039	N.S.
STR030	23	14	10.150	11.118	N.S.
STR013	24	15	9.818	11.117	N.S.
STR015	25	26	9.602	9.539	N.S.
STR035	26	28	9.000	8.944	N.S.
STR019	27	32	8.677	7.831	N.S.
STR014	28	33	8.634	7.276	$p<.05$
STR029	29	29	7.901	8.519	N.S.
STR017	30	27	7.503	9.500	$p<.05$
STR036	31	18	7.115	11.0278	$p<.001$
STR032	32	35	7.036	6.584	N.S.
STR037	33	17	7.005	11.0282	$p<.001$
STR008	34	34	6.850	7.221	N.S.
STR007	35	19	6.479	10.960	$p<.001$
STR006	36	37	6.432	4.904	$p<.05$
STR038	37	36	6.042	5.958	N.S.
STR034	38	39	5.958	4.831	N.S.
STR033	39	38	4.762	4.873	N.S.

APPENDIX C: SUMMARY OF STRESS ITEMS BY CATEGORIES

Financial
1. Not having money for bills, social activities, living expenses.
2. Contributing money to help support the immediate family.
3. Uncertainty of receiving financial aid, i.e., grants, loans, work-study.
4. Finding employment that will not jeopardize academics, i.e., part-time, summer.
5. Being obligated to repay student loans.
6. Parents' willingness to provide personal income information for financial-aid applications.
7. Lack of parents' contribution for financial support.

Academic
8. Being asked to verbally participate in class.
9. Enrolling in school and not having adequate English reading, writing, and speaking skills.
10. Teachers treating you differently than other students.
12. Not meeting personal expectations for academic achievement.
13. Not meeting parents'* expectations for academic achievement. *("Parents" implies any adults that might have raised you.)
14. Not meeting teachers' expectations for academic achievement.
15. Attempting to get higher GPA than peers.
16. Receiving lower GPA than peers.
18. Taking "unmeaningful/irrelevant" courses.
19. Approaching a teacher, staff member, or administrator to resolve an issue, conflict, get assistance, etc.
20. Taking a test.
21. Writing a paper.
22. Going through the process of applying to college or graduate school.
23. Uncertainty of being accepted into college or graduate school.

Familial
17. Being told by parents to attend or not to attend school.
24. Having a conflict with family members.
27. Family members having health problems.
28. Family members having personal problems.
29. Family disapproval of social life style.

Personal
11. Peers treating you differently than other students.
25. Having health problems.
26. Having personal problems.
30. Conflicts with changing personal values.
32. Making friends with people from different backgrounds and/or values.

33. Presenting friends of different ethnic or social groups to your immediate family.
34. Meeting parents of friends from other ethnic or social groups.
35. Seeking help with your personal or academic problems.
36. Asking for a date.
37. Difficulty getting a date.
38. Letting someone know you disagree with them.
39. Enrolling in school and feeling different (isolated, alienated, not belonging).

NOTES

1. CESI (which appears in appendix A) was constructed in collaboration with Hervey Sweetwood, formerly of the Life Stress Department of the Veterans Administration Hospital, La Jolla, California, and was based on work done by Holmes and Rahe (1967) and by Paykel, Myers, and Dienelt (1969). The instrument consists of forty-one typical events that undergraduates had reported to be stressful. Of these, thirty-nine are included in this report. (The other two, items 40 and 41 on the index, related to language skills and were not found to be statistically significant.) The instrument was cross-validated with psychologists and social workers at the University of California at San Diego, who agreed that these events frequently led students to seek help from the University's psychological services. A test-retest reliability (Chronbach's alpha) run was performed on the instrument using two academic classes of thirty undergraduates at the University of California, San Diego.

2. During interview sessions, Chicano students maintained that financial concerns would be the main reason that they might have to leave the university.

3. The primary source of funding for Chicano students in our sample is through the campus financial-aid office. According to 1975 College Entrance Examination Board data, the majority of Chicanos (65 percent) were receiving financial assistance at their respective campuses compared to 26 percent of Anglo students. A representative 65 percent of the Chicano students in our sample were funded by financial aid.

4. There were virtually no differences in stress scores between the UC students and the CSU students; only one of the thirty-nine items correlated significantly: UC students were more concerned about "adjusting to a new school environment."

REFERENCES

Astin, A. W. (1971). *Predicting academic performance in college: Selectivity data for 2,300 American colleges.* New York: Free Press.
Astin, A. W. (1975). *Preventing students from dropping out.* San Francisco: Jossey-Bass.

Cannon, W. B. (1929). *Bodily changes in pain, hunger, fear and rage.* New York: D. Appleton.

Casso, H. (1975). Higher education and the Mexican-American. In G. Tyler (Ed.), *Mexican-American Tomorrow.* Albuquerque: University of New Mexico Press.

Coleman, J. C. (1973). Life stress and maladaptive behavior. *American Journal of Occupational Therapy, 27*(4), 169–180.

Cope, R. G., & Hannah, W. (1975). Revolving college doors: The causes and consequences of dropping out, stopping out, and transferring. New York: Wiley-Interscience.

Cuéllar, A. J., & Moore, J. W. (1970). *Mexican Americans.* Englewood Cliffs, NJ: Prentice-Hall.

Dohrenwend, B. S., & Dohrenwend, B. P. (1970). Class and race as status related sources of stress. In S. Levine & N. A. Scotch (Eds.), *Social stress.* Chicago: Aldine.

Dohrenwend, B. S., & Dohrenwend, B. P. (1974). *Stressful life events: Their nature and effects.* New York: Wiley.

Hernández, N. G. (1973). Variables affecting achievement of middle school Mexican American students. *Review of Educational Research, 43*(1), 1–41.

Holmes, T. H., & Rahe, R. H. (1967). The social readjustment scale. *Journal of Psychosomatic Research, 11,* 213.

Howard, L. R. (1960). The subjective meaning of stress. *British Journal of Medical Psychology, 33,* 185.

Keefe, S. E., Padilla, A. M., & Carlos, M. L. (1978). The Mexican American extended family as an emotional support system. In J. M. Casas & S. E. Keefe (Eds.), *Family and mental health in the Mexican American community,* Monograph No. 7. Los Angeles: Spanish Speaking Mental Health Research Center, UCLA.

Lazarus, R. S. (1970). Cognitive and personality factors underlying threat and coping. In S. Levine & N. A. Scotch (Eds.), *Social stress.* Chicago: Aldine.

Levi, L. (1971). The psychosocial environment and psychomatic disease. In L. Levi (Ed.), *Society, stress, and disease,* Vol. 1. London: Oxford University Press.

López, R. W., Madrid-Barela, A., & Macías, R. (1976). *Chicanos in higher education: status and issues.* Monograph No. 7. Los Angeles: Chicano Studies Center Publications, University of California, Los Angeles.

Meyer, A. (1951). The life chart and the obligation of specifying positive data in psychopathological diagnosis. In D. E. Winters (Ed.), *The collected papers of Adolf Meyer.* Baltimore: Johns Hopkins University Press.

Muñoz, D. & García-Bahne, B. (1978). A study of the Chicano experience in higher education. Final report for the Center for Minority Group Mental Health Programs. National Institute of Mental Health, Grant No. NN24597-01. University of California, San Diego.

Murillo, N. (1971). The Mexican American family. In N. Wagner (Ed.), *Chicanos.* St. Louis: Mosby.

Paykel, E. S., Myers, J., & Dienelt, M. (1969). Life events and depression. *Archives of General Psychiatry, 21,* 753–760.

Rahe, R. H. Epidemiological studies of life change and illness. (1975). *International Journal of Psychiatric Medicine, 6,* 133–146.

Selye, H. A. (1956, July 4). A syndrome produced by diverse nocuous agents. *Nature,* pp.138–153.

Selye, H. (1956). *The stress of life.* New York: McGraw-Hill, 1956.

Selye, H. (1974). *Stress without distress.* New York: Lippincott, 1974.

Selye, H. (1978, March). (Interviewed by Laurence Cherryl). On the real benefits of eustress. *Psychology Today,* pp. 78–93.

Sheatsley, P. B., & Feldman, J. (1964, summer). The assassination of President Kennedy: Public reaction. *Public Opinion Quarterly, 28,* 189–215.

U.S. Commission on Civil Rights. (1978). Social indicators of equity for minorities and women. Washington, DC: U.S. Government Printing Office.

Vásquez, M. J. (1978). Chicana and Anglo university women: Factors related to their performance, persistence, and attrition. Unpublished dissertation, University of Texas at Austin.

6 | The Latino Science and Engineering Student: Recent Research Findings

JOSÉ P. MESTRE

The representation of Hispanics in professional technical fields is disproportionately low in comparison to the Hispanic representation on the mainland United States. The extent of this underrepresentation is detailed in a publication of the National Center for Education Statistics entitled *The Condition of Education for Hispanic Americans* (Brown, Rosen, Hill, & Olivas, 1980). For example, the enrollment statistics for 1978 show that, out of all Hispanics attending college on the mainland, the percentages enrolled in engineering and the physical sciences were 2.4 percent and 0.8 percent, respectively; in comparison, the percentages of whites enrolled in engineering and the physical sciences (out of the total white undergraduate enrollment) were 5.2 percent and 1.5 percent, respectively. The situation is even worse at the postgraduate level—the corresponding percentages of postgraduate enrollments for Hispanics on the mainland in engineering and the physical sciences are 1.5 percent and 1.4 percent, compared to 4.2 percent and 3.1 percent for whites.

The causes of this underrepresentation are many and varied. In terms of undergraduate enrollments, only 2.8 percent out of all undergraduates attending four-year programs in 1978 were Hispanic, despite the fact that Hispanics comprised 5.6 percent of the mainland population. High school dropout rates also contribute to the problem, since Hispanics between the ages of fourteen and nineteen are twice as likely not to have completed high school as nonminority students in the same age group. Socioeconomic status (SES) measures indicate large disparities between Hispanics and whites. Given the fact that SES has been

Work supported in part by National Institute of Education Grant No. G-79-0094. The contents do not necessarily reflect the position, policy, or endorsement of the National Institute of Education.

157

shown to correlate with educational aspirations and academic preparedness (Sewell, 1971; Sewell & Hauser, 1975), Hispanics have a decided disadvantage (Ramírez & Castañeda, 1974; Vásquez, 1982). Furthermore, recent disclosures by the Educational Testing Service have revealed that Hispanics are underprepared in mathematical and verbal skills as measured by performance on the Scholastic Aptitude Test (SAT) ("Board Says . . .," 1982). However, some researchers have recently expressed concern about the validity of the SAT for use with Hispanic students (Durán, this volume; Mestre, 1981).

The purpose of this article is to report on a series of research studies conducted with Hispanic college students enrolled in science and engineering programs. Although Hispanic college students have not been "popular" for use as research subjects, there is much to be learned by studying this particular group. First, what we learn about the difficulties that these students experience during various problem-solving tasks should provide data useful in designing effective intervention programs at the precollege level. In addition, we can study how and to what extent below-average language proficiency interferes in the problem-solving process. Lastly, such studies will help illuminate the role of language, and especially of bilingualism, in the development of cognitive skills.

With few exceptions, the underlying theme in all of the studies discussed here is the interplay of language in problem solving. Educators in the sciences agree that one of the most difficult steps in the problem-solving process is the translation of the problem statement into the appropriate symbolic or mathematical notation. Not only does the ability to correctly solve a problem hinge on accurately translating the problem, but it is precisely in this step that most errors occur—errors that are often the result of inappropriate interpretations of textual information contained in the problem statement.

Before proceeding, I offer a word of caution. As indicated above, the role of SES in studies investigating the cognitive performance of minority populations is important. That SES is an important factor in the studies reported here is not at issue; however, the *extent* to which SES mediates performance in the mathematics- and language-proficiency measures used is not clear. It is therefore important to keep in mind the possible confounding role of SES on the results reported in this article.

REVIEW OF THE LITERATURE

As has already been mentioned, the number of studies that have investigated problem solving with bilingual populations is few. The oldest and perhaps the best-known study using Puerto Rican bilingual subjects was conducted by the International Institute of Teachers College of Columbia University (1926). This study found that the English mathematical problem-solving ability of twelfth-grade Puerto Rican bilinguals educated in Puerto Rico was significantly below that of U.S. twelfth-graders, despite the fact that the Puerto Rican students had been receiving mathematics instruction in English since the fifth grade. Similar findings were reported by Macnamara (1967), who reviewed numerous studies of arithmetic reasoning among bilinguals. Macnamara concluded that bilinguals appear to have more difficulties than monolinguals in solving mathematics problems that require semantic processing, even when the language of the problems was also the language used for instruction. There did not appear to be any differences, however, between bilinguals and monolinguals in problem-solving performance on arithmetic problems requiring no semantic processing.

Similar findings were obtained by Kellaghan and Macnamara (1968) in a study of the problem-solving skills of Irish fifth-standard primary students. They found a weaker performance in problems requiring substantial amounts of semantic processing, if the problems were given in the students' weaker language. Not only were the problems equated for number of words across the Irish and English versions, but students had displayed an understanding of each separate component of the problems' statements in their weaker language. Another finding from this study was that problem-reading time was longer in the weaker language by factors ranging from 1.4 to 1.7, a finding consistent with other studies (Lambert, Havelka, & Gardner, 1959; Kolers, 1966). These results suggest that the linguistic processes mediating the decoding process necessary for understanding a problem at a sufficiently high level to be able to solve it go beyond simple semantic decoding. Macnamara (1967) explained these findings by pointing out that longer decoding times in the weaker language imply greater difficulties with that task, thereby placing an added burden on a short-term memory that is already limited both in the quantity of information it can store and in the length of time for which it can store it. This additional burden on short-term memory has a confounding effect on solving problems in a weaker language.

A more recent investigation by DeÁvila and Duncan (1981) studied the performance of 903 children from nine distinct ethnolinguistic groups on various academic, cognitive, and linguistic tasks. The single best predictor of academic performance found in this study was language proficiency, indicating that the difficulties encountered by the students in performing the various tasks may have been linguistic rather than intellectual in nature. In an investigation with Hispanic and Anglo ninth-graders enrolled in Algebra I, Mestre and Gerace (1985) found that Hispanic and Anglo students alike had a difficult time verbalizing the procedure they used in solving word problems, even when they could operationally obtain the solutions to the problems. This ability to verbalize was poorest among those Hispanics who were below average in language proficiency. Results from this study also revealed that the syntax of a problem was a very important factor in determining problem-solving difficulty, and that Hispanics who were below average in language proficiency often did not understand word problems well enough to attempt a solution. Further, even though errors caused by misinterpreting a phrase or word in a problem were committed by all students, the Hispanic group was more prone to this type of error.

The evidence thus supports the premise that language proficiency mediates complex cognitive tasks. An explanatory hypothesis espoused by Cummins (1979) takes into account the effect of language proficiency on cognitive functioning. Cummins's "linguistic threshold hypothesis" posits that "there may be a threshold level of linguistic competence which bilingual children must attain both in order to avoid cognitive deficits, and to allow the potentially beneficial aspects of becoming bilingual to influence their cognitive growth" (1979, p. 229). The actual threshold level is not defined in absolute terms, since it depends on the individual and on the demands of the cognitive task in question. Cummins does define three types of bilingualism. The first, "semilingualism," is characterized by a below-threshold level of linguistic competence in *both* languages. In semilingualism, both languages are sufficiently weak to impair the quality of interaction between the student and the educational environment. The negative effects of semilingualism are no longer present in "dominant bilingualism," which is characterized by an above-threshold level of competence in *one* language. Dominant bilingualism is supposed to have neither a negative nor a positive effect on cognitive development, although it could have a negative effect on cognitive functioning in tasks that impose substantial linguistic demands on the weaker language. The last category, "additive bilingualism," is one conducive to positive cognitive effects. Additive bilingualism is characterized by above-threshold competence in both languages.

The Hispanic college students in the studies I am about to review appear to be semilingual in the Cummins sense. Although no single piece of evidence gives incontrovertible proof that poor language skills militate against successful problem-solving, we will present numerous findings that, collectively, lend strong support to this view. At the conclusion of this paper, suggestions are listed to combat some of the extant problems encountered by Hispanic students who wish to pursue technical fields.

REVIEW OF RESEARCH STUDIES

The studies discussed here were conducted during the 1979–1982 academic years. Although the number and ethnicity of the subjects who participated varied from study to study, the approximate breakdown of the ethnicity of the Hispanic participants was fairly consistent across studies. Half the Hispanics were of Puerto Rican descent, while the remaining half were of South American, Central American, or Caribbean descent. Approximately one-third of the Puerto Rican group consisted of students who were living in Puerto Rico and came to the mainland for the express purpose of attending college, then returned to Puerto Rico during the summer months. Another third of the Puerto Rican group, as well as most of the non-Puerto Rican Hispanics, had immigrated to the mainland during their precollege years. The remaining one-third of the Puerto Rican group was born and raised on the mainland. Many of these students were dominant English speakers. Further details on the subjects used in our studies can be found in the references cited throughout this paper.

All our studies also included a control group of Anglo students. This permitted us to assess how factors such as language proficiency, academic preparation, and socioeconomic status affected problem-solving performance, and college performance as measured by grade-point average, across the two groups.

Academic Preparation: The Overall Picture

One of the studies conducted (Mestre, 1981) was an evaluation of the students' academic preparation in verbal and mathematical skills. Several tests covering language proficiency, mathematical computation, and word-problem-solving proficiency were administered to the students. Given that I was also interested in identifying any possible differences in performance across language, and that there is a paucity of advanced testing instruments in parallel English-Spanish forms, I was forced to develop several mathematical testing instruments. A brief description of all testing instruments discussed in this paper is given in the Appendix. The mathematics tests that will be discussed in this section are the Test of General Ability–Computation (Guidance Testing Associates, 1962a), the Formula Translation Examination, the Short Algebra Inventory, and the Word Problem Inventory. The language-proficiency tests consist of the Test of Reading and Prueba de Lectura (Guidance Testing Associates, 1962b). We will also show student performance on the Scholastic Aptitude Test (Educational Testing Service, 1942–1985).

The means and standard deviations on these tests for sixty Hispanic science and engineering majors, and for a corresponding group of seventy-three Anglo science and engineering majors, are shown in table 6.1. Also shown in table 6.1 is each group's college grade-point average (GPA). Table 6.2 displays the Pearson correlation coefficients among all ten variables.

Table 6.1 shows that the Hispanic group was academically underprepared in comparison to the Anglo group. In the Test of Reading and the Prueba de Lectura, the Hispanic group showed a balanced performance across English and Spanish; only eleven students showed a performance dissimilar enough across English and Spanish to be deemed "unbalanced." However, the Anglo group had a decided advantage in English-language proficiency as measured by the Test of Reading; the Anglo group was also better prepared in mathematical, manipulative, and computational skills as measured by the Short Algebra Inventory

Table 6.1:   Means and Standard Deviations on Testing Instruments

| | | Bilinguals $N=60$ | | | | Monolinguals $N=73$ | |
| | Max. | Spanish | | English | | English | |
Exam	Score	Mean	S.D.	Mean	S.D.	Mean	S.D.
Grade-point average*	4.0	—	—	2.33	.77	2.62	.73
TOR—Vocabulary	45	29.0	9.0	29.8	7.5	36.0	4.0
TOR—Speed of Comprehension	30	11.5	4.8	10.9	4.5	18.0	4.3
TOR—Level of Comprehension	50	23.0	7.9	24.8	8.0	35.1	6.1
TOGA— Computation	26	10.4	4.8	10.4	4.8	14.5 ($N=52$)	5.5
Short Algebra Inventory	40	22.4	8.8	19.3	9.3	30.3	7.5
Word Problem Inventory	30	10.7	5.6	9.3	4.5	16.3	4.6
Formula Translation Examination	14	5.1	4.6	5.2	4.3	9.5	4.4
SAT Verbal	800	—	—	327 ($N=26$)	96	482 ($N=62$)	71
SAT Math	800	—	—	435 ($N=26$)	128	597 ($N=62$)	73

NOTE: From Mestre (1981, p. 1260). Reprinted by permission of *Educational and Psychological Measurement*.

*The GPAs of the total student population and the engineering student population are 2.63 and 2.59, respectively.

and the Test of General Ability–Computation. Given the large differences between the Anglo and Hispanic groups in academic preparation, it is not surprising to find a statistically significant difference (.05 level) in college performance between these two groups, as measured by GPA.

There is also an interesting pattern from the correlation coefficients of table 6.2. First, the GPA of the Hispanic group is more strongly correlated with the three language-proficiency measures of the Test of Reading than is the GPA of the Anglo group. Not surprisingly, this pattern persists for mathematical measures requiring substantial amounts of linguistic proficiency, such as the Word Problem Inventory and Formula Translation Examination. However, it is surprising to find the strong and persistent correlations between the three Test of Reading language measures and the mathematical tests requiring almost no linguistic proficiency, such as the Test of General Ability–Computation and the Short Algebra Inventory. Although the larger variances among these measures for the Hispanic group shown on table 6.1 necessarily imply larger correlation coefficients for this group, trying to correct for this effect results in the Hispanic group maintaining much stronger correlation coefficients between the Test of General Ability–Computation and the Short Algebra Inventory, and the three language-proficiency measures of the Test of Reading (see, for example, Hopkins & Glass, 1978, p. 141, eqn. 8.1, for a way to correct for large differences in variance between samples when computing correlation coefficients).

Mathematical Decoding

The results presented in the last section provide a general picture of the academic preparedness of Hispanic students—general in that nothing is known about the specific kinds of difficulties that the students are having. In this section, I will explore the problem-solving process in more detail. In particular, the translation process from textual to symbolic representations will be explored. Only by investigating some of the errors committed by the students in the translation process will we be able to sort out those errors that stem from difficulties with language from those that stem from difficulties with mathematics.

I will begin by discussing the performance on several problems from the Formula Translation Examination. The "students and professors" problem from this test (see Appendix) is one that has attracted much attention in recent mathematics educational research. The reason for this attention is that, even though it is a relatively simple problem, Anglo engineering students have inordinate difficulties solving it. For example, Clement, Lochhead, and Monk (1981) have shown that in the "students

(Continued on page 166)

Table 6.2: Pearson Correlation Coefficients Among Variables

Variables	1	2	3	4	5	6	7	8	9	10
1. GPA	1									
2. TOR—Vocabulary	48***	1								
	48***									
	26*									
3. TOR—Speed of Comprehension	23*	70***								
	30*	60***	1							
	14	46***								
4. TOR-Level of Comprehension	40***	71***	71***							
	36**	64***	74***	1						
	13	53***	47***							
5. TOGA—Computation[a]	40***	25*	18	37**						
	40***	37**	48***	36**	1					
	-04	-01	18	06						
6. Short Algebra Inventory	43***	41***	30**	45***	69***					
	32**	40***	46***	33**	81***	1				
	31**	05	13	17	47***					

	C1	C2	C3	C4	C5	C6	C7	C8	C9	C10
7. Word Problem Inventory	44***	37**	29*	47***	57***	54***	1			
	49***	53***	36**	41***	56***	63***	1			
	36***	24*	27*	17	42***	60***				
8. Formula Translation Examination	32**	36**	12	29*	45***	48***	44***	1		
	37**	44***	33**	31**	46***	46***	53***	1		
	38***	27*	16	12	17	27*	26*			
9. SAT—Verbal[b]	—	—	—	—	—	—	—	—		
	12	52**	64***	63***	55**	49**	47**	54**	1	
	35**	64***	59***	61***	24	23*	27*	26*		
10. SAT—Math[b]	—	—	—	—	—	—	—	—	—	
	42*	55**	54**	51**	74***	85***	87***	74***	59***	1
	53***	45***	34**	29*	45***	63***	65***	41***	48***	

NOTE 1: From Mestre (1981, p. 1261). Reprinted by permission of *Educational and Psychological Measurement*.
NOTE 2: The first, second, and third of the entries correspond to bilinguals taking Spanish version of tests, bilinguals participating in English version of tests, and monolinguals, respectively. Decimal points have been omitted; *p. <.05, **p<.01, ***p<.001 level.

[a] $N = 52$ for monolinguals.
[b] $N = 62$ for monolinguals and $N = 26$ for bilinguals.

and professors" problem, 37 percent out of a sample of 150 Anglo freshman engineering majors answered the problem incorrectly. A full two-thirds out of all incorrect answers consisted of students writing the answer 6S = P, where the variables appear in the reverse order for the correct answer, 6P = S. In problems containing a slightly more complicated relationship between the variables (e.g., ". . . for every seven students there are two professors . . ."), the percentage of students committing the variable-reversal error increased dramatically.

Clement et al. (1981) were able to show that few, if any, of the variable-reversal errors stemmed from a misreading of the problem. In clinical interviews with over twenty students, none indicated that they believed there were more professors than students in the "students and professors" problem. The errors appeared to stem from misconceptions concerning the structure and interpretation of algebraic statements and from the process by which one translates from natural language to symbolic language. The actual mechanism used by most students who committed the variable-reversal error consists of using a sequential left-to-right translation of the problem statement. Hence the phrase "six times as many students" becomes 6S, and by equating this to P, students believe that they have set up the appropriate relationship. From looking at the equation 6S = P, it is clear why it is very tempting to misinterpret its meaning as "six times as many students as professors," rather than its correct mathematical meaning: Multiplying the number of students, S, by 6 gives the number of professors, P—an obvious contradiction from what is stated in the problem. In other words, students are using the *variables* S and P, which are supposed to represent the *numbers* of students and professors, as *labels* for "students" and "professors."

In the fourteen-question Formula Translation Examination that we administered to a group of forty-three Hispanic engineering students, we found results similar to those obtained by Clement et al. However, the Hispanics committed the variable-reversal error almost twice as frequently as a group of fifty-two Anglo engineering students tested. More importantly, the Hispanic group exhibited certain types of errors that were not committed by the Anglo group. Table 6.3, taken from Mestre, Gerace, and Lochhead (1982), details the performance of these two groups of students on the Formula Translation Examination and its Spanish counterpart. The three entries on table 6.3 correspond to Hispanics on the Spanish and English versions of this test, and Anglos, respectively. Each entry denotes the total number of students from that group in the respective categories shown and is followed in parentheses by the percentage that this number constitutes of the total number of students in the group. The row labeled "χ^2" is the result of a 2 × 2 chi-

Table 6.3: Performance on Formula Translation Tests

| | Problem Number | | | | | | | | | | | | | |
	1	2	3	4	5	6	7	8	9	10	11	12	13	14
Correct	18(41.9)	16(37.2)	16(37.2)	24(55.8)	8(18.6)	10(23.3)	10(23.3)	15(34.9)	14(32.6)	18(41.9)	31(72.1)	8(18.6)	10(23.3)	7(16.3)
	14(32.6)	19(44.2)	17(39.5)	22(51.2)	8(18.6)	17(39.5)	6(14.0)	19(44.2)	21(48.8)	19(44.2)	29(67.4)	5(11.6)	14(32.6)	8(18.6)
	35(67.3)	39(75.0)	33(63.5)	44(84.6)	23(44.2)	45(86.5)	33(63.5)	40(76.9)	38(73.1)	35(67.3)	44(84.6)	22(42.3)	37(71.2)	30(57.7)
Variable-reversal error	20(46.5)	23(53.5)	24(55.8)	11(25.6)	26(60.5)	26(60.5)	23(53.5)	23(53.5)	19(44.2)	20(46.5)	6(14.0)	26(60.5)	8(18.6)	25(58.1)
	23(53.5)	20(46.5)	19(44.2)	8(18.6)	28(65.1)	19(44.2)	24(55.8)	19(44.2)	17(39.5)	17(39.5)	5(11.6)	28(65.1)	5(11.6)	18(41.9)
	16(30.8)	13(25.0)	19(36.5)	4(7.7)	27(51.9)	3(5.8)	18(34.6)	11(21.2)	13(25.0)	17(32.7)[1]	6(11.5)	28(53.9)	4(7.7)	19(36.5)
Other error	5(11.6)	4(9.3)	3(7.0)	6(14.0)	7(16.3)	0(0)	9(20.9)	4(9.3)	8(18.6)	4(9.3)	4(9.3)	5(11.6)	21(48.8)	9(20.9)
	6(14.0)	4(9.3)	7(16.3)	11(25.6)	5(11.6)	1(44.2)	12(28.0)	5(11.6)	4(9.3)	4(9.3)	3(7.0)	3(7.0)	15(34.9)	5(11.6)
	1(1.9)	0(0)	0(0)	3(5.8)	2(3.9)	3(5.8)	1(1.9)	1(1.9)	1(1.9)	0(0)	1(1.9)	0(0)	10(19.2)	2(3.9)
No answer	0(0)	0(0)	0(0)	2(4.7)	2(4.7)	0(0)	1(2.3)	1(2.3)	2(4.7)	1(2.3)	2(4.7)	4(9.3)	4(9.3)	2(4.7)
	0(0)	0(0)	0(0)	2(4.7)	2(4.7)	1(2.3)	1(2.3)	0(0)	1(2.3)	3(7.0)	6(14.0)	7(16.3)	9(21.0)	12(27.9)
	0(0)	0(0)	0(0)	1(1.9)	0(0)	0(0)	0(0)	0(0)	0(0)	0(0)	1(1.9)	2(3.9)	1(1.9)	1(1.9)
χ^2	11.4	9.4	5.4	11.9	6.3	21.9	23.1	10.7	5.3	3.7	.9	8.8	8.4	8.5
p	.001	.005	.025	.001	.025	.001	.001	.005	.025	N.S.	N.S.	.005	.005	.005

NOTE 1: From Mestre, Gerace, & Lochhead (1982). Reprinted by permission of the *Journal of Research in Science Teaching*, © 1982, John Wiley & Sons, Inc.

NOTE 2: The three entries correspond to bilinguals in Spanish, bilinguals in English, and monolinguals in English, respectively. The number of students is followed in parentheses by the percentage this number constitutes of the total.

square analysis between the Hispanic group and the Anglo group in the Formula Translation Examination, taking into account the number correct versus the total number wrong in all categories. The significance level of the chi-squares is given as "p" in table 6.3.

To investigate the non-variable-reversal errors in more detail, we interviewed nine Hispanics and eleven Anglos, all randomly selected from the two groups. These students were asked to "think aloud" while solving the "students and professors" problem, as well as other problems from the Formula Translation Examination. There were five types of errors uncovered during the interview sessions that were different from the variable-reversal error. These errors were committed only by the Hispanics interviewed, and several appear to be interpretational errors deriving from difficulties in understanding the problem statement. For example, in the "students and professors" problem, some Hispanics wrote 6S = 6P. These students explained that the phrase "as many students as professors" implies that there is an equal number of each, that is, S = P. The "six times" in front of the statement was interpreted to mean that each side of S = P should be multiplied by 6. A full description of these nonstandard errors can be found in Mestre et al. (1982).

Other detailed findings of the students' performance on some of the problems from the Word Problem Inventory suggest that the difficulties experienced by many of the students are linguistic and not mathematical in nature. For example, in the "carpenter" problem (see Appendix), the error rate for Hispanics and Anglos was similar, namely, 57 percent and 42 percent, respectively. One type of error was made almost exclusively by the Hispanic group and accounted for 35 percent of all errors. It consisted of interpreting the first sentence in the problem, "a carpenter bought an equal number of nails and screws for $5.70," to mean that an equal amount of money was spent by the carpenter on nails and screws out of the total $5.70 spent. This interpretation resulted in the carpenter purchasing 95 screws and 147.5 nails. In the equivalent Spanish problem about "lápices y plumas" (i.e., "pencils and pens"), there was an error rate of 31 percent for the Hispanic group. Why the error rate in Spanish was slightly more than half of what it was in English is not clear—it may be due to the fact that the Spanish version is somewhat easier to work out by trial and error (a procedure used by some students); or perhaps the students found the Spanish version easier to understand. In either case, the type of error equivalent to the misinterpretation in the English version, in this case consisting of interpreting the problem to mean that an equal amount of money was spent on pens and pencils out of the total $.84 spent, accounted for 47 percent of all errors.

It therefore appears from the evidence at hand that subtleties in language construction, jargon, and so on increase the likelihood of problems being misinterpreted by Hispanic bilinguals. These misinterpretations are not caused by an unfamiliarity with vocabulary, per se. What is clear is that these students often translate a problem into mathematical terminology incorrectly, yet the interpretation is totally consistent with their own understanding of what the problem is asking. The result is a solution that is algebraically correct but suffers from an inappropriate translation from natural language to mathematical language.

Performance as a Function of Verbosity

Although we have demonstrated instances where the performance of Hispanics on word problems is adversely affected by inappropriate interpretations of phrases in the problem statement, the search for particular phrases or constructions that are apt to cause semantic difficulties is a tedious process. One can never predict with assurance whether a phrase will be prone to misinterpretation by students.

In an attempt to measure the effect of language comprehension within a mathematical problem-solving context, another pair of word-problem tests was constructed. Each test contained ten problems and required only a knowledge of elementary algebra, since the intent was to assess the likelihood of language-related difficulties, not to measure mathematical prowess. In the Terse Test, the problems were asked using simple, terse language. In the Verbose Test, the problems were embellished with technical jargon. Every problem in the Terse exam had a verbose counterpart in the Verbose exam—that is, the pair of problems had exactly the same mathematical content. A sample pair of equivalent problems from the Terse and Verbose exams is shown in the Appendix.

Both exams were given to sixty Hispanic science and engineering majors and to a corresponding group of seventy-three Anglos. The results are contained in table 6.4. As table 6.4 indicates, Spanish versions of the Terse and Verbose Tests were administered to the Hispanic group. The differences in performance between the Terse and Verbose scores were statistically significant in all three cases. It appears that the Hispanic group's performance on the Spanish versions was worse than their performance in the English versions; the difference mean was also larger in Spanish than in English for the Hispanic group, indicating more difficulties in Spanish.

I hasten to point out that reliability measures for these tests show that they are better instruments for the Hispanic group than for the Anglo group. The Cronbach alpha coefficients for the Terse exam for Anglos, and for Hispanics in English and in Spanish, are .34, .72, and

Table 6.4: Effect of Verbosity on Problem-Solving Performance

| | Hispanic N = 60 | | | | Anglo N = 73 | |
| | Spanish | | English | | English | |
	Mean	S.D.	Mean	S.D.	Mean	S.D.
Terse	6.87	2.01	7.82	1.99	9.26	.94
Verbose	4.40	2.39	6.45	2.51	8.56	1.30
D = Terse- Verbose	2.47*	1.72	1.37*	1.44	.70*	1.28

*$p < .01$

.68, respectively; for the Verbose exam, the corresponding alpha coefficients are .34, .75, and .74. The low reliability coefficients for the Anglo group were caused by a disproportionate distribution of the variance among the test items. There was little variance among most items for this group, and most of the overall variance can be attributed to two items in the Terse exam and to three items in the Verbose exam. I therefore believe that the difference-mean between the Terse and Verbose Tests for the Anglo group is not so much a measure of the direct effect of language comprehension upon performance as it is a measure of the likelihood of making silly errors due to the indirect effect of language comprehension. That is, because of the larger processing load placed on short-term memory caused by the increased amounts of language processing necessary in working out the Verbose Test, there is a greater chance of a "slip" resulting in a silly error.

On the other hand, I interpret the high reliability on both Spanish and English versions of the Terse and Verbose Tests for Hispanics to mean something else. The high alpha coefficients on the Terse Test mean that the item variances were not disproportionately distributed among just a few items but were somewhat uniformly distributed; these items were of "adequate" mathematical difficulty for the Hispanic group. The fact that the mathematical level of the Terse Test was not unchallenging for the Hispanic group, in combination with the large difference means between the Terse and Verbose exams, indicates that the difference means for this group are a measure of an effect apart from, and also in addition to, the likelihood of making a silly error. It is my contention that this additional effect is due to the direct interference of language in solving the verbose problems. That is, the combined load placed on short-term memory by both mathematical and linguistic demands in the verbose problems results in a larger gap between the performance in the terse and verbose problems for this group.

Effect of Double Negatives
and Biasing on Logic Problems

My discussions of how language interacts with problem solving have thus far been restricted to one content area—mathematics. Another content area where language comprehension plays an important role is logical reasoning. I do not believe that it would take much argument to convince the reader that ability to reason logically is a skill that can be usefully transferred to many problem-solving settings; whether it is writing a polemic essay or devising a strategy for attacking an intricate mathematical problem, in order to succeed in the task, the arguments or strategies adduced must be governed by proper logic.

A brief review of some of the extant literature on syllogistic reasoning reveals that subjects often use logical rules that are not valid. For example, in categorical syllogisms (i.e., those that begin "all A's . . .," "no A's . . .," or "some A's . . .") subjects appear to prefer a conclusion that has the same form as the premises. For example, subjects are more likely to accept as valid the syllogism on the left than the syllogism on the right:

Some A's are B's.	Some A's are B's.
<u>Some B's are C's.</u>	<u>Some B's are C's.</u>
Some A's are C's.	All A's are C's.

This led Woodworth and Sells (1935) to propose the "atmosphere hypothesis," which states that quantifiers such as *some* and *all* used in syllogisms create an atmosphere in which subjects are apt to accept as valid conclusions with the same quantifiers.

Other research by Johnson-Laird and Steedman (1978) has revealed that subjects are more likely to accept an invalid conclusion linking A to C if they can form a continuous thread linking A to B and B to C. Thus, subjects are more likely to accept as valid the syllogism on the left-hand side above than the following syllogism:

Some B's are A's
<u>Some C's are B's</u>
Some A's are C's.

Subjects have also been known to read more into a premise than is logically allowed (Henle, 1962; Chapman & Chapman, 1959). For example, "all A's are B's" is often interpreted to mean "A is the same as B," while "some A's are B's" is interpreted to mean "some A's are B's but not all A's are B's and further, not all B's are A's." Another logical pitfall for subjects concerns the issue of "pragmatic deduction." In pragmatic deduction subjects trade sound, logical approaches for pragmatic truisms that are in accord with the situation in the real world (Chapman and Chapman, 1959; Henle, 1962; Reder, 1976).

One recent study by Durán (1981) investigated the logical-reasoning skills of Puerto Rican bilingual college students. Several logical-reasoning instruments, some dealing with syllogisms, were administered to the students in both English and Spanish. Standardized measures were also administered to evaluate the students' language proficiency in both English and Spanish. The results of this study showed that performance on logical-reasoning tests in each language can be significantly predicted by language-proficiency measures in the language of the tests. Duran also found that the performance pattern was similar across languages for English-Spanish pairs of equivalent tests.

In addition, logical-reasoning research on semantics indicates that negative sentences are harder to comprehend than affirmative sentences. Whether measured by reaction time (Just & Carpenter, 1971; Carpenter & Just, 1975; Trabasso, Rollins, & Shaughnessey, 1971), or by ability to recall (Miller, 1962; Mehler, 1963; Clark & Card, 1969), or by ability to verify (Wason, 1959, 1961; Anderson & Reder, 1974), there is abundant evidence that negative sentences give subjects more difficulties. Further, increasing the number of negations appears to create successive decrements in comprehension (Sherman, 1976; Johnson-Laird, 1970; Legrenzi, 1970).

The role of double negatives in the Spanish language takes on particular significance. In Spanish, certain constructions containing double negatives retain the negative meaning—something that is not found in (grammatically correct) English. Thus, the grammatically correct translation of the statement "I do not want any money" into Spanish is "yo no quiero ningún dinero," which, when literally translated back into English, becomes "I do not want no money." A question that immediately comes to mind is whether Hispanics are more likely to misinterpret doubly negated statements when solving problems because of this logical inequivalance between the two languages. If so, this would have adverse ramifications for Hispanic students, since the use of double negatives in the English language is not infrequent.

In view of the research findings above, and of the inequivalence between the English and Spanish languages concerning the meaning of certain double-negative constructions, a study of the logical-reasoning skills with Hispanic technical students appeared to hold promise for extracting valuable insights, both into the thought processes used by the students and into the possible existence of language-interference effects. To probe some of these questions, we constructed two multiple-choice Logic Tests containing nine problems each, one in English and the other in Spanish. These tests were administered to sixty Hispanics and seventy-four Anglos. Sample problems from the English Logic Test are given in the Appendix.

The general form of six of the problems in this test was

If it is [false, not true] that [all, not all, some] A are [not] B, then we can conclude that

    a. Some A are [a form of] B
    b. All A are [a form of] B
    c. All A are [a form of] B
    d. All A are [a form of] B

where A is a noun class (e.g., college graduates, basketball players) and B is a descriptive category (e.g., people who earn less than $10,000 a year, people who are less than six feet tall). Two of these problems contained only one negation, while the remaining four problems contained two negations. In addition, the four problems containing two negations were constructed as two pairs of structurally equivalent problems; however, there was one "biased" problem in each of the two pairs, since the correct answer was arranged to be counterintuitive to the situation that exists in the "real world" (e.g., one biased answer was "all basketball players are less than six feet tall"). The other problem in the pair was unbiased in that it had a "neutral" answer (e.g., the answer "all fig trees grow more than six inches a year"). These four problems were designed to assess the students' proclivity to resort to "pragmatic deduction" as a means of obtaining an answer.

Of the remaining three problems in the Logic Test, two involved the interpretation of a Venn diagram. The last problem asked the students to determine whether the statement "I do not want no money" meant that money was or was not wanted. Although it could be argued that the statement is of questionable grammatical construction, it does carry the same meaning as "I do want money," albeit in a less forceful fashion. This problem should clearly illustrate whether Hispanics are likely to interpret statements containing double negations differently than Anglos.

The means, standard deviations, and reliability coefficients for the Logic Tests are shown in table 6.5a. The Cronbach alpha was computed using only problems 1 through 8 of the tests, since these were all problems with four multiple-choice answers; problem 9, the "money" question, contained only two multiple-choice answers and was not included in the reliability analysis. Shown in table 6.5b is a breakdown of the English version of the Logic exams by problem, showing the percentage of each group responding correctly. The entries in the column labeled Chi^2 are

Table 6.5a: Results of Logic Tests

| | Hispanic N = 60 | | Anglos N = 74 |
	Spanish	English	English
Mean	3.85	4.10	5.59
Standard deviation	1.68	2.18	1.73
Cronbach α	.47	.59	.54

NOTE: Maximum score on each test is 9.

Table 6.5b: Detailed Breakdown of Problems, English Version, by Percentage of Subjects With Correct Responses

Problem Number	Problem Type	Hispanics	Anglos	Chi²
1	One negation	55.0	79.7	9.4*
2	One negation	60.0	60.8	0.
3	Two negations biased (paired w/6)	13.3	17.6	.4
4	Venn diagram	53.3	86.5	17.9*
5	Two negations biased (paired w/ 8)	13.3	27.0	3.8
6	Two negations unbiased (paired w/ 3)	33.3	48.6	3.2
7	Venn diagram	78.3	91.9	5.0*
8	Two negations unbiased (paired w/ 5)	28.3	54.0	9.6*
9	Two negations	60.0	91.9	19.4*

*Significant beyond the .05 level

the result of a 2×2 chi-square analysis between the Hispanics and the Anglos, taking into account the number correct versus the number wrong for each problem.

Table 6.5b shows significant differences in performance between the Anglo and Hispanic groups in problems 1, 4, 7, 8, and 9; the differences in problems 5 and 6 approach significance. We found it surprising that significant differences between Anglos and Hispanics emerged in only two out of the five problems containing two negations, namely, problems 8 and 9. On the surface, these results appear to indicate that there are no persistent observable differences in the way Anglos and Hispanics interpret double negations. I find an alternate explanation more credible. It is evident from table 6.5b that on the other three problems containing two negations, namely, problems 3, 5, and 6, both Hispanics and Anglos performed extremely poorly—in fact, the performance on biased problems 3 and 5 for both Hispanics and Anglos was at, or below, the level one would expect by randomly guessing the answer. It appears that problems 3, 5, 6, and 8 were too difficult for differences in performance between the two groups due to double negations to be observed.

Returning to problem 9 concerning the interpretation of "I do not want no money," the significant differences in performance between the Anglo and Hispanic groups may be due to the logical inequivalence in the meaning of double negations between English and Spanish. In this problem, the percentage of the Hispanic students who interpreted the double negation as an overall negation was 40 percent, compared to only 8 percent for the Anglo group. The results in this problem illustrate that Hispanics may interpret double negations in English as they would have in Spanish. Another possible explanation is that Hispanics are using nonstandard English interpretations of double negations more often than Anglos.

There is evidence that problem bias had a pronounced adverse effect on performance. Although equivalent problems 3 and 6, and 5 and 8 proved to be extremely difficult for all the students, performance on these problems indicates that Hispanics and Anglos alike resorted to "pragmatic deduction" on biased problems 3 and 5. Table 6.6 shows the effect of bias in the English version of the logic exam in more detail. As is evident from table 6.6, the differences in performance between the biased problems and the unbiased problems were statistically significant in the obvious direction for both groups. It thus appears that students are not likely to select answers that conflict with real-world truth values.

There is also evidence in support of the "atmosphere hypothesis," as manifested by the students' proclivity to choose answers containing the quantifier *some* when the problem statement contained the quantifier *some* or *not all*. A detailed breakdown of the students' responses is given

Table 6.6: Effect of "Pragmatic Deduction" on Questions 3, 5, 6, and 8 of English Logic Test (Means and Standard Deviations)

	Biased Questions #3 & #5 Combined	*Unbiased Questions* #6 & #8 Combined	*Difference—Mean* (#6,#8)–(#3,#5)	*t = Statistic* *Difference–Mean*
Hispanic ($N=60$)	.27 (.48)	.58 (.77)	.32 (.68)	3.6*
Anglo ($N=74$)	.46 (.69)	1.03 (.76)	.57 (.81)	6.0*

*$p<.001$

in table 6.7 for problems 5 and 8 (which begin "if it is not true that some . . .") and problems 3 and 6 (which begin "if it is false that not all . . ."). This time I have also included the Hispanic group's performance in the corresponding Spanish problems. Taking into consideration only the three incorrect choices for these four problems, we can see that students who chose an erroneous answer preferred the choice that starts "some . . ." by a large margin. The chi-square statistic in table 6.7 is a significance test among the three wrong answers for each problem; the null hypothesis was taken to be that all three wrong answers had an equally likely probability of occurrence. As we can see, the resulting chi-squares favor the rejection of the null hypothesis in favor of the atmosphere hypothesis. It thus appears that a substantial percentage of the

Table 6.7: Test of "Atmosphere Hyphothesis" on Questions 3, 5, 6, and 8 of English and Spanish Logic Tests

	Question Number			
	3	5	6	8
Hispanics in Spanish				
Correct response	(c)6	(a)7	(c)13	(c)9
Response with "some . . ."	(a)37	(b)31	(a)39	(b)37
Wrong "all . . ." response	(b)5	(c)5	(b)5	(a)4
Wrong "all . . ." response	(d)12	(d)15	(d)3	(d)10
Chi² on wrong answers	31.4*	20.2*	52.2*	36.4*
(Degrees of freedom = 2)				
Hispanics in English				
Correct response	(c)8	(d)8	(d)20	(c)16
Response with "some . . ."	(a)35	(b)37	(a)29	(a)32
Wrong "all . . ." response	(b)8	(a)5	(b)7	(b)8
Wrong "all . . ." response	(d)9	(c)10	(c)4	(d)4
Chi² on wrong answers	27.0*	34.2*	28.0*	31.3*
(Degrees of freedom = 2)				
Anglos in English				
Correct response	(c)13	(d)20	(d)36	(c)40
Response with "some . . ."	(a)42	(b)33	(a)28	(a)26
Wrong "all . . ." response	(b)9	(a)12	(b)5	(b)3
Wrong "all . . ." response	(d)10	(c)9	(c)5	(d)5
Chi² on wrong answers	34.7*	19.0*	27.8*	28.6*
(Degrees of freedom = 2)				

NOTE: The chi² test assumes a null hypothesis that has the wrong answers distributed equally among the three incorrect responses.
*$p < .001$

students we tested preferred to have the quantifier in the problem statement match the quantifier in the answer they select.

In order to investigate the cognitive processes employed by the students in solving these types of logic problems, we conducted clinical interviews with a total of seventeen students, eight from the Hispanic group and nine from the Anglo group. These interviews revealed that many students employed "rules" in a mechanical fashion to solve these problems, rather than attempting to rephrase and understand the meaning of each problem in order to select the most suitable answer. Only one procedure employed by students consistently yielded the correct answer. This procedure can be summarized as follows:

> Find the innermost negation. Then remove this negation by paraphrasing from that point to the end of the statement. Repeat this procedure until all negations are removed and the result is an affirmatively phrased statement.

This procedure is best illustrated with an example. In problem 3 concerning the earning potential of college graduates (see Appendix), it would work as follows:

> "Not all college graduates earn less than $10,000 per year" means there must be some that earn more than, or exactly, $10,000 per year. But if this is false, then all college graduates must earn less than $10,000 per year.

Only two of the students interviewed, both from the Anglo group, consistently applied this procedure successfully.

Far more frequently used than the above procedure were rules that were efficacious in obtaining the correct answer in some of the problems but resulted in specious logic when applied blindly to all problems. Five rules were clearly identified that students used singly or in "packages" of two or more at a time. These rules consisted of the following: (1) The phrase *not all* can always be replaced with the word *some*. (2) Problems beginning with *not all* or *some* must have answers beginning with the quantifier *some*; this rule is just the "atmosphere hypothesis." (3) In problems where the world is dichotomized into two complementary and exhaustive categories, stating that some of a particular group is in one of the categories implies that there must be some in the complementary category.[1] (4) Negations can always be canceled in pairs. (5) When all else fails, use either intuition or experience in finding a suitable answer; this rule is equivalent to "pragmatic deduction."

The following two examples illustrate how students applied some of the rules above to problem 3. One popular approach was to apply rules 1 and 2, thereby arriving at the (erroneous) answer "some college gradu-ates earn more than $10,000 a year." A second, more convoluted ap-proach by which some students arrived at this same answer starts with an application of rule 1 with the result "it is false that some college gradu-ates earn less than $10,000 a year." This is immediately followed by a liberal application of rule 4; that is, rule 4 allows "it is false" to convert "less than" to "more than," making the final answer "some college gradu-ates earn more than $10,000 a year."

It should be pointed out that neither group differed appreciably in which of the five rules were used or in how they were applied. Although the two groups used these rules with approximately the same frequency, the percentage of correct responses exhibited during the interviews re-flected the percentage of correct answers for each group as a whole, as shown in table 6.5.

Effect of Problem-Solving Speed
Upon Performance

One often neglected skill related to successful problem solving that has not been mentioned is problem-solving speed. In our roles as instructors we often neglect to address speed because we are much more interested in students' ability to solve problems correctly, and not so much in their ability to do so in record speed. However, a complaint voiced by many of the Hispanics in our studies is that they often do not have adequate time to finish all of the problems given in the fifty minutes of the typical "hour exam," especially when they spend considerable time attempting to un-derstand what is being asked.

I would like to illustrate the effect of speed in mathematical problem solving. Before doing so, I will start by quantifying how the Hispanics and Anglos in our studies differed in reading-comprehension speed. In the Speed of Comprehension section of the Test of Reading, students are required to read a sentence from which a word has been deleted and then select from among five choices that word which best fits within the context of the sentence. The section is designed to measure the speed and accuracy with which a student can read and understand a sentence. The disparity in performance between the Hispanic and Anglo groups in this section as shown on table 6.1 is largely due to the ability of the Anglo group to answer significantly more problems. In the six minutes allowed for this section, the average number of problems attempted per student was 20.5 for the Anglo group and 15.3 for the Hispanic group.

The effect of problem-solving speed in a mathematics test such as the Word Problem Inventory is shown in figure 6.1. The bar graph area

Figure 6.1: Breakdown of Performance in the Word Problem Inventory

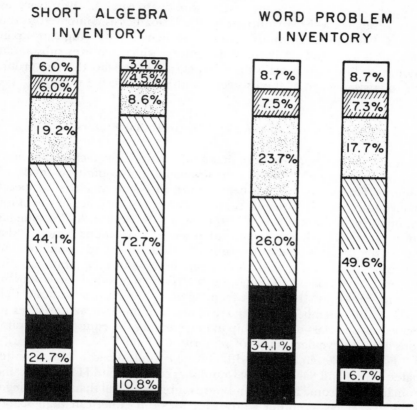

SHORT ALGEBRA INVENTORY

	HISPANIC	NON-MINORITY
Miscellaneous	6.0%	3.4%
Arithmetic Errors	6.0%	4.5%
Problems Set Up Incorrectly	19.2%	8.6%
Correct Responses	44.1%	72.7%
Questions Not Reached	24.7%	10.8%

WORD PROBLEM INVENTORY

	HISPANIC	NON-MINORITY
Miscellaneous	8.7%	8.7%
Arithmetic Errors	7.5%	7.3%
Problems Set Up Incorrectly	23.7%	17.7%
Correct Responses	26.0%	49.6%
Questions Not Reached	34.1%	16.7%

KEY

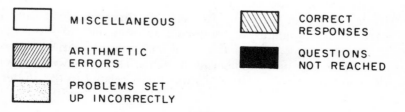

- MISCELLANEOUS
- ARITHMETIC ERRORS
- PROBLEMS SET UP INCORRECTLY
- CORRECT RESPONSES
- QUESTIONS NOT REACHED

179

is representative of the total number of problems for the exam. From the "questions not reached" category, it is clear that time restrictions adversely affected Hispanics much more than Anglos. Over twice as many problems were left untried by the Hispanics as compared to the Anglos. Thus the significantly better performance of the Anglo group in a test such as the Word Problem Inventory, which requires substantial amounts of linguistic processing, is largely due to the fact that this group gets to answer more of the problems within the allotted time.

Academic, Socioeconomic, and Motivational Factors

Thus far, no mention has been made of nonacademic factors that have been shown to influence the achievement and aspiration levels of students. For example, it has been known for some time that socioeconomic status (SES) is positively correlated with academic achievement for nonminority students (Sewell, 1971; Sewell & Hauser, 1975). Similar studies that have shown significant positive correlations between SES and academic achievement for minority students are too numerous to cite. Since minority groups dominate the low income brackets, low academic achievement has often been attributed to ethnic-group membership. However, the results from some recent studies indicate that ethnic-group membership, per se, is not as important as measures of socioeconomic-class membership in determining the educational aspirations and achievement levels of minority students.

For example, in a study with college-bound Mexican American females, Buriel and Sáenz (1980) found that college-bound Chicanas came from higher-income families and were more bicultural than non-college-bound Chicanas. Another study with Mexican American high school students by Bender and Ruiz (1974) showed that class membership was more significant than race in determining levels of achievement and aspirations. In yet another study with Puerto Rican, black, and Anglo adolescents, Dillard and Perrin (1980) found that after controlling for ethnic-group membership and sex, factors associated with socioeconomic background are very influential as predictors of career aspirations, career expectations, and maturity.

In view of the confounding effects that factors such as SES can have on academic achievement, we conducted an evaluation of several academic, socioeconomic, and motivational background characteristics of our Hispanic science and engineering students. To do this, we designed a questionnaire that probed three distinct areas related to the students' background:

1. *Academic Preparation.* This section of the questionnaire consisted of eight questions aimed at clarifying the students' high school preparation in science and mathematics.
2. *Motivational Factors.* The six questions in this section were designed to isolate factors that had been influential in motivating the student to pursue a technical career. Some of the factors included were high school counseling, role models, and parental influence.
3. *Socioeconomic Factors.* This section consisted of six questions pertaining to areas such as family income, the number and types of "technical toys" the student owned while growing up, and student employment experience.

The questionnaire format was in both open-coded and checklist style. Whenever possible, student responses were placed into two mutually exclusive categories (e.g., family income levels less than $20,000 per year, and more than $20,000 per year). When a question did not lend itself to two mutually exclusive categories, we devised the smallest number of categories necessary to exhaust all types of responses made by the students. The questionnaire was administered to forty-nine Hispanics and fifty-three Anglos, all of whom had participated in the studies discussed above. The statistical analysis consisted of cross-tabulating the answers by group and evaluating the resulting chi-squares for significance at or beyond the .05 level. More details on this study can be found in Mestre and Robinson (1983).

Most of the similarities between the groups appeared in the Academic Preparation and Motivational Factors sections of the questionnaire. For example, responses to the questions under Academic Preparation revealed that there were no significant differences between the two groups in high school grade-point average. Under Motivational Factors, approximately the same number from each group indicated that they had decided to enter a technical field between the ages of fourteen and eighteen and that they knew friends or relatives employed in technical fields. The number of students in each group who claimed to have discussed career choices with their parents was also comparable. Only two similarities in Socioeconomic Factors between the two groups emerged—the majority of the students from both groups indicated that their mothers held no occupation outside the home. Similarly, those mothers from both groups who held employment outside the home held nontechnical jobs.

The statistically significant differences between the two groups are shown in table 6.8. Most differences emerged under the Socioeconomic

Table 6.8:   Differences Between the Groups in the Three Categories Surveyed

					N	
Question Topic	*Categories*	χ^2	*df*	*p*	*Hispanic*	*Anglo*
Academic Preparation						
Numbers of science courses completed in high school	a. ≤3 b. >3	7.58	1	.05	49	53
Motivational Factors						
Received career counseling in high school	a. Yes b. No	13.48	1	.0005	44	50
Reasons for deciding to pursue technical fields	a. Encouragement and interest b. Interest only c. Other	15.01	2	.0005	48	52
Socioeconomic Factors						
Father's occupation	a. Technical b. Nontechnical	8.35	1	.01	41	49
Family yearly income	a. ≤$30,000 b. >$30,000	7.80	1	.01	41	49
Number of technical toys owned	a. ≤5 b. >5	5.91	1	.05	45	50
Held part-time employment during high school	a. Yes b. No	9.08	1	.005	47	51

NOTE: From Mestre & Robinson (1983, table 1). Reprinted by permission of *Vocational Guidance Quarterly*.

Factors category. In areas such as family income, number of technical toys owned while growing up, and part-time employment prior to entering college, the Anglo group had a decided advantage. In view of the dismal representation of Hispanics in professional technical fields to which I alluded earlier, it is not surprising that many more of the Anglo fathers than the Hispanic fathers held occupations in technical fields.

One other comparison was performed. The Hispanic group was divided into a high-income group (those from families with incomes greater than $20,000 per year) and a low-income group (those from families with incomes less than $20,000 per year). Comparisons were then made, using simple *t*-tests, between the performance of these two Hispanic subgroups on the Short Algebra Inventory, Word Problem Inventory, Formula Translation Examination, Test of General Ability–Computation, and the Test of Reading. The two subgroups' college performances, as measured by grade-point average, were also compared. The *t*-tests resulted in statistically significant differences in the obvious direction between low- and high-income Hispanics in the Word Problem Inventory, Formula Translation Examination, Test of Reading– Vocabulary, and grade-point average. There were not enough low-income Anglos in our sample to conduct a similar comparison for this group.

As in numerous other studies, our findings suggest that socioeconomic factors are influential in the academic achievement of the Hispanic technical college students that participated in our studies. It is interesting to note that the only statistically significant difference between the Hispanic and Anglo groups under Academic Preparation was in the number of science courses taken while in high school; the Hispanic group averaged 3.61 science courses, while the Anglo group averaged 4.06 science courses. This difference in itself cannot be responsible for the mathematical underpreparedness exhibited by the Hispanic group, except perhaps indirectly, through SES or other variables. That is, the fact that many of the Hispanics in our sample came from low income brackets means that there is a greater likelihood that the education received by these students in their community schools was not on a par with the education received by the middle-class Anglo students. Thus, equivalent high school grade-point averages or equivalent course loads might not imply equivalent academic preparation.

SUMMARY AND DISCUSSION

Before summarizing the findings of the studies reviewed and discussing their implications, I would like to discuss some limitations with the work reviewed. Needless to say, our findings involve a complex interplay of cultural, economic, linguistic, environmental, and educational factors. Although our studies have identified some central issues in the education and background characteristics of Hispanic college students, there is a danger that the findings may be interpreted as encompassing a wider spectrum than is warranted. I therefore caution the reader to take careful note of the following points:

1. Because our samples are small, we can never make any statements that would be as widely applicable as statements deriving from studies conducted with large national samples. However, the kinds of questions that can be studied with large samples are very different from the detailed questions one can investigate with small samples. Although large-sample studies are excellent

in providing gross features, small-sample studies can provide details that are useful in thinking about pedagogical questions.

2. Since there have been so few studies focusing on issues covering Hispanic college students, and even fewer focusing on Hispanic technical college students, there is a need for more research that will help replicate our findings as well as provide us with new information that will aid in forming a well-rounded picture of the current situation.

3. Finally, there is no such thing as the "typical Hispanic." The education issues relevant for first-generation Mexican immigrants are very different from those that are relevant for the Chicanos of the West and Southwest, for the Cubans that emigrated twenty years ago, or for the Puerto Ricans living in New York City. Although the difficulties being faced by the Hispanics that participated in our studies are very probably similar to those being faced by other Hispanic technical college students in other parts of the country, there is no reason to expect a perfect overlap.

In summary, our findings indicate that the Hispanic technical college students that participated in our studies are underprepared in comparison to Anglo technical college students. The areas in which Hispanics displayed underpreparation are algebraic skills, language skills, and problem-solving skills requiring substantial amounts of linguistic processing. We also found large differences in SES between the Hispanics and the Anglos of our studies. Finally, our findings indicate that various errors committed by the Hispanics in solving mathematics and logic problems are the result of semantic difficulties and not necessarily the result of difficulties in the content area.

To appreciate the role of language in the problem-solving process more fully, it would help to consider the five steps one goes through in solving a mathematics problem:

1. Understanding the problem
2. Developing a strategy of attack
3. Translating the problem into the appropriate mathematical terminology
4. Solving the mathematically translated problem
5. Checking the answer

With slight variation, these are the five steps that most would agree take place during problem solving. The steps in which language plays a crucial role are numbers 1 and 3. It is in these two steps that misinterpretations will result in errors before the problem is actually solved. It is our opinion that technical students with language deficiencies, such as the Hispanics of our studies, would benefit from problem-solving courses that stress these two steps. Work in these two areas not only will help the students develop skills that are transferable to almost any problem-solving domain but also will allow the instructor to identify and address errors deriving from semantic difficulties.

The notion that language may have an effect on cognitive processes (not just for bilingual populations) is not new. For example, according to Vygotsky (1962), many facets of intellectual functioning are intimately related to language acquisition. Vygotsky also claims that the internalization of language induces a restructuring of many mental processes. In relation to problem solving, he states that problem-solving strategies become more rational and sophisticated when they can be verbalized.

Another view, that of Whorf (1956), states that the language we speak can set certain limits or constraints on our perception. Perhaps the justification for this view derives more from cultural effects than from linguistic effects; that is, it may well be that cultural experiences are as important as linguistic experiences in forming our perceptions. The difficulty in the Whorfian hypothesis lies in how to distinguish between these two effects.

What is clear is that many Hispanic students are enrolling in technical college programs with language deficiencies that place them at a disadvantage when compared with their Anglo peers. Perhaps some of these linguistic problems inadvertently originate at the primary and secondary levels of schooling. Many transitional bilingual programs are allowed three years to prepare students of limited English proficiency for a level where they can be mainstreamed. At the end of three years, these programs turn out students who, although linguistically competent to function in the mainstream curriculum, are not linguistically proficient at a level where they can favorably compete academically with Anglo students.

A more lamentable situation is that there is no natural mechanism by which these students can improve their language-proficiency level. For example, Anglo children can have their English-language skills reinforced in the home, whereas Hispanic students who speak Spanish at home do not get similar reinforcement. Anglo children may enjoy reading books and magazines, whereas Hispanic children may not be able to maintain interest in reading books and magazines if they do not understand the nuances of the English language, or if their reading speed is slow enough to cause them to be bored by the pace at which they can process the "action" in the text.

It appears that there is a decided need for more research in evaluating supplemental instructional approaches for improving the verbal and quantitative deficiencies of limited-English-proficiency students. I say "supplemental" since this would not require drastic modifications in the traditional instructional formats used in schools. For example, it is conceivable that microcomputers could be extremely effective if used in supplemental instructional programs designed to improve the vocabulary, reading-speed, reading-comprehension, mathematical, and problem-solving skills of these students. Students with language or mathematical deficiencies could be asked to spend their "study periods" working with microcomputers on modules covering language skills or mathematical skills. The fact that students seem to enjoy spending lots of time working on microcomputers and the affordability of microcomputers for school systems indicate that this approach has the potential to offer substantial educational relief for students with deficiencies, without being a threat to teachers.

APPENDIX: DESCRIPTION OF TESTING INSTRUMENTS

1. *Formula Translation Examination—English and Spanish.* These two tests contained fourteen questions each and were designed to evaluate the students' ability to read a sentence stating a relationship between two variables and then write an equation to express that relationship. Sample question from the English and Spanish versions of the Formula Translation Examination are given below:

English   Write an equation using the variables S and P to represent the following statement: "There are six times as many students as there are professors at this university." Use S for the number of Students and P for the number of professors.

Spanish   Escriba una ecuación usando las cantidades I y M para representar esta declaración: "En esta universidad hay seis veces más ingenieros que matemáticos." Use I para representar el número de ingenieros y M para el número de matemáticos.

2. *Short Algebra Inventory.* There were two Short Algebra Inventory tests in English and Spanish, each containing twenty questions. The problems required a knowledge of basic algebra, and demanded very little semantic processing on the part of the student. Two problems from the English version appear below:

$$\text{Solve for } x \text{ and } y: \quad \begin{aligned} 2x + y &= 2 \\ x - 3y &= -27 \end{aligned}$$

$$\text{Factor the following:} \quad 4x^2 + 10x - 6$$

3. *Word Problem Inventory.* This instrument consisted of two equivalent English and Spanish versions of a fifteen-question test. Problems on both versions required substantial amounts of semantic processing. Sample problems from these two tests are shown below:

English   In an engineering conference, 9 meeting rooms each had 28 participants and there were 7 participants standing in the halls drinking coffee. How many participants were at the conference?

     A carpenter bought an equal number of nails and screws for $5.70. If each nail costs $.02 and each screw costs $.03, how many nails and how many screws did he buy?

Spanish   Un muchacho compra el mismo número de lápices que de plumas por $.84. Cada lápiz vale $.05 y cada pluma vale $.07. ¿Cuántos lápices y cuántas plumas ha comprado?

4. *Terse and Verbose Tests.* These instruments consisted of four ten-problem tests—two Verbose tests, one in English and the other in Spanish, and two Terse tests, one in English and the other in Spanish. For either language, the Terse and Verbose tests were mathematically equivalent; that is, each problem in the Terse

test had a mathematically equivalent problem in the Verbose test. However, as their names imply, the problems in the Terse tests were stated concisely, while the problems in the Verbose test were embellished with technical jargon, much of it irrelevant in obtaining the solution to the problem. Two equivalent sample problems, one from the English Terse test, the other from the English Verbose test, are given below:

Terse   In a wholesale hardware store, 45 high-intensity light bulbs sell for $50. At a local hardware store, the same light bulb sells for $1.10 each. What is the difference in price between buying 45 light bulbs at the two stores?

Verbose   Albert Einstein, the renowned theoretical nuclear physicist, showed that energy and mass could be thought of as equivalent quantities. Thus particles that are bound together should have a different rest mass than the same particles taken separately. Suppose that a collection of 45 bound particles is determined to have a rest mass of 50 MeV. Careful measurements also show that each of the particles, when examined on its own, has a rest mass of 1.1 MeV. Calculate the difference in rest mass between the 45 bound particles and the 45 unbound particles.

5. *Logic Tests.* These consisted of two nine-problem tests, one in English and the other in Spanish. The problems in these tests were of two types: (1) those requiring the student to read a statement containing one or two negations and to select from four multiple choices the answer that best matched the original statement, and (2) those requiring the student to interpret a Venn diagram. Four problems of the first type were constructed to be pairwise equivalent in structure; however, in one problem of the pair, the answer contradicted real-world truth values; these problems were termed "biased" (see problem 3 below with answer "c"). In the other problem of the pair, the answer was "neutral"; these problems were termed "unbiased" (see problem 6 with answer "d"). Problem 9 shown below was the only problem containing only two multiple choices.

Problem 3   If it is false that not all college graduates earn less than $10,000 a
(biased)   year, then it must be true that
    a. Some college graduates earn more than $10,000 a year.
    b. All college graduates do not earn less than $10,000 a year.
    c. All college graduates earn less than $10,000 a year.
    d. All college graduates earn more than $10,000 a year.

Problem 6   If it is false that not all fig trees grow more than 6 inches per year,
(unbiased)   then it must be true that
    a. Some fig trees grow less than 6 inches per year.
    b. All fig trees do not grow more than 6 inches per year.
    c. All fig trees grow less than 6 inches per year.
    d. All fig trees grow more than 6 inches per year.

Problem 9   The statement "I do not want no money" implies:
  a. I want some money.
  b. I do not want some money.

6. *The College Board Scholastic Aptitude Test* (Educational Testing Service, 1942–1985).

7. *Test of Reading–Level 5, and Prueba de Lectura–Nivel 5* (Guidance Testing Associates, 1962).   These two language instruments are intended to be equivalent versions, one in English and the other in Spanish. The three topics covered in these two tests are Vocabulary, Speed of Comprehension, and Level of Comprehension.

8. *Test of General Ability–Level 5, Part III–Computation* (Guidance Testing Associates, 1962a).   The Test of General Ability–Computation is a nonverbal computation test covering addition, subtraction, multiplication, and division of both whole numbers and fractions.

NOTE

1. An example of applying this erroneous rule is interpreting the statement "not all college graduates earn less than $10,000 a year" to mean "some college graduates earn less than $10,000 a year *and* some college graduates earn exactly or more than $10,000 a year."

REFERENCES

Anderson, J., & Reder, L. (1974). Negative judgments in and about semantic memory. *Journal of Verbal Learning and Verbal Behavior, 13,* 664–681.

Bender, P. S. & Ruiz, R. A. (1974). Race and class as differential determinants of underachievement and underaspiration among Mexican-Americans and Anglos. *Journal of Educational Research, 68,* 51–55.

Board says minority-group scores helped push up averages on SAT. (1982, October 20). *Chronicle of Higher Education,* pp. 1,10.

Brown, G. H., Rosen, N. L., Hill, S. T., & Olivas, M. A. (1980). *The condition of education for Hispanic Americans.* Washington, DC: National Center for Education Statistics.

Buriel, R. & Sáenz, E. (1980). Psychocultural characteristics of college-bound and non-college-bound Chicanas. *Journal of Social Psychology, 110,* 245–251.

Carpenter, P. A. & Just, M. A. (1975). Sentence comprehension: A psycholinguistic processing model of verification. *Psychological Review, 82,* 45–73.

Chapman, L. J. & Chapman, J. P. (1959). Atmosphere effect reexamined. *Journal of Experimental Psychology, 58,* 220–226.

Clark, H. H. & Card, S. K. (1969). The role of semantics in remembering comparative sentences. *Journal of Experimental Psychology, 82,* 545–553.

Clement, J., Lochhead, J., & Monk, G. S. (1981). Translation difficulties in learning mathematics. *American Mathematical Monthly, 88,* 286–290.

Cummins, J. (1979). Linguistic interdependence and the educational development of bilingual children. *Review of Educational Research, 49,* 222–251.

DeÁvila, E. A., & Duncan, S. F. (1981). The language minority child: A psychological, linguistic, and social analysis. In J. E. Alatis (Ed.), *Georgetown University Round Table on Languages and Linguistics, 1980: Current issues in bilingual education.* Washington, DC: Georgetown University Press.

Dillard, J. M. & Perrin, D. W. (1980). Puerto Rican, Black, and Anglo adolescents' career aspirations, expectations, and maturity. *Vocational Guidance Quarterly, 28,* 313–321.

Durán, R. P. (1981). Reading comprehension and the verbal deductive reasoning of bilinguals. In R. P. Durán (Ed.), *Latino language and communicative behavior.* Norwood, NJ: Ablex.

Educational Testing Service. (1942–1985). *College Board Scholastic Aptitude Test.* Princeton, NJ: ETS.

Guidance Testing Associates. (1962a). *Test of General Ability,* Level 5, Advanced Form CE. San Antonio, TX.

Guidance Testing Associates. (1962b). *Test of Reading,* Level 5. San Antonio, TX.

Henle, M. (1962). On the relation between logic and thinking. *Psychological Review, 69,* 366–378.

Hopkins, K., & Glass, G. (1978). *Basic statistics for the behavioral sciences.* Englewood Cliffs, NJ: Prentice-Hall.

International Institute of Teachers College, Columbia University. (1926). A survey of the public educational system of Puerto Rico. Bureau of Publications, Teachers College, Columbia University, New York.

Johnson-Laird, P. N. (1970). Linguistic complexity and insight into a deductive problem. In G. B. Flores d'Arcais & W. J. M. Levelt (Eds.), *Advances in psycholinguistics* (pp. 334–343). Amsterdam: North Holland.

Johnson-Laird, P. N. & Steedman, M. (1978). The psychology of syllogisms. *Cognitive Psychology, 10,* 64–99.

Just, M. A., & Carpenter, P. A. (1971). Comprehension of negation with quantification. *Journal of Verbal Learning and Verbal Behavior, 10,* 244–253.

Kellaghan, J., & Macnamara, J. (1968). Reading in a second language in Ireland. In D. Jenkinson (Ed.), *Reading Instruction: An international forum—Proceedings of the 1st World Congress on Reading* (pp. 231–240). Newark, DE: International Reading Association.

Kolers, P. A. (1966). Reading and talking bilingually. *American Journal of Psychology, 79,* 357–376.

Lambert, W. E., Havelka, J., Gardner, R. C. (1959). Linguistic manifestations of bilingualism. *American Journal of Psychology, 72,* 77–82.

Legrenzi, P. (1970). Relations between language and reasoning about deductive rules. In G. B. Flores d'Arcais & W. J. M. Levelt (Eds.), *Advances in psycholinguistics* (pp. 322–333). Amsterdam: North Holland.

Lochhead, J. (1980). Faculty interpretations of simple algebraic statements: The professor's side of the equation. *Journal of Mathematical Behavior, 3,* 29–37.

Macnamara, J. (1967). The effects of instruction in a weaker language. *Journal of Social Issues, 23,* 121–135.

Mehler, J. (1963). Some effects of grammatical transformations on the recall of English sentences. *Journal of Verbal Learning and Verbal Behavior, 2,* 346–351.

Mestre, J. P. (1981). Predicting academic achievement among bilingual Hispanic college technical students. *Educational and Psychological Measurement, 41,* 1255–1264.

Mestre, J. P. (1986). Teaching problem-solving strategies to bilingual students: What do research results tell us? *International Journal of Mathematics Education in Science and Technology, 17.*

Mestre, J. P., Gerace, W. J., & Lochhead, J. (1982). The interdependence of language and translational math skills among bilingual Hispanic engineering students. *Journal of Research in Science Teaching, 19,* 399–410.

Mestre, J. P., & Gerace, W. J. (1985). A study of the algebra acquisition of Anglo and Hispanic ninth graders: Research findings relevant to teacher training and classroom practice. *Journal of the National Association for Bilingual Education (NABE Journal), 10,* (1).

Mestre, J.P., & Robinson, H. (1983). Academic, socioeconomic, and motivational characteristics of Hispanic college students enrolled in technical programs. *Vocational Guidance Quarterly, 31,* 187–194.

Miller, G. A. (1962). Some psychological studies of grammar. *American Psychologist, 17,* 748–762.

Ramírez, M., & Castañeda, A. (1974). *Cultural democracy, bicognitive development, and education.* New York: Academic Press.

Reder, L. M. (1976). The role of elaborations in the processing of prose. Unpublished doctoral dissertation, University of Michigan.

Sewell, W. H. (1971). Inequality of opportunity for higher education. *American Sociological Review, 36,* 793–809.

Sewell, W. H., & Hauser, R. M. (1975). *Education, occupation, and earnings: achievement in the early career.* New York: Academic Press.

Sherman, M. (1976). Adjectival negation and the comprehension of multiply-negated sentences. *Journal of Verbal Learning and Verbal Behavior, 15,* 143–157.

Trabasso, T., Rollins, H., & Shaughnessey, E. (1971). Storage and verification shapes in processing concepts. *Cognitive Psychology, 2,* 239–289.

Vásquez, M. J. T. (1982). Confronting barriers to the participation of Mexican-American women in higher education. *Hispanic Journal of Behavioral Sciences, 4,* 147–165.

Vygotsky, L. S. (1962). *Thought and language.* Cambridge: MIT Press.

Wason, P. C. (1959). The processing of positive and negative information. *Quarterly Journal of Experimental Psychology, 11,* 92–107.

Wason, P. C. (1961). Response to affirmative and negative binary statements. *British Journal of Psychology, 52,* 133–142.

Whorf, B. *Language, thought and reality.* Cambridge: Wiley, 1956.

Woodworth, R. S., & Sells, S. B. (1935). An atmospheric effect in formal syllogistic reasoning. *Journal of Experimental Psychology, 18,* 451–460.

7 | New Directions for Research on Spanish-Language Tests and Test-Item Bias

MARÍA PENNOCK-ROMÁN

Psychometric research on the potential sources of unfairness in aptitude and achievement tests can be classified into three broad areas, as identified by Flaugher (1970): test content, test environment, and test use. The studies on fairness in test content include, for example, the analysis of individual items, the adequacy of tests translated into Spanish, and the use of nonverbal types of items. The second category of research comprises investigations of the effects of testing conditions, examiner characteristics, types of instructions to examinees, and test speededness. Research on fair test use has focused on models of fair selection and the clarification of societal values concerning selection.

In this paper, test-content issues for Hispanics will be reviewed. The objective is twofold: (1) to identify gaps in the research and unresolved issues of particularly high priority and (2) to suggest ways of overcoming the methodological difficulties in these areas associated with the diversity of Hispanic subgroups and the resultant small sample sizes per subgroup. Studies on the differential predictive validity of college aptitude tests using the traditional regression approach or of the "criterion problem" are not covered here, since they are so thoroughly discussed in the article by Durán in this volume; in addition, I will review research on fair test use in another paper in this book.

CROSS-CULTURAL AND CROSS-LANGUAGE TESTING

Cross-Cultural Testing

In her review of approaches to cross-cultural testing, Anastasi (1982, pp. 286–287) has grouped existing methods into several types. One involves the choice of content that is common to many cultures; it is exemplified by nonverbal reasoning tests such as Cattell's Culture Fair Intelligence Test. A second approach involves the standardization of tasks that maximize cultural differences. The latter have been used to dramatize how individuals' skills are influenced by the cultural milieu in which they are reared. A recent example of this approach is the BITCH Test (Black Intelligence Test of Cultural Homogeneity), for which items were selected on the basis of maximal empirical differences in black-white performance. Other, earlier examples given by Anastasi (1982) include a Footprint Recognition Test standardized on Australian aborigines and a Draw-a-Horse Test standardized on Pueblo Indians. Still a third approach has involved the translation and adaptation of existing tests for use in other cultures, such as the many versions of the Wechsler Intelligence Scales adapted for various countries.

These approaches, in most circumstances, are severely limited in their applications. Nonverbal tests simply do not measure the same kinds of skills as do verbal tests and often do not predict school performance as well as verbal tests. The consensus among most psychologists and psychometricians is that these tests, if anything, have increased the disparities in mean performance between minority and majority individuals (Samuda, 1975; Olmedo, 1977). Culture-specific tests have also demonstrated little predictive validity for criteria outside the given culture. Furthermore, translations of existing tests have many problems as well. There is no guarantee that the degree of difficulty of any item will be preserved when it is translated. In addition, it is difficult to choose specific terms that will have identical common meanings across the dialects in a given language. To illustrate this point, consider a hypothetical item that could have been developed by a Nigerian psychometrician. An analogies item might ask: "In what way are a *tap* and a *cork* alike?" Perhaps a Nigerian student would have little difficulty in responding that both are necessary to fill the bathtub with water. However, Americans would probably be baffled by the unfamiliar use of the term *tap* to indicate a bathroom faucet and *cork* to indicate a bathroom stopper.

On the other hand, the misuses of translations of the Wechsler scales into Spanish are far from hypothetical. Most Hispanic psychologists can cite examples such as the following: A South American child was initially misclassified as emotionally disturbed because of his response to a question concerning the similarity between an orange (*una china*) and a banana (*un guineo*). He replied that both were human. It turns out that his response was perfectly logical because, in most of the Spanish-speaking world, a *china* is a resident of China and a *guineo* is a resident of Guinea, West Africa. The more common words for orange and banana outside of Puerto Rico are *naranja* and *banano*.[1] Translating intelligence-test items based on content from outside the school environment is particularly difficult; it is in the names of articles in the home and the flora and fauna of a country that the linguistic divergence is most likely to occur among variations of the same language.

A fourth category of construction of cross-cultural tests, which has been virtually ignored in U.S. texts on psychometrics, involves the development of a culture-specific measure to ensure predictive validity within the targeted culture, rather than group differentiation. The next sections summarize the research on two tests in Spanish developed in Puerto Rico: the Prueba de Aptitud Academica (PAA) and the Prueba de Admisión para Estudios Graduados (PAEG).

The Prueba de Aptitud Académica

As is pointed out by Durán (1983), the PAA, which is designed and administered by the Puerto Rican Office of the College Board, is quite successful in predicting undergraduate scholastic performance in Puerto Rican universities, where instruction is primarily in Spanish. Some U.S. mainland admissions committees use the PAA as supplemental information to the SAT to be used in borderline cases. Other than the study by Boldt (1969), very little empirical research has been done on the PAA outside of Puerto Rico. Some unpublished studies with small sample sizes have shown that it has moderate predictive value for estimating the college performance of Puerto Rican students in U.S. colleges on the mainland (J. Dieppa, personal communication, August 1982). This line of research is extremely interesting because it investigates how generalizable the predictive validity of one test normed in one language environment can be toward prediction of criteria in the context of another language. Although the PAA is a better measure of ability than the SAT for Puerto Rican high school students whose best language is Spanish, the SAT would probably have higher predictive validity for U.S. mainland colleges, since it reflects the proficiency in English needed to absorb the course materials and lectures.

Alderman (1981) demonstrated that Puerto Ricans' performance on the SAT could be predicted with an accuracy almost as high as the SAT's reliability ($R = .86$ to .89) using a combination of the PAA and any one of three different measures of English proficiency used in the study. Eighty percent of the variance in SAT-V scores among these students could be explained by three components: about 44 percent was accountable to ability as measured by the PAA; 29 percent was due to the addition of English language test; and 7 percent was due to an interaction between the PAA and English proficiency. Although the effects of second-language proficiency on measuring aptitude in the second language were pointed out by Sánchez (1932a, 1932b, 1934a, 1934b) five decades ago,

Alderman's study was the first to quantify the separate components for Spanish speakers. This quantification is important because it underscores how substantial the language-proficiency component can be when measuring aptitude. These results leave no doubt that low proficiency in the language of the test can lead to a sizable underestimate of ability. However, the actual estimates of the percentages of variance attributable to each component are not necessarily generalizable to bilingual samples with different language histories because they depend on the distribution of levels of English proficiency among participants.

Perhaps this type of breakdown could be extended to the prediction of grade-point average in college for bilinguals. Following Alderman's approach, one could investigate how well the PAA and an English-language proficiency test predict college success on the mainland, examining the predictors separately and in combination. However, the study of the predictive validity of this test outside Puerto Rico involves several problems. One is that validity studies usually require a minimum sample size of about three hundred subjects before one can estimate with confidence the predictive validity of a test in one situation. Puerto Rican high school students distribute themselves sparsely over a large number of U.S. universities, so that it is very unlikely that one would get as many as three hundred in one place even in a four-year span. Nevertheless, new statistical techniques based on empirical Bayes procedures enable validity studies to be carried out even with small individual sample sizes at each university; Rubin (1980) has described an example of this approach.

A second problem is that no records are kept of the patterns of Puerto Rican students' enrollment in U.S. mainland colleges (J. Dieppa, personal communication, August 1982). Locating these students is further complicated by the fact that college registrars do not keep separate tabulations on Puerto Ricans from the island as opposed to those residing in the continental United States. One would need the separate counts because only those from the island have PAA scores. These logistical problems are, of course, surmountable. Now, with the right kinds of statistical tools (i.e., empirical Bayes estimators), a validity study of this type would be very useful for the improvement of measurement for at least one segment of Hispanic college students.

The Prueba de Admisión para Estudios Graduados (PAEG)

The PAEG, which is a newer test than the PAA, was designed by the Educational Testing Service (ETS) for the Graduate School Council of

Puerto Rico. It was initially developed for use in selection decisions for law schools and graduate schools of business and education in Puerto Rico. The first experimental forms of the test were administered in 1972–73 and were found to have good psychometric properties. They represented a substantial improvement over the use of the English-language tests—the Law School Admission Test (LSAT), the Admissions Test for Graduate School in Business (ATGSB), and the Graduate Record Examinations (GRE). For example, the validity coefficient for predicting first-year GPA in law school (academic year: 1973–74) rose from .39, using the LSAT as a single predictor, to .48, using the PAEG as a single predictor. The correlation between the two tests was surprisingly high ($r = .77$; P. P. Woodford, personal communications, January–May 1983). This value is noticeably higher than the correlation of .67 found by Alderman (1981) between the SAT-V and the PAA for a sample that was heterogeneous in English skills. Since he demonstrated that the correlations between the two tests increased with level of English-language proficiency, one could speculate that the law school students taking the PAEG had to be quite proficient in English for such a high intercorrelation to be found. It is likely that self-selection for English-language skills occurred because the LSAT scores were being used for purposes of admission at that time.

The finding of a .39 correlation between an aptitude test in English and achievement in a Spanish environment is a rather interesting empirical finding in itself. It confirms that an aptitude test in one language can have predictive validity for achievement in another language, given a (presumably) high proficiency in both languages. These data raise the following questions: Among bilinguals equally fluent in both languages, would the LSAT and PAEG be equally good predictors of GPA, or would there still be a language-specific advantage for the PAEG? How much could the LSAT-GPA correlations be improved if English-language proficiency could be partialed out of the LSAT as an irrelevant source of variance? Studies addressing these issues would elucidate the interacting effects of language proficiency, bilingualism, and aptitude on achievement.

Like the PAA, the PAEG in combination with an English-proficiency test may be an improvement over the GRE for the prediction of graduate school grade-point averages at U.S. mainland universities for graduates of Puerto Rican institutions. The restriction of range in the level of ability and grade-point averages of these candidates may pose an additional problem to the feasibility of pursuing validity studies. On the other hand, the sample sizes of graduate school candidates might actually be bigger than those seeking undergraduate degrees.

Research on the PAA and PAEG
for Other Spanish-Language Populations

For U.S.-born Hispanics, the potential usefulness of these Spanish-language tests is greatly limited because only a very small segment of the nation's school-aged Hispanic population is literate in Spanish (Nielsen & Fernández, 1981). From another perspective, the generalizability of the PAA and the PAEG could be studied in U.S. mainland colleges with other non–Puerto Rican student populations that are proficient and literate in Spanish. It would also be interesting to use these tests with students in other Latin American countries to see how well they predict scholastic performance at colleges in these countries. Since the lexicon used for the PAA and the PAEG is the more formal, standard Spanish that is common to academic texts throughout Latin America, one would expect it to be relatively free of the regional variations that hamper the use of the Puerto Rican translation of the Wechsler scales. It would probably require fewer modifications than tests translated from English.

The PAEG is already used in the selection of candidates for the Latin American Scholarship Program for American Universities (LASPAU) in Cambridge, Massachusetts (P. P. Woodford, personal communications, January–May 1983). The applicants to this program are usually professors from Latin American universities who wish to pursue graduate studies in the United States (K. Sellew, personal communications, spring 1983). After taking the PAEG and an English-proficiency test, the selected candidates are trained in English until they reach the desired level of fluency. At that point, they take the Test of English as a Foreign Language (TOEFL) and apply to graduate schools. Usually, the schools accept the PAEG results in lieu of the GRE. Since the LASPAU keeps complete records of its students' progress in graduate schools, a validity study on the PAEG with this group would be feasible. On the other hand, the generalizability of these findings to other groups would be limited to bilinguals who have attained the level of English proficiency that LASPAU ensures for its graduates. Such a study would also have to contend with the aforementioned problems of restriction of ability range and small sample sizes at each university.

A Classificatory Framework
for Cross-Language Validity Studies

It is useful to outline all of the different possible variations on the validity studies that one can identify for Spanish-English bilinguals in order to classify past and future research in table form. Table 7.1 shows a cross-classification of potential research designs resembling a 5 × 2 × 2

Table 7.1: Validity Studies Classified by Language of Test and of Instruction for Bilinguals Who Vary in Language Dominance

Type of Bilingualism		Language of Instruction			
		Spanish		English	
		Aptitude Test		Aptitude Test	
		Spanish	English	Spanish	English
Spanish dominant in academic areas	I	1	6	11	16
	II	2	7	12	17
Proficient in both	III	3	8	13	18
	IV	4	9	14	19
English dominant in academic areas	V	5	10	15	20

NOTE: The cross-hatched cells identify the most common kinds of validity studies that have already taken place.

analysis-of-variance table. One dimension is the type of language dominance that one has for academic tasks, which is shown here with five levels, from Spanish-dominant to English-dominant. Then there are two levels each for the language of the examination and the language of instruction. The latter could be extended to more than two levels, if various combinations of the languages were used for instructional purposes. The cells that are cross-hatched indicate types of designs that have already been used; these studies have usually included several levels of language proficiency in each analysis, without separating subjects by level.

As Durán points out in his article, the 1981 College Board data indicate that more than 93 percent of Chicanos and 90 percent of Puerto Ricans taking the SAT have responded to the Student Data Questionnaire that English is their best language. These results are probably generalizable also to Hispanics taking the American College Tests (ACT), given that ratings of proficiency in English are generally higher than ratings of proficiency in Spanish for high-school-aged Hispanics residing in the U.S. (Nielsen & Fernández, 1981). Therefore, existing studies on the SAT and the ACT validities at U.S. universities for Hispanics residing in the United States have been conducted mostly with English-dominant bilinguals; they can be classified into cells 19, 20, and possibly 18. Similarly, the validity studies for the PAA can be classified into cells 1, 2, and possibly 3. The use of the LSAT and GRE for Puerto Rican institutions belongs in cells 7, 8, and possibly 6. The foregoing cells are cross-hatched in the table. Future studies of graduates of Puerto Rican or Latin American institutions attending U.S. mainland schools suggested here would be classified into cells 11–13 if the PAA, the PAEG, or an equivalent were used and into cells 16–18 if English-language tests were used. To complete the picture, one might study the use of Spanish-language aptitude tests for English-dominant bilinguals on the U.S. mainland (cells 14–15) to see if they improve prediction over the usual English-language tests. Studies in cells 4, 5, 9, and 10 might be useful for Latin American or Puerto Rican universities that attract U.S. English-dominant students (e.g., medical schools in México).

The foregoing collection of designs provides a comprehensive research framework for the study of bilingualism and achievement. In practical terms, the application of Spanish-language tests may help to identify talent among the small segment of the U.S.-born population that is literate in Spanish. Though these tests merit much empirical research, an equal or higher priority should be given to the investigation of methods of improving existing English-language tests for use with Hispanic students. In the next section, research pertaining to one of the newer approaches—the minute examination of test content at the item level (i.e., item-discrepancy investigations)—is reviewed.

DETECTING DISCREPANT ITEMS

Discrepancy, Bias, and Unfairness

As is pointed out by Shepard (1982), the terms *bias* and *unfairness* do not have consistent meanings from one author to another. In this article, I will use the term *item discrepancy* rather than *item bias* to keep the concepts of statistical discrepancy and unfairness as separate as possible. Angoff (1982) has pointed out that most of our statistical techniques for detecting anomalous items are best described as item-discrepant methodologies rather than item-bias methods: "[T]he presence or absence of bias [in the sense of unfairness] is unavoidably a matter of human judgment, for which the statistical analysis is only a useful tool . . . item fairness and test fairness are concepts and characteristics that must be evaluated in terms of the purpose of the instrument and its intended use, not solely on the basis of the bare statistics" (p. 114).

An item is said to be *discrepant* if individuals with equal ability but from different groups have different probabilities of answering the item correctly. (The choice of criteria to define *ability* will be discussed later.) A discrepant item may not be judged "unfair," in the same ways that "unfair" items are not necessarily statistically discrepant. These distinctions between the source of a discrepancy and the relevance of the group difference to the skill being measured have been made by Scheuneman (1982). Each is viewed as a separate dimension when classifying the discrepancies in items. On the one hand, the source of a discrepancy can reflect a real difference between groups in (a) experience and training or (b) ethnic culture, language, or values. On the other hand, these differences can be classified along a second dimension as to whether the difference between groups is (a) related to the ability measured or (b) not related to the ability measured. Hence, a group difference on an item can be classified into one of four categories, as seen in table 7.2.

I concur with Scheuneman's view that the determination of "unfairness" should depend only on the relevance of the difference to the skill being measured. Thus, differences of types III and IV, those *unrelated* to the skill being measured, are clearly sources of *unfairness* in items. Differences of types I and II, which are related to the skill being measured, can be judged to be "fair," but only after a careful examination of the content validity of the item. Some examples may help to illustrate these distinctions.

Table 7.2: Sources of Unexpected Performance Differences Between Groups

	Experience and Training	Ethnic Culture or Values
Related to ability measured	I	II
Not related to ability measured	III [a]	IV [a]

NOTE: From Scheuneman (1982, Table 7.1, p. 186). Reproduced with permission of the publisher, Johns Hopkins University Press.
[a] Items in these categories would be considered biased.

Breland, Stocking, Pinchak, & Abrams (1974) found that items requiring familiarity with square roots on a mathematics achievement test were relatively more difficult for Hispanic, black, and American Indian high school students than for non-Hispanic whites. The source of the discrepancy in all likelihood reflects a real deficiency in the students' knowledge of basic concepts necessary for success in mathematics courses. In my view, such an item is "fair," because the test is one measuring *achievement*. On the other hand, in a test of *reasoning skill*, the inclusion of items that involve knowledge of square roots would be "unfair," because it is desirable that reasoning be measured as independently as possible from specific content. Similarly, Breland et al. (1974) and Alderman and Holland (1981) found that Hispanics performed relatively better than other groups on vocabulary items that contained Spanish cognates. In Nielsen and Lerner's (1982, p. 3) words, "[bilinguals have] easier access to a difficult . . . more abstract, cultivated lexicon . . . than a [monolingual] . . . English speaker." In my view (different from that of Breland et al.), this discrepancy is "fair" if the vocabulary tests sample Latin-origin words representatively, in numbers that reflect the frequency of their occurrence in academic texts. On the other hand, Spanish cognates that are unusually difficult and obscure for English monolinguals are out of place in an analogies test, since reasoning tests should be as independent as possible of vocabulary level. In sum, "fairness" is ultimately a matter of judgment, an evaluation of content validity, which is often difficult to make.

A Priori Judgments Versus Statistical Indexes of Bias

Several studies have shown that panels of reviewers have usually failed in their attempts to identify by inspection those items that are *statistically* discrepant across ethnic groups (Shepard, 1982). Although Judge Grady in the *PASE v. Hannon* decision (1980) singled out several items on the Wechsler Intelligence Scales for Children–Revised (WISC-R) as being particularly biased, the specific items that actually did show statistical discrepancies among black, Mexican American, and non-Hispanic white students tested by Sandoval (1979) "revealed no logical pattern" (p. 923). In a study by Sandoval and Miille (1980), black, Mexican American, and non-Hispanic white (hereafter called "white" or "Anglo") college students were asked which items would be more difficult for black children than for white children on the WISC-R. These students were no more successful than Judge Grady in identifying the relatively more difficult items for the various groups of children.

Furthermore, even subject-matter experts are unsuccessful in identifying statistically discrepant items. Plake (1980) found that, for items on a mathematics test "[t]he [expert] raters predicted twice as many bias instances and biased items as were found by the statistical method. The raters themselves showed a tendency to disagree in the direction of a predicted biased item nearly as often as they agreed" (p. 403). Alderman and Holland (1981) found that linguistic experts were unable to predict which items on the Test of English as a Foreign Language would show the largest differential performance across various language groups. Disparities between judgmental ratings and statistical indexes have also been found on the Test of Standard Written English when subject-matter experts were asked to predict item difficulties for unselected students (Béjar, 1981).

Scheuneman (1982) attributes the lack of agreement between judgmental and statistical methods to the complexity of the issue. "[A] large number of different kinds of problems . . . can yield unexpected performance results. Even if reviewers were aware of all of these problems, reviewing items on more than one or two criteria simultaneously is extremely difficult to do well" (p. 194). This point is supported by Murray and Mishra (1983), who found that the degree of agreement between Anglo and Mexican American judges varied according to the criteria used to rate items. When test items were rated according to "familiarity with item language," there was a high degree of agreement between the two groups of judges. On the other hand, using the criteria of "opportunity to learn item content," there were statistically significant differences in ratings between the groups for sixteen out of forty-six items. Berk (1982) suggests that *a priori* judgmental and statistical methods "are tapping different kinds of bias" (p. 4). Scheuneman (1982) adds that "what reviewers see—offensive material, stereotypic representation, uneven coverage of content from a minority perspective—is important and should be corrected on moral and ethical grounds" (p. 194). Shepard (1982) points out that objectionable items may not lead to observable decrements in performance, because minority groups may be aware of the expected right answers. In addition, "empirical methods for detecting bias are insensitive to any delayed or pervasive reduction in performance caused by perceived unfairness in the questions. Apart from the issue of bias, ambiguous items conceivably could frustrate examinees enough to lessen their scores on subsequent items. Similarly, one can imagine that offensive items or items entirely foreign to an examinee's experience could harm motivation and attention on later test questions" (p. 22).

Hence, test publishers maintain systematic programs of analysis for test items, as described by several authors in Berk (1982, chap. 9). Angoff (1982) explains that the consensus seems to be that "proper methods of test development require extensive and careful judgmental review. . . . The role of [statistical] methods . . . is to serve only as a further check, in the event that one or more biased items may have escaped the attention of the reviewers" (p. 96). An extensive review of the judgmental procedures in use by Tittle (1982) points to the need for more research to establish the main categories that judges use in classification of items and to identify the characteristics of the "best" judges.

Before we can demonstrate that particular judgmental methods have greater validity than others, it is necessary to establish accurate and consistent statistical indexes of bias that will serve as criteria to evaluate these methods. However, there are methodological difficulties in doing this kind of research because the statistical techniques used are not designed to be confirmatory statistical methods. We seem to have an abundance of exploratory methods that can be used to identify group differences but few, if any, that can confirm or disconfirm specific predictions. Once the best judgmental methods are identified, raters can then be trained so as to achieve a high degree of interjudge agreement. Without a sufficient number of judges or a high enough degree of concordance among raters, the reliability of the ratings would be too low to predict statistical bias consistently. In sum, future research on *a priori* judgments of bias must address two issues: (1) achieving reliable, consistent *a priori* ratings and (b) finding appropriate statistical indexes to confirm predictions of bias.

How Large a Discrepancy Constitutes Unfairness?

There is currently no consensus among researchers concerning how large a discrepancy in test-item performance among groups should be considered nontrivial (Alderman & Holland, 1981; Shepard, Camilli, & Averill, 1981; Angoff, 1982). There is general agreement, however, that statistical significance alone is an insufficient criterion. For small sample sizes, one is likely to miss detecting biased items. Also, "any level of item-by-group interaction can attain statistical significance with enough cases. . . . [T]he level of significance chosen for this purpose is purely arbitrary and often reflects only the predilections of the investigator. What is needed is simply a well-rationalized index that expresses the degree, or amount, of item-by-group interaction reflected by the item in question and a sufficiently large sample size to insure a reasonable level of stability" (Angoff, 1982, p. 113).

Shepard at al. (1981) used an inspectional technique to compare several different methods of detecting item discrepancies to see how well they agreed in finding biased items. They rejected the alternative of comparing the ten or twenty most extreme items identified by each method. Arbitrary cutoffs do "not properly model our sense that biased items should be clearly discrepant from the pattern set by other items on the test" (p. 352). Instead, they identified outliers by gaps in the distributions of item values and found that "[t]he number of items identified as biased by this inspectional technique differed by method and by data set" (p. 353). Thus, the lack of agreement concerning how large a discrepancy must be in order for an item to be declared biased presents many methodological difficulties. It makes the comparison of different statistical techniques and the judgment of overall bias very arbitrary.

Various statistical techniques for detecting item discrepancies will now be described and compared. Some methods have been shown clearly to be less adequate than others, although they continue to be commonly used because of practical considerations. In addition, as has been noted, the items that are identified as biased by one method are not always so identified by others. Hence, any evaluation of studies that assess the numbers of discrepant items on tests must first examine the technical details and appropriateness of the methods used in each study.

An Evaluation of Current Statistical Methods for Identifying Item Discrepancy

There are currently more than a dozen different statistical methods proposed for the detection of item discrepancy, and the number keeps growing. (See Burrill, 1982, and Rudner, Getson, & Knight, 1980b, for comprehensive overviews, and Jensen, 1980, chap. 9, pp. 432–453, for detailed descriptions of computational methods.) Mellenbergh (1982) has grouped existing methods into two basic classes. The first class of methods, which emerged earlier, examines how the probability of a correct response for an item varies by group. This category is exemplified by Angoff's delta-plot method. The more recently proposed second class of methods, exemplified by the item-characteristic curve techniques, takes into account the distribution of ability in all groups and looks at the probability of a correct response in each group as a function of ability. Several authors have reviewed existing methods, but much research still needs to be done with emerging techniques. Some published critiques have been theoretical (Lord, 1977); others have been based on computer-simulated data (Rudner, Getson, & Knight, 1980a), while still others have used "real" data (Shepard et al., 1981; Ironson & Subkoviak, 1979; Stricker, 1982). The second class of methods (those that take into account ability level, particularly the three-parameter item-characteristic curve [ICC-3]) is considered superior by many researchers (Hunter, 1975; Mellenbergh, 1982; Lord, 1977; Stricker, 1982).

However, the most widely applied methods to detect item discrepancies belong to the first category and involve the calculation of item-difficulty values, that is, p values (percent correct) for each different group. These p values are then usually transformed into normal deviates (called deltas) or by an arcsin transformation. Of the twenty-three ETS studies of item discrepancy reported by Carlton and Marco (1982) for which the statistical method was listed, eighteen had used the delta method proposed by Angoff (see Angoff, 1982, for a recent overview), and two had used an analysis-of-variance method (ANOVA), which usually involves the arcsin transformation. Angoff's method is also widely used by Science Research Associates (Raju, 1982). The ANOVA procedure is frequently used by the Riverside Publishing Company (publishers of the Iowa Tests of Basic Skills) and by the American College Testing Program, in combination with other methods (Coffman, 1982; Handrick & Loyd, 1982). Most of the studies evaluating subjective ratings of item bias against statistical methods (e.g., Sandoval & Miille, 1980; Plake, 1980) have also used an ANOVA test of differences in transformed item difficulties. The studies by Loyd (1980, 1982) involving Chicanos also used the ANOVA technique.

In view of their popularity, it is disturbing to learn that these methods can be inaccurate, as pointed out by the aforementioned critiques. In some instances, item discrepancies are found where none exist, while in other circumstances, underlying anomalies are not detected. When groups differ substantially in average ability score, items that have good discrimination between low- and high-scoring examinees will have substantially different p values, which will make an item that is not discrepant appear to be anomalous. Angoff (1982) has conceded the existence of this problem and has suggested that the method be applied only when groups are matched beforehand on ability.

Failure to detect discrepant items, however, cannot be corrected by matching the groups. The transformed item difficulty (TID) methods are unable to detect certain types of interactions between group and ability level that affect item performance. In cases where one group is favored at low levels of ability and the other group performs differentially better at the high end of the ability scale, the overall p values of the item in the two groups will be approximately equal, and no discrepancy will be detected even if the groups are matched (see Lord, 1977, figs. 6 and 7). Furthermore, when item discrepancies tend to occur at either of the extreme ends of ability level, where there are relatively few observations, the p values will reflect the results on the bulk of the cases, and the discrepancies will not appear to be large (see Lord, 1977, fig. 8).

Simulation studies based on computer-generated data have shown that the TID methods are insensitive to bias in item discrimination but reflect biases in difficulty levels quite adequately (Rudner et al., 1980a; Merz & Grossen, 1979). Their results tend to agree moderately well with those of other techniques, but on the whole, TID methods do not perform as well as the ICC-3 and chi-square methods, which will be discussed subsequently. The adequacy of the TID methods depend in part on just how frequently group-by-ability-level interactions are found. The little evidence that exists suggests that these interactions are relatively frequent in ethnic-group comparisons and less frequent in gender-group comparisons (Stricker, 1981).

In the aforementioned simulation studies, the various indexes of bias based on the ICC-3 technique have demonstrated the most sensitive and accurate detection of item discrepancy even when interactions of group by ability level are present. The greater rigor of the ICC-3 approach stems from its power to take into account how performance varies by ability level, enabling one to examine group differences at each level of ability, throughout the spectrum. Nevertheless, this method is less popular than the TID approaches because it is complex and extremely costly to apply. Furthermore, the ICC-3 requires that the ability level be estimated on at least forty items and sample sizes of at least 1,000 to (preferably) 2,000. These conditions can be met only by very large testing programs and for relatively long, homogeneous tests. Heterogeneous tests such as the Wechsler scales, which must be analyzed separately by subtest, have too few items in each subtest for this type of approach.

Given the practical limitations of the ICC-3 and the flaws of the TID approaches, many alternative techniques have been proposed that control for ability. There are two basic types: those treating underlying ability as a continuum, and contingency-table methods that separate ability level into discrete categories. One method that treats ability as a continuum but eliminates the restrictive statistical assumptions of the ICC-3 method is Dorans and Kulick's (1983) "standardization" technique. It uses an item-characteristic function that is based on the empirical item and score distributions and not the theoretical normal ogive or logistic distributions. This method is very new, and there are no published studies evaluating it with simulated data or contrasting it with other techniques to date. Its authors recommend it only for very large sample sizes, in order to have all or almost all categories of total score well represented (N. J. Dorans, personal communication, fall, 1982); therefore, it is impractical for most testing programs.

Stricker (1981, 1982) evaluated an inexpensive method that computes the partial correlation between subgroup membership and item performance after partialing out total score. It is probably applicable to total sample sizes as small as 400 subjects. However, Stricker admits that, like the TID methods, its "main drawback, . . . in contrast to the ICC index, [is that] it cannot identify items which change in their functioning . . . favoring a subgroup at one point and penalizing it at another" (1981, p. 3). When he applied it to data on the GRE, it agreed closely with the ICC results for gender comparisons but not for the ethnic-group comparisons.

Linn and Harnisch (1981) proposed a small-sample alternative to the ICC-3, which Doolittle (1983) has synopsized as follows: "To calculate the index, the item and ability parameters of the . . . [ICC-3] model are estimated for the *total* sample. The two groups are then separated. The difference is taken between each examinee's probability of correctly answering the item and the examinee's actual response to the item. . . . This difference is then standardized and averaged over the examinees in each group" (p. 6). Linn and Harnisch also suggested estimating the ICC-3 parameters on the majority group alone and not the total sample, because the use of the total sample might tend to deflate the magnitude of the bias indexes. The total-sample method fared well in comparison with other techniques evaluated by Doolittle (1983); the method based on majority-group parameters was not included in Doolittle's study.

Another approach to controlling for ability level in examining item performance is represented by a variety of contingency-table analysis methods (see Ironson, 1982, for a review). These include a modified chi-square procedure (Scheuneman, 1979), a full chi-square procedure (Camilli, 1979; Nungester, 1977), other chi-square models (Marascuilo & Slaughter, 1981), log-linear models (Alderman & Holland, 1981; Mellenbergh, 1982), and an application of the del statistic (Watkins, 1983; Pennock-Román, 1984). Unlike the ICC-3 and others above, the contingency-table methods categorize the ability distribution into several classes (usually five to ten). These approaches have the advantages of being able to examine ability level by group interactions, relatively low cost, and the requirement of much smaller sample sizes than the ICC-3. Nevertheless, they can run into problems when the ability categories are too narrow or too gross. In the former case, the marginal frequencies become small, and the expected values drop below the minimum levels that statisticians consider adequate. (Depending on which statistician one consults, the required minimum value should be unity or five for chi-square methods.) When categories are too gross, the matching of ability level between two groups is less than optimal, because there is too much heterogeneity in ability within each category. When two groups differ widely in mean score, false item discrepancies that are artifacts of the gross categorization can be detected (Dorans, 1982). Despite these problems, Scheuneman's (1979) modified chi-square procedure has been found to agree fairly closely with ICC-3 results (Rudner et al., 1980a; Shepard et al., 1981; Ironson & Subkoviak, 1979; Intasuwan, 1979; Rudner & Convey, 1978). The other methods have not been so thoroughly studied.

Judging by Monte Carlo simulation studies of the del statistic in other applications (Hildebrand, Laing, & Rosenthal, 1977), modifications of the del method for detecting item discrepancy are likely to be more robust against small sample sizes and skewed marginal frequencies than alternative contingency-table techniques. The statistic has the additional advantage of being able to function as both a confirmatory method of *a priori* prediction and an exploratory method. Moreover, it supplies an overall index that measures how discrepant an item is. This index is scale-free, like a correlation coefficient.

Currently, contingency-table methods are regarded as inferior to the ICC-3 because simulation studies have shown greater accuracy for the latter. On the other hand, the chi-square methods are somewhat superior to Angoff's TID technique when evaluated in terms of agreement with the ICC-3 results.

The chi-square methods generally reproduce the ICC-3 results more closely than do the TID methods. Ironson and Subkoviak (1979) found that the signed Scheuneman modified chi-square indexes correlated .54 to .82 with the ICC-3 indexes in the four relatively unspeeded subtests of the battery, whereas Angoff's TID indexes correlated .32 to .69 with the ICC-3 results on these subtests. The percent agreement for the twenty-four most biased items among methods was 54.2 percent between the ICC-3 and chi-square procedures and 33.3 percent between the ICC-3 and TID procedures. Shepard et al. (1981) found that, when blacks and whites were compared, the signed indexes for ICC-3 correlated .66 with full chi-square indexes and .30 with Angoff's indexes. For the Chicano-white comparison, the correlation between full chi-square and ICC-3 was .68 and the corresponding TID and ICC-3 correlation was .51. Despite the closer agreement between chi-square and the ICC-3, the TID methods have been used far more frequently (probably because they were introduced earlier).

The best techniques for studying item discrepancy at this point in time appear to be the indexes based on ICC-3 theory, given the following conditions: The test should have at least forty items that measure only one dimension (factor); and the sample size should be large (preferably at least 2,000). When these conditions are not met, it is unclear from the research so far whether the ICC-3 method is superior to contingency-table or TID methods. Perhaps the ICC-3 methods are still more accurate than alternatives even when its parameters are not optimally measured (H. Wainer, personal communication, November 1983). On the other hand, the ICC-3 parameters are very costly (and sometimes impossible) to estimate; the LOGIST program that estimates its parameters takes many interactions, and its estimates do not always converge, even when the aforementioned conditions are met. Therefore, these methods are practical only for the largest and most prosperous testing programs.

When it is not feasible to use the ICC-3 methods, the best alternatives at this time appear to be the full or modified chi-square procedures. However, small sample sizes or skewed marginals may cause expected values to be too small in some applications. Other contingency-table methods, such as the del statistic, normally resolve these difficulties, but much research still needs to be done to evaluate the del and other alternative methods.

Unfortunately, the ICC-3 and chi-square methods have rarely been applied to Hispanic-Anglo comparisons (one exception is the study by Shepard et al., 1981); the majority of published studies including U.S. Hispanic samples have tended to use a variety of TID methods (Breland et al., 1974; Loyd, 1980, 1982; Sandoval, 1979; Sandoval & Miille, 1980; Sinnott, 1980). Given the aforementioned limitations of the TID methods, much of this early research on Hispanics should be regarded as methodologically flawed and must be interpreted with caution; the results are of dubious value if groups have not been matched on ability beforehand or if there is reason to believe that group-by-ability-level interactions are likely to have occurred.

External Versus Internal Criteria
to Define Ability

One characteristic that almost all of the current item-discrepancy methods share is that they use the total score on the test as the measure of ability, an internal criterion. Items are declared biased if, relative to any given total score, the probabilities of passing an item differ by group. Thus Shepard et al. (1981) note that the methods cannot escape an inherent circularity—if the items are biased, the total test score is likely to be biased and is thus a poor measure of ability. Given these limitations, Burrill (1982) points out that "[w]hat the process can do is improve the homogeneity of the test being constructed. . . . Although most researchers have conceived of item bias procedures as improving validity, it may be more realistic to visualize them as concerned more with internal consistency or reliability—a necessary, but not sufficient, prerequisite of validity" (pp. 173–174).

Using external criteria will help, but only if the external criteria are free of the same bias that affects the items and if they reflect the same ability as the items do. The study by Shepard et al. (1981) illustrates some of the problems in finding appropriate external criteria. Several statistical methods were applied to the Lorge-Thorndike tests (verbal and non-verbal) using the usual internal criterion (total score). For an external criterion, they repeated all of the analyses but substituted scores from the Raven's Progressive Matrices for the total score on the test being analyzed. They found that "[p]redictably, the estimation difficulties with the external criterion were worse for the verbal test than for the nonverbal test since the Raven's reflects the same factor as the nonverbal test" (p. 341). Another problem was that the Raven's test was too easy for this population, which led to a lack of differentiation in the upper end of the ability scale. This effect led to finding more biased items than with the internal criterion. The gross categorizations at the upper end of ability led to the inclusion of persons of various ability levels in one category. The more "able" ones, as measured by total score on the Raven's, in these categories passed the harder items more frequently. Because the more "able" ones were more likely to be the white examinees, this pattern gave the harder items a greater likelihood of appearing biased.

One way around this problem has been suggested by Sinnott (1980). She proposed an iterative procedure to modify the delta-plot method in which the line is recalculated several times as necessary. First, one identifies discrepant items in the usual way. Then the new line is recalculated based on the nondiscrepant items of the first analysis. Item-discrepancy indexes are then calculated for *all* of the items in a second analysis (the discrepant ones are readmitted) using the recalculated line. Any discrepant items in this second analysis are eliminated from the recalculation of the line for the third analysis. This process goes on until no more new discrepant items are identified.

A Posteriori Interpretations of Discrepant-Item Performance

Although some authors claim that it is uncommon to find adequate interpretations for observed statistical item discrepancies (Stricker, 1982; Burril, 1982), Scheuneman (1982) gives many examples of logical findings. Sometimes the anomaly is due not to the content of the item itself but to differences in test naiveté or test-taking strategies among the various groups. For example, directions that are more ambiguous for some groups than others can lead to a pattern whereby one group tends to miss relatively more frequently the items at the beginning of a section. Unfamiliarity with particular words in the instructions can also lead to having one group consistently pick out the wrong choice, regardless of the item (such as picking a synonym when an antonym is called for). Some items in which minority groups did relatively well turned out to be ones where the "testwise" cues, presumably used by the majority group, led to a particular distractor that was wrong. In other words, the cues (of which the minority students were less aware) helped the majority group in most items but led them astray on others. Other items reflected differential effects of speededness.

Loyd (1982) also found interpretable results on the American College Test for Anglo-Hispanic differences in items on the English Usage and Social Studies Reading subtests. On the English Usage reading passages, there were six discrepant items, three favoring Anglos and three favoring Hispanics. Two of the three items favoring Anglos involved skill in punctuating or adequately placing adjectives and adverbs in a series. These discrepant items appeared to be sensitive to linguistic features that may have been more difficult for Spanish bilinguals. On the Social Sciences Reading test, there were seven discrepant items, three favoring Hispanics and four favoring Anglos. Two of the four favoring Anglos required knowledge of the subject matter that was not contained in the reading passage. Thus, the latter finding suggests a deficiency in the educational background of the Hispanic candidates that made these items relatively more difficult. Also, as mentioned before, Spanish cognates sometimes lead to a performance advantage for Hispanic groups on vocabulary tests (Breland et al., 1974; Alderman & Holland, 1981).

These examples illustrate the uses of a posteriori inspection of discrepant items. It is an aid in identifying content invalidities and ambiguities in test instructions and format. In addition, it can serve as a diagnostic tool for identifying weaknesses and strengths in the backgrounds of individuals from diverse groups, including gaps in the acquisition of basic concepts, test naiveté, and sometimes linguistic advantages. Perhaps it is at the item level of analysis that controversies over the effects of bilingualism can be resolved. The foregoing examples illustrate both positive and negative effects of Spanish-English bilingualism. Possibly, some of the answers to questions concerning the benefits of bilingualism depend on the specific kinds of items sampled by a given task.

Hence, a posteriori analyses are particularly valuable in many respects and quite challenging. Scheuneman (1982) gives several important guidelines about a posteriori procedures. A key factor is having a large pool of items grouped by specific types to detect trends: "If the tests analyzed contain 50 to 75 items, which are typical test lengths, . . . the chance of a sufficient number of items being presented to detect the pattern is considerably reduced. . . . Other differences can best be understood by contrasting items with high or low bias indices or items that appear to be biased in opposite directions" (pp. 193–194).

Future Research on Item Discrepancy

Item-discrepancy research is a relatively new approach to the study of bias; the bulk of studies have been published in the last ten years. Consequently, the information that we have at this time is far from complete. Very few studies have included samples of Hispanics when contrasting the item performance of ethnic groups. For example, out of sixteen studies at the ETS of item discrepancy across ethnic groups reported by Carlton & Marco (1982) only two included U.S. Hispanics. Furthermore, the majority of analyses of Hispanic-Anglo differences have used TID methods, which are inferior to the ICC-3 techniques. There is a great need for more research on item discrepancy involving Hispanic samples. College aptitude tests have less predictive validity for Hispanics than for whites (see Durán's article), and the search for the causes of this difference must include careful statistical and judgmental analyses of item content.

Where feasible, the statistical techniques used in future studies should be based on the ICC-3 model; these methods have the best record so far in identifying discrepancy in simulated test-item data. Unfortunately, these methods have many practical limitations, particularly when samples are small. In cases where it is not feasible to use the ICC-3 model, chi-square methods are a better alternative than TID techniques. However, there are some situations where even chi-square methods will not be appropriate if marginal frequencies are skewed. Therefore, the search for a simpler, more robust, and less expensive small-sample statistical technique for detecting item discrepancy must go on. The ideal method should have the following additional features: sensitivity to group-by-ability-level interactions; a scale-free index that measures the degree of item discrepancy independently of sample size; ease in incorporating multiple variables; and the capacity to confirm a priori predictions of discrepancy. Wainer believes that such a tall order can only be filled with Bayesian estimation methods applied to latent-trait theory (H. Wainer, personal communication, November 1983). Contingency-table methods also seem promising and would be less expensive.

A flaw that has been common to most applications of item-discrepancy techniques has been the use of total score as the measure for ability. These procedures can identify only the relative discrepancy of items; they cannot detect a pervasive bias in the test. Therefore, future research attempting to link item content to group differences in predictive validity or regression-line intercepts should incorporate ability criteria that are external to the test, such as grade-point average. In this manner, particular items may be identified that are causing the differential predictive results. However, the use of grade-point average may present some additional methodological problems. Even if all students' grades could be assumed to be on the same scale, some assumptions (e.g., unidimensionality) of the current statistical methods could be violated.

Once a highly valid procedure (or combination of methods) is developed, work should proceed to identify the characteristics of discrepant items that lead to real biases, that is, content or format features unrelated to the trait being measured. This approach will entail a breakdown by test characteristics and by subject variables. Critical subject characteristics to be included are age in relation to grade, oral proficiency and literacy in Spanish and English, country of origin, and geographical residence. Often Hispanics are older than majority students in their own grade. If sampling was done by age (as in the National Assessment of Educational Progress), then the source of item discrepancies might simply be due to a difference in grade level because the Hispanic children were one or two grades behind their age cohorts. Owing to the diversity of Hispanic subgroups, one cannot assume that the results for Chicanos, island Puerto Ricans, continental Puerto Ricans, Cubans, and other Hispanics will have similar patterns.

The work of Nielsen and Fernández (1981) suggests that Puerto Ricans and Chicanos have very similar covariance structures relating background variables to test scores but that Cubans diverge from that pattern. More research of this nature needs to be done, for it is desirable to identify the conditions under which groups can be merged in order to enhance the sample size and increase the sensitivity (statistical power) to test critical hypotheses. It would be desirable also to identify which variables can best account for subgroup differences in test-item performance. For example, literacy in Spanish may be one critical variable that distinguishes Cubans from other Hispanics. If literacy in Spanish facilitates learning the formal Latin-origin terms in English, one would expect Cubans and island Puerto Ricans (who are more often taught to read in Spanish), to have an advantage over other groups in vocabulary items containing these words. The identification of such variables can help to uncover the causes and sources of group differences, rather than merely flagging the group differences that may exist.

The features of items that lead to group differences must also be systematically identified. Schmeiser (1982) suggests that the characteristics of items be varied experimentally in order to see if one can produce or eliminate sources of bias in reproducible ways. These procedures would enable us to verify hypotheses derived from a posteriori analyses and to develop general principles about sources of item bias. Such a framework would be useful to test development specialists who supervise the writing and editing of test items. Multivariate, confirmatory statistical methods will be necessary to evaluate these theories of bias. The methodology of judgmental procedures also needs further study. Currently, reviewers of test items often disagree with each other in their evaluations of bias and with statistical indexes of bias. Some of these problems may be due to the presence of more than one dimension; instead of one overall rating of bias, there should be separate ratings for distinct aspects of the item.

Not all of the unresolved issues are methodological, however. How discrepant must an item be before it is flagged for inspection? By what criteria should we judge whether the content of a discrepant item is related to the trait being measured and is, therefore, "fair"? Questions of this sort cannot be settled by psychometric research alone, because they involve values. A societal consensus is required. The inescapable fact is that fairness in all aspects of testing is ultimately a question of values.

SUMMARY

The objective of this paper was to identify directions for substantive and methodological research on test-content issues for Hispanics. Obviously, the gaps are many. Very little has been done to investigate within the context of an English environment the high-quality aptitude tests in Spanish developed by the College Board and ETS for use in Puerto Rico. Item-discrepancy research on Hispanics has usually employed statistical techniques that are less than optimal; these studies, therefore, are of questionable value. In fact, much empirical work on item discrepancies should probably be redone, especially the studies on subjective ratings, because better methods are available now. The value of research on test content with Hispanics extends beyond its relevance to test fairness. There are many interesting questions about bilingualism, aptitude, and achievement that can be addressed. With the Spanish-language aptitude tests we could investigate cross-language validity, that is, how well abilities measured in one language can predict achievement in the context of another language. Examples have been found of discrepant test items where bilingualism created an advantage, and others where it created a disadvantage. Perhaps some of the controversies that abound in the research on bilingualism and aptitudes can be resolved by analyzing item discrepancies.

An experimental approach to the proposed research has been advocated. Cross-language validity studies should systematically vary the language that is dominant in examinees, the language of the test, and the language of instruction. Item-discrepancy research should vary the features of item content and format to see which ones lead to bias in reproducible ways. Many subject variables, such as language proficiency and country of origin, need to be included in order to identify the sources of group differences.

Some methodological problems have been solved, but others remain. Empirical Bayes estimation methods have made small-sample validity research more feasible. On the other hand, the lack of enrollment records of island Puerto Ricans at continental U.S. universities impedes the study of the tests developed in Puerto Rico. The soundest methods for detecting item discrepancy are indexes based on the three-parameter item-characteristic curve model; unfortunately, they have many practical limitations. Much research still needs to be done to evaluate alternative techniques. Current methods cannot detect a pervasive bias in a test if total score is used to measure ability level and no external criteria are included.

We are still very far from having a theory that can predict reliably what items on a test will be discrepant. Subjective ratings and indexes of item discrepancy have often failed to agree. Ideally, we would want to be able to explain why items show discrepancies. However, when there is high agreement among judges that an item is biased, these ratings have value even if the item shows no statistical discrepancies. The face validity of an item is important for the morale and cooperation of examinees, even if it does not demonstrably affect the test performance of individuals. Unfortunately, some studies have shown poor interrater agreement on judgments of bias. The generalizability of judges' responses to those of test takers is, therefore, questionable. Perhaps the main conclusion that we can draw from research thus far is that the study of bias in item content is extremely complex. Future research should focus on the survey of values concerning fairness in addition to the improvement of statistical techniques.

NOTE

1. This example was cited by Dr. Haydee Montenegro González at the meeting of the Association for Puerto Rican Scientists and Engineers, Bethesda,

MD, April 1981. She was able to correctly identify the child as normal when he was referred to her for psychological evaluation.

REFERENCES

Alderman, D. L. (1981). *Language proficiency as a moderator variable in testing academic aptitude.* TOEFL Research Report 10. Princeton, NJ: Educational Testing Service.

Alderman, D. L., & Holland, P. W. (1981). *Item performance across native language groups on the Test of English as a Foreign Language.* TOEFL Research Report 9. Princeton, NJ: Educational Testing Service.

Anastasi, A. (1982). *Psychological testing.* New York: Macmillan.

Angoff, W. H. (1982). Use of difficulty and discrimination indices for detecting item bias. In R. A. Berk (Ed.), *Handbook of methods for detecting test bias* (pp. 96–116). Baltimore, MD: Johns Hopkins University Press.

Béjar, I. I. (1981). *Subject matter experts' assessment of item statistics.* Research Report 81–47. Princeton, NJ: Educational Testing Service.

Berk, R. A. (1982). *Handbook of methods for detecting test bias.* Baltimore, MD: Johns Hopkins University Press.

Boldt, R. F. (1969). *Concurrent validity of the PAA and SAT for bilingual Dade County high school volunteers.* Statistical Report 69–31. Princeton, NJ: Educational Testing Service.

Breland, H. M., Stocking, M., Pinchak, B. M., & Abrams, N. (1974). *The cross-cultural stability of mental test items: An investigation of response patterns for ten sociocultural groups.* Project Report 74-2. Princeton, NJ: Educational Testing Service.

Burrill, L. E. (1982). Comparative studies of item bias methods. In R. A. Berk (Ed.), *Handbook of methods for detecting test bias* (pp. 161–179). Baltimore, MD: Johns Hopkins University Press.

Camilli, G. (1979). A critique of the chi-square method for assessing item bias. Unpublished paper, Laboratory of Educational Research, University of Colorado, Boulder.

Carlton, S. T., & Marco, G. L. (1982). Methods used by test publishers to "debias" standardized tests: Educational Testing Service. In R. A. Berk (Ed.), *Handbook of methods for detecting test bias* (pp. 278–313). Baltimore, MD: Johns Hopkins University Press.

Coffman, W. E. (1982). Methods used by test publishers to "debias" standardized tests: Riverside Publishing Company/Houghton Mifflin. In R. A. Berk (Ed.), *Handbook of methods for selecting bias.* (pp. 240–255). Baltimore, MD: Johns Hopkins University Press.

Doolittle, A. E. *The reliability of measuring differential item performance.* Paper presented at the annual meeting of the American Educational Research Association, Montreal, April 1983.

Dorans, N. J. (1982). *Technical review of SAT item fairness studies: 1975-1979.* Unpublished Statistical Report 82-90. Princeton, NJ: Educational Testing Service.

Dorans, N. J. & Kulick, E. (1983). *Assessing unexpected differential item performance of female candidates on the December 1977 administration of the SAT and TSWE.* Research Report RR 83-9. Princeton, NJ: Educational Testing Service.

Durán, R. P. (1983). *Hispanics' education and background: Predictors of college achievement.* Princeton, NJ: Educational Testing Service.

Flaugher, R. L. (1970). *Testing practices, minority groups, and higher education: A review and discussion of the research.* Research Bulletin 70-41. Princeton, NJ: Educational Testing Service.

Handrick, F. A., & Loyd, B. H. (1982). Methods used by publishers to "debias" standardized tests: The American College Testing Program. In R. A. Berk (Ed.), *Handbook of methods for selecting bias* (pp. 272–278). Baltimore, MD: Johns Hopkins University Press.

Hildebrand, D. K., Laing, J. D., & Rosenthal, H. (1977). *Prediction analysis of cross-classifications.* New York: Wiley.

Hunter, J. E. (1975, December). *A critical analysis of the use of item means and item-test correlations to determine the presence or absence of content bias in achievement test items.* Paper presented at the National Institute of Education Conference on Test Bias, Maryland.

Intasuwan, P. A. (1979). A comparison of three approaches for determining item bias in cross-national testing. Doctoral dissertation, University of Pittsburgh, 1979. *Dissertation Abstracts International, 40,* 2613A. (University Microfilms No. 79–24, 720.)

Ironson, G. H. (1982). The use of chi-square and latent trait approaches for detecting item bias. In R. A. Berk (Ed.), *Handbook of methods for detecting test bias* (pp. 117–160). Baltimore, MD: Johns Hopkins University Press.

Ironson, G. H. & Subkoviak, M. (1979). A comparison of several methods of assessing item bias. *Journal of Educational Measurement, 16,* 209–225.

Jensen, A. R. (1980). *Bias in mental testing.* New York: Free Press.

Linn, R. L., & Harnisch, D. C. (1981). Interaction between item content and group membership on achievement test items. *Journal of Educational Measurement, 18,* 109–118.

Lord, F. M. (1977). A study of item bias using item characteristic curve theory. In N. H. Poortinga (Ed.), *Basic problems in cross-cultural psychology* (pp. 19–29). Amsterdam: Swits & Vitlinger.

Loyd, B. H. (1980, April). *An investigation of differential item performance by Anglo and Hispanic pupils.* Paper presented at the annual meeting of the American Educational Research Association, Boston.

Loyd, B. H. (1982, March). *Analysis of content-related item bias for Anglo and Hispanic students.* Paper presented at the annual meeting of the American Educational Research Association, New York.

Marascuilo, L. A., & Slaughter, R. E. (1981). Statistical procedures for identifying possible sources of item bias based on χ^2 statistics. *Journal of Educational Measurement, 18,* 229–248.

Mellenbergh, G. J. (1982). Contingency table models for assessing item bias. *Journal of Educational Statistics, 7,* 105–118.

Merz, W. R., & Grossen N. (1979, April). *An empirical investigation of six methods for examining test item bias.* Paper presented at the annual meeting of the National Council on Measurement in Education, San Francisco. (Final report submitted to the National Institute of Education, Grant NIE-G-78-0067, California State University, Sacramento, 1979.) (ERIC Document Reproduction Service No. ED 164 610.)

Murray, A. M., & Mishra, S. (1983). Judgment of item bias in the McCarthy Scales of Children's Abilities. *Hispanic Journal of Behavioral Sciences, 5,* 325–336.

Nielsen, F., & Fernández, R. M. (1981). *Hispanic students in American high schools: Background characteristics and achievement.* Report submitted to the National Center for Education Statistics, Contract OE-300-78-0208, National Opinion Research Center, Chicago.

Nielsen, F., & Lerner, S. J. (1982, October). *Language skills and school achievement of bilingual Hispanics.* Manuscript submitted for publication.

Nungester, R. J. (1977). An empirical examination of the models of item bias. Doctoral dissertation, Florida State University, 1977. *Dissertation Abstracts International, 38,* 2726A. (University Microfilms No. 77-24, 289.)

Olmedo, E. L. (1977). Psychological testing and the Chicano: A reassessment. In J. L. Martínez, Jr. (Ed.), *Chicano psychology* (pp. 175–195). New York: Academic Press.

Parents in Action on Special Education (PASE) et al. v. Joseph P. Hannon, General Superintendent of Schools in Chicago et al., No. 74C3586 (N.D., Ill., July 7, 1980).

Pennock-Román, M. (1984, April). *Confirming a priori hypotheses of item bias using the del statistic.* Paper presented at the annual meeting of the American Educational Research Association, New Orleans.

Plake, B. S. (1980). A comparison of a statistical and subjective procedure to ascertain item validity: One step in the test validation process. *Educational and Psychological Measurement, 40,* 397–404.

Raju, N. S. (1982). Methods used by test publishers to "debias" standardized tests: Science Research Associates. In R. A. Berk (Ed.), *Handbook of methods for selecting bias* (pp. 261–272). Baltimore, MD: Johns Hopkins University Press.

Rubin, D. B. (1980). Using empirical Bayes techniques in the law school validity studies. *The Journal of the American Statistical Association, 75* (372), 801–827.

Rudner, L. M., & Convey, J. J. (1978, March). *An evaluation of select approaches for biased item identification.* Paper presented at the annual meeting of the American Educational Research Association, Toronto. (ERIC Document Reproduction Service No. ED 157 942.)

Rudner, L. M., Getson, P. R., & Knight, D. L. (1980a). A Monte Carlo comparison of seven biased item detection techniques. *Journal of Educational Measurement, 17.*

Rudner, L. M., Getson, P. R., & Knight, D. L. (1980b). Biased item detection techniques. *Journal of Educational Statistics, 5,* 213–233.

Samuda, R. J. (1975). *Psychological testing of American minorities: Issues and consequences.* New York: Harper & Row.

Sánchez, G. I. (1932a). Group differences and Spanish-speaking children: A critical review. *Journal of Applied Psychology, 16,* 549–558.

Sánchez, G. I. (1932b). Scores of Spanish-speaking children on repeated tests. *Journal of Genetic Psychology, 40,* 223–231.

Sánchez, G. I. (1934a). Bilingualism and mental measures: A word of caution. *Journal of Applied Psychology, 18,* 765–772.

Sánchez, G. I. (1934b). The implications of a basal vocabulary for the measurement of the abilities of bilingual children. *Journal of Social Psychology, 5,* 395–402.

Sandoval, J. (1979). The WISC-R and internal evidence of test bias with minority groups. *Journal of Consulting and Clinical Psychology, 47,* 919–927.

Sandoval, J., & Miille, M. P. W. (1980). Accuracy of judgments of WISC-R item difficulty for minority groups. *Journal of Consulting and Clinical Psychology,* 1980, *48,* 249–253.

Scheuneman, J. D. (1979). A method of assessing bias in test items. *Journal of Educational Measurement, 16,* 143–152.

Scheuneman, J. D. (1982). A posteriori analyses of biased items. In R. A. Berk (Ed.), *Handbook of methods for detecting test bias.* (pp. 180–198). Baltimore, MD: Johns Hopkins University Press.

Schmeiser, C. B. (1982). Use of experimental design in statistical item bias studies. In R. A. Berk (Ed.), *Handbook of methods for detecting test bias* (pp. 64–95). Baltimore, MD: Johns Hopkins University Press.

Shepard, L. A. Definitions of bias (1982). In R. A. Berk (Ed.), *Handbook of methods for detecting test bias* (pp. 9–30). Baltimore, MD: Johns Hopkins University Press.

Shepard, L., Calmilli, G., & Averill, M. (1981). Comparison of procedures for detecting test-item bias with both internal and external ability criteria. *Journal of Educational Statistics, 6,* 317–375.

Sinnott, L. T. (1980). *Differences in item performance across groups.* Research Report 80-19. Princeton, NJ: Educational Testing Service.

Stricker, L. J. (1981). *A new index of differential subgroup performance: Application to the GRE aptitude test.* Research Report 81-13. Princeton, NJ: Educational Testing Service.

Stricker, L. J. (1982). Identifying test items that perform differentially in population subgroups: A partial correlation index. *Applied Psychological Measurement, 6,* 261–273.

Tittle, C. K. (1982). Use of judgmental methods in item bias studies. In R. A. Berk (Ed.), *Handbook of methods for detecting test bias* (pp. 31–63). Baltimore, MD: Johns Hopkins University Press.

Watkins, M. P. (1983, April). *An application of the del statistic to detect differential item performance on the Test of English as a Foreign Language.* Paper presented at the annual meeting of the American Educational Research Association, Montreal.

8 | Prediction of Hispanics' College Achievement

RICHARD P. DURÁN

This article examines issues and trends of research findings regarding prediction of Hispanics' undergraduate college achievement in selective colleges, and it also suggests directions for improvement in existing approaches. The first portion of the article focuses on the use of high school grades and college admissions test scores to predict early college grades in selective college institutions. Basic assumptions underlying use of measures are discussed, as are characteristics of Hispanics' performance on measures. The emphasis of the first part of the article is on the question of population validity in the prediction of grades for nonminority college students versus Hispanic college students. The main issue is whether existing research evidence using correlation methods or regression methods shows us that we can predict college grades in a similar manner and to a similar level of accuracy for both nonminority and Hispanic populations. No attempt is made to discuss technical details of procedures, nor is there any attempt to describe alternative statistical frameworks other than the procedures described.

The weight of current research findings suggests that high school grades and admissions test scores do not do as good a job at predicting Hispanics' college grades as they do for nonminority students. This conclusion, however, does not invalidate the use of high school grades and admissions test scores for Hispanics; it does suggest that we need to understand how differences between Hispanic and nonminority students should affect the interpretation of admissions information and also how our conception of different measures of college aptitude and college achievement affects the ability to predict success in college for Hispanics. The implication for admissions policy is that college admis-

---

This report is based on research supported by the College Board. Researchers are encouraged to express freely their professional judgment in the conduct of such projects; therefore points of view or opinions stated do not necessarily represent official College Board positions or policy.

sions staff need to be very cautious in interpreting Hispanics' admissions profiles. High school grades and admissions test scores have their place in evaluating Hispanics' preparation for college, but they should be examined critically, with due weight given to other factors that may affect their interpretation.

The second part of this paper is devoted to discussion of a broader conceptual framework for improving prediction of Hispanics' college success, and this will entail development of additional indicators of college ability and college success. This broader framework also includes identification of interventions that might benefit Hispanics' chances for success in college. Ideally, a broader framework would help admissions staff in applying more critical judgment to the value of high school grades and admissions tests in making admissions decisions regarding Hispanics. In addition, a broader framework would permit institutions to investigate empirically what sorts of additional information about Hispanics and about institutions can help predict Hispanics' success in their local college context and how interventions might affect Hispanics' college success.

PREDICTIVE VALIDITY STUDIES

Predictors of College Achievement

Not all college institutions are alike. Colleges vary in the importance they place on candidates' previous academic achievement and college aptitude test scores. Almost all selective four-year institutions rely heavily on high school grades or rank in high school class and college aptitude test scores as primary evidence of candidates' preparation for the academic demands of college.

Among admissions staff, the importance of high school grade-point average or rank in high school class is weighed judgmentally in terms of students' areas of study in high school, and sometimes by the academic reputation of a high school. High school grade-point average and rank in high school class based on grades have the advantage that they are numerical measures and, as such, embody objective quantitative characteristics that should be interpreted in the same manner by different persons. High school grade-point average and rank in high school class also have a cumulative and representatively stable character; they reflect a history of academic achievement rather than just a one-shot evaluation of academic skills.

High school grade-point average and rank in high school class as predictors of college aptitude also have some limitations, and these limitations are of special significance to minority populations such as Hispanics. Achievement information alone, based on high school grades or rank in high school class, is incapable of indicating whether students' performance has been moderated by the quality of schooling and students' opportunity to learn in classroom settings. Such information is also incapable of capturing personal and background characteristics of students that influence opportunity to learn, given the characteristics and resources of a school. Thus, if we wish to be sensitive to factors moderating students' achievement in high school, we must go beyond simple numerical measures of high school achievement.

Research findings from the National Longitudinal Study of the High School Class of 1972 suggest that Hispanics overall are not achieving at the same level in high school as are non-Hispanics (U.S. Department of Education, 1980). Figure 8.1, for example, indicates that His-

Figure 8.1: Academic Achievement of High School Seniors

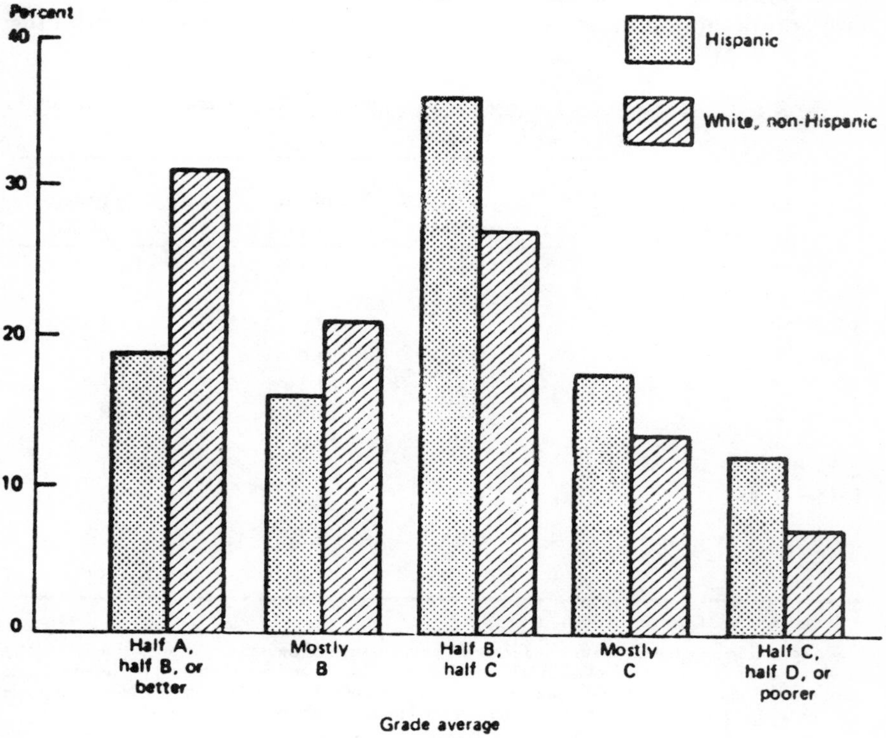

SOURCE: Brown et al. (1980).

panics tended to earn lower grades in high school than did non-Hispanic white students. A similar but less dramatic pattern of grade differences also obtains for Hispanic and non-Hispanic white students who aspired to go to college and who took the Scholastic Aptitude Test. Table 8.1, based on the report *Profiles: College-Bound Seniors, 1983* (Ramist & Arbeiter, 1984), indicates a small difference in the high school grade-point average of whites versus Mexican Americans and Puerto Ricans residing in the fifty states and the District of Columbia. Closer inspection of table 8.1, however, reveals that a noticeable difference occurs in the proportion of whites versus Hispanics who earn a grade-point average of 3.0 and above; about 60 percent of whites earned a grade-point average of 3.0 or better as compared to about 55 percent of Mexican Americans and about 47 percent of Puerto Ricans. Such differences, when examined more closely for the proportion of persons in the highest grade-point average categories above 3.0, imply that Hispanics are less likely than whites to meet high school grade standards for admission among highly selective college institutions.

As mentioned previously, areas of high school study are an important adjunct to evaluating high school grades. Table 8.2, taken from the

Table 8.1:   Self-Reported High School Grade Averages of Hispanic and White SAT Test Takers in 1982–83

Overall High School Grade Average[a]	Percent Mexican Americans	Percent Puerto Ricans[b]	Percent Whites (non-Hispanics)
3.75–4.00	12.1	8.1	16.5
3.50–3.74	11.2	8.9	12.4
3.25–3.49	13.2	10.9	13.4
3.00–3.24	18.1	18.8	17.6
2.75–2.99	13.2	14.1	12.1
2.50–2.74	13.1	15.3	11.9
2.25–2.49	9.0	10.6	7.6
2.00–2.24	6.1	7.7	5.4
Under 2.00	4.1	6.1	3.2
Mean GPA by group	3.01	2.89	3.09
N	15,496	7,959	701,345

SOURCE: Ramist & Arbeiter (1984).

[a] Calculated by weighting the latest self-reported grade in each of the six subject areas (English, Mathematics, Foreign Languages, Biological Sciences, Physical Sciences, and Social Studies) by the number of years of study in the subject and dividing by the total number of years of study in all six subjects. If a grade was not reported in a subject, that subject was not used in the calculation of overall grade average.

[b] Puerto Ricans in the 50 states and District of Columbia only.

College Board data for 1982–83 (Ramist and Arbeiter, 1984), summarizes difference in high school areas of study for Mexican Americans, Puerto Ricans, and whites. As the table shows, Hispanic SAT test takers in 1982–83 were almost 15 percent less likely than white test takers to have been enrolled in college-preparatory programs during high school. Almost 80 percent of whites had such a background versus about 65 to 67 percent of Hispanics. Particularly important is the length of prior study of English and mathematics; 94 percent of whites have studied English for four or more years, while about 88 percent of Mexican Americans have studied this much English. Ninety percent of Puerto Ricans have studied four or more years of English, but this figure probably also reflects Puerto Ricans' exposure to English-as-a-second-language training among Puerto Rican test takers who have had some schooling in Puerto Rico. Moreover, with regard to length of mathematics study, 65 percent of whites have studied mathematics for four or more years as compared to a little over 50 percent of Hispanics. The data suggest that Hispanics show nearly a 15 percent disadvantage in mathematics experience in comparison to whites.

A level of four years or more of English and mathematics study is

Table 8.2:   Areas of High School Study, 1982–83 College Board Data on SAT Test Takers

	Mexican Americans	Puerto Ricans [a]	White Non-Hispanics
Percentage enrolled in academic or college preparatory programs	67.3	65.2	79.9
Percentage with four years or more of English	88.3	90.4	94.0
Percentage with four years or more of mathematics	53.5	50.1	65.3
Average number of years of foreign language	1.99	2.36	2.27
Average number of years of biological sciences	1.31	1.38	1.39
Average number of years of physical sciences	1.50	1.64	1.87
Average number of years of social studies	3.06	3.15	3.24

SOURCE: Ramist & Arbeiter (1984).
[a] Puerto Ricans in the 50 states and District of Columbia only.

used for the foregoing comparisons for a good reason. Students who are candidates for the most selective colleges are likely to show a more intensive background in English and mathematics than are other college candidates. English and mathematics study are often assumed to be the most important and most generalizable areas of high school study; they are more likely to be studied sequentially over a longer period of years, and they also emphasize training in academic skills that are required across a wide range of academic study areas in college.

Table 8.2 also shows data on the average number of years of study spent by students in foreign languages, biological sciences, physical sciences, and social studies. The average length of study in these areas tends to be just a little longer for whites than for Hispanics. The data of table 8.2 do not convey to us differences in the academic track of students; these data do not reveal whether Hispanics and whites have received the same quality and intensity of instruction in the areas indicated.

The high school data also indicate that Hispanics who take the SAT tend to show lower high school grades and less intensive academic study in core areas related to college work than do whites. From the point of view of college admissions staff evaluating high school credentials, Hispanic college candidates for selective institutions tend to show lower college qualifications than nonminority college candidates.

Longitudinal educational survey research suggests that high school experiences and background of Hispanics can differ from the experiences and background of nonminority students. It may be that such differences are allied not only with evidence of lower high school academic achievement among Hispanics versus white non-Hispanics but also with more inaccuracy in use of such information for prediction of college achievement for Hispanics than for whites. Consider, for example, figure 8.2, drawn from data from the National Longitudinal Study of the High School class of 1972 (Brown, Rosen, and Olivas, 1980). The figure reports differences between Hispanic students' replies to survey questions concerning various factors that interfere with their high school work. Both Hispanics and whites reported in significant numbers that "money worries," "family obligations," "poor place to study," and "parents' disinterest" were impediments to high school work. Hispanics, however, were 15 to 20 percent more likely than whites to respond that the factors cited were a detriment to high school work. Whether or not similar data would obtain for Hispanics and nonminority students planning attendance at selective college institutions is an open question meriting further investigation based on the 1972 NLS educational survey data base or perhaps based on the more recent High School and Beyond longitudinal data base. There is the possibility, then, that Hispanics' high

Figure 8.2: Factors Interfering with School Work of High School Seniors

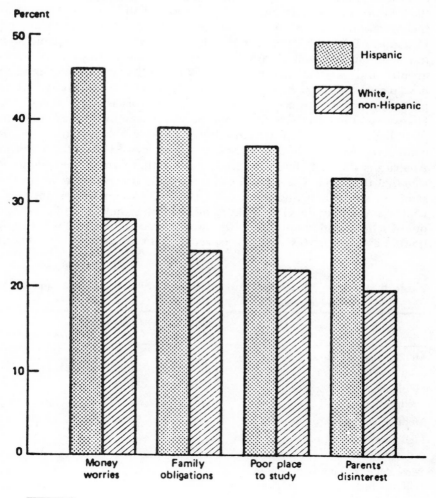

Source: Brown et al. (1980).

school achievement may show more variation than would be expected because of the effects of home and family obligations and concerns.

College Board data (Ramist and Arbeiter, 1984) from 1982–83 suggest that there are both similarities and differences in the nonacademic characteristics of Hispanic and white non-Hispanic test takers. In considering such similarities and differences, it is essential to note that the populations represented are not representative of high school students as a whole. This is particularly so for Hispanics, since Hispanics who take the SAT are a very select and small subsample of all Hispanics because of the operation of factors that inhibit receipt of a quality education among Hispanics. Table 8.3 compares Hispanics and white non-Hispanic SAT test takers in 1982–83 on answers to several survey questions of background and personal characteristics. White college candidates tend to have parents with more education than Hispanics. On the average, white parents demonstrate access to college, while this is not the case for Hispanics—the latter showing averages influenced by a failure to complete high school. White parents show a considerable advantage in income level, $31,200, in comparison to Hispanics—$19,600 for Mexican Americans and $14,700 for Puerto Ricans. Other data in the table indicate that the family sizes of white and Hispanic students were about the same for students taking the SAT in 1982–83. About 10 percent more white than Hispanic SAT test takers indicated that they worked part time out of school, and among those who worked, about an equal number of hours was spent in this endeavor (seven to eight hours per week). About

Table 8.3: College Board Background Data on 1982–83 Hispanic and White Non-Hispanic SAT Test Takers

	Mexican Americans	Puerto Ricans[a]	White Non-Hispanics
Median years of father's education	12.0	12.0	14.3
Median years of mother's education	11.8	11.9	13.5
Median parental income	19,600	14,700	31,200
Median number of parent dependents	4.8	4.3	4.3
Percentage working part time in high school	52.7	52.6	62.6
Mean number of part-time work hours outside of school	7.3	7.4	7.8
Percentage planning to request financial aid for college	87.7	89.7	73.5
Percentage indicating English is not their best language	7.4	9.7	1.8

SOURCE: Ramist & Arbeiter (1984).
[a] Puerto Ricans in the 50 states and District of Columbia only.

15 percent more Hispanics than whites indicated that they planned to ask for financial aid to attend college; from 88 to 90 percent of Hispanics had such plans, as opposed to 74 percent of whites. All told, the figures cited indicate clearly that 1982–83 Hispanic test takers were not as economically able as whites to plan pursuit of a college education.

Hispanics in 1982–83 were more likely than whites to answer no to the question "Is English your best language?" Almost 10 percent of Puerto Ricans and a little over 7 percent of Mexican Americans answered this question no. These figures compare to a no answer for under 2 percent of white examinees. The figures suggest that a small but significant proportion of Hispanic test takers face the prospect of college education in their less familiar language—English. It is possible, however, that many subtle and important features of English-language familiarity are not reflected in the language question cited. Sociolinguistic research I reviewed (Durán, 1983) indicated that some Hispanics could maintain that they were more familiar with English than Spanish and still manifest limited familiarity with English occurring in academic settings. Limited familiarity with English in academic settings could be manifested not only in lack of familiarity with academic vocabulary, reading skills, and written usage but also in oral comprehension and speaking skills required in academic settings. Research indicates that Hispanics' school achievement may be limited both by students' English familiarity and, just as significantly, by the negative attitudes and negative attributions of teachers toward Hispanic students in academic interactions (Durán, 1983; Buriel, 1983). Hispanic students' academic preparation for college may be limited in a number of ways by lack of compatibility between students' language background and the language environment of high school (and later on, college). Some Hispanic students may be quite resourceful in overcoming such incompatibilities, while others may not be so resourceful. The resulting variation in this accommodation could affect the interpretation of high school grades (and also test scores) as predictors of college achievement.

A hypothesis to be drawn from reviewing Hispanics' high school achievement in relation to their background is that Hispanics' high school grades and areas of study may not be as valid measures of college preparation as are those of white non-Hispanics. Overall, Hispanics' patterns of achievement and areas of study indicate that they are less prepared for study in highly selective colleges than white non-Hispanics. In addition, however, there is evidence to suggest that background heterogeneity and heterogeneity in high school experiences among Hispanics may lead to variation in the usefulness of high school achievement measures as predictors of college achievement.

College Admissions Test Scores

Two college aptitude tests are used widely in admissions to selective institutions: the American College Testing Program (1980) college admissions test (ACT) and the College Board Scholastic Aptitude Test. While the tests differ in terms of their structure and the scores they report, they both are described as tests of developed academic abilities needed for college. College admissions test scores, like high school grade-point average, have an advantage in being numerical. Presumably, the same numerical value of a test score for a given candidate should signify the same level of college potential for admissions staff at different colleges with similar academic standards. Since the ACT and SAT are administered nationally, scores on each of these tests ought to be comparable across all candidates taking the same test. Numerical comparison is much less tenable with high school grades, since the quality of high schools, the difficulty of study areas, and the grading standards applied may differ from student to student. Just like high school grade-point average, college admissions test scores have inherent limits. They are incapable of indicating how much they are influenced by background and schooling factors that spuriously affect test performance. These limitations will be discussed later.

Table 8.4 displays mean ACT test scores in 1978–79 for a large sample of self-identified Mexican American/Chicano students, Puerto

Table 8.4:   Mean ACT Scores and Standard Deviations in 1978-79 for Representative Samples of Hispanic and Caucasian American/White Students

Group	ACT Subtest				
	English	Mathematics	Social Studies	Natural Sciences	Composite
Mexican American/Chicano students—sample: $N = 931$	14.1 (5.2)	12.6 (6.7)	12.5 (6.5)	16.6 (5.9)	14.1 (5.2)
Puerto Rican/Spanish-speaking American students—sample: $N = 190$	14.5 (5.6)	13.7 (7.3)	14.0 (7.2)	17.5 (6.2)	15.1 (5.8)
Caucasian American/white students—sample: $N = 34,172$	19.1 (4.9)	19.0 (7.3)	18.7 (6.9)	22.4 (6.0)	19.9 (5.4)

SOURCE: American College Testing Program (1980, pp. 90-91, 93). Reprinted by permission of the publisher.

NOTE: Sample sizes given arise from a 10 percent random sampling of the full population of examinees in 1978–1979 who enrolled in college as freshmen 1979. Parentheses enclose standard deviations.

Rican/Spanish-speaking American students, and Caucasian American/ white students. (The ethnic category labels given are the same as those used by the American College Testing Program.) Average standardized scores for each group are shown for each four subtest areas and also for a composite score across areas. Scores on all subtests and the composite score have a range from a low of 1 to a high of 36. The entries in parentheses beneath scores are the standard deviations of the scores. Examination of table 8.4 reveals that both Hispanic subgroups scored about one standard deviation below Caucasion American/white students in all subscore areas. Puerto Rican/other Spanish-speaking students scored slightly higher than Mexican American/Chicano students in all subtest areas and on the composite score.

Table 8.5 displays SAT verbal and mathematics test scores in 1982– 83 for self-identified Mexican Americans, Puerto Ricans, and whites.[1] Standardized scores on each section vary between 200 and 800. Standard deviations of scores for each group and subscore are indicated in parentheses. The data in table 8.5 indicate that white non-Hispanics scored about three-quarters of one standard deviation higher than Mexican Americans and Puerto Ricans. Mexican Americans scored slightly higher than Puerto Ricans on both verbal and mathematics subscores. Taken at face value, the ACT and SAT test data cited suggest that Hispanics seeking enrollment in selective colleges show less college aptitude than white non-Hispanic college candidates. Questions of construct and content validity aside, the pattern of differences between Hispanics and whites on test scores is consistent with the interpretation of differences

Table 8.5: Mean Scholastic Aptitude Test Scores 1982–83 for Hispanics and Whites (Non-Hispanics)

Group	Verbal	Mathematics
Mexican Americans	375 (S = 100)[a] (N = 15,315)	417 (S = 105) (N = 15,314)
Puerto Ricans[b]	365 (S = 107) (N = 7,479)	397 (S = 108) (N = 7,479)
Whites	443 (S = 102) (N = 685,219)	484 (S = 114) (N = 684,957)

SOURCE: Ramist & Arbeiter (1984).

[a] Standard deviations (S) are given in parentheses along with sample sizes (N).
[b] Puerto Ricans in the 50 states and District of Columbia only.

reported earlier concerning high school grades and years of study in important academic study areas.

As with measures of high school achievement, one may raise questions about the usefulness of admissions test scores as predictors of Hispanics' college achievement. Admissions test scores result from isolated encounters with a test. Test scores thus do not have a cumulative history of repeated assessment over high school years as is the case with high school grade-point average. Since tests are encountered only in isolated situations, they are subject to all the personal and situational factors that limit the reliability of assessment for any variable measured on a single occasion or on just very infrequent occasions.

The instructions for taking a test and the elementary content of test items ought to be equally intelligible to all examinees, regardless of background. A further concern is that the speed or pace of an admissions test is not excessive across populations, so that ability to answer items is not affected by "racing" or inability to reach an item. Limitations in interpreting test scores for a population may result when we are not confident that test items are measuring exactly and only those skills they are supposed to assess for that population (Osterlind, 1983).

A review of the foregoing question suggests that some Hispanics' admissions test behavior may be influenced by familiarity with academic English, personality factors, and speededness (Durán, 1983). The extent and intensity of such influences are not well understood or documented at this point. Results across studies vary. There is a fair amount of evidence that, by and large, SAT admissions test items measure the same abilities across Hispanic and nonminority populations, although language familiarity and speededness can affect this interpretation. The results thus far seem clearest for the language-familiarity question. Alderman's (1981) research, for example, indicated that SAT scores of Spanish-dominant Puerto Ricans, tested in Puerto Rico, were more related to their Prueba de Aptitud Académica scores (the Spanish version of the SAT) as students' proficiency in English rose. The relationship between SAT and PAA scores was more unstable when students had less English-language proficiency. As one might suspect, low English-language familiarity might also lower scores on English-language college aptitude tests. Table 8.6, taken from 1982–83 College Board data, shows the median SAT verbal and mathematics test scores of Mexican Americans, Puerto Ricans, and white non-Hispanics broken down according to a yes versus no answer to the question, "Is English your best language?"

As the table 8.6 data indicate, Hispanics who indicated that English was not their best language earned lower SAT scores than other Hispanics; these Hispanics, as expected, also earned much lower SAT scores

Table 8.6: Hispanic and White Non-Hispanic SAT Verbal and Mathematics Median Scores in Relation to Answers About English as Best Language (1982–83 SDQ Question 38)

Group	SDQ Question 38 Response: English as Best Language	Percentage of a Group	Median SAT Verbal Score[b]	Median SAT Mathematics Score[b]
Mexican Americans	Yes	92.6	374	407
(N = 16.438)[a]	No	7.4	290	360
Difference in medians to yes/no responses			80	47
Puerto Ricans[c]	Yes	90.3	365	385
(N = 8.089)	No	9.2	282	337
Difference in medians to yes/no responses			83	48
White Non-Hispanics	Yes	98.2	439	481
(N = 706,923)	No	1.8	360	443
Difference in medians to yes/no responses			79	38

SOURCE: Ramist & Arbeiter (1984).

[a] N is based on those examinees who responded to SDQ question 38 *and* who had an SAT verbal section score.

[b] Median scores rather than mean scores are reported since the tabulations reviewed used only median statistics.

[c] Puerto Ricans in the 50 states and District of Columbia only.

than white non-Hispanics who indicated that English was their best language. As mentioned previously, there is the possibility that some Hispanics who answer yes to the question "Is English your best language?" may be persons whose familiarity with academic English is not commensurate with the English-language background and English-language familiarity of non-minority-group white students. Thus the data from table 8.6 confirm the possibility that low levels of English-language familiarity may depress SAT scores, but this does not inform us fully about the underlying issue. The data do not reveal how examinees' SAT performance changes as a function of their degree of English-language proficiency.

Other College Candidate Information

In addition to the high school record and college aptitude test scores, other widely used pieces of information are weighed by admissions staff of selective institutions, including the candidate's letter of application, letters of recommendation, and in some instances oral interview performance. Apparently, very little apart from ancedotal knowledge is known about how such information affects the admission of Hispanics to college. Among the important advantages of the additional forms of information is that they can help establish candidates' maturity and motivation for college and its academic demands. In addition, such information can assist a college in ascertaining personal qualities of candidates that may not be directly related to academic endeavors but might contribute to the well-roundedness and representativeness of a college community, should a candidate be admitted. Recent research by Willingham and Breland (1982) indicates that information on the personal qualities of candidates can be useful in deciding the nonacademic characteristics of admittees but that such information has less value than the high school record and admissions test scores in predicting college grades. Willingham and Breland's work was not intended as a study of minority access to institutions per se. Hence, one may legitimately suggest that the issue of how best to use personal qualities in minority admissions to college is an area in need of further research. Given the unequal educational opportunity that Hispanics face prior to college, evidence shows that personal qualities such as motivation to achieve may be very useful as indicators of Hispanics' ability to succeed in college.

The use of letters of intent, letters of recommendation, and interview information in the actual process of admissions decision making is difficult to research. Moll (1979), in an account of the admissions decision-making process for private colleges, suggests that the process itself has characteristics affected by the nature of institutions, institutional policies, and the social interaction of admissions staff in admissions decision making. The manner in which admissions staff evaluate the relative importance of the high school record, college admissions test scores, and personal characteristics of candidates is often not a rational decision-making process. How Hispanics fare in this process, given their tendency to present lower high school grades and admissions test scores, is not well documented. There is a persistent belief among many Hispanic students and educators that too much importance is placed by admissions staff on high school grades and admissions test scores relative to other information on Hispanic candidates. Also, admissions staff unfamiliar with Hispanics' social, cultural, and historical background may be unable to provide a sensitive interpretation of Hispanic candidates' personal characteristics indicative of college potential. Further discussion is given to some of these concerns in the last section of the paper.

Predictive Validity Research

This section presents a discussion of findings of research studies using high school grade-point average (or rank in class) and college admissions test scores to predict Hispanics' and white non-Hispanics' early college grades.[2] A fuller discussion of studies and findings is given in Durán (1983) and to some extent in Breland (1979). College grades earned early in a college experience—typically in the first year—are a commonly adopted indicator of propensity to succeed in college. Predictive validity studies most often follow a model using high school grade-point average (or rank in high school class) and college admissions test scores as variables predicting college grade-point average.

Early college grade-point average has the advantage of being a quantitative measure and hence is capable of being interpreted in an identical numerical manner by different observers. The temporal proximity of early college grades to high school experience is an important quality enhancing the use of information based on performance at the high school level in predicting college grades. It is a well-known phenomenon of social science research that relationships among variables that are collected across different points in time grow weaker as the interval separating points of measurement increases. In the case of college grades and information gathered in high school this decrease in relationship among variables results from changes, growth, and learning in individuals in college that stem from experiences after leaving high school. As will be mentioned in the last part of this paper, more attention ought to be given to such college experience factors—particularly those that are allied with Hispanics' success in college.

College grades have some disadvantages, just as high school grades do. College grades may not reference similar levels of achievement across different subject-matter areas of study, and idiosyncrasies in course requirements also affect interpretation of grades earned. Furthermore, grades may not reflect the same levels of achievement across different institutions. Predictive validity studies typically deal with the latter limitation by being based only on single institutions; predictive validity studies, however, seldom deal with the other confounding factors indicated. Early college grades have a disadvantage in not spanning an extended period of college study; they are inadequate as a proxy variable for actual graduation and for progress in meeting significant academic requirements en route to graduation that are an integral part of coursework. Factors such as planning of course load, appropriate sequencing and selection of courses, and cultivation of contact with faculty and teaching assistants may be critical academic determinants of achievement in college.

Table 8.7, taken from Durán (1983), displays median correlations of high school grade-point average (labeled HSR) and college admissions test scores with early college grades for samples of Hispanic and white college students based on the studies referred to in note 2. The median correlations are based in part on an earlier survey of Breland (1979), but they also include new data from studies not previously reviewed by Breland in his population validity survey of studies involving blacks, Hispanics, and whites.

The median correlations displayed in table 8.7 indicate that there is less of a relation between college grades and predictor measures for Hispanics than for white non-Hispanics. The median correlations between high school grade-point average and college grade-point average indicate that high school grades did not predict college grades among Hispanics as well as they did among whites; this result was somewhat unexpected given Breland's (1979) earlier results, also shown in table 8.7. Data in table 8.7 also show that verbal college admissions test scores, mathematics college admissions test scores, and a composite of high school grades and admissions test scores all were less well related to college grades for Hispanics than for whites. These results are entirely consistent with Breland's earlier findings, which involved a smaller number of studies. While the total number of independent analyses on Hispanics that were reviewed is small, and while more research is needed,

Table 8.7: Median Correlations Between College Predictor Measures and College Grades

| | Group | | |
| | Breland Review | | This Review[b] |
Predictor	White	Chicano	Hispanics[c]
High school record (HSR)	.37(32)[a]	.36(8)	.30(14)
Verbal test scores	.37(45)	.25(9)	.25(16)
Quantitative test scores	.33(45)	.17(9)	.23(16)
HSR and admissions test scores	.48(61)	.38(25)	.38(31)

[a] Number of independent analyses over studies is indicated in parentheses.

[b] Includes the same analyses in Breland (1979), plus additional results not cited in Breland but cited in new studies reviewed here. The review appears in Durán (1983).

[c] Hispanics in the 50 states and District of Columbia only.

there appears to be enough evidence to suggest that the patterns of association that are reported are real.

Use of regression analysis to predict college grades from high school grades and admissions test scores is the most common procedure by which to evaluate how well grades can be preducted. Because of the theoretical connection between the R statistic and the results of a regression analysis, the entries in the bottom row of table 8.7 are reflective of how well high school grades and verbal and mathematics test scores predicted Hispanics' and whites' college grades in the regression analyses of the studies reviewed. The bottom-row entries indicate that combining information about high school grades and admissions test scores in ethnic specific regression equations leads to less accurate prediction of Hispanics' college grades. In terms of the college grade-point average variance accounted for, Hispanics' college grades were predicted 9 to 10 percent less accurately than were whites' grades.

One of the strengths of the regression analysis approach is that it allows analysis of whether Hispanics' grades would be systematically underpredicted or overpredicted had high school grade-point average and admissions test scores been weighed in the same fashion as was the case for whites at the same institutions. When this concern was investigated by Durán (1983), no consistent evidence was found that Hispanics' grades were primarily underpredicted versus overpredicted across the studies reviewed. Patterns of overprediction or underprediction of Hispanics' college grades relative to whites' grades are idiosyncratic; they are very sensitive to the characteristics of institutions, to differences in the curriculum experiences of Hispanics versus non-Hispanics, and to the range of academic and personal characteristics of students.

Taken in toto the results cited suggest that Hispanics' college grades are less well predicted than those of whites but that the reasons for this difference are not allied with a consistent bias in the direction of prediction. The most sensible interpretation is that heterogeneity among Hispanics and their characteristics, and heterogeneity in Hispanics' college experiences, moderates the relationship between high school grades and test scores with early college grades. This moderation ought to be less pronounced for white students. This hypothesis would suggest that we need to learn more about how personal and background characteristics of Hispanics interact with high school achievement, admissions test performance, and college achievement in order to sort out the degree to which we can expect accurate prediction of grades. In addition, this hypothesis suggests that we ought to give more attention to alternative ways in which we can represent and assess Hispanic students' preparation for college and success in college. This added attention is necessary in order to develop information that can be used by college admissions staff in better evaluating the potential of Hispanic college candidates.

NEW DIRECTIONS

The prediction of Hispanics' college achievement is influenced by the manner in which this question is framed. The most serious shortcoming in present procedures used to formulate this question is that they are unduly insensitive to the characteristics and educational experiences of Hispanic college candidates that may moderate prediction of their college achievement. In order to cope with the resulting inequities it is necessary to create a broader framework within which to conceptualize the problem of prediction. The problem may be broken into three parts:

- Deciding which kinds of information about Hispanic students and their precollege experiences are needed to improve prediction of college potential
- Deciding which kinds of information about Hispanic experiences in college and college environments best represent achievement or moderator variables for predicting achievement
- Deciding how to link information on precollege and college characteristics of Hispanics into prediction schemes for college achievement

In no small part, the attempt to derive an improved framework for prediction of Hispanics' college achievement is a sociopolitical one. This is so because the socioeconomic and educational characteristics of Hispanics are depressed relative to the nonminority population of the United States. The educational access problems faced by Hispanics in the United States have their roots in a larger historical and social arena that reflects the struggles that ethnic-minority persons have faced in dealing with American life. These circumstances for Hispanics are distinctive from those of European ethnic immigrant groups, since Hispanics as a whole have a continuing and deep sociocultural and historical interaction with the rest of the Hispanic populaces of the American continents. The assimilation "problem" of Hispanics will not vanish as succeeding generations of Hispanics living in the United States become anglicized. Total assimilation will not occur in the foreseeable decades, since the population rise of Hispanics in the United States will continue to reflect immigration from Latin America of Hispanic persons aspiring to settle and live in the United States. This pattern of immigration in the future may be even more complex than it is now, and this may have unforeseen impacts on the education of Hispanics in the United States.

Our ability to comprehend what factors limit U.S. Hispanics' access to college, in the present as well as in the future, will need to be based on sound knowledge of the population characteristics of Hispanics and of the diversity of these characteristics. The fact that Hispanics differ among themselves and differ overall from nonminority U.S. persons in ways that have a significant relation to educational attainment means that the problem of predicting college aptitude may need to be approached in somewhat different ways across nonminority white and Hispanic populations. For example, in evaluating the information in admissions test scores of nonminority students, we need not worry about previous exposure to English and how this may affect the interpretation of admissions test scores. On the other hand, we need to take this factor into account in the case of Hispanics.

Nationally based educational-survey research over the past decade has begun to shed light on some significant experiential and background characteristics of Hispanics related to opportunity to learn prior to college. The results of such research are important as an empirical base by which to establish factors moderating Hispanics' preparation for college. National educational-survey data and descriptive data from college admissions testing programs are giving us the clear message that Hispanics' college preparation is not commensurate overall with the degree of college preparation of nonminority students. While we need to be sensitive to factors among Hispanics that moderate scholarly achievement and development of college aptitude prior to college, we must own up to the fact that many Hispanics are academically less prepared for college than nonminority students. Owning up to this fact should not be a passive matter. As we sharpen our understanding of what factors influence Hispanics' and other minority students' educational opportunity, we may be able to design high school and college institutional environments and academic interventions that will aid persons in better pursuing their chosen academic studies given their current academic aptitudes.

Improving Knowledge of Predictors of College Achievement

High school grades and college admissions test scores are likely to remain basic and important measures of college aptitude for the foreseeable future. Problems in the interpretation of such information primarily arise for Hispanics when these measures are low enough to be used as the basis for making a decision to exclude Hispanics from admissions consideration. We need to conduct research on procedures for guiding admissions staffs' interpretation of Hispanics' high school grade information and admissions test scores. One outcome of such research might be to develop a procedural manual for reviewing the characteristics of Hispanics excluded from admissions consideration because of high school grades and test scores. The objective of this manual, which might be computerized, would be systematically to review the background of Hispanic candidates in order to identify those persons whose academic credentials are possibly underestimated. For example, the following factors might be reviewed:

- Candidates' language background and English-language proficiency
- Candidates' exposure to schooling in Spanish and academic achievement in Spanish contexts
- High educational aspirations and high achievement motivation that are coupled with lower high school grades and admissions test scores than expected
- Higher than expected high school grades or admissions test scores given parents' educational background and income
- The presence of financial and other obligations to family during high school coupled with higher than expected high school grades and admissions test scores.

The foregoing list of suggestive factors all might be useful in identifying factors that could moderate the interpretation of candidates' high school achievement and admissions test scores. In addition, however, there might be another set of factors that reflect Hispanic students' academic aptitude in ways not reflected well by high school grades and admissions test scores. Such factors might include the following:

- Significant school and home or community activities involving use of academic and subject-matter skills related to schooling
- Frequency of voluntary participation in counseling programs and other programs exposing students to significant academic environments (e.g., visits to libraries, museums, science exhibits)
- Development of significant literacy skills in Spanish and functional utilization of these skills at advanced levels

The systematic availability of information such as has been described is problematic, but it could be realized in two ways. First, in college application materials self-identified Hispanic students might be requested to fill out a computer-readable questionnaire touching on the topics mentioned. Other relevant information might be supplied in computer-readable data made available by testing programs; this information might come from student background questionnaires filled out by students when they take an admissions test. Second, to the extent feasible, admissions staff reviewing Hispanic students' letters of application or interview proceedings might quickly and easily code computer-readable forms indicating relevant information of the sort cited. The entire system would operate on readily available microcomputers at minimal expense.

The heart of the kind of system envisioned would be the computer algorithms that would suggest which students merited and did not merit further admissions consideration. The development of the appropriate questionnaire system and computerized admissions aid described would be a nontrivial, value-laden task that would need to be accomplished with extreme care. At present it is only possible to suggest that such a system could be developed and that if it were developed it might significantly help in making the admissions decision-making process more rational and valid for Hispanics. There are many conceptual questions that would need to be carefully thought through, and research would be needed to establish the validity of such a system.

Improving Knowledge About College Achievement

As discussed earlier in this paper, there are inherent limits in viewing college achievement in terms of early grades in college. This is not at all to say that early college grades are invalid measures of achievement; obviously, they are valid. It seems clear, however, that a more comprehensive picture of college achievement should draw on additional measures. Other academic measure areas such as the following might be included:

- Ability to graduate
- Advanced-level course performance
- Ability to accomplish significant course requirements and academic activities required in advancing toward graduation
- Academic-related accomplishments outside of course work and required activities that occur in college or community settings

Indices and measures for the foregoing sorts of accomplishments might not be as predictable from high school grades and admissions test scores as are first- and second-year college grades; this possibility, however, does not diminish their value as areas for assessing college achievement. This is so for Hispanics and other minority students because some of these students may need to grow academically in college at a steeper rate than will other nonminority students. Hence, Hispanics' and other minority students' pattern of accomplishment in college may show a sustained effort to accelerate development of academic skills that may not be reflected very well if concern is focused only on grades earned in the first two years of college. Because of this possibility, as an additional concern, it also would be unwise to suggest that speed factors, such as speed in completing a degree or speed in meeting degree objectives, should serve as valid measures of college achievement for all minority students.

Apart from a richer set of indices for academic achievement in college, there is an acute need for measures that reflect students' personal growth characteristics in college and institutional characteristics that affect educational opportunity. Factors such as the aforementioned will moderate students' opportunities to achieve in college. These are not at all trivial matters for Hispanic students, since their sociocultural characteristics, educational experiences, and early educational aspirations may vary so much from what is the norm for nonminority students. Institutional characteristics, such as services related to financial aid, study assistance, and counseling and the sociocultural climate of a college community may be very critical determinants of Hispanics' success in college. Moderating factors such as those mentioned may have more of an effect on some Hispanics' ability to achieve in college than academic credentials presented at the conclusion of high school.

At present we do not have an extensive base of research to inform us about the effect of personal and institutional moderator variables on Hispanic students' achievement in college. However, as reflected in the contributions to this volume, such a base is beginning to emerge. As mentioned in the final section, one of the exciting prospects of such research and other needed research is that it might help us go beyond merely improving prediction of Hispanics' success in college. The next steps would include interventions designed to promote development of Hispanics' college aptitude and success in college.

Improving Prediction of College Achievement

By its very nature, the topic of prediction of college achievement engenders concern for what will occur in the future as a result of what has occurred in the past. The issues discussed in the last two sections suggest that in order to improve prediction of Hispanics' college achievement, we need to extend the range of the kinds of information that we consider to be predictors of college aptitude and also our criterion measures of college achievement. In addition, we need to draw attention to factors that moderate the interpretation of college academic predictor measures and factors that moderate Hispanics' ability to demonstrate achievement in college. The goal of improving prediction of Hispanics' college achievement ought to be built on research findings that investigate connections between high-school-based predictors and moderator variables with college-based achievement measures and moderator variables. The problem of prediction as thus conceived is multivariate in nature. The approaches for investigation, however, could be either statistical research or case-study observational research.

Statistical research might use multivariate statistical methodology to investigate relationships between high-school-based and college-based measures. Such research would have a strong exploratory orientation because at present we do not know the strength of relationships among many of the variables involved, nor do we know the best measurement procedures to follow in operationalizing variables. It is almost certain to prove desirable to work with single institutions as a basic unit of study, though statistical metaanalysis techniques might be used to investigate trends across institutions. It is likely to emerge since students' achievement in college and admissions criteria are very much tied to the characteristics of particular institutional environments.

Case-study research appears to be very important, and perhaps it should be a prelude to highly quantitative research. The purpose and direction of case-study research would be to document carefully what is occurring to Hispanics on selective college campuses. Such field research needs to identify how Hispanics are treated and how they fare in the college admissions process, how Hispanics adjust to college life, and whether Hispanics are successful in college endeavors. Case-study research can be a rich resource for developing knowledge needed to operationalize significant variables for quantitatively oriented research such as that described earlier.

Design of Interventions

Recent research in the area of instructional psychology has begun to suggest that once we know a lot about factors that affect students' learning we can then begin to explore ways in which education might be tailored to individuals with different learning characteristics and aptitudes (e.g., see Snow, 1982). At the forefront of the field there is now a belief that what we call "intelligence" itself may be increased by appropriate interventions based on cognitive-psychology research findings (see Detterman & Sternberg, 1982). At the present this emerging field has yet to contend with socio-cultural and linguistic background factors, but the problems of addressing these additional factors are not insurmountable (see Durán, 1985). Snow (1982) suggests that current conceptions of college aptitude should not be narrow and that they should include allowances for motivational and personality variables that affect ability to learn. By opening up the range of factors we consider relevant to Hispanics' college aptitude, we are thus recognizing a richer field of influences on development of college aptitude. In the case of Hispanics we may find that deliberate manipulation of experiences in high school or college would have a positive effect on their college admissions and college achievement. Predictive validity research of the sort that has been described might form the foundation for interventions we might design. Unlike attempts to influence admissions test scores by coaching, we might directly address the accelerated teaching of thinking and language skills required in college in a way that would be more sensitive and effective than the traditional curricula of high school or college.

NOTES

1. In addition to the SAT, the Admissions Testing Program of the College Board currently administers thirteen separate achievement tests along with a written placement test known as the Test of Standard Written English. Hispanics' recent performance on these tests is not discussed in the present paper; the interested reader is referred to the publication *Profiles: College-Bound Seniors, 1983* (Ramist & Arbeiter, 1984). It should suffice to note that Hispanic subgroups performed lower on these tests than white non-Hispanics and that the pattern of differences was of similar magnitude as reported for SAT score differences.

2. The studies reviewed were as follows: D. S. Calkins & R. Whitworth, *Differential prediction of freshman grade point average for sex and two ethnic classifications at a southwestern university* (El Paso: University of Texas at El Paso, 1974; available as ERIC ED 102-199); N. Dittmar, *A comparative investigation of the predictive validity of admissions criteria for Anglos, Blacks, and Mexican-Americans,* unpublished doctoral dissertation, University of Texas at Austin, 1974; R. E. Goldman & B. Hewitt, "An investigation of test bias for Mexican-American college students," *Journal of Educational Measurement, 12,* no. 3 (Fall 1975), 187–196; R. Goldman & B. Hewitt, "Predicting the success of black, Chicano, oriental and white college students," *Journal of Educational Measurement, 13,* no. 2 (1976), 109–117; R. Goldman & M. Widawski, "An analysis of types of errors in the selection of minority college students," *Journal of Educational Measurement, 13,* no. 3 (1976), 185–200; R. Goldman & R. Richards, "The SAT prediction of grades

for Mexican-American versus Anglo-American students of the University of California, Riverside," *Journal of Educational Measurement, 11,* no. 2 (1974), 129–135; R. Lowman & D. Spuck, "Predictors of college success for the disadvantaged Mexican-American," *Journal of College Student Personnel, 16,* (1975), 40–48; J. P. Mestre, "Predicting academic achievement among bilingual Hispanic college technical students," *Educational and Psychological Measurement, 41,* (1981), 1255–1264; C. Scott, *Longer-term predictive validity of college admission tests for Anglo, Black and Mexican-American students* (Albuquerque, NM: New Mexico Department of Educational Administration, University of New Mexico, 1976); M. J. Vásquez, *Chicano and Anglo university women: Factors related to their performance, persistence and attrition,* unpublished doctoral dissertation, University of Texas at Austin, 1978; J. Warren, *Prediction of college achievement among Mexican-American Students in California,* College Board Research and Development Report (Princeton, NJ: Educational Testing Service, 1976).

REFERENCES

Alderman, D. (1982). Language proficiency as a moderator variable in testing academic achievement. *Journal of Educational Psychology, 74*(4), 580-587.

American College Testing Program. (1980). *College student profiles: Norms for the ACT assessment.* 1980–81 ed. Iowa City, IA: ACT.

Breland, H. (1979). *Population validity and college entrance measures.* Research Monograph No. 8. New York: College Entrance Examination Board.

Brown, G. H., Rosen, N., Hill, S., & Olivas, M. A. (1980). *The condition of education for Hispanic Americans.* Washington, DC: National Center for Educational Statistics.

Buriel, R. (1983). Teacher-student interactions and their relationship to student achievement: A comparison of Mexican-American and Anglo-American children. *Journal of Educational Psychology, 75*(6), 889–897.

Detterman, D., & Sternberg, R. (Eds.). (1982). *How and how much can intelligence be increased.* Norwood, NJ: Ablex.

Durán, R. P. (1983). *Hispanics' education and background: Predictors of college achievement.* New York: College Entrance Examination Board.

Durán, R. P. (1985). Influences of language skills on bilinguals' problem solving. In S. Chipman, J. Sigel, & R. Glaser (Eds.), *Thinking and learning skills: Vol. 2. Current research and open questions* (pp. 187–207). Hillsdale, NJ: Erlbaum.

Moll, R. *Playing the private college admissions game.* New York: Penguin Books. (1979).

Osterlind, S. (1983). *Test item bias.* Beverly Hills, CA: Sage.

Ramist, L., & Arbeiter, S. (1984). *Profiles: College Bound Seniors, 1983.* New York: College Entrance Examination Board.

Snow, R. (1982). The training of intellectual aptitude. In D. Detterman & R. Sternberg (Eds.), *How much can intelligence be increased* (pp. 1–37). Norwood, NJ: Ablex.

Willingham, W. W., & Breland, H. M. (1982). *Personal qualities and college admissions.* New York: College Entrance Examination Board.

9 | Fairness in the Use of Tests for Selective Admissions of Hispanics

MARÍA PENNOCK-ROMÁN

In this paper, psychometric models for fairness in selective admissions will be evaluated and contrasted with current practices at institutions of higher learning. Studies of these models will be reviewed from the perspective of their usefulness for making selection decisions about Hispanic and female applicants. In addition, the societal values implicit or explicit in these models concerning the use of group membership will be discussed in light of the institutional objectives that selective admissions traditionally have served. Recommendations will be offered for future debate and research on these issues.

Hargadon (1981) claims that "[a]s a subject that invites debate and controversy, tests and their uses must rank with religion, politics, and sex" (p. 1113). The statement is particularly appropriate for the uses of tests to make selection decisions in postsecondary education. As Haney (1981) points out, "considerations of group parity and fair selection ultimately are determined by social political values. . . . [W]hile the social role of standardized testing often is both advocated and challenged in technical terms, the prominent social concerns surrounding standardized testing, both now and in the past, are rooted in matters of social and political values" (p. 1032). Given the central role of these values in any discussion of fair test use, it seems appropriate to list here the goals of selective admissions processes and the justification for giving some weight to group membership, such as race or gender, in the admissions process.

MAJOR ARGUMENTS FOR THE USE OF GROUP-MEMBERSHIP INFORMATION IN SELECTIVE ADMISSIONS

Willingham and Breland (1977) identified three broad purposes that are served by selective admissions: (1) "To enroll successful students," (2) "to serve other institutional purposes" (e.g., filling up programs that have

246

ample staff and facilities, meeting the needs of orchestra and athletic teams, and maintaining or changing the diversity and balance in its student body in order to enhance the educational climate and health of the institution); and (3) "to serve other social purposes" (e.g., developing talent and research capability in particular fields, maintaining a continuous supply of graduates to the various professions and service to the public, and promoting affirmative action) (p. 71). In the discussion that follows, it will be argued that giving some weight to group-membership identification in this process is necessary to all three of these major purposes.

Manning (1977) contends that consideration of diversity and professional service are the most important justifications for treating race as a relevant factor in admissions. However, for completeness he presents six additional major arguments, some of which he believes have merit, but which are somewhat less compelling. Completeness in presenting these views is of interest "for the reason that opponents of such a policy often cite only one or two such arguments and then, having demolished these, conclude that the issue is settled" (p. 33).

The eight justifications that are discussed below are based in large part on Manning's essay. Some points have been reordered here to correspond more closely to the three purposes served by selective admissions as cited above. The major divergence from his report is in the discussion of test bias; his essay predates the reviews of differential validity and prediction upon which this paper is based. Points 2 and 3 have been supported with additional citations, but the remaining justifications, 4 through 8, are a synthesis of Manning's statements. I believe that the last two are the least appealing.

1. Differential Prediction. Knowledge of minority- or gender-group membership is necessary in order to interpret the test scores that are used to predict who will be successful students.

As demonstrated by Breland (1979) and Durán (1983), standardized test scores are clearly less predictive of the college performance of Hispanics than of non-Hispanic whites (hereafter called "whites" or "Anglos"). Median validity coefficients for whites were higher by approximately .10. Hence, test scores are more ambiguous as predictors of college performance for Hispanics. When dealing with mental measurements, one often forgets that, unlike physical measurements, they do not necessarily measure the same underlying dimensions (constructs) in all persons. Since differential prediction does exist by ethnic and by gender groups (e.g., see Linn, 1982), the same score, say a 500 on the verbal Scholastic Aptitude Test (SAT-V), has a different meaning for various groups in terms of its relationship to college grades. For Hispanics, it predicts a wider range of possible grade-point averages than it does for whites. For women, it implies a systematically *higher* grade-point average than it does for males. For example, other things being equal, females with SAT-V scores of 500 as a group are more "able" in the sense of latent criterion performance than are males with scores of 500 (Breland, 1979; Linn, 1982).

There is also evidence that using long-term versus short-term criteria magnifies subgroup differences in predictive validity coefficients. A recent study by Hathaway (1984) of Columbia University Law School students showed that the Law School Admissions Test had lower correlations with law school marks for males than for females and that the difference in correlation was much larger for third-year grades than for first-year grades. For the small ($N = 46$) sample of minority students (which included eleven Hispanics), the correlation between LSAT and grades dropped from $r = .51$ the first year to $r = .17$ for the third year. The decrease in correlation for majority students was smaller, from $r = .35$ to $r = .28$.

On the other hand, Powers (1984a) found few significant differences in predictive validity coefficients for minority versus majority groups in twenty-three law schools. Most of the differences between the groups occurred in the intercept value of the regression systems because minority students had lower law school grades than predicted (i.e., they had a lower intercept value than majority-group students). However, the degree of overprediction was small, especially when the criteria used were second- and third-year-averages.

After examining three-year trends in grades at the twenty-three law schools, Powers (1982, 1984b) suggested various explanations that could account for these findings. He found that the grades of black and Chicano students improved much more than the grades of white students between their first and third years of law school. The mean difference in grades between minority and white students narrowed by the third year. Powers evaluated several alternative explanations for the differential improvements. He was able to test three hypothesized causes directly through statistical analyses: decreases in the reliabilities of grades, statistical artifacts such as "ceiling" or "floor" effects on grades, and patterns of enrollment in courses. All three were found to be unlikely sources of the differential improvement. Although minority and majority students had different preferences in specializations, the courses that minorities chose were not systematically easier ones. On the other hand, it was not possible to test whether the differences could be due to artifactual changes in the units of measurement of grades.

Powers suggested two other more likely hypotheses for further study. Curricular differences between the first and third years could lead to changes in the nature of the skills required for successful academic performance. In addition, minority students may differentially improve in their study skills and self-confidence through their "own initiative or from effective institutional support systems" (1982, p. 14). Powers concluded that "the differential improvements of minority students would seem to provide further justification to admitting minority and other disadvantaged students with lower admission credentials" (1982, pp. 15–16).

If one institutional goal is to enroll successful students as measured by grade-point average, then information that consistently moderates how well grades can be predicted (e.g., group membership) ought to be taken into consideration. Perhaps future research will enable us to eliminate the need for separate-group predictions by identifying and assessing those characteristics of the individual that mediate subgroup differences. Although a thorough review of the possible causes of differential prediction is beyond the scope of this chapter, several points will be mentioned to outline the complexity of the issue.

Bias in test content cannot be the sole cause, because the results for high school grade-point average (HS-GPA) parallel those of aptitude tests; that is, college grade-point average (C-GPA) for females is more closely related to HS-GPA than for males and less related to high school record for Hispanics than for Anglos (American College Testing Program, 1973; Breland, 1979; Linn, 1982; Durán, 1983). These differences are often attributed to noncognitive factors (e.g., in his article for this volume, Durán points to resourcefulness as an individual characteristic that may influence the differential prediction of grades for Hispanics). Personality characteristics are difficult to measure with objectivity; self-report instruments can easily be faked in the desirable direction. Furthermore, when data on personal qualities are gleaned from standard admissions forms, the improvement in prediction of freshman grades is only very slight beyond that achieved by using test scores and HS-GPA (Willingham & Breland, 1982, chaps. 3, 9).

On the other hand, there is evidence that cognitive factors not measured by multiple-choice tests may help explain differential prediction. Breland and Griswold (1981) found that females wrote significantly better essays for the English Placement Tests (EPT) than did males with comparable scores on the multiple-choice subtests of the EPT, the verbal and mathematical sections of the Scholastic Aptitude Tests, and the Test of Standard Written English. The results for Hispanics varied by score level. At moderately low levels of multiple-choice test scores, Hispanics wrote worse essays than Anglos; at other score levels for the predictors (high, moderately high, or very low), there were no differences in essay quality between Hispanics and Anglos. Since essay tests are still common in many classes in college, these results suggest that some of the differences in validity and regression slopes may be due to an unmeasured, cognitive variable—writing ability. More research needs to be done to verify this finding.

Therefore, given the limitations of our present instruments and knowledge, it is justifiable to use race, ethnicity, and gender to modify predictions concerning which students will have high grades because subgroup identification has demonstrable effects on the efficiency and accuracy of such predictions.

2. *Insufficiency.* Although high school grades and test scores are generally good predictors of college grade-point average, they do not reflect a broad enough spectrum of talents for success in occupations and the professions.

Cardoza (1982) has expanded this point:

> If we change the criterion variable to occupational success, then perhaps the introduction of new predictor variables would make sense. Take for example, two doctors, an Anglo and a Chicano, who have received equivalent medical training. Suppose that they are both practicing in a hospital which provides services in the Chicano community. Which doctor would be more successful? Probably the Chicano doctor because he has a better understanding of their complaints and symptoms and [would], therefore, be more accurate in his diagnosis than would the Anglo doctor. The MCAT would not have been able to predict this type of success. (p. 46)

In other words, minority persons bring to their professions special sensitivities and communication skills that go unmeasured by traditional academic credentials but are necessary for "success" in working with minority populations. This kind of success, while difficult to quantify, is at least as important as achieving good grades. Therefore, insufficiency exists in the measures used for both selection and the criteria of "success."

3. *Diversity.* According to Heath (1968), "[t]he two most powerful determinants producing change in the undergraduate and alumni samples were their roommates and the intellectual atmosphere and traditions of the college" (p. 197). Hence, a culturally diverse student body is necessary to enhance the educational experiences of students. In addition, the inclusion of racial and ethnic minority students is an essential first step toward change in racist attitudes among mainstream students. The work of Nahemow and Lawton (1975) has shown that living in very

close residential propinquity (e.g., same floor) can promote friendships that cross traditional racial and age barriers.

In sum, diversity in the student body is an essential aspect of a desirable college environment.

4. Professional Service. Increasing ethnic and racial minorities in medicine, law, and other professions is one way to improve the supply of professionals serving minority populations (assuming minority professionals are more likely to serve their own group). Whereas the "insufficiency" argument stresses the *quality* of services to minority populations, the emphasis here is on increasing the *quantity* of professionals who choose to work with these populations.

5. Leadership. It is desirable to expand the number of minority persons who are available to assume positions of leadership in a variety of professions and to serve as role models for minority youth.

6. Remediation. Rather than shutting out those minority students who are victims of ineffective schools, colleges should provide remedial programs for educationally disadvantaged students.

7. Reparations. Manning (1977) expresses this viewpoint concisely: "the 'collective guilt' of white society . . . for two centuries of injustice and cruelty . . . toward racial and ethnic minorities requires reparation through deliberately extending preferential treatment" (p. 39).

8. Accommodation to Political Stress. Special admissions programs for minority students are one means of assuring the public that genuine efforts toward open access to education for minorities do occur.

It is evident that the reasons for incorporating group-membership information in selection decisions vary not only in their appeal but also in the implications that they have for determining which characteristics are desired, how much weight to give, and in the ways to use these characteristics. For example, if the emphasis is on remediation or reparation, the implication is that one should focus on measuring the degree of disadvantage of the candidates in order to select those minority-group members who are victims of inequities in the educational system. If, on the other hand, diversity and providing more minority leaders and role models are the main goals, then minority-group members are sought out whether or not they are disadvantaged. Unfortunately, most debates about fair-selection methods have not explicitly discussed the particular values that they assume are the goals of admissions processes. In the discussion that follows, it will be seen that critiques of various methods have tended to confound value differences with technical issues. The next section reviews briefly some of the proposed fair-selection models and the values that they implicitly embody.

DESCRIPTION OF FAIR-SELECTION MODELS

Fair-selection models have been described and contrasted thoroughly by a number of authors (Olmedo, 1977; Linn, 1973; Ledvinka, Markes, & Ladd, 1982; ACT, 1973; Petersen & Novick, 1976; Jensen, 1980). All of the models assume the following: There is one, unidimensional criterion Y, such as college grade-point average (C-GPA), that measures "success," either in college or in a job. A predictor X exists, which can be a linear combination of variables, that has demonstrable validity for estimating Y in advance. The various models differ in how they specify that acceptance or cutting scores on X be derived in order to decide who scores high enough on X in order to be admitted. Since the relationship between predictors and the criterion is far from perfect, some selection decisions will turn out to be correct preclassifications of candidates, and others will turn out to be errors. For simplicity, the models are usually presented as "threshold" models, which assume that the criterion can be dichotomized into "success" or "failure" (such as C-GPAs that are above a "C" grade value vs. C-GPAs that are below "C" value). When the criterion is dichotomized, there are four potential outcomes: two that are correct decisions and two that are errors. "True positives" are persons who were admitted and performed well on the criterion (i.e., correct acceptances). In contrast, "false positives" are persons who performed poorly on the criterion after they were admitted (i.e., wrong acceptances). "True negatives" are persons who were *not* actually admitted but who would have *failed* on the criterion had they been admitted (i.e., correct rejections). "False negatives" are persons who were *not* actually admitted but who would have *succeeded* had they been admitted (i.e., incorrect rejections).

Figure 9.1 presents these outcomes for both the minority-group and the majority-group candidates. The symbols A_i and B_i, $i = 1, 4$, represent proportions of candidates in the various outcomes, numbered to correspond to areas in a graph of a bivariate frequency distribution. Adding A_1 to A_4 and B_1 to B_4 gives the proportions admitted from each group (the selection ratios within each group); adding A_2 to A_3 and B_2 to B_3 gives the proportions rejected from each group. Success ratios are the proportions who succeed on Y; that is $A_1 + A_2$ and $B_1 + B_2$.

The various rules for setting cut scores for X for each group can be specified as follows:

Single-Group Regression Model. The same cutting score is used for each group. This cutting score is the value of the predictor that best estimates the minimum criterion performance when groups are combined. Hence, group membership is ignored in the selection process.

Figure 9.1: Selection Outcomes for Majority- and Minority-Group Candidates

Selection Decision

Majority Group

Actual Outcome in College Grades

	High	Low	Selection Ratio
Admit because x exceeds or equals cut score	True Positives A_1	False Positives A_4	$A_1 + A_4$
Rejects because x is below cut score	False Negatives A_2	True Negatives A_3	
	Success Ratio = $A_1 + A_2$	Failure Ratio = $A_3 + A_4$	

Model	Ratio
Thorndike's Constant Ratio	$(A_1 + A_4)/(A_1 + A_2) = (B_1 + B_4)/(B_1 + B_2)$
Cole's Conditional Probability	$A_1/(A_1 + A_2) = B_1/(B_1 + B_2)$
Equal Impact	$A_1 + A_4 = B_1 + B_4$

Minority Group

Actual Outcome in College Grades

	High	Low	Selection Ratio
Admit because x exceeds cut score	True Positives B_1	False Positives B_4	$B_1 + B_4$
Reject because x is below cut score	False Negatives B_2	True Negatives B_3	
	Success Ratio = $B_1 + B_2$	Failure Ratio = $B_3 + B_4$	

Converse Model	Ratio
Converse Constant Ratio	$(A_3 + A_2)/(A_3 + A_4) = (B_3 + B_2)/(B_3 + B_4)$
Converse Conditional Probability Model	$A_3/(A_3 + A_4) = B_3/(B_3 + B_4)$

Note: The proportions are calculated _within_ groups. That is $A_1 + A_2 + A_3 + A_4 = 1$; $A_5 + A_6 = 1$; $B_1 + B_2 + B_3 + B_4 = 1$; $B_5 + B_6 = 1$.

Separate-Groups Regression Model. Separate within-group regressions are used to select the cutoffs for each group separately that best predict the minimal desired criterion level in each group. The criterion levels defining "success" are the same in all groups. Usually, only two groups are considered and the model is referred to as the two-groups regression model. (If all groups have identical regressions, this becomes the single-group model.)

Equal-Risk Model. (Einhorn & Bass, 1971.) This model is similar to the separate-groups-regression model, but it differs in that the probability of success pertaining to a given test score for each of the different subgroups is also considered rather than just the applicants' predicted criterion score.

The Darlington Model. (Darlington, 1971.) This model is the same as the separate-groups-regression model except that the "desirable" criterion-level performance is defined differently for each group. One states explicitly that if the desirable minimum criterion-level performance for majority candidates is Y, then the desirable minimum performance for the minority group is $Y - K$, where K is a positive number that is determined subjectively and is open to debate.

The Thorndike Model. (Thorndike, 1971; also known as the constant-ratio model.) Cut scores are set separately for each group such that the selection ratios are proportional to the success ratios in each group. (See figure 9.1 for an explanation of proportions in the selection classifications.)

The Cole Model. (Cole, 1973; also known as the conditional-probability model.) Successful applicants must have the same probability of selection in all groups. (See figure 9.1 for an explanation in terms of proportions in the selection classifications.)

Expected-Utility Models. (Gross & Su, 1975; Petersen, 1974; Petersen & Novick, 1976.) This approach applies the methodology from statistical decision theory to psychometric selection. For each group, a number ("utility value') is assigned to each selection outcome (e.g., false negatives) that represents a measure of the "importance" or relative desirability of this outcome. If one outcome, such as "true positives," is considered more desirable in the minority group than for the majority group, then a higher utility value is assigned to this outcome in the minority group as compared to the majority group. The model can be expressed also in terms of "losses" rather than utilities. In this case, one may consider that certain errors in selection (e.g., false negatives) represent a more serious loss for one group than another. The critical aspect is that the specification of the preference of one group over another is made explicitly and that these preferences are expressed in terms of the value or loss associated with each of the selection errors and correct decisions. The assignment of these numerical values is subjective and open to debate. Once these numbers are specified, the procedure derives (usually separate) cutoff values for each group that maximize the "expected utility" of selection, an overall index that is a function of both the predicted criterion and group membership.

Equal-Impact Model. Separate cut scores are set such that the selection ratios are the same across groups, regardless of differences in average criterion scores across groups. This model was evaluated by Ledvinka et al. (1982) in terms of its long-term impact on minority representation in an employment setting.

Quota Model. Specified proportions of majority and of minority-group candidates are selected, regardless of differences in average criterion scores across groups. Usually, quotas are set to be equal to the proportion in the applicant pool, or in the population at large.

In order to evaluate these models fully, one can view them from the following perspectives: What values, implicit or explicit, do they place on group membership and the various selection outcomes? What impact would they have on minority admissions to colleges and on minority employment? What technical shortcomings do they have, and how serious are these shortcomings?

VALUES REFLECTED IN FAIR-SELECTION MODELS

The models represent a full spectrum of viewpoints concerning the legitimacy of group membership as a variable in the selection process. At one extreme is the single-group regression model, which forgoes the use of group membership altogether and concentrates exclusively on a narrowly defined criterion of success. At the other extreme are the quota and equal-impact models, which concentrate almost exclusively on group membership as the critical variable and use the criterion of "success" only to make selection decisions *within* groups.

The separate-groups regression, equal-risk, Thorndike, and Cole models all use group membership as a means of clarifying the prediction of a narrowly defined "success," a psychometric approach. However, they resolve ambiguities in a different manner. In general, when differential prediction exists between the groups in question, the Thorndike and Cole models resolve ambiguities so as to give the benefit of the doubt to the *applicants* in the group with poorer predictors. The separate-groups regression and equal-risk models resolve ambiguities in the direction that favors the *selecting institution* (assuming that the narrowly defined "success" is the only institutional goal). These points will be demonstrated later, with hypothetical selection situations.

The Darlington model and the "utilities" approach also allow the simultaneous use of both group-membership information and maximization of the prediction of the criterion for success, but with greater flexibility in the use of the group membership. Group membership is not necessarily seen as a variable that assists prediction but as a valued characteristic in its own right. In the case of the Darlington model, selection decisions are defined as an explicit trade-off between group representation and high future criterion scores. In utility models, the "value" of group membership is also explicitly defined, and the object is to maximize prediction success subject to these differential weights reflecting these values. Hence, these two selection approaches, like the equal-impact and quota models, leave room for considerations of group membership that reflect the positive value of diversity, or the needs for minority leaders, professional services, reparations, exceptions for the disadvantaged, or political expedience. However, unlike the equal-impact and quota models, the predictions of "success" are not necessarily ignored.

Another way to categorize the models is to consider how they view the various selection outcomes and whether some selection errors are seen as more serious than others. Gross and Su (1975) compared the two-groups regression, equal-risk, Thorndike, Cole, and Darlington models with respect to selection outcomes under several hypothetical situations within a decision-theoretic framework. They calculated the implicit values for each selection outcome, assuming that false positives were equally undesirable in the majority and minority groups. Given this restriction, they found that the two-groups regression and equal-risk models were highly similar and that they tended to weigh all errors equally or almost equally in both groups. A false negative in the majority group was *equally* undesirable in the majority and minority groups. In contrast, the Darlington, Thorndike, and Cole models, for most hypothetical situations, implicitly viewed false negatives as involving a greater loss for minority members. In other words, they considered it a worse mistake to reject a potentially successful minority candidate than to reject a potentially successful majority candidate. The extent to which false negatives were considered a worse mistake for minorities varied depending on the accuracy of prediction and differences in mean values on the criterion. If the validity was lower in the minority group, the scale was tipped toward the minority group. The minority group was also favored if the mean criterion score was lower for the minority group.

Petersen and Novick (1976) criticized the greater concern that the

Thorndike and Cole models imply toward false negative selection errors as compared to false positive selection errors. They defined converse-constant ratio and converse-conditional-probability models that focused on the probability of failure rather than the probability of success on the criterion (see figure 9.1). They demonstrated that these converse models could not be satisfied simultaneously with their corresponding model under most conditions. In their view, "a definition of selection fairness can only be satisfactory if one considers . . . both sides (selection-success and rejection-failure)," (p. 22). In this sense, they believe that the Thorndike and Cole models and their converse are "internally" contradictory and "incoherent."

In response to this criticism, Sawyer, Cole, and Cole (1976) argued that the "converse models are expressions of different values than those expressed by the original rules [of the Thorndike and Cole models]. They certainly do not represent logical contradictions to the rules, as Petersen and Novick suggest" (p. 74). In the views of Sawyer et al. it is justifiable to be less concerned with fairness to potential failures than to potential successes. "Although someone might have such utility functions, people's verbal expressions of fairness in selection rarely include an exclusive concern for fairness to potential failures. It is much more common to feel that special assurance of fairness is owed exclusively to potentially successful candidates" (p. 74). Cronbach, Yalow, and Schaeffer (1979) pointed to the agreement of policymakers with the latter view: "Novick and Petersen object to the [concept of adverse impact on satisfactory applicants] because it ignores the outcome for workers who would be unsatisfactory if hired; but policy-makers and the courts do not see this as an important aspect of fairness" (p. 8).

This discussion of concern over errors in selection versus rejection clearly centers on social and philosophical values. However, Petersen and Novick (1976) have referred to it as an issue pertaining to logic, and in a later paper, Novick and Petersen (1976) discussed it under the heading of "Technical Issues." The debate about fair selection has often been clouded by confusions of this sort between social values and technical issues. On the other hand, some of the Novick-Petersen criticisms of the "group-parity" models have been truly technical ones, and they will be taken up later.

It is evident that psychometricians disagree widely in the points of view concerning the legitimacy of using group membership, except for purposes of aiding psychometric prediction of a criterion. Novick and Petersen (1976) expressed the view that group-parity concepts of selection fairness (such as the Cole and Thorndike models) are "unconstitutional," and they have advocated a focus on individual characteristics such as degree of disadvantage rather than on gender or race. Evans (1977) and Manning (1977), however, have pointed out that a focus on disadvantage would not substantially increase minority representation in law schools or undergraduate institutions.

CONSEQUENCES OF FAIR-SELECTION MODELS

The outcomes of applications of the models have been viewed as a trade-off between maintaining a desirable balance in the representation of groups and maintaining the "quality" of selected individuals at a given level. In these cases, "quality" has been defined in terms of the probability of "success" or as a function of the criterion score. Usually, the criterion has been narrowly specified, such as grade-point average in universities, and it has not measured the kinds of qualities identified by Cardoza (1982; e.g., Chicano doctors' empathy with Hispanic patients).

If one adopts a "threshold" utility model, grade-point average is dichotomized; the focus is on the percent of cases that have college GPAs above a specified, acceptable level. If one adopts a linear or continuous utility model, then grade-point average is viewed as a continuous variable whose overall level at a university can be upgraded or downgraded. The derivations have been based on various hypothetical situations and also on actual empirical data from colleges. Rarely have all models been compared at once, but there is substantial overlap between reports.

Hypothetical Selection Situations

Four studies will be discussed here: Cole (1973), Hunter, Schmidt, and Rauschenberger (1977), Cronbach et al. (1980), and Ledvinka et al. (1982). In the hypothetical selection situations to be reviewed, several parameters have been either fixed or systematically varied. These include the proportion of minorities in the applicant pool; the proportion of selected applicants (selection ratio); the difference in validities between majority and minority groups; the size of the validity coefficient in each group; the mean difference in criterion scores between majority and minority groups; the mean difference in predictor scores between groups; and the difference in slope intercepts between the minority and majority regressions. All of these researchers have held the standard deviations for predictors and criteria to be equal in the two groups. A contrast among the situations studied is provided in summary form in table 9.1. Cole's study was the only one in which the models were examined with unequal validities.

Table 9.1: Comparison of Studies on the Consequences of Fair-Selection Models

	Theoretical				Empirical
	Cole (1973)	Hunter et al. (1977)	Cronbach et al. (1980)	Ledvinka et al. (1982)	ACT (1973)
ASSUMPTIONS					
Size of validity coefficients	.2 to .7	.10 to 1.00	.4	.3 to .5	Various values derived from data
Difference in validity (majority—minority)	0, .2, -.2, .5	0	0	0	Various values derived from data
Mean difference on criterion variable y (majority—minority)	0, .5 SD_y, 1.0 SD_y, -.8 SD_y	.5 SD_y	.5 SD_y	0 to .5 SD_y	Various values derived from data
Utility function to measure "quality"	Threshold	Linear	Threshold	—	—
Proportion of minority applicants	.20	.00 to 1.00	.20	Derived from data = .225	.20
Selection ratio	.20	.10 to .50	.50	.2 to .5	.50
TYPES OF MODELS					
Two-group regression	X	X[a]		X[a]	X
Equal risk	X	X[a]		X[a]	X
Single-group regression	X				X
Thorndike	X	X			X
Cole	X		X		X
Darlington	X	X			
Quota models		X	X[b]	X	
Equal impact			X	X	

[a] Although the authors quote only one model, under the assumptions of equal validities and equal SDs the two-group regression and equal-risk models have the same effects. Hence, the result quoted for two-group regressions would also apply to the equal-risk model.

[b] It is possible to find the results for quota models in their figures, although they are not discussed explicitly.

259

In Cole's study (1973), the equal-risk and two-groups-regression models gave identical results when regression lines were parallel (and standard deviations equal). Otherwise, when slopes varied, the equal-risk model tended to set higher cutoff scores for the minority group than the separate-groups regression model when the minority slope was smaller. That is, when prediction is *poorer* in the minority group, the equal-risk model is very "conservative" and admits even fewer minorities. The Thorndike and Cole models admitted many more minorities than the equal-risk or regression models under most circumstances, especially when the accuracy of prediction was *lower* in the minority groups. Usually, the Thorndike and Cole models were very close to each other in numbers of minority applicants. The results for the Darlington model can be made to be very "liberal" depending on the value set for K. In Cole's study (1973), the value set for K led to high numbers of minorities admitted, higher than the Thorndike and Cole models except when the intercepts varied. The single-group-regression model, in comparison to the two-groups regression model, tended to disfavor minorities in one situation (when minority intercept was higher) and to favor minorities in other situations, but it was usually considerably less "liberal" than the Thorndike and Cole models. In sum, the two-groups regression and equal-risk models led to very few, *if any*, minorities being selected, especially when prediction was poor.

These conclusions are limited, however, to the situations and combinations of parameters generated by Cole, which included a selection ratio of .20; moderate, not high, validities; and a proportion of .20 of minorities in the applicant pool. These assumptions are fairly realistic except, perhaps, for the very low selection ratio; most undergraduate institutions admit much higher proportions of applicants, although self-selection may make the effective institutional selection ratio smaller than it appears. When the criterion scores (measures of success) of the selected groups were examined, she found that the expected percentages of persons with acceptable criterion scores among minorities admitted were smaller than or equal to that of the majority selectees, in almost all cases for all models. These "success rates" for the Darlington, Thorndike, and Cole models were usually lower than those for the equal-risk or separate-groups regression model, by about .10 to .30, when prediction was poorer for the minority group. In other words, more minorities would be at risk to have unacceptable criterion scores, such as low grades, using these models, but the differences in risk were not always large. Compared to the two-groups regression, the single-group regression model also led to higher rates of "at-risk" minority students; these risks were comparable to the Darlington, Thorndike, and Cole models.

Hunter et al. (1977) and Cronbach et al. (1980) extended some of Cole's comparisons to other selection parameters and functions, including selection ratios of .5 and .1, other utility functions, different values for proportions of minority applicants, and additional validities (see table 9.1). For the situation that Cronbach et al. consider typical, the Thorndike and Cole models differ from the equal-risk model in two ways: The expected percentage of selectees with acceptable criterion scores is slightly lower, and the number of minority acceptances is dramatically larger. In other words, the equal-risk model achieves a small gain in the percentages of persons with high criterion scores (e.g., GPAs) at the expense of dramatically curtailing the number of minority admissions.

Ledvinka et al. (1982) applied a human resource model to simulate the long-term impact of the equal-risk, Thorndike, equal-impact, and quota selection models on minority employment. They concluded that "[t]he simulation shows that the fairness standard implicit in the federal selection guidelines (Cleary's [two-groups] regression model) would have a worse effect on black employment than would the implicit fairness standard typically used by employers (similar to Thorndike's constant-ratio model)" (p. 18). Over 30 years, assuming a .20 selection ratio and a validity of .30, the cumulative impact of the two-groups regression model, if applied, would actually erode black employment from .6 percent, 5.2 percent, and 33 percent, respectively, in the professional, technical, and clerical job classes to .4 percent, 2.1 percent, and 2.1 percent, respectively. In contrast, the Thorndike model would redistribute black employees so that after thirty years, 16.6 percent, 14.5 percent, and 14.8 percent would be represented in the professional, technical, and clerical job classes. The pattern was much the same when the selection ratio was set at .50. When the higher validity ($r = .50$) was used, which is a less realistic number, the difference between the Thorndike and two-groups regression models was substantial, though not as dramatic.

Ledvinka et al. also investigated the long-term impact of quota models. One interesting finding was that even if one black was hired for every white, "it would take at least six years . . . to bring the black employment in all job classes of this organization up to the population parity figure of .225. . . . This is note-worthy in light of the fact that the federal government . . . operates under the expectation that minority underutilization will be remedied within five years" (p. 26).

One limitation of the Ledvinka et al. simulation is that validities were assumed to be equal for both groups. One could extrapolate, however, from Cole's (1973) finding that the two-groups regression was highly conservative when prediction was poorer in the minority group.

Therefore, it is likely that if validities were lower in the minority group, the drop in minority hiring would be even more severe if the equal-risk model were used as the standard of selection.

Selection Situations Based on Empirical Data

The ACT Technical Report (1973), whose main authors were Cole and Hanson, presented the effects of various models if applied to the admissions in the thirty-five colleges that they surveyed. The predictors included ACT and SAT tests and high school grades. They examined the impact of the different models for women, minorities, socioeconomic status, and age groups. All validities and parameters were estimated from the real data, except for the proportion of minorities (which was assumed to be .20) and the selection ratio (which was assumed to be .50).

One surprising finding concerns the effect of the two-groups regression and equal-risk models on women. It was found that the use of these models would "result in selection of 67 percent women and 33 percent men [in the typical class]" (p. 273). This result occurred because validities were typically higher for women, and the two-groups and equal-risk models favor the group with the better prediction. The single-group regression, Thorndike, and Cole models would result in the selection of *more men* than the two-groups regression and equal-risk models, with classes fairly evenly divided between men and women. The analyses by racial-ethnic groups showed that the equal-risk and two-groups-regression models would have admitted fewer minorities than the single-group-regression, Thorndike, and Cole models. It should be pointed out that studies of Chicano-Anglo comparisons were relatively rare among the thirty-five colleges; most analyses involved blacks and whites.

The Consequences of the Models by Ethnicity and Gender

In general, the research on fair selection has concentrated on typical selection situations for blacks and whites and has tended to ignore other groups such as women, Hispanics, and Asians. The effects on these groups can be approximated with the tables from Hunter et al. (1977), where the various proportions of minorities were varied. In the case of gender comparisons, women would be considered the "majority" group because their criterion scores are generally higher. The main limitation of these tables is their assumption of equal validities in the two groups, which is unrealistic for women and Hispanics. Petersen and Novick (1976) have pointed out that for Japanese Americans (who have higher mean predictor and criterion scores than the majority population) the Thorndike and Cole models lead to *fewer* minorities being selected than do the equal-risk and two-groups regression models. Hence, the impact of the various models depends on the regression characteristics of that group. A model that leads to favorable effects for one group may lead to unfavorable results for another.

TECHNICAL WEAKNESSES
OF THE THORNDIKE AND COLE MODELS

Petersen and Novick (1976) have pointed out that the most statistically sound decision-making procedure involves the maximization of only the conditional probability of success, given test score and the utility of that success. "It does not involve any of the marginal or conditional probabilities used by Thorndike [or] Cole. . . . From this point of view, the fundamental fallacy in each of these models is that they are based on the *wrong conditional probability*" (p. 25). The end result is that the degree of preference given to any one group varies as a function of predictive accuracy and the size of the mean differences between groups. This approach can lead to inadvertent inconsistencies in policies at the same institution if there should be a secular change in regressions and marginal distributions. In other words, the utilities are not constant across situations.

EXPLICITNESS OF THE VALUES
INHERENT IN EACH MODEL

Only the Darlington, equal-risk, and expected-utility models express the preference (or nonpreference) given to the various selection outcomes explicitly. This feature is a desirable one since it permits a public debate concerning these issues. The Thorndike and Cole models have been criticized because they do not define these utilities with enough explicitness (Petersen & Novick, 1976). Although they openly define fairness in terms of group parity, the degree of preference for each group and the utilities for selection errors and correct decisions are not easily derived from the models.

The least explicit model, however, is the single-group regression model. When differential prediction exists, the use of a single-group-regression model gives preference to the group that is overpredicted (i.e., has a smaller slope intercept), while ostensibly ignoring group-membership information. Consequently, it has been criticized by both opponents and proponents of group-parity concepts. Jensen (1980) objects to it because it is "an inefficient and biased selection procedure having the statistical properties of a *quota* system, with the added disadvantage that its utilities are inexplicit and inadvertent" (p. 420). The ACT Technical Report (1973), which advocated the Cole model, points out that the single-group regression model produces "accidental favoritism of varying amounts" and that "[i]f such favoritism is desirable, there are [more] rational, explicit methods to implement it" (p. 249).

CURRENT PRACTICES IN SELECTING INSTITUTIONS AND FAIR-SELECTION MODELS

Breland and Ironson (1976) added irony to the heated debate over fair-selection models with their comparison between the University of Washington Law School's selection practices in 1971 and several psychometric models. They applied the Thorndike, Cole, and equal-risk models to fit the selection data that had become public as a result of the DeFunis suit against the University of Washington Law School on the issue of preferential admissions for minorities. Breland and Ironson found that the most "liberal" selection models (Thorndike's and Cole's), would, at best, admit 16 percent of the minority applicants who applied, whereas thirty-seven out of seventy minority applicants were actually selected (53 percent). In contrast, the percent of white applicants to be selected was 17–18 percent according to the models, while the actual percentage selected was 15 percent in the first cut for selectees. Breland and Ironson concluded that "[o]bviously, then, the values represented by the psychometric models are very different from the values represented by the admissions committee's actions" (p. 97). "One suspects that the solution to the broad social dilemma that *DeFunis* represents is not to be found in psychometric models. . . . Had there been only as many as 333 minority applicants to the University of Washington Law School in 1971, rather than only 70, then Cole's . . . model of selection fairness would have provided not only a fair (by one definition) but a sufficient solution" (p. 98). They also suggested other ways to increase the numbers of minority selectees: tutoring and coaching minority students on the tests, the development of "new measures capable of assessing a wider range of competencies" (p. 98), and a revision of instructional approaches in professional education.

It is difficult to assess how typical the minority and majority selection ratios were at the University of Washington Law School in comparison to those of other law schools and higher education institutions.

There have been very few studies on admissions processes for under-graduate, graduate, law school, medical school, and graduate business admissions. In a review of selective admissions processes for various types of institutions, Skager (1982) cited no more than one or two studies on admissions research for each level of postsecondary admissions. A few exceptional institutions have made their alternate admissions proce-dures public (see Fuller, McNamara, & Green, 1978, for examples of seven medical schools and law schools and Willingham & Breland, 1982, for undergraduate colleges). Willingham and Breland (1977) find, how-ever, that "[e]ven with details usually unavailable . . . one finds that a complete understanding of law school admissions procedures is some-what elusive. It is perhaps more useful to turn to data on the actual outcomes of procedures nationally" (pp. 102–103). This point was sup-ported by a comparison of actual admissions to stated institutional goals in their later study of undergraduate colleges (Willingham & Breland, 1982). For example, the policy intentions of institutions did not fully match selection decisions concerning extracurricular accomplishments of students.

Data on actual enrollments also have their limitations (Abramowitz, 1975; Arce, 1976; López, Madrid-Barela, & Macías, 1976). Often the figures presented for professional schools are totals for all law schools or medical schools, and these aggregate figures can misrepresent individ-ual selection ratios. For example, Gordon (1979) reported that in 1977–78, forty-three out of forty-eight private medical schools had selection ratios below .10, whereas the aggregate figures showed that 45 percent of the applicants received at least one offer of admission (Skager, 1982).

Highly Selective Undergraduate Institutions

Willingham and Breland (1977) summarized the results for the Consor-tium on Financing Higher Education (COFHE), which includes thirty institutions that are very selective, such as the Ivy League colleges, the Seven Sisters, and prestigious state universities. They found that individ-ual selection ratios at these schools in 1974 were rarely below .25 and that the average selection ratio was about .45. According to the authors, there were "virtually no difference[s] between minority and nonminority ac-ceptance rates" (p. 79). These near-equal figures represent some prefer-ence for minorities since the minority students scored an average of 75 points below nonminorities on the verbal SAT.

Setting aside possible objections to the equal validities and other assumptions in the simulation of Hunter et al. (1977), one can compare the empirical selection ratios for these institutions (both approximately

.45) with the prediction from an application of Thorndike's selection rule given in their tables. For validities of .30 to .60, the Thorndike model would admit about 32.6 percent of minority candidates and 51.9 percent of majority candidates. In contrast, the two-groups regression model would admit between 6.1 percent to 22.5 percent of minority applicants, depending on the validity coefficients. Hence, the average empirical selection ratio for COFHE institutions appears to be substantially more liberal than that specified by the two-groups regression model and somewhat more liberal than the Thorndike model. These departures are in the same direction as those in the University of Washington Law School, but are not as dramatic.

It is interesting to note that minority students applying to the COFHE institutions in 1974 did not "typically come from impoverished backgrounds" (Willingham & Breland, 1977, p. 79), although their parents' income was substantially below that of white applicants. Also, the proportions of minority applicants and accepted applicants to these institutions were 11.1 percent and 10.8 percent, respectively. This latter figure is several percentage points below the national percentage of minorities enrolled in 1974 at four-year colleges (14.1 percent).

The smaller representation of minority students in COFHE schools reflects self-selection trends; minority students apply and enroll more often in the less selective four-year schools than their white counterparts of the same ability level (Baily & Collins, 1977). Hence the .20 figure for the proportion of minority applicants used in many simulation studies is an unrealistically high figure for most universities, especially the highly selective ones; the number of minority applicants is typically much lower. In this regard, the most realistic simulation study has been one by Hunter et al. (1977), which included proportions of minority applicants below .2 and a selection ratio of .5.

Although a thorough discussion of the factors leading to choices in college applications is beyond the scope of this paper, one point is worth noting. The term *self-selection* is a misnomer because institutions do play an active role in this process through their recruitment policies, financial-aid programs, and informational brochures. Applications to colleges are the result of a complex interaction between the students' and institutions' characteristics. These include the students' financial need compared with the colleges' tuitions and aid packages; the students' academic credentials compared with average test scores and class standings at the institutions; and the students' geographical mobility and the colleges' locations, among other things (Willingham & Breland, 1982; Ihlanfeldt, 1980).

Data on the percentage of accepted women applicants at COFHE institutions were not reported by Willingham and Breland (1977), probably because the figures would have been skewed by the institutions that were traditionally women's colleges. However, the American College Testing Program, in its 1973 survey of undergraduate institutions, concluded that "[t]he [two-groups] regression model, commonly used and defended in questions of racial bias, is not commonly used in matters of sex probably because its use results in classes of 67 percent women on the average. . . . [Q]uotas appear to be in wide use" (p. 272).

Aggregate Selection Ratios
for Law and Medical Schools

Evans (1977) and Willingham and Breland (1977) provide admissions data for law and medical schools that show acceptance rates for minorities and women. Overall, law schools and medical schools are considerably more selective than undergraduate institutions, and the applicants are self-selected for high test scores and undergraduate grade-point averages (UGPAs). The figures shown are aggregated over schools, in that they reflect the percentage of applicants receiving an offer from at least one school. Evans (1977) reported that for law schools in 1976, 59 percent of whites received at least one acceptance in contrast to 39 percent for blacks and 47 percent for Chicanos. If one examines the percentages after breaking down the applicants according to their score on the Law School Admission Test (LSAT), it is evident that at score intervals below 500, acceptance rates for blacks and Chicanos were two to four times higher than for whites. At higher score intervals, the minority acceptance rates tended to be somewhat higher than for whites, but the difference was generally small. These figures cannot be compared directly with the results at the University of Washington Law School because aggregate selection ratios do not accurately reflect proportions accepted for individual institutions.

Evans made an interesting observation when he compared minority applicants and trends in selectivity from 1961 to 1976, when law schools became increasingly selective:

> Although the number of spaces available in first-year classes has increased somewhat, the number and quality (in terms of LSAT and UGPA) of those seeking admission has increased far more rapidly. [Therefore], the quality, in terms of LSAT and [UGPA], of first-year law students is much higher today [in 1976] than it was 10–15 years earlier. . . . (p. 634)

> Although the LSAT scores and UGPA records of accepted blacks and Chicanos are lower, on the whole, than the corresponding numerical measures

for accepted nonminority applicants, these accepted minority students cannot for this reason be regarded as less than fully qualified for law study. They rank, on these predictors, equal to or higher than the average of all law students enrolled 15 years ago. (p. 566)

On the other hand, the acceptance rates for women (in 1976) showed no evidence of preferential treatment toward women for admission to law school. Overall, a higher percentage of women applicants were accepted (60 percent vs. 56 percent) but only because women law applicants had higher grade-point averages. For each level of test score crossed with each level of college grade-point average, the percent of women receiving at least one acceptance was about equal to that for men. Hence, the equality of these proportions suggests that a single-group regression model was used rather than an equal-risk model. As explained earlier, this practice by the schools ostensibly gives equal treatment regardless of gender, but its true effect is to give preference to males when validities are lower for males. Linn (1982) found that validities for the LSAT were higher for females and the female slope intercept was somewhat higher, also.

The medical school data (Willingham & Breland, 1977) show that medical schools were even more selective than law schools, admitting only 36 percent of applicants overall. The applicants were so highly self-selected that the mean scores of the rejected candidates were generally quite high. In 1975–1976, the percentage of all minority applicants (except for Asians, Commonwealth Puerto Ricans, and Cubans) admitted was higher than the percentage of white applicants admitted. Specifically, while 37 percent of whites were admitted to at least one medical school, 42 percent of blacks, 52 percent of Chicanos, and 43 percent of mainland Puerto Ricans were admitted. The mean score on all subsections of the MCAT for *accepted* minority applicants and the mean undergraduate GPA was usually below the mean score of *rejected* white applicants. Specifically, the average MCAT on the verbal subsection for nonaccepted whites was 533, whereas the accepted blacks, Chicanos, and mainland Puerto Ricans averaged 479, 508, and 522 on the same test (Gordon, 1977, cited in Willingham & Breland, 1977). Hence, it is evident that medical schools were admitting larger percentages of minorities than specified by even the most liberal fair-selection models. Data on percentages of women were not reported for medical schools by Willingham and Breland.

Despite the generally lower test scores and undergraduate GPAs of minorities accepted, the "success rate" among accepted minorities was generally high. For law schools, 83 percent of minorities and 90 percent of whites were promoted to their second year in 1975 (Willingham & Breland, 1977, p. 100). For medical schools in 1971, 81 percent of blacks, 85 percent of American Indians, 93 percent of Chicanos, and 96 percent of Puerto Ricans were promoted with their class, compared with 96 percent of whites (Willingham & Breland, 1977, p. 200). Hence, the preference for minorities increased only slightly the rates of attrition or failure to promote.

AN EVALUATION OF FAIR-SELECTION MODELS

It is evident that the evaluation of a selection strategy must encompass many criteria—the reasonableness of its definition, the desirability of its consequences for all subpopulations, its technical soundness, and the explicitness of the values it embodies. Singly, each of these criteria can lead to a misleading conclusion about a strategy when other criteria are ignored. The equal-risk model, for example, has great appeal from some of these perspectives. It maximizes the "quality" (i.e., GPA) of the pool of selectees in that it has many desirable technical features, such as minimizing *all* selection errors equally, using the "right" conditional probability distribution, and having situationally consistent, explicit utilities. However, when its consequences are examined closely, one sees that the increase in GPA of the selectees compared to competing models is small under most realistic circumstances, while the decrease in minority representation is sizable, on both a short-term and a long-term basis.

On the other hand, as noted by Petersen and Novick (1976), one should also be cautious about accepting models simply because they increase the representation of one group.

> [W]e might well contend that it is generally not appropriate to evaluate the correctness of a model solely on the basis of the pleasantness or unpleasantness of its implications but, rather, that one must look carefully at the logical structure of the model. One must be sure that the model is getting the right results for the right reasons. If the models are giving the right results for the wrong reasons, it may well be possible that, in some other circumstances, wrong answers will be forthcoming. . . . [I]ndeed . . . [the Cole and Thorndike] models sometimes can produce most undesirable results that could, in fact, be used to justify discrimination against [Japanese Americans and women]. (p. 24)

The flaws identified in the Thorndike and Cole models are that their utilities for the various selection outcomes are incompletely specified and that they fail to follow generally accepted principles in statistical decision theory. Many of these same criticisms can also be applied to the single-group regression model.

Among current methods, expected-utility models with explicitly defined preferences for targeted groups are potentially the soundest method, when considered across multiple criteria. It should be noted that the equal-risk model can be specified as an expected-utility model that sets utilities equal in two groups, that is, one that states no preference for one group over another. The class of utility models advocated here is more general than the special case of the equal-risk model. The Darlington model is also useful, although its utilities for the various selection outcomes are not as explicitly specified. Unfortunately, little research has been done to investigate the consequences of these models when various parameters are manipulated. Investigations using the Darlington model, for example, have set the value of K at only one number and have not shown the effects on selection outcomes for alternative values of K. The only well-investigated expected-utility model has been the equal-risk model.

One approach that seems promising is the application of utility models to derive tables and graphs like the ones published by Hunter et al. (1977) and Cronbach et al. (1980). Admissions committees can use these results to see how particular selection ratios for minorities would affect the overall grade-point average of the selectees, and the expected difference in success rates among the majority and minority selectees whose scores are near the cutoff value that corresponds to their respective groups. This difference in success rates is called the "difference in quality at the margin" by Cronbach and his colleagues (p. 698).

In some respects, however, all current methods share certain limitations that stem, in part, from a failure to consider some of the most compelling reasons for affirmative action. If diversity in the student body and the provision of quality services to minority populations are important criteria for undergraduate and professional institutions, then academic credentials cannot be considered the only variable to be predicted. In a sense, all current selection fairness strategies are oversimplistic because they have a unidimensional dependent variable, usually operationally defined as grade-point average.

In the Thorndike and Cole models, this exclusive concentration on the college or professional school grade-point average ties the degree of preference given to a group directly to the prediction of grades. The Darlington and expected-utility models are the only ones that set the degree of preference for one group a priori, apart from the prediction of GPA. However, when the "quality" of selected individuals is measured according to these latter models, the outcome is viewed only in terms of success on grades.

This so-called criterion problem has been considered inescapable. The value of diversity and of effective service to minority populations has been viewed as difficult to quantify objectively without using self-report methods that are easily faked. In contrast, some attempts have been made to quantify "disadvantagement" (e.g., Astin, 1978). This task of defining and measuring the construct of disadvantage is undoubtedly easier, given that educational, occupational, and income information lends itself to quantifications. Perhaps the absence of measures to quantify the *positive* contributions of minorities to the professions is not solely due to measurement problems. After all, difficulties in quantification have not stopped personality theorists (though one might question some of their instruments). The preponderance of references to reparations, remediation, and disadvantage in the literature on fair test use suggests that most of these authors have a myopic view of affirmative action that restricts the goals to remediation and reparations for past discrimination.

A comparison of the actual outcomes by admissions committees and the prescriptions of fair-selection models yields several interesting contrasts. Despite the many limitations of actual admissions data, some careful conclusions can be drawn. It appears that committees admit greater numbers of minorities than prescribed by even the most liberal selection models; the same does not appear to be the case for the admission of women. The percentage of students who persisted or were promoted (i.e., "success rates") in the resulting classes has dropped somewhat in comparison to "success rates" of white selectees, but not dramatically. These outcomes generally validate the predictions of simulations by Hunter et al. (1977) and Cronbach et al. (1980).

On the other hand, the assumptions of these and other simulation models have been unrealistic for educational institutions in several respects. One is the failure to incorporate differential prediction systems, which are fairly well documented for women and Hispanics. Another is that the percentage of minority applicants that actually apply to highly selective institutions is much lower than the theoretical number (.20) assumed by the models. For undergraduate institutions, selection ratios of .40 or below are accompanied by percentages of minority applicants usually below 11 percent.

Studies of admissions processes (e.g., Fuller et al., 1978) reveal that admissions committees have to deal with a much greater variety of group-membership variables than ethnicity, disadvantage, or gender; additional characteristics include past employment, veteran status, state residency, service in Peace Corps or VISTA, and physical handicaps, to name a few. Current approaches to fair selection models are oversimplistic because they treat group membership as a univariate dichotomy and therefore do not provide guidelines for *combining* preferences for the different characteristics. For example, in an expected utility model, one may specify separate utilities for ethnicity, veteran status, and physical handicaps—but how does one apply them to a handicapped Hispanic veteran who is a state resident?

Another curious inconsistency in the literature on selection models is that the concept of group parity is attacked almost exclusively when it applies to race or ethnicity but not to state residency and other characteristics. Haney (1981) comments on this point when referring to the use of state residency to select National Merit semifinalists.

> This [method of determining semifinalists] raises the interesting question of how it is that while the National Merit Competition has employed a primitive group-parity approach (it might even be called a quota system) for more than 20 years, group-parity models of fair selection (including parity in terms of characteristics such as race and sex) generally seem to have gained little credibility in the testing literature. The contrast is especially intriguing [when one considers that] . . . the group-parity adjustments . . . actually are fairly substantial. For the 23rd competition in 1978, qualifying scores between low and high scoring states varied by two thirds of a standard deviation. (p. 1032)

Although Haney implies that there is societal opposition to explicitly stated group-parity concepts with respect to gender, in actual practice there is widespread acceptance of selection procedures that could be said to favor males. Many undergraduate institutions and law schools apply the single-group regression model to males and females combined, a procedure that functions, in effect, as a disguised group-parity model. On the surface, this practice appears to give the same opportunities for both sexes because equal cutoffs for test scores and prior grades are used for both groups; however, as explained earlier, it can be considered to favor males because men achieve a lower criterion academic performance than women given the same qualifications.

FUTURE RESEARCH ON FAIR TEST USE

One of the highest priorities of future research should be to extend the approaches that pose the fair selection issues in terms of a trade-off between achieving a high traditional measure of selectees' academic quality and adequate representation of minorities, men, and women (Cole, 1973; Hunter et al., 1977; Cronbach et al., 1980). This type of framework is likely to lead to higher acceptance rates for minorities than most models prescribe in situations where the decreases in the average expected grade-point average of a class would be small. To guarantee that the results will be useful, however, psychometricians should begin to study more closely the types of decisions and situations that academic admissions committees actually face, in order to build more realistic models and simulations. Current models fail to provide for ways to incorporate discrete multivariate group-membership data. The combinations of selection ratios, proportion of minority applicants, and validity coefficients frequently do not reflect typical situations, particularly for admissions for Hispanics, Asians, and women.

The determination of how much "loss in quality" (i.e., average GPA) among selectees should be tolerated by an academic institution in order to increase minority representation is a question of values, not psychometrics. Policy guidelines with respect to this issue can be established by reviewing societal goals, psychometric considerations, and current institutional practices. The recommendations by the Carnegie Council on Policy Studies in Higher Education (1977) represent a successful effort of this type. One of their most useful suggestions concerned the setting of minimum levels for admissions requirements at which students would have a reasonable chance of completing the course work without a reduction in academic standards. The Council advocated using the level of applicants' grades and test scores that were considered acceptable in the mid-1960s when competition for admissions to graduate and professional schools was less intense but successful professionals were being trained. These earlier admission requirements were substantially lower in some fields such as law as shown by Evans (1977). By setting the minimum acceptable cutoffs for admissions at these earlier levels, the pool of minority applicants receiving consideration could be enlarged while maintaining a high probability of successful completion of the program by enrolled students.

Other considerations that can be added to the Council's list are the trade-offs that many institutions currently make between predicted high GPA and the achievement of other goals, such as providing education for state residents and maintaining balanced sex ratios. For example, according to the equal-risk model, only 33 percent of males at current undergraduate institutions should be accepted (see ACT, 1973). The near-equal sex ratios at most institutions imply that the average "quality" of the selected students is less than it would be if more females were admitted. Since this decrease in average GPA is widely accepted, we could use this number to set limits for what is considered a "tolerable" drop in quality. Similar estimates could be derived by examining the trade-offs made by selective state universities when more "qualified" out-of-state residents are rejected in favor of state residents. Even if these "losses in quality" turn out to be small, scrutiny of these practices would be enlightening. It would bring to the debate of fair selection issues a necessary awareness concerning the widespread use of group-parity concepts that go unchallenged in our society when they are applied to groups defined by characteristics other than race or ethnicity.

At the undergraduate level, the problem of self-selection is even more critical than how to help admissions committees determine who is to be admitted. A large part of the problem is that minority students tend to apply to two-year institutions and to the least selective four-year institutions. Research should concentrate on ways to counsel minority students to take standardized tests and apply to higher-quality institutions.

Ideally, future research should challenge the view that academic performance is the only criterion for success by developing measures of competence other than grades. For example, medical or law schools could consider evaluating how well their graduates communicate with minority patients or clients and how effectively they serve these populations. In this manner, the selection problem would become a multivariate multiple regression paradigm where several measures of quality are to be predicted. Cutting scores could then be set to maximize these qualities simultaneously. In this way it might be possible to identify and validate individual characteristics of minority students that are predictors of these other kinds of "success." The predictors could include, for example, fluency in conversational Spanish or black English. This approach could conceivably eliminate the need for preferences based on group membership alone, rather than on an individual's assets. Realistically speaking, however, it is unlikely that the "criterion problem" will ever receive the attention and effort that it has so long deserved.

REFERENCES

Abramowitz, E. (1975). *Equal opportunity for Blacks in U.S. higher education: An assessment.* Report No. 1. Washington, DC: Institute for the Study of Educational Policy, Howard University.

American College Testing Program. (1973). *Assessing students on the way to college.* Technical Report, Volume 1. Iowa City, IA: ACT.

Arce, C. H. (1976). *Historical, institutional, and contextual determinants of Black enrollment in predominantly White colleges, 1946 to 1974.* Unpublished doctoral dissertation, University of Michigan.

Astin, A. W. (1978). Quantifying "disadvantagement." In A. W. Astin, B. Fuller, & K. C. Green, (Eds.), *Admitting and assisting students after Bakke: New direc-*

tions for higher education (Vol. 6, No. 3. pp. 75–84). San Francisco: Jossey-Bass.

Bailey, J. P., Jr., & Collins, E. F. (1977, April). *Entry into postsecondary education.* Paper presented at the annual meeting of the American Education Research Association, New York City.

Breland, H. M. (1979). *Population validity and college entrance measures.* Research Monograph 8. New York: College Entrance Examination Board.

Breland, H. M., & Griswöld, P. A. (1981). *Group comparisons for basic skills measures.* College Board Report No. 81-6. New York: College Entrance Examination Board. (Also ETS RR No. 81-21.)

Breland, H. M., & Ironson, G. H. (1976). DuFunis reconsidered: A comparative analysis of alternative admissions strategies. *Journal of Educational Measurement, 13,* 89–99.

Cardoza, D. (1982). *Culture fairness and prediction models: Is there an answer?* Unpublished paper, University of California, Riverside.

Carnegie Council on Policy Studies in Higher Education. (1977). *Selective admissions in higher education.* San Francisco: Jossey-Bass.

Cole, N.S. *Bias in selection.* (1972). American College Testing Research Report 51. Iowa City, IA: American College Testing Program.

Cole, N. S. (1973). Bias in selection. *Journal of Educational Measurement, 10,* 237–255.

Cronbach, L. J., Yallow, E., & Schaeffer, G. (1979, October). *Setting cut scores in selection: A mathematical structure for examining policies.* Project Report 79-A7. Palo Alto, CA: Institute for Research on Educational Finance and Governance.

Cronbach, L. J., Yallow, E., and Schaeffer, G. (1980). A mathematical structure for analyzing fairness in selection. *Personnel Psychology, 33,* 693–704.

Darlington, R. B. (1971). Another look at "culture fairness." *Journal of Educational Measurement, 8,* 71–72.

Durán, R. P. (1983). *Hispanics' education and background: Predictors of college achievement.* Princeton, NJ: Educational Testing Service.

Einhorn, H. J., & Bass, A. R. (1971). Methodological considerations relevant to discrimination in employment testing. *Psychological Bulletin, 75,* 261–269.

Evans, F. R. (1977). Applications and admissions to ABA accredited law schools: An analysis of national data for the class entering in the fall of 1976. LSAC-77-1, Princeton, NJ: Law School Admissions Council.

Fuller, B., McNamara, P. P., & Green, K. C. (1978). Alternative admissions procedures. In A. W. Astin, B. Fuller, & K. C. Green (Eds.), *Admitting and assisting students after Bakke: New directions for higher education* (Vol. 6, No. 3. pp. 1-28). San Francisco: Jossey-Bass.

Gordon, T. L. (1977). *Descriptive study of medical school applicants, 1975–76.* Washington, DC: Association of American Medical Colleges.

Gordon, T. L. (1979). Study of U.S. medical school applicants, 1977–78. *Journal of Medical Education, 54,* 677–702.

Gross, A. L., & Su, W. (1975). Defining a "fair" or "unbiased" selection model: A question of utilities. *Journal of Applied Psychology, 60,* 345–351.

Haney, W. (1981). Validity, vaudeville, and values: A short history of social concerns over standardized testing. *American Psychologist, 36,* 1021–1034.

Hargadon, F. (1981). Tests and college admissions. *American Psychologist, 36,* 1112–1119.

Hathaway, J. C. (1984). The mythical meritocracy of law school admissions. *Journal of Legal Education, 34,* 86–96.

Heath, D. H. (1968). *Growing up in college.* San Francisco: Jossey-Bass.

Hunter, J. E., Schmidt, F. L., & Rauschenberger, J. M. (1977). Fairness of pyschological tests: Implications of four definitions for selection utility and minority hiring. *Journal of Applied Psychology, 62,* 245–260.

Ihlanfeldt, W. (1980). *Achieving optimal enrollment and tuition revenues: A guide to modern methods of market research, student recruitment, and institutional pricing.* San Francisco: Jossey-Bass.

Jensen, A. R. (1980). *Bias in mental testing.* New York: Free Press.

Ledvinka, J., Markes, V. H., & Ladd, R. T. (1982). Long-range impact of "fair selection" standards on minority employment. *Journal of Applied Psychology, 67,* 18–36.

Linn, R. L. (1973). Fair test use in selection. *Review of Educational Research, 43,* 139–161.

Linn, R. L. (1982). Ability testing: Individual differences, prediction, and differential prediction. In A. K. Wigdor & W. R. Gardner (Eds.), *Ability testing: Uses, consequences and controversies, Part II* (pp. 335–387). Washington, DC: National Academy Press.

López, R. W., Madrid-Barela, A., & Macías, R. F. (1976). *Chicanos in higher education: Status and issues.* Monograph No. 7. Los Angeles: Chicano Studies Center, University of California.

Manning, W. H. (1977). The pursuit of fairness in admissions. In Carnegie Council on Policy Studies in Higher Education, *Selective admissions in higher education.* San Francisco: Jossey-Bass.

Nahemow, L., & Lawton, P. M. (1975). Similarity and propinquity in friendship formation. *Journal of Personality & Social Psychology, 32,* 205–213.

Novick, M. R., & Petersen, N. S. (1976). Towards equalizing educational and employment opportunity. *Journal of Educational Measurement, 13,* 77–88.

Olmedo, E. L. (1977). Psychological testing and the Chicano: A reassessment. In J. L. Martínez, Jr. (Ed.), *Chicano psychology.* (pp. 175–195). New York: Academic Press.

Petersen, N. S. (1974). An expected utility model for "optimal" selection. *ACT Technical Bulletin,* No. 24, Iowa City: The American College Testing Program, 1974.

Petersen, N. S., & Novick, M. R. (1976). An evaluation of some models for culture-fair selection. *Journal of Educational Measurement, 13,* 3–29.

Powers, D. E. (1982). *Differential trends in law school grades of minority and non-minority law students.* Research Report RR-82-1. Princeton, NJ: Educational Testing Service.

Powers, D. E. (1984a). Predicting law school grades for minority and nonminority students: Beyond the first-year average. (Report LSAC-81-1). In Law

School Admission Council, *Reports of LSAC Sponsored Research: Vol. IV, 1978–1983* (pp. 261–300). Princeton, NJ: Author.

Powers, D. E. (1984b). Differential trends in law grades of minority and nonminority law students. *Journal of Educational Psychology, 76,* 488–499.

Sawyer, R. L., Cole, N. S., & Cole, J. W. L. (1976). Utilities and the issues of fairness in a decision theoretical model for selection. *Journal of Educational Measurement, 13,* 59–76.

Skager, R. (1982). On the use and importance of tests of ability in admission to post-secondary education. In A. K. Wigdor & W. R. Gardner (Eds.), *Ability testing: Uses, consequences, and controversies, Part II* (pp. 286–314). Washington DC: National Academy Press.

Thorndike, R. L. (1971). Concepts of culture-fairness. *Journal of Educational Measurement, 8,* 63–70.

Willingham, W. W., Breland, H. M., & Associates. (1977). The status of selective admissions. In Carnegie Council on Policy Studies in Higher Education, *Selective admissions in higher education.* San Francisco: Jossey-Bass.

Willingham, W. W., & Breland, H. M. (1982). *Personal qualities and college admissions.* New York: College Entrance Examination Board.

III | Economics and Stratification

10 | Financial Aid for Hispanics: Access, Ideology, and Packaging Policies

MICHAEL A. OLIVAS

Despite its importance in the administration of financial aid, relatively little is known about packaging policy. Billions of dollars are distributed each school year through public and private programs, and nearly all colleges and universities assemble financial-aid "packages" for students, whose eligibility is computed by third-party form processors. Yet, even with major investments in financial assistance—and increasing research and policy analyses on the topic of financial aid—scant attention has been paid to the economic, equity, or policy dimensions of packaging. This omission is anomalous, for the major federal higher education legislative debates have been over financial aid, whether establishment of massive grant and loan programs, the expansion of these programs to "middle-income" students, or federal efforts to trim back costs in the financial-aid programs.

Researchers have little record of public debate on packaging issues, because there is no national consensus on packaging policy. Institutions have wide discretion to combine resources according to institutional priorities, within broad governmental and College Scholarship Service guidelines. A federal task force attempted to identify acceptable guiding principles for distribution of financial aid and conceded defeat: "the existence of several similar but yet distinctive concepts has instead served more to confuse matters, perhaps even deterring the development of a full coordinated approach to the award of various student assistance monies" (Department of Health, Education and Welfare, U.S. Office of Education, 1973). These pessimistic conclusions, drafted more than ten years ago, have worsened over the decade. Low-income students have been particularly hard hit by uncertainty over financial-assistance policy and actual cutbacks in aid amounts, since their families frequently have fewer resources, including information about available funds (Olivas, 1981a).

PURPOSE OF THE STUDY

This study has as its purpose the establishment of current baseline data on receipt of financial aid by disadvantaged Hispanic students. The balance of this paper analyzes the findings of these data, noting in particular the patterns of aid awards, the "packages" of Hispanic students; it also attempts to measure the relationships between student characteristics and financial aid received. It examines institutional financial-aid administration policies in assembling packages for Hispanics and assesses the impact of governmental-aid policies upon these students. Finally, it discusses models for aid awards based upon public policy objectives and recommends several packaging policies for use by aid administrators. There is a popular ideology that suggests that "need-based" awards help economically disadvantaged students, and the data examined in this study both support and refute this ideology. Given the inchoate nature of the ideology, little data-based research on packaging has been attempted, and no compelling theoretical frameworks have emerged. Another reason packaging "theory" has been so atheoretical is that many institutions treat their financial-aid administration mechanically (frequently on a first-come-first-served basis) rather than theoretically or philosophically.

DATA

A serious deterrent to previous packaging research has been the extensive data problems inherent in such an undertaking. While these problems—confidentiality (Comment, 1976), accuracy of student-reported items, and underenrollment of low-income students (Olivas, 1982)—plague all packaging studies, the small number of Mexican American and Puerto Rican students has posed acute problems for measuring the effects of financial assistance upon this population.[1]

The data examined in this study are files from the country's largest Hispanic Talent Search (a federally funded counseling program), an eleven-city project that annually counsels 16,000 Hispanic students. Because of federal record-keeping requirements for the program, extensive data are gathered for each student; owing to the complex nature of financial applications, many personal and family items are necessary, including parental income and other confidential data. A sample of 521 complete files was compiled, each containing a thirty-item counselor questionnaire, a notarized parental confidential statement or IRS return, a high school transcript, an official test score (except where scores were imputed),[2] a notification-of-aid award, and other personal information such as letters or application essays. Family-income guidelines for the Talent Search Program require that at least two-thirds of clients served be from low-income families. The 521 files were Mexican American and Puerto Rican full-time, first-time students in 1979–80. With program guidelines and Hispanic poverty, it was not surprising to find that 77 percent of the students in the sample came from families with 1978–79 incomes of less than $15,000;[3] over 60 percent of the families had incomes of less than $10,500. Income quartile measurements conform to 1972 National Longitudinal Survey categories of low (below $7,500), lower middle ($7,500-$10,500), upper middle ($10,500-$15,000), and high (over $15,000).

RESEARCH FINDINGS

The most striking single finding is the small extent to which any packaging is being performed for Hispanics: Over 60 percent of all the students received only one source of aid, almost exclusively Basic Educational Opportunity Grants, known as Pell Grants since 1981 (see table 10.1). Pell Grants as a major component of multiple sources were also evident, for 95 percent of multiple sources included a Pell Grant award. Single-source aid was evident at all income levels, ranging from 54 percent of lower-middle to 65 percent of upper-middle students receiving only one source of aid. The pattern of single-source aid by SAT scores was less evenly distributed across all score levels;[4] the lowest score category had 62 percent of its students with single-source aid, while the three higher score categories ranged from 44 percent to 77 percent with single-source aid—almost exclusively Pell Grant and Supplemental Educational Opportunity Grant awards.

The evidence of little packaging for Hispanic students contrasts both with earlier studies of Hispanic student aid and with current packaging practice for all students. In 1972–73, 52 percent of Hispanic aid packages were single source, but only 23.4 percent of all packages were solely grant awards; there was evidence that work-study (10.3 percent), loans (14.7 percent), and benefits (3.7 percent) were significant components of Hispanic financial-aid packages, at all income levels and for attendance at all types of institutions (Wagner & Rice, 1977, table IV-15). A 1978 study of student assistance reported that even students from the lowest-income families attending the least expensive schools averaged $158 of nongrant federal aid in their average package of $1,079 (*Condition of Education*, 1980, table 4.17). The Cooperative Institutional Re-

Table 10.1: Distribution of Financial Aid According to Type of Aid, by Family Income and SAT score, for Entering Full-Time Freshman Hispanic Students, 1979–80

	Total Aided Freshman	Single Type Only				More Than One Type	
		Grant	Work	Loan	Benefit	With Grant	Without Grant
	100	60.0	*	*	*	34.7	4.0
	(521)	(313)	(1)	(1)	(4)	(181)	(21)
Family Income Quartile [a]							
Low		59.4	*	*	1.2	33.6	5.1
	232	(138)	(1)	(0)	(3)	(78)	(12)
Lower middle		52.4	*	*	1.2	42.6	3.6
	82	(43)	(0)	(0)	(1)	(35)	(3)
Upper middle		64.7	*	*	*	31.8	3.4
	88	(57)	(0)	(0)	(0)	(28)	(3)
High		63.0	*	*	*	33.6	2.5
	119	(75)	(0)	(1)	(0)	(40)	(3)
SAT Score [b]							
Low		60.2	*	*	*	33.9	4.4
	430	(259)	(1)	(1)	(4)	(146)	(19)
Lower middle		63.1	*	*	*	36.8	*
	57	(36)	(0)	(0)	(0)	(21)	(0)
Upper middle		44.0	*	*	*	52.0	4.0
	25	(11)	(0)	(0)	(0)	(13)	(1)
High		77.7	*	*	*	11.1	11.1
	9	(7)	(0)	(0)	(0)	(1)	(1)

* <1.0%

[a] Income quartiles calculated from student-reported income interval estimates: Low = less than $7,500; Lower middle = $7,500 to $10,500; Upper middle $10,500 to $15,000; High = over $15,000.

[b] Students are grouped according to SAT-equivalent scores; Low = less than 800; Lower middle = 800 to 950; Upper middle = 950 to 1,100; High = over 1,100.

search Program (CIRP) data revealed that only 31.5 percent of all freshmen received a BEOG, only 7.2 percent a SEOG, and 13.2 percent a guaranteed student loan (Astin, King, & Richardson, 1979, pp. 57–58). It is clear, then, that grant aid has risen dramatically for all students, in all institutions and for all income levels. Hispanic data, however, reveal a strikingly different pattern in the students' extraordinary reliance upon grants, to the near exclusion of other forms of aid.

Table 10.2: Average Total Aid Received by Entering Full-Time Freshman Hispanic Aid Recipients by Median Family Income and Institutional Type and Control, 1979–80

Institutional Type	Median Family Income				
	Under $7,500	$7,500– $10,500	$10,500– $15,000	$15,000 & over	ROW TOTAL
Public 4-year	2251	2530	1725	1406	1959
Public 2-year	1805	1476	1109	950	1482
Private 4-year	3243	4356	4705	3514	3835
Private 2-year	2885	3301	2333	2409	2784
Other	1859	1971	2145	1998	1942
TOTAL	2125	2362	1830	1548	1981

Table 10.2 disaggregates the data by median family income and the type of institution attended. Cross-tabulations show several trends: In each income quartile, more money went to students attending, in descending order, private four-year, private two-year, public four-year, and public two-year colleges. Additionally, students from low- and lower-middle-income families received more aid than did students from upper-middle- and high-income families; curiously, however, except for students in public two-year institutions, in each institutional type the lowest-income students received less aid than did students in the lower-middle category; the mean difference was more than $200 per student. Closer analysis of twenty of the files showed this difference was not due to the lowest-income students' having the lowest costs but rather to lower aid awards and higher expected personal contributions. One of the assumptions of financial-aid distribution is that the neediest students receive the most assistance, within the limits of institutional costs. It could have been expected, then, that within institutional types, the amounts to students would slope downward, with the highest aid awards going to the students in the lowest category. In these data, only the public two-year colleges showed such a pattern, with private four-year colleges showing a tendency to award proportionately more aid to higher-income students.

Attending a public two-year college meant that students were less likely to receive aid. As table 10.3 indicates, fewer students attending public community colleges received aid than did students attending other institutions, and in the important grant category, a significant difference in grant receipt was evident. This finding corroborates other research on the practice of community colleges in financial-aid administration (Augenblick & Hyde, 1979; Harris, 1976; Hyde, 1979). As table

Table 10.3: Hispanic Financial Aid Recipients According to Type of Aid, by Institutional Type and Control (Percent Distribution), 1979–80

Institutional Type	Financial Aid	Grants or Scholarships	Term-time Earnings	Loans	Benefits
Public 4-year		92.4[a]	22.8	21.1	4.2
	(222)	(219)	(54)	(50)	(10)
Public 2-year		83.6	2.8	1.4	9.9
	(195)	(178)	(6)	(3)	(21)
Private 4-year		95.6	21.7	32.6	2.2
	(45)	(44)	(10)	(15)	(1)
Private 2-year		96.0	12.0	4.0	8.0
	(25)	(24)	(3)	(1)	(2)
Other		85.3	0.0	11.8	11.8
	(34)	(29)		(4)	(4)
TOTAL		89.0	13.2	13.2	6.8
	(521)	(494)	(73)	(73)	(38)

NOTE: Numbers in parentheses are actual cases.
[a]Horizontal percentage totals may exceed 100%.

10.4 shows, public two-year colleges are the sector most reliant upon federal financial aid for Hispanic students and the sector with the least discretionary (nonfederal) and mixed-discretionary aid. This reliance upon federal funds is a major shift since Hispanic packaging data in 1972–73, when the federal sources of aid were 39 percent, nonfederal 21.6 percent, and mixed sources 39.4 percent (Wagner & Rice, 1977, table IV-20). Inasmuch as Hispanic students are disproportionately enrolled in public two-year colleges (Olivas, 1979), this distribution of assistance suggests that enrollment patterns may inhibit complete access to financial-aid resources; the extraordinary reliance upon federal funds may also mean that federal cutbacks in financial-aid programs have disproportionately affected community colleges and Hispanic students.

PACKAGING AS IDEOLOGY

In the main, the data in this study reveal that financial aid is being distributed to Hispanic students on the basis of "need." The distribution system evidently is working, *if* the criterion is that lower-income students are to receive larger aid awards. However, while this equity principle is a

Table 10.4: Distribution of Financial Aid According to Source, by Institutional Type and Control, for Entering Full-Time Freshman Hispanic Students (Percent Distribution), 1979–80

Institutional Type	Federal Only	Nonfederal and Federal	Nonfederal Only
Public 4-year (222)	61.3 (136)	34.7 (77)	4.1 (9)
Public 2-year (195)	78.5 (153)	19.5 (38)	2.0 (4)
Private 4-year (45)	26.6 (12)	55.6 (25)	17.8 (8)
Private 2-year (25)	16.0 (4)	80.0 (20)	4.0 (1)
Other (34)	76.5 (26)	17.6 (6)	5.9 (2)
TOTAL (521)	63.5 (331)	31.8 (166)	4.6 (24)

NOTE: Numbers in parentheses are actual cases.

fundamental premise of financial-aid distribution, it is surely not the sole criterion. Student choice among institutions, public support to the private sector, and aid to "middle-income" families are just as surely premises of the existing financial-aid system. Susan Nelson has succinctly summarized these indices: "In short, what is the standard against which the actual distribution of student aid can be judged? There is no clear answer to this question, though the choice of a standard crucially affects the verdict" (Nelson, 1980, p.1).

It may be that a single standard does not exist, as crucial as the choice of standard clearly is. And while politically glib justifications for aid to education and increased financial-aid programs may invoke a "societal good" rationale, less debate has centered upon which societal good is to be subsidized and which is not. The passage of the Middle Income Assistance Act typified the view that "middle-income" families deserved more support.[5] However, just as the excessive costs of medical education have called into question the federal investment in subsidizing more medical schools and doctors, so are massive quasi-entitlement programs such as Pell Grants and student loan authorities being reexamined by budget cutters.

Consider several packaging scenarios, based upon different public policy fiscal presumptions. Assume that higher education is determined to be an *individual* good, the benefits of which accrue solely to the recipient. In such a case, self-help or reimbursable aid would be the appropriate packaging strategy; work-study, loans, and personal resources (which may include family savings) would be packaged, and loan terms could be arranged so that the government did not subsidize deferred repayment. A second scenario assumes that a more highly educated citizenry is solely a social benefit and that education for all persons is a *community* contribution. This presumption would entirely subsidize tuition, living expenses, and perhaps forgone income. No self-help, save eventual participation in the tax system, would be required, on the assumption that this scheme would subsidize itself over time. Yet another scenario, a variation of the second case, would reward persons with certain characteristics, on the assumption that society needed to educate more of these persons, whether honor students, minorities, veterans, doctors, or whichever recipients were deemed worth subsidization. This more targeted social-benefit theory could use packaging as a focused mechanism for achieving the good. Many other such scenarios could be envisioned in either pure or mixed versions, and financial-aid packages could be assembled to effectuate the policies by indexing awards to choice of curriculum, grade-point averages, student characteristics, or a mix of qualifications.

These scenarios do exist and are routinely employed by institutions for assembling millions of packages each year (Windham, 1976, 1980). However, as noted earlier, the complexity of award administration and the lack of consensus on aid or packaging principles have precluded more thoughtful theoretical approaches to public policy on student financial assistance. Several packaging models are summarized in figure 10.1, according to the mix of aid and public policy objectives.

Anyone familiar with higher education institutions will recognize case IV, the mixed-purpose package, as the most common type of aid award, reflecting several purposes and delivery systems. Yet the Hispanic data detailed in this study reflect almost a pure II or III, depending upon whether grants are characterized as societal benefits or targeted group benefits. In truth, they are both. It is also true that Pell Grants, as the cornerstone of federal higher education policy, are a major component of wealthier students' packages. This role may not reflect ambivalence so much as it reflects the mixed purposes (and mixed economy) that federal policies serve in the financing of student assistance. Always reluctant to legislate in language explicitly spelling out "minority" entitlement, Congress has frequently employed "need" as a criterion, even when majority students have participated disproportionately (Olivas, 1982; Windham, 1980). If administered well, such indirection may yet improve minority access.

Figure 10.1: Financial Aid Packaging Models

I. Individual benefit
    · Work-study
    · Unsubsidized loans
    · Personal and family resources

II. Societal benefit
    · Subsidized grants
    · Subsidized loans
    · No charges

III. Individual or group characteristic benefit
    · Subsidized grants according to specific
      characteristic
    · Loans subsidized according to specific
      characteristic
    · Personal resources indexed according to
      specific characteristic

IV. Mixed-purpose packages
    · Work-study
    · Loans
    · Grants
    · Award for characteristics
    · Personal and family resources

POLICY IMPLICATIONS FOR HISPANIC ACCESS

Even if the welcome verdict is that lower-income Hispanic students fare relatively well, there are clear signs within these data that the maldistribution of Hispanic students throughout the postsecondary system and the high reliance upon single-source federal aid could augur problems. While the data base replicates the distribution of Hispanic students by institutional type, the concentration of students in two-year institutions raises serious concerns about widespread access to the system; moreover, the concentration is even more striking when it is known that twenty-one institutions enroll a quarter of all Hispanic students in the fifty states and the District of Columbia (Brown et al., 1980, p. 119). In this study, public two-year colleges are the most dependent upon federal funds to distribute financial assistance to Hispanics, exceeding even "other" schools such as proprietary and postsecondary adult basic education centers (tables 10.4 and 10.5); these institutions use less discretionary aid in Hispanic packages, owing to little endowment or institutional aid resources. Because needy students will probably attend only institutions where they receive an aid award, Hispanic students may be dissuaded from attend-

Table 10.5:   Packaging of Federal Aid to Aided Entering Full-Time Freshman Hispanics by Student and Family Attributes, 1979–80

		Percentage of Aided Full-Time Freshmen		
	Total Aided Freshmen	Receiving Federal and Nonfederal Aid	Receiving Federal Aid Only	Receiving Nonfederal Aid Only
All aided freshmen	521	33.0	63.5	3.5
Family Income Quartile[a]				
Low	232	30.2	67.7	2.2
Lower middle	82	42.7	56.1	1.2
Upper middle	88	31.8	63.6	4.5
High	119	32.8	60.5	6.7
SAT Score[b]				
Low	430	31.2	67.2	1.6
Lower middle	57	38.6	52.6	8.8
Upper middle	25	44.0	36.0	20.0
High	9	55.5	33.3	11.1

[a] Income quartiles calculated from student-reported income interval estimates: Low = less than $7,500; Lower middle = $7,500 to $10,500; Upper middle = $10,500 to $15,000; High = over $15,000.
[b] Students are grouped according to SAT-equivalent scores: Low = less than 800; Lower middle = 800 to 950; Upper middle = 950 to 1,100; High = over 1,100.

ing private four-year colleges where aid is more readily available to wealthier students and more discretionary institutional aid awards are made. Moreover, the low SAT scores and the large percentage of Hispanics who do not take standardized tests may preclude the students from being eligible for most private four-year institutions, unless colleges are willing to employ other criteria or qualitative indices.

Another problem may be the extraordinary reliance of Hispanic students upon Pells, almost to the exclusion of other forms of aid. The dangers are twofold: government cutbacks in Pells and unpackaged aid's effect upon student persistence. Pell Grant awards were scaled back from a maximum of $1,800 in 1979–80 to $1,670 in 1981–82 (Budget bill . . . , 1981), and institutions not accustomed to packaging aid awards have required Hispanics to make up the difference by parental contributions or summer earnings. With the poverty and lack of summer job opportunities for minority youth, this gap may not be made up by all students. In particular, two-year colleges continue to underutilize campus-based financial-aid programs (Gladieux, 1975; Nelson, 1980). Equally serious, the lack of comprehensive, multisource packages may have a detrimental effect upon Hispanic persistence. There is compelling evidence that different types of aid facilitate persistence, for reasons that are not fully understood (Astin, 1975; Jensen, 1981). College work-study participation, in particular, seems to improve the likelihood that students will remain in school, perhaps because the regular earnings require students to budget their money (whereas grants made in lump sum do not enforce such frugality), or because the contact with a supervisor makes students feel a part of the system, or because a meaningful skill is acquired.

It is difficult to recommend an increased emphasis upon loans, because the 1972 evidence suggested that Hispanic students took on disproportionately large levels of indebtedness (*Condition of Education,* 1980, table 5.17). Although the data in this study reveal small participation in loan programs, institutions frequently use loans as an increasingly large share of packages, on the assumption that the longer a student is in college, the larger the share of reimbursable aid should be. If this unarticulated packaging is in effect, then data on Hispanic juniors and seniors may reveal more participation in loan programs. Even though these data differ significantly from CIRP baseline data on freshman packages, what may be operating is institutional decisions to award Hispanics—who tend to have lower grades, test scores, and persistence levels than do majority students—grant packages that do not require reimbursement or take time that could be used for study. Inasmuch as Hispanic students tend to come from lower income families and to express more economic concerns than do majority students,[6] aid administrators should consider whether moderate work-study or cooperative education programs might afford more psychosocial benefits than merely awarding single-source grant packages. The federal cutbacks under Gramm-Rudman legislation may force such considerations upon colleges, and aid administrators should work with institutional researchers to assess the effect of packaging upon low-income students.

One obvious limitation of these data is that only enrolled students are studied (and these students had counseling assistance), and there is no practical way to know how many students were discouraged from attending college because of their inability to receive technical assistance, to negotiate the aid application process, or to secure aid. However, it is intuitively obvious that students from low-income families have fewer resources to spend on college, and in many ways, the aid system compensates for this imbalance by packaging larger awards to needier students. Concentrating upon those Hispanic students who do make it into the system ought not to blind educators to the major access barriers that remain or to lull observers into believing that the financial-aid system—however equitable toward needy students—can itself remedy historic exclusion. Nonetheless, it is evident that financial-aid packaging can be a powerful means of increasing access to postsecondary education. At a time when fundamental educational fiscal issues are being debated, packaging theory remains strangely ignored, even though the assembling of financial aid at the institutional level holds considerable promise as a major redistributive public policy intervention point.

NOTES

1. In the fifty states and the District of Columbia, Hispanic undergraduates were 3.5 percent of U.S. full-time enrollments in 1978 (Brown, Rosen, Hill, & Olivas, 1980, table 3.09). Additional Hispanic education data issues are examined in Olivas (1981b, 1981c).

2. Approximately 30 percent of the files required imputation of standardized test scores, derived from a method that assigned scores to students within income categories (Doermann, 1976). For additional information on the data base, see Panel on Student Financial Need Analysis (1971).

3. Filers must report the previous year's income. Financial data are in 1979 constant dollars, unless otherwise noted.

4. This was undoubtedly affected by the imputation of scores for the non–test takers, as well as the few students (thirty-four) with combined SAT scores above 950 (of a possible 1600).

5. Yet the legislation's upper-income limits seem to mischaracterize "middle income."

6. Data on high school seniors show considerable differences between white and Hispanic student concerns. Hispanic seniors expressed more concern over money problems (45.5 percent to 27.4 percent for white students) and family obligations (39.3 percent to 23.6 percent; Brown et al., 1980, table 2.16).

REFERENCES

Aspira. (1976). *Social factors in educational attainment among Puerto Ricans in U.S. metropolitan areas, 1970.* New York: Aspira.

Astin, A. (1975). *Preventing students from dropping out.* San Franciso: Jossey-Bass.

Astin, A. (1976). Determining racial enrollments in post-secondary education. In E. Abramowitz (Ed.), *Proceedings from the National Invitational Conference on Racial and Ethnic Data* (pp. 16–41). Washington, DC: Institute for the Study of Educational Policy.

Astin, A. (1979). *The impact of student financial aid programs on student choice.* Los Angeles: Higher Education Research Institute.

Astin, A., King, M., & Richardson, G. (1979). *The American freshman: National norms for fall 1979.* Los Angeles: University of California at Los Angeles.

Atelsek, F., & Gomberg, I. (1975). *Student assistance: Participants and programs, 1974–75.* Washington, DC: American Council on Education.

Augenblick, J., & Hyde, W. (1979). *Patterns of funding, net price and financial need for postsecondary education students.* Denver, CO: Education Commission of the States.

Baird, L. (1976). *Using self-reports to predict student performance.* New York: College Entrance Examination Board.

Bingham, R. (1970). Financial aid packaging: Student serving or institution serving? *NACAC Journal, 15,* 23–25.

Bonilla, F., & Campos, R. (1981). A wealth of poor: Puerto Ricans in the new economic order. *Daedalus, 110,* 133–176.

Bowman, J. (1974). *Accuracy of parents' taxable income reports for the 1972–73 processing year* (mimeographed). New York: College Entrance Examination Board.

Boyd, J., & Fenske, R. (1976). Financing of a college education: Theory and reality. *Journal of Student Financial Aid, 6,* 13–21.

Breland, H. (1979). *Population validity and college entrance measures.* New York: College Entrance Examination Board.

Brown, G., Rosen, N., Hill, S., & Olivas, M. (1980). *The condition of education for Hispanic Americans.* Washington, DC: National Center for Education Statistics.

Brown, R. (1976). *Equity packaging of student financial aid* (mimeographed). New York: College Entrance Examination Board.

Budget bill makes broad changes in postsecondary law. (1981, August 14). *Higher Education Daily,* pp. 3–4.

Comment. (1976). The confidentiality of university student records: A common law analysis. *Brigham Young University Law Review, 20,* 477–486.

The condition of education. (1980). Washington, DC: National Center for Education Statistics.

Creech, F. (1974). *A vocational reevaluation of the base year survey of the high school class of 1972, Part 1* (mimeographed). Princeton, NJ: Educational Testing Service.

Davis, J., & Van Dusen, W. (1978). *Guide to the literature of student financial aid.* New York: College Entrance Examination Board.

Department of Health, Education and Welfare, U.S. Office of Education Task Force on Management of Student Assistance Programs. (1973). *Preliminary report.* Washington, DC: DHEW/USOE.

Doermann, H. (1976). The future market for college admission. In *A role for marketing in college admissions* (pp. 1–53). New York: College Entrance Examination Board.

Fields, C., & Le May, M. (1973). Student financial aid: Effects on educational decisions and academic achievement. *Journal of College Student Personnel, 14,* 425–429.

Gladieux, L. (1975). *Distribution of federal student assistance: The enigma of the two-year colleges.* New York: College Entrance Examination Board.

Harris, M. (1976). *A study of the relationship between financial need and student withdrawal among state-grant recipients enrolled at community colleges in Ohio.* Unpublished doctoral dissertation, University of Pittsburgh.

Hecht, L. (1980). *Using SAT scores in awarding Illinois State scholarships: A psychomet-*

ric feasibility study. Unpublished manuscript, Princeton, NJ, Educational Testing Service.

Higher Education Act of 1965, Title IV, Subpart 4; 45 CFR 159.

Huff, R. (1975). Institutional financial aid resources. In *Perspectives on financial aid* (pp. 168–179). New York: College Entrance Examination Board.

Hyde, W. (1979). *The equity of the distribution of student financial aid.* Denver, CO: Education Commission of the States.

Jackson, G., & Weathersby, G. (1975). Individual demand for higher education: A review and analysis of recent empirical studies. *Journal of Higher Education, 6,* 623–652.

Jensen, E. (1981). Student financial aid and persistence in college. *Journal of Higher Education, 52,* 281–294.

Kehoe, J. (1981). Migrational choice patterns in financial aid policy making. *Research in Higher Education, 14,* 57–69.

Mahard, R. (1978). *The influence of high school racial composition on the academic achievement and college attendance of Hispanics* (mimeographed). Santa Monica, CA: Rand.

Modu, C. (1980). *Discussion paper on the use of SAT scores in awarding Illinois State scholarships.* Unpublished manuscript, Princeton, NJ, Educational Testing Service.

Modu, C., & Stern, J. (1975). *The stability of the SAT score scale.* Princeton, NJ: Educational Testing Service.

National Commission on the Financing of Postsecondary Education. (1973). *Financing post-secondary education in the United States.* Washington, DC: U.S. Government Printing Office.

National Commission on the Financing of Postsecondary Education. (1974). *A context for policy research in financing postsecondary education.* Washington, DC: U.S. Government Printing Office.

National Task Force on Student Aid Problems. (1975). *Final report.* Brookdale, CA: NTFSAP.

Nelson, S. (1980). *Community colleges and their share of student financial assistance.* New York: College Entrance Examination Board.

Olivas, M. (1979). *The dilemma of access.* Washington, DC: Howard University Press.

Olivas, M. (1981a). Information access inequities in voucher plans. *Journal of Law and Education, 10*(4), 441–465.

Olivas, M. (1981b). *Research on Hispanic education: Students, finance, and governance.* Stanford, CA: Institute for Research on Educational Finance and Governance.

Olivas, M. (1981c). *Financial aid: Access and packaging policies.* Stanford, CA: Institute for Research on Educational Finance and Governance.

Olivas, M. (1982). Federal higher education policy: The case of Hispanics. *Educational Evaluation and Policy Analysis, 4*(3), 301–310.

Panel on Student Financial Need Analysis. (1971). *New approaches to student financial aid.* New York: College Entrance Examination Board.

Poston, D., & Alvirez, D. (1973). On the cost of being a Mexican American worker. *Social Science Quarterly, 53*, 697–709.

Rossman, J. (1979). *Private returns on investment in education: An analysis of returns to Mexican Americans graduating from Texas A&I University* (mimeographed). Springfield, VA: National Technical Information Service.

Sechrist, L., & Phillips, M. (1979). Unobtrusive measures: An overview. In L. Sechrist (Ed.), *Unobtrusive measurement today* (pp. 1–18). San Francisco: Jossey-Bass.

Stevens, G. (1980). Invasion of student privacy. *Journal of Law and Education, 9*, 343–352.

Tierney, M. (1980). Student matriculation decisions and financial aid. *Review of Higher Education, 3*, 14–25.

Valdivieso, R. (1980). Federal policy, segregation and language in the schooling of Puerto Ricans. *Metas, 1*, 1–11.

Wagner, A., & Rice, L. (1977). *Student financial aid: Institutional packaging and family expenditure patterns* (mimeographed). Washington, DC: College Entrance Examination Board.

Windham, D. (1976). Social benefits and the subsidization of higher education: A critique. *Higher Education, 5*, 237–252.

Windham, D. (1980). *The benefits and financing of American higher education: Theory, research, and policy.* Stanford, CA: Institute for Research on Educational Finance and Governance.

11 | Chicanas and Chicanos: Barriers to Progress in Higher Education

MARÍA A. CHACÓN
ELIZABETH G. COHEN
SHARON STROVER

It is well known that Chicanos[1] and other groups from predominantly low socioeconomic backgrounds exhibit generally depressed rates of enrollment and persistence in colleges and universities. The question to be addressed in this chapter is, Do Chicanas (Mexican American females) encounter certain barriers related to their sex as well as obstacles stemming from their membership in an oppressed minority? In other words, do these women experience a double disadvantage in higher education? Our research sought to compare the experience of Chicanas and Chicanos, to identify barriers to their progress, and to understand how these barriers operate in higher education. This paper reports a multivariate analysis of a sample of Mexican American women and men attending five different institutions of higher education.

Literature on the Chicana is relatively recent and is not extensive. Mirande and Enríquez give a good historical overview in their book *La Chicana: The Mexican-American Woman* (1979). In 1982, the *Hispanic Journal of Behavioral Sciences* devoted an entire issue to research articles on Hispanic women. In this issue, Sally J. Andrade discusses the problem of social science stereotypes of the Mexican American woman; she focuses upon family-role stereotypes, fertility rates, and labor-force participation (1982). *Twice a Minority: Mexican American Women* (1980) edited by Margarita Melville is a collection of essays including some on gender roles and cultural conflict. Also of interest is "Employment and Education of Mexican American Women: The Interplay of Modernity and

This study was sponsored by the Center for Research on Women at Stanford University and was supported by the Ford Foundation.

Ethnicity in Eight Families" (1980) by Maxine Baca Zinn. The summer 1980 issue of *Frontiers: A Journal of Women Studies* contains a bibliographic survey on the Chicana as well as a review essay of six reference works on Mexican American women by Cordelia Candelaria.

Most relevant to our research question are the large-scale surveys of educational attainment and rates of college enrollment, completion, and attrition. These data provide a general picture of the status of the Mexican American female in comparison to Anglos, other Hispanic subgroups, and Mexican American males. Where possible, we have cited statistics that differentiate persons of Mexican origin from those of other Spanish origin. The data that are available on Chicanas show that they are the poorest group and have the lowest levels of educational attainment. They are the least likely to hold professional positions, and they have high levels of unemployment (U.S. Bureau of the Census, 1979). When data are based on all individuals over eighteen, the educational attainment of Mexican American women is so low, in comparison with other subgroups, as to suggest that they do indeed suffer from a double set of barriers.

Mexican Americans are underrepresented in higher education in comparison to their proportions in the population of states where they reside (Western Interstate Commission on Higher Education, 1980). Hispanics as a group have a lower probability than Anglos of enrolling in college. In 1977, the percentage of eighteen- to thirty-four-year-old Hispanics enrolled in college was 11.8 percent compared to 16.6 percent for Anglos (National Center for Education Statistics, 1980, p. 138). Astin, in a recent analysis of data on minorities in higher education, cites high rates of dropout from high school as the single most important factor accounting for the underrepresentation of Chicanos, Puerto Ricans, and Indians in college (1982). Using data from current population surveys of the Census Bureau, Astin finds that from 1974 to 1978, the percentage of Chicanos aged twenty to twenty-five who dropped out of high school was 49.7 percent. This is markedly higher than the comparable statistic of 29.4 percent for blacks and 17.8 percent for other whites (1982).

While the rate of college completion for Mexican-origin men is low compared to that of other groups, it is nearly twice as high as that of Mexican-origin women (U.S. Bureau of the Census, 1979). Mexican-origin women have the lowest completion rate among all Spanish and non-Spanish origin groups. These statistics do not reveal the absolute increases in the number of Hispanic college women during the decade of the 1970s. C. Arnold, analyzing U.S. Census Bureau statistics on school enrollments from 1968 to 1981, found a sharp increase in the number of Hispanic women enrolled in college. The 1972 total of 117,000 increased to 252,000 in 1981. This sharp increase in absolute numbers represented only a small increase in the proportion of all women who were enrolled in college (from 3 percent to 3.9 percent); this is because of the overall rise in college enrollments of all women during these years (U.S. Bureau of the Census, 1968, 1972, 1979, 1981). Older women were the fastest-growing part of the college population in 1972–1981. Parallel increases in the enrollment of older men seem to have occurred prior to 1970 (Arnold, 1983).[2]

Hispanics, once enrolled in college, generally show extremely high rates of attrition. The National Center for Education Statistics (1980) reports that four years after enrolling in college, only 10 percent of Hispanic men and 12 percent of Hispanic women hold the baccalaureate degree as compared to 38 percent of Anglo men and 42 percent of Anglo women. Many Hispanics are enrolled in two-year colleges, where they are undertaking vocational training or are planning a terminal A.A. degree. Moreover, minority-group students are likely to take longer than four years to complete a baccalaureate program. Anglo-Hispanic differences in rates of attrition all but disappear if these two factors are taken into account (Astin, 1982).

It is not clear whether there are differential rates of attrition for Mexican American men and women. Available research shows conflicting results. A 1977 NCES study (1977b), shows rates of withdrawal from four-year colleges for Hispanic females that are the lowest of all groups examined (cited in Olivas, 1979, p. 44). In a regression analysis of two follow-up studies, Astin (1982) controls on type of institution and other personal characteristics. He finds being a woman is negatively related to persistence among Chicanos.

BARRIERS IN HIGHER EDUCATION

What barriers to finishing a college education have been identified for Chicanos? How are they related to barriers for students from other backgrounds? Astin (1982) finds that even when student characteristics are controlled statistically, minority students' chances of persistence are negatively related to starting out at a community college (p. 99). Fully 85 percent of California Chicano high school students who decide to enter higher education will enter a two-year college (Walsh, 1980). An NCES study finds that nationwide fewer than one-third of community college students eventually transfer to four-year schools (1977a).

Very different kinds of students enter two-year schools in comparison to those who enter four-year schools. For this reason it is very difficult to estimate the singular effect of entering a two-year college. In a study of the open admissions policy in the City University of New York, Alba and Lavin (1981) attempted to measure the contextual effect of attending a community college among a specially selected sample. Only students who had applied to the four-year schools in the system were included in the analysis. Some of these students had been accepted and some had been rejected; students who were rejected were told that they would be given easy transfer to the four-year college after they had completed their first two years. There were no systematic differences in academic or background characteristics between those assigned to the four-year and two-year schools. A follow-up study showed that those who attended the four-year school made much more timely progress toward their degrees. This result occurred despite the fact that the great majority of both groups preferred and were placed within the liberal arts curriculum. Furthermore, there were sharp distinctions between two-year colleges as to the probability of a timely completion of one's degree at the end of four years.

In summary, Chicanos along with other minorities are concentrated in two-year colleges. Within these institutions many students elect programs that do not lead to any academic degree. This factor alone helps to account for "failure" to receive the degree in large-scale surveys. There appears to be some contextual effect of entering a two-year program, even if one is in the liberal arts curriculum. However, there is no compelling evidence that this barrier acts any differently for Chicanos than for other minorities or for Anglos.

The second major barrier is one of age and work status. In reviewing studies of persistence, Daigle (1979) found that older students and those who have heavy responsibilities on paid jobs are less likely to persist. The first and second barriers are highly related, because the population attending the two-year colleges is older and more likely to be working. However, studies of students at public four-year colleges reveal that their students are older than conventional college students and often work at least part time. These older college students do not have the same probabilities of completing their programs in timely fashion or of completing their program at all.

The third barrier stems from the socioeconomic background of the student. The fourth barrier, academic performance, is difficult to disentangle from the effects of lower socioeconomic status. Astin finds in a large and careful longitudinal study that the most "dropout-prone" freshmen are those with poor high school academic records, low aspirations, poor study habits, relatively uneducated parents, and small-town origins (Astin, 1975). He also finds that although poor academic performance is a powerful predictor of dropout, many students with poor academic records do manage to persist in college. In a synthesis of earlier research, Tinto (1975) concludes that SES is inversely related to dropout even when IQ is taken into account. Vásquez (1982) examined factors that influenced and mediated grade-point average, persistence, and attrition of Chicana and Anglo University of Texas women. The results of a discriminant analysis showed that socioeconomic status was one of the three major variables that contributed to differences between the "successful" and "nonsuccessful" groups. Empirical findings on the relationship of SES to GPA in college for Chicanos are not fully consistent: Muñoz and García-Bahne (1977) found no association in their sample of Chicanos at four California universities.

The picture emerging from these studies is that socioeconomic background has an indirect effect on persistence that is mediated by academic performance. Students who enter college from lower SES backgrounds have lower GPAs in both high school and college. In a series of regressions on two longitudinal samples of college students, Astin (1982) found that among student characteristics, student high school grades are the most consistent and substantial predictors of persistence for Chicanos.

There is abundant evidence that Chicano high school students score more poorly in English achievement tests than their Anglo counterparts (Espinosa, 1975; Carter & Segura, 1979). This situation is aggravated by the segregation of minorities into urban high schools where academic standards are low and attendance is sporadic.

In attempting to compare the experiences of Chicanas and Chicanos in higher education, one must explore whether or not there are differences in the extent to which they experience these major barriers to persistence. The analytic task is complicated by the intercorrelation of such variables as the type of college attended, SES background, age, work status, and academic performance. A multivariate approach to data analysis is clearly required; in this paper we use a path analysis to examine simultaneously the effects of sex and the known barriers to persistence on the rate of progress students are making in completing their programs. Path analysis also permits us to test ideas about causal interconnections between the barriers.

DESIGN OF THE STUDY

In order to carry out the multivariate analysis we chose a design that would allow us to examine the impact of gender on a student's progress

and the major barriers to persistence that had been identified in previous research. Chicanas attending five different colleges, varying in
student selectivity, answered a mail questionnaire in the fall of 1980 or
after the beginning of the second semester in 1981. The five schools in
our sample were all located in California; they included an extremely
selective private university, one highly selective campus from the University of California system, one community college, a four-year urban
campus of the state university system, and a second state university
campus that draws students from a more rural area.

We selected a large sample[3] of students of Mexican descent, focusing
on females but including a smaller male sample for comparison at three
of the five campuses. Freshmen, sophomores, juniors, and seniors were
surveyed. The sample used for analysis consisted of 508 women at five
campuses and 160 men at three campuses.

Because the design was cross-sectional, the dependent variable was
progress in one's college program rather than persistence, as in the
major earlier studies. Previous studies had pointed to the importance of
age and hours of work as negative predictors of persistence. Hours of
paid work and hours of domestic labor were thought of as fixed time
costs in a social system external to the campus. Many Chicanas in higher
education are older students with major domestic obligations. The ante-
cedent variables of fixed costs in the external social system were indicated
by hours of paid work and hours of domestic labor. We included an
index of academic functioning because previous research had shown it to
be an important predictor of persistence. In addition, respondent's age,
parental education and occupation, marital status, number of children,
and a number of other demographic variables were ascertained.

This design permitted us to examine the joint and separate impact
of sex, fixed time costs, academic difficulties, and institutional context
on progress in one's academic program. It also permitted us to test the
prediction that fixed time costs would have a powerful direct impact on
successful completion of college for this population.

Measures

Program Progress. Program progress, the dependent variable, measured
progress over time toward completion of a degree-granting or vocational college program. We included in the multivariate analysis all respondents except those who said they were taking only one or two courses and
were not interested in completing any particular program. The program
progress index included self-assessment of whether one would drop out
temporarily; self-assessment of whether one would drop out permanent-

ly; length of time away from school if education had already been interrupted; frequency of postsecondary interruptions; number of units taken the previous term (if enrolled); patterns of school enrollment (moving from school to school, "reverse" transfers from four- to two-year schools, and so forth); and self-assessment of the likelihood of needing extra time to complete one's program. The alpha value for this index was .673, indicating a high degree of internal consistency. The emphasis on timely progress toward one's program goals was selected because previous studies such as those of Astin (1972) had shown that a strong predictor of eventual dropout was previous stopout and failure to make timely progress toward one's degree.

Fixed Time Costs. In order to measure fixed time costs in family and work situations, we asked the respondents how many hours they spent weekly in domestic labor and paid work. Domestic labor was defined as the number of hours spent on child care, care of the elderly, cooking, cleaning, or doing other domestic work.

Freedom from Academic Difficulty. We did not attempt to measure the respondent's ability or aptitude; we were more interested in the existence of academic problems that could seriously impede progress through the institution. The issue is one of attaining a degree or credential rather than one of outstanding academic performance. Therefore, the index is called Freedom from Academic Difficulty; the items included self-assessment of preparation in comparison with other students; current GPA; evaluation of high school preparation; report of academic probation; the occurrence of leaving school for academic reasons; self-rating on understanding and writing English; and self-ratings on ability to write papers, understand books, and give oral reports. The reliability of this index was .768.

Background Variables. Socioeconomic status was an index computed on the basis of father's education, mother's education, and father's occupation. Occupation was coded into six categories ranging from major professional and managerial to unskilled labor; clerical, sales, and service were combined into one category. When data on one of the three variables were missing, values were assigned; for example, when father's occupation was missing, the mean value of father's occupational score was ascertained for other individuals whose fathers had the same amount of education; and this value was assigned in place of missing data. Other background variables were age, marital status, number of children, and sex.

RESULTS

Table 11.1 reports basic statistics on age, SES, hours of domestic labor, and hours of paid work of Chicanos and Chicanas at the five different campuses. In addition to these background variables, average ratings for the variable "freedom from academic difficulty" are also reported. The type of student at each of the five campuses shows wide variability. Students at the private university have the highest SES rating and are the youngest. They also put in much less time in paid work and domestic labor. The University of California campus is similar, but with somewhat lower SES scores and higher average age and hours of domestic and paid work. The males and females at the private university were not significantly different from each other on any of these variables. The community college is in sharp contrast; not only were both men and women

Table 11.1: Average Values for Major Predictors of Degree Progress for Men and Women, by Campus

	Private University		Urban State		University of California		Community College		Rural State	
	Mean	N	Mean	N	Mean	N	Mean	N	Mean	N
Freedom from Academic Difficulty										
Women	3.76	(54)	3.50	(95)	3.68	(101)	3.49	(69)	3.66	(131)
Men	3.76	(85)	*		*		3.41	(36)	3.63	(59)
All	3.76		3.5		3.68		3.45		3.65	
Domestic Hours										
Women	4.37	(54)	14.32	(90)	7.54	(100)	22.25	(67)	12.40	(59)
Men	4.37	(83)	*		*		9.09	(32)	7.83	(128)
All	4.37		14.32		7.57		13.54		10.11	
Hours Paid Work										
Women	7.18	(56)	17.24	(96)	7.87	(101)	26.06	(71)	13.55	(132)
Men	7.36	(85)	*		*		33.14	(36)	14.23	(60)
All	7.27		17.24		7.87		29.6		13.89	
SES										
Women	9.46	(85)	6.66	(96)	8.35	(101)	5.42	(71)	5.53	(60)
Men	10.12	(56)	*		*		5.77	(36)	6.03	(132)
All	9.79		6.66		8.35		5.59		5.78	
Age										
Women	19.53	(56)	23.26	(96)	21.01	(101)	30.21	(71)	22.91	(58)
Men	20.02	(85)	*		*		27.83	(35)	23.35	(131)
All	19.78		23.26		21.01		29.02		23.13	

*No sample.

much older and of lower SES, but they worked many more hours; furthermore, there were large sex differences. Women averaged 22.25 hours per week in domestic labor as compared to 9.09 for men; women averaged 26.06 hours per week of paid labor compared to men's 33.14; and the women were older than the men (30.21 years versus 27.83 years). The two state university campuses were midway between the community college and the UC campus on most background variables. Of these two campuses, students spent more time in paid and domestic labor at the urban campus and were also a little older; women were 23.3 compared to an average age of 22.91 for women at the rural campus. The SES background at the rural state university campus was closer to that of the community college because the fathers of many students were rural farm laborers with little formal education.

An examination of the age distribution of our respondents in comparison to the age distribution for all students at three of the campuses showed no marked differences. Our sample at the community college had an average age of 29; the average age of all students at that campus was 28. As in Daigle's earlier study (1979), there were many students over 21 at the state university system campuses; our sample had an average age of 23, while the average age for all students at both the state university campuses was between 22 and 23. There is no basis for arguing that Chicanos were older than the average student on their respective campuses. Rather, there are important age differences in the type of students these different campuses recruit. Because Chicanos are more likely to attend community colleges, Chicanos in higher education, as a group, are likely to be older than Anglo college students, as a group.

Domestic Labor

Women reported a high average number of domestic hours at three of the five campuses. In the entire sample of women, there were only 148 who were either married or divorced. Of those who had children, there were only 13 women out of 508 in the entire sample who had more than two children.

Table 11.2 contrasts the average hours of domestic labor for men and women at the three campuses where we had male and female respondents. The table breaks down these figures by whether or not the respondents were married and had children. Women put in many more hours of domestic labor than men. Single women, married women, and women with children nearly always put in double the amount of domestic labor as did men in similar marital or parental circumstances. Single women averaged 7.8 hours per week to single men's 4.7; married women

Table 11.2:   Average Domestic Hours and Average Program Progress for Men and Women According to Marital Status and Parental Status

Sex	Campus	Status	Domestic Hours	Program Progress
Men	(Comm. coll., private univ., rural state)	Married, divorced, separated	13.6	3.2
		Single	4.7	3.8
		Children	16.8	3.2
		No children	5.2	3.8
Women	(Comm. coll., private univ., rural state)	Married, divorced, separated	26.0	3.1
		Single	7.8	3.8
		Children	31.5	3.2
		No children	7.2	3.8
Both	All campuses	Married, divorced, separated	22.8	3.1
		Single	7.8	3.8
		Children	28.6	3.2
		No children	6.7	3.8

averaged 26.0 hours to married men's 13.6; women with children averaged 31.5 hours per week compared to men with children, who averaged 16.8 hours.

Table 11.3 documents mean domestic hours for both men and women in different age categories and marital status by campus. Even when age is held constant, there are clear campus differences, but these differences are not always consistent according to marital and parental status. It is interesting that single students at the urban state campus who were in the 23–30 age group reported an average of 17.8 hours of domestic labor, much more than at any other campus. It was also the case that 44.7 percent of the women at this campus reported living with their families, a higher proportion than at any other campus. The most heavily obligated were the students under 22 who had children and who attended community college, an average of 48 hours per week.

Predictors of Program Progress

The mean scores on program progress were significantly different at the different campuses. At the private university, the score was significantly

Table 11.3: Average Hours of Domestic Labor by Age and Marital Status, by Campus, Men and Women Combined

Age & Status	Private University	Urban State	University of California	Community College	Rural State
18-22 yrs.					
Single	4.07(125)	9.94(52)	6.2(80)	8.78(28)	7.38(106)
Married	6.25(8)	17.75(4)	9.75(4)	12.5(2)	8.63(8)
Married w/					
children	(0)	3.0(1)	(0)	48.0(1)	40.0(1)
23-30 yrs.					
Single	10.00(4)	17.8(12)	4.71(7)	10.0(12)	6.83(30)
Married	(0)	8.6(5)	15.0(2)	20.6(10)	12.72(11)
Married w/					
children	(0)	39.8(5)	24.23(4)	12.4(10)	34.4(10)
31 + yrs.					
Single	(0)	9.5(2)	(0)	(0)	7.5(2)
Married	(0)	9.0(2)	(0)	12.5(6)	3.33(3)
Married w/					
children	(0)	36.0(5)	19.6(3)	31.3(30)	32.23(13)
TOTAL CASES	(137)	(88)	(100)	(99)	(184)

higher than at any other campus ($t = 13.16$; $p<.001$). The UC campus was next highest, closely followed by the rural state university campus, the urban state campus, and, at the bottom, the community college campus. The average score for program progress at the community college was 3.17, while the comparable figure at the private university was 4.14. The t value for the comparison of program progress at the community college versus all the other campuses was -10.44; $p<.001$. These campus differences were expected from previous research. Of considerable interest is the fact that there were no statistically significant differences between men and women at the three campuses where samples of both sexes were drawn. Average scores for program progress are given for men and women in table 11.4.

All of the variables chosen for consideration proved to be significantly correlated with program progress. Table 11.5 reports the relevant intercorrelations. Age and hours of domestic and paid work were all negatively correlated with program progress, while SES and freedom from academic difficulty were positively correlated with program progress. These predictor variables were also clearly related to each other.

Table 11.4: Mean Degree Progress Score for Men and Women on Five Campuses

	Private University	Urban State	University of California	Community College	Rural State
Women	4.16	3.58	3.76	3.18	3.68
Men	4.10	*	*	3.15	3.72
All	4.14	3.58	3.76	3.17	3.69

*No sample.

Table 11.5: Intercorrelation of Program Progress and Its Predictors ($N = 614$)

	Age	Domestic Labor	Paid Work	SES	Freedom from Academic Difficulty	Program Progress
Age	1.00	.41***	.46***	−.28***	−.14***	−.46***
Hours Domestic Labor		1.00	.12**	−.20***	−.18***	−.35***
Hours Paid Labor			1.00	−.17***	−.03	−.40***
SES				1.00	.30***	.20***
Freedom from Academic Difficulty					1.00	.31***
Program Progress						1.00

** $p < .01$
*** $p < .001$

Older students worked more hours of both types, were from lower SES backgrounds, and had more academic difficulties.

Multivariate Analysis of Program Progress

After careful study of intercorrelations at each campus, we chose to construct a path model that would incorporate type of campus and sex along with the variables that had been predicted to affect program progress. Dummy variables represented campus type in this model. Type 1 is the private university. The mean progress score for the rural state university was not significantly different from that of the UC campus. Therefore, these two campuses were combined for the analysis and are referred to as type 2. Type 4 is the community college. All are compared to the reference category of type 3—the urban state campus with a score on program progress in the middle of the range. Sex is included in the model as a dummy variable. This model is pictured in figure 11.1.

The model in figure 11.1 includes the predicted paths with significant path coefficients.[4] Where the direction of the relationship was not specified, the correlation coefficients are presented with a double-headed arrow. The first features to be noted in this model are the strong paths between school type and the most powerful predictor variables. There were strong correlations between SES and school type. The paths between schools and hours of paid labor and hours of domestic labor were also clearly delineated, with strong negative paths between these variables and the private university, the University of California campus, and the rural state university campus. The standardized betas were −.11 for the regression of domestic hours on type 2 and −.21 for hours of paid work. Similarly, for type 1, the standardized betas were −.17 for the regression of domestic hours and −.28 for hours of paid work. In contrast, the path coefficient between type 4 (community college) and hours of paid work was positive (.17). In this model, type 4 was not a statistically significant predictor of hours of domestic labor. We found in earlier

Figure 11.1: Antecedents of Program Progress

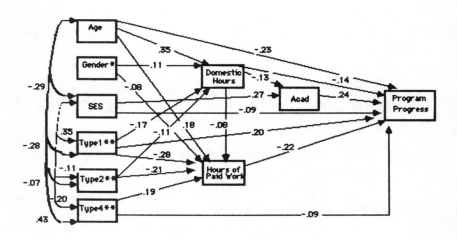

#Female=1 ; Male=0

##Type1=Private university ; Type2=Rural State and U.C.; Type4=Community College
Reference category=Type3, Urban State

analyses that if age were omitted from the predictors of domestic labor, type 4 had a statistically significant beta weight. Age, it will be recalled, is closely related to attendance at a community college. The failure of type 4 to work as a predictor in this model is undoubtedly due to multicollinearity.

The effect of sex on program progress was entirely indirect. Being female meant a higher level of domestic labor; domestic labor had a strong negative path to program progress and to freedom from academic difficulty. Being female also related negatively to hours of paid work, another strong negative factor in program progress.

The effect of SES on program progress was largely mediated by the measure for freedom from academic difficulty. SES had a strong positive effect on freedom from academic difficulty; its only direct effect on program progress was small and in the opposite direction from what one would expect ($-.09$). As in other studies, academic performance variables were powerful predictors of program progress, holding other variables constant ($+.24$).

Holding school type and freedom from academic difficulty constant, three major negative factors in program progress were age, hours of paid work, and hours of domestic labor. Although these variables were correlated, they appear in the model with significant path coefficients suggesting that they have independent effects on the dependent variable.

The type of school one attends has strong direct and indirect effects. Type 1, the private university, had a strong direct effect on program progress ($+.20$) as well as indirect effects through its negative relationship to domestic and paid labor. Type 4, the community college, had a smaller direct effect ($-.09$) on program progress and powerful indirect effects through age and paid labor.

In review, the effect of sex on program progress was indirect; it was mediated by women's putting in more hours of domestic labor and somewhat fewer hours of paid work. Domestic labor also had an indirect effect on program progress through the negative relationship of domestic labor to freedom from academic difficulty. Freedom from academic difficulty, as one would expect, was a powerful precursor of program progress. Both indicators of fixed time costs in external social systems had strong negative effects on program progress. With all these predictors of program progress held constant, campus type showed *an independent direct effect* on program progress: It was positive at the private university and negative at the community college for students who had the same scores on all the other predictors. Age had a direct and negative impact on program progress. The total amount of variance accounted for by the regression of program progress on its predictors in the path model is .40.

Other Sex Differences

There were two other sets of findings of interest that reflected differences in the experience of the sexes with respect to higher education. These findings concerned the reported level of parental support and the experience of situational stress.

Parental Support.   On the whole, the degree of support from parents for attending college appeared to be good for both sexes. We did, however, find differences between men and women in reported support from parents. Men were significantly more likely than were women to report that their mothers and fathers were very supportive of college attendance. Sixty-eight percent of the women reported that mothers were very supportive while 81 percent of the men chose this response ($t = 3.20$; $p<.001$). The corresponding figures for supportiveness of fathers were 63 percent for women and 77 percent for men ($t = 2.83$; $p<.05$). Few parents were reported to be opposed to college attendance for their children, but again the proportion of discouragement was greater for women than for men.

Stress.   Stress was measured by a series of items describing various situations such as "not being as well prepared academically as other students." As in an earlier study of stress among Chicano students (Muñoz & García-Bahne, 1977) the conceptualization of stress was situational; and the items covered social, financial, academic, and familial situations. Chicanas in the earlier study reported consistently higher stress than Chicano men on twenty-eight of the thirty-nine items on the Muñoz and García-Bahne instrument. In our study, the wording and format of the questions were different, and there were many fewer items. For each item, students were asked to select one of the following six choices: "I haven't experienced this"; "I experienced this, but it was not stressful"; "it was a little stressful"; "it was moderately stressful"; "it was very stressful." We factor-analyzed responses to the stress-related items and found three main factors that we named academic stress, social stress, and financial stress.

We created scales for each stress factor based on the item's factor coefficient and found that women and men were very different in their experience of stress in all three areas, with women consistently scoring higher on the stress factors than men. Item by item, women scored higher on the level of reported stress on all but one of the thirteen items designed to measure stressful experiences. Table 11.6 gives six of these items arranged in order of the percentage of respondents who reported these experiences as very stressful. The percentages of respondents reporting stress are divided by sex. On a different analysis examining the relationship between sex and level of stress, only two of these items showed statistically significant sex differences. These items were not being prepared academically and not having enough money. Most of the items yielding higher proportions reporting stress were in the academic area. Because women reported higher grade-point averages for both high school and current academic work than did men, it was somewhat surprising that they also reported greater stress in this area.

DISCUSSION

Conventional and Unconventional College Experience

The college experience of this sample of Chicanas and Chicanos varied enormously. At one end of the spectrum was an eighteen-year-old living in a dormitory and attending a highly selective university. At the other end was a thirty-year-old woman taking care of her household, holding a part-time job, and attempting to acquire a college degree by taking six units a semester in evening classes at the local community college. The more selective the campus, the younger and more middle-class was the population of students. Older students were more likely to come from a lower SES background and were more likely to report difficulties in their academic work, particularly difficulties in reading and writing English.

Table 11.6: Proportions of Men and Women Reporting Stress on Items Most Generally Reported as Stressful

| | Women | | Men | |
Item	%	N	%	N
Not being prepared academically	39	194	31	50
Being in a competitive place	36	177	27	42
Loss of self-confidence	36	178	28	44
Not having enough money	32	158	23	37
Not being able to help family	32	159	22	34
Speaking up in class	30	149	18	29

Furthermore, older students tended to have many more fixed obligations in terms of paid work and domestic duties.

This heterogeneity within the Chicano population was clearly related to the dependent measure of the pace of progress in completing one's program. Furthermore, the use of a path analysis revealed that demographic characteristics, work obligations, academic performance, and differences in type of college attended were *independent predictors* of progress. Despite the intercorrelation of variables such as age, academic difficulty, hours of paid work, and hours of domestic labor, each of these factors tended to predict program progress even when all the others were held constant.

College Experience of Men and Women

Domestic Labor. Gender did not have a direct impact on program progress in the path model: There was no significant difference in the rate of progress of men and women in the sample as a whole or within the three campuses with a male and female sample. Gender had an impact *indirectly* through its influence on hours of domestic labor. Women put in many more hours of domestic labor than men. And domestic labor had a sharp, direct, and negative impact on program progress $(-.14)$. In addition, domestic labor had an equally strong negative impact on the variable called Freedom from Academic Difficulty $(-.13)$, a factor with a strong positive path to program progress $(+.24)$. Thus hours of domestic labor had both a direct and an indirect effect on program progress.

Being female meant that one worked fewer hours for pay than men; and hours of paid work were another major negative predictor of program progress $(-.22)$. This result should not be taken to mean that women did not work for pay; 39 percent of the men worked more than 30 hours per week and 30 percent of the women worked this much. Besides taking courses, many women, especially at the community college, held paying jobs in addition to their domestic work. At the community college the combined number of hours of domestic and paid work per week for women was 48.3, while for men it was 42.2. Across the whole sample the average figure for combined responsibilities was 26.5 for women and 25.3 for men.

Who were these women who were putting in so many hours of domestic labor? They were especially likely to be attending the community college, where the average age for women was 30.21 in comparison to 27.8 for men. They were also more likely to come from a lower SES background than the men at the community college—community college women had the lowest average value for the SES index of any group in the study.

There was a strong relationship, as can be seen in table 11.3, between being married, having children, and putting in many hours of domestic labor. In evaluating this association, it is important to remember that there were many more single than married students in this sample, even in the age range of 23–30. Only among those 31 or older were most of the students married. Furthermore, there were only 13 women with three or more children in the sample. Thus one should not view this sample as filled with women who married at a young age and bore many children.

A careful examination of table 11.3 shows that single women age 23–30 attending the urban state university and single men and women attending the community college were averaging a relatively high number of domestic hours. These were campuses in which many students lived with their families; probably many of these students fulfilled domestic duties in connection with their status as an older member of the household. A UC campus woman described the role conflict stemming from her positions as family member and student:

> About my only problem related to college is not having family support in terms of them understanding the amount of time I need to dedicate to reading, studying, reviewing, etc. Because I live at home, I must still participate in everything that my family does. If I don't, a lot of tension results. But my family certainly doesn't discourage my college attendance.

The number of hours of domestic labor was positively associated with several variables that suggest why domestic responsibilities were a detriment to academic performance in the path model. Of the variables that make up the index of Freedom from Academic Difficulty, domestic labor was closely related to reported difficulties with reading and writing the English language. The presence of these difficulties combined with a heavy domestic obligation evidently does not leave enough hours in the day to complete the work to be done. This time problem is reflected in the correlation between reported stress in managing time and hours of domestic labor. A final fact helps to fill out this picture of the time factor: The number of hours of domestic labor was uncorrelated with the number of units taken, while the number of hours of paid work clearly was negatively related to the number of units taken. Hours of paid work, unlike the hours of domestic labor, were uncorrelated with the index of academic difficulty. Although their progress was significantly slowed, those who worked more hours for pay avoided academic problems by cutting down on the number of units.

In review, these relationships suggest that women who put in many hours of domestic labor were more likely to be women who had to spend much more time in doing their assigned schoolwork. This need for extra time for schoolwork along with their sense of domestic obligation produces a time bind in which we must suppose that schoolwork loses out and the chances of academic failure are increased. The time problem is exacerbated by the curious invisible character of hours of domestic labor; in deciding how many units to take, those who labor at domestic tasks evidently don't take into account how many hours they have free for study. Rather than cutting down on their usual level of domestic work, they simply add schoolwork to everything else.

Parental Support.   Women reported less parental support for going to college than men, particularly support from their mothers. These differences were statistically significant despite the fact that over 60 percent of the sample reported their parents as very supportive and only a small fraction reported any kind of parental opposition.

Stress.   Women reported more stress than men. We approached this finding with caution, thinking that higher levels of reported stress might be due to a general tendency for women to be more willing than men to report psychic difficulties (Klerman & Weissman, 1980). However, in an earlier study, Muñoz and García-Bahne (1977) found sex differences for Chicanos but *not* for Anglos. We interpret the findings on stress as indicating that Chicanas do indeed experience more stress. Our conclusion is consistent with the findings of the earlier study and with the conclusion of the review on the controversy concerning sex differences in reports of stress by Klerman and Weissman (1980).

Type of College Versus Type of Student.   The Chicanas who attended community college were more likely to experience every one of the barriers we have discussed. In addition to all the barriers encountered by males, these women experienced additional obstacles because of their age and higher levels of domestic obligations. Because of the strong interrelationship between type of institution and the kind of student who attends them, we reach the limits of what a path model can accomplish in disentangling the institutional effects from the characteristics of the student.

It is difficult to obtain an independent estimate of the power of any single predictor when it is highly related to other predictors in the same regression equation—the problem of multicollinearity. The best way to think about the effects of the community college context is that there is probably some direct effect, but there are large indirect effects where the impact of the community college is mediated by variables such as age, SES, domestic labor, and paid work.

Lacking a theoretical framework, it is impossible to tell where demographic characteristics and fixed time costs of individuals who attend the community college end and variables pertaining to institutional climate and school policies begin. We did find that the level of social integration of the community college was markedly lower than any of the other campuses. The community college students made less use of support services than students at the other campuses. This might be a function of a school where support services are offered during the day while over half the students attend classes at night. There are also few residential facilities around which colleges can structure student activities. Or, alternatively, it could be a function of age. Older students with many other obligations have no time to spend in social interaction and in extracurricular activities on campus.

For community college students, there seemed to be several factors locking students into a pattern of taking fewer units and working many hours. Older students have greater financial needs and more responsibilities with respect to their families; forgone wages are thus of greater importance for older than for younger students. Beyond these life circumstances is the lack of financial support available for part-time college attendance. Ninety-four percent of the students at the community college campus received no aid from loans; 86 percent received no aid from grants; and 77 percent received no aid from parents.

Community college students had high aspirations but were making exceedingly slow progress toward their educational and occupational goals. Fifty-five percent at this campus were taking less than six units per semester. Counseling concerning the length of time they would take to achieve their goals at the present rate of progress or counseling concerning the importance of intensive remedial work seemed either unavailable, insufficiently used, or not sufficiently directive. It was clear from the data analysis that many community college students needed to do intensive remedial coursework. Unless there were some way for them to take courses on a more intensive basis, they were unlikely to succeed in their educational aspirations.

The very structure of the community college with its "easy in, easy out" procedures undoubtedly makes for much more erratic patterns of college attendance. In contrast, the urban state university required students who were enrolled in a degree program to maintain a requisite number of units and to make a certain degree of progress; otherwise they were placed on academic probation. The private university had the strongest set of policies and procedures affecting academic progress and did not allow students to attend part time. The number of hours they could work for pay was restricted. Furthermore, in the case of poor grades, there was a system of procedures to diagnose the difficulty and to prescribe remedial assistance. Financial aid was designed to make full-time attendance possible. No matter what controls were added to the path model, the private university continued to have a strong favorable effect on program progress (.20).

In this discussion we have stressed the impact of different requirements concerning the number of units taken. We do this because the index of program progress contains number of units taken last term as one of its constituent variables. Thus this index is likely to be influenced by procedural and structural differences between campuses such as we have described.

Limitations of the Study

Cross-Sectional Design. Measures were taken only at one point in time, so the study is like a snapshot of any one campus. In order to study actual persistence, a longitudinal design is preferable. The index of program progress does not directly measure persistence. It is a large set of highly intercorrelated variables that have high predictive value for persistence and program completion. Furthermore, the variables themselves capture the rate of progress; and it is undeniably true that unless one makes adequate progress, one is unlikely to complete the program. A second limitation of a cross-sectional design is that it cannot reveal very well what formal support systems do to help students who have academic difficulties. We could only document their reported use of support services.

Measurement Problems. It should be noted that the measure of academic performance does not contain test scores or transcript data. It contains only self-report items. On the other hand, the index called Freedom from Academic Difficulty does contain items concerning reported language difficulties that correlated well with having been on academic probation and having a lower GPA. The index had excellent reliability and good predictive validity.

This paper has stressed the effects of domestic labor. However, the hours of domestic labor were estimated with a single item in the questionnaire. Thus we have no information on the reliability and validity of this measure. Recent studies of domestic labor typically use more elaborate measures requiring subjects to keep logs of their activities (Robinson, 1980; Nelson, 1980; Berk & Shih, 1980). Studies of higher education have never asked this question; our results suggest that it should be included in questionnaires to older students in higher education and that in future studies there should be more attention to problems of its measurement.

Effects of Age. Age was correlated with almost all the predictor variables in this study. Yet in the path analysis it maintained a strong, direct, and negative impact on Program Progress ($-.23$), with all the other predictors controlled. In interpreting the strength of this relationship, one should keep in mind that the dependent variable of program progress contains variables such as "number of times stopped out" and "length of absences from school." Clearly, one has to be older to attain a high score on these two items. Thus some, but not all, of the relationship between age and program progress is due to the logical relationship of these variables.

Effects of SES. The major impact of SES on program progress is indirect, mediated by Freedom from Academic Difficulty. The path analysis did, however, yield a small direct effect of SES on program progress. The path coefficient had, surprisingly, a negative rather than a positive value ($-.09$). It is hard to interpret such a figure, and it may well be a product of multicollinearity (the high level of intercorrelation) among predictors such as SES, age, domestic labor, hours work, and freedom from academic difficulty.

Sampling. The path model involved five campuses, but there were male samples at only three of the campuses. Path analysis of the same model for the three campuses where we had both male and female samples produced substantially the same results as the model for five campuses. This suggests that the effects of gender were not biased by the absence of males at certain campuses.

Generalizability. In the absence of a theoretical framework that specifies conditions under which the observed relationships hold on other campuses, we have no way of estimating the extent to which these findings generalize to other campuses. We can only speculate that, given equally diverse institutions and student sample, a similar study conducted elsewhere would come up with essentially the same results.

DIRECTIONS FOR THE FUTURE

Domestic Labor

This may be the first study to detect the impact of domestic labor on persistence in higher education. Obviously these results do not clearly imply what might be done about this barrier to higher education. We don't even know whether this is an effect more characteristic of minority women or whether it would also be found among older Anglo women. This sample of Chicanas contained many women who had entered college some years after high school graduation. However, only nine women reported using services designed for the reentry woman. Reentry offerings vary by campus but typically include services that would be relevant for this population, such as academically geared tutorials and workshops, leadership or assertiveness training, child care, and support groups. Discussions with college officials and counselors at the campuses with many older students (twenty-two and older) revealed that they did not perceive domestic labor as a barrier and had not given it much thought.

There are several things that, at minimum, might be recommended for such campuses. One is to provide services geared to younger women who may be only twenty-five but are nonetheless reentry. In addition, minority women should be made to feel at home in such programs, perhaps by minority staffing and more relevant program offerings. Third, campus support staff would do well to open discussions with women students on how they perceive and manage their domestic obligations. As long as the problem remains invisible, there is little chance of moderating its effect.

Age

If many of the older students had been reached in high school and given guidance about higher education and career prospects, they would have made much more rapid progress in college. Young girls in particular need to meet adult Chicanas who have interesting jobs requiring higher education. Special efforts need to be made because in the ordinary course of events lower-social-class Chicana girls are unlikely to meet such women or to receive much information about career options and career paths. They need to acquire a clearer idea, earlier in their schooling, of what kind of high school preparation will be necessary for success in higher education. Early outreach, apprenticeship, and work-study programs for young women might be very effective in meeting this goal.

Miseducation

In many ways this study is a documentation of the miseducation of language-minority youth who enter school with weak skills in English. The students who were reporting lingering difficulties with the English language were largely educated in this country, and twelve years of education had clearly failed to remediate the problem for a number of students in the sample. Thirty-six percent of the entire sample perceived their high school preparation as "poor." Forty-eight percent considered it "average," and only 16 percent considered it "excellent." It is clear that schools need the funds to launch intensive programs of writing and reading comprehension for language-minority youth who want to attend college but who clearly lack the requisite skills. However, this must not be done by the techniques of tracking these students into low-level programs where they fail to receive the math, science, and English skills necessary for college entrance and performance.

Community Colleges

Policy issues surrounding the community college are especially critical for women. Arnold's (1983) analysis of census figures[5] reveals that the recent growth in college enrollments for women is concentrated in the two-year college. More women than men enroll in community colleges. If this holds true for the Chicana, then we have a double impact of sex and ethnicity pushing her toward the community college.

In order to evaluate the effectiveness of the community college in meeting the needs of older women, we need to understand in more detail why they are selecting these institutions and how it relates to their plans for labor force participation. For a reentry woman with financial and domestic obligations, a short technical training program may offer the best way to enter the labor force without too long a period of foregone income. Her heavy obligations make the number of years spent in training a critical variable to be considered. She needs to reach as soon as possible the point where she has only to juggle domestic and work responsibilities rather than having to play the three roles of household worker, paid worker, and student. Anything that can speed up the time spent in the training program or any way to provide some salary during the training period would be of great assistance to such women.

Meeting the needs of overburdened women in technical and vocational programs is quite different from meeting the needs of men without the same domestic obligations or from meeting the needs of students from lower SES backgrounds who aspire to the bachelor's degree. At the present time, community colleges are not well suited to meeting the needs of students from a low socioeconomic background who aspire to a B.A. or B.S. degree. At the four-year state university campuses we studied, there were intensive financial, academic, and social support systems available. In addition, many of these support services were specifically oriented to minority needs. As long as this situation continues, it would seem that students who can meet the admissions requirements would be far better off attending a four-year campus than the local community college. For those who do not yet meet admissions requirements or for those who must attend college closer to home for the first two years, much closer coordination between the four-year and two-year colleges is essential.

Both men and women who have aspirations to transfer to a four-year college require special treatment. They need much more guidance about which courses are transferable and which are not. They would benefit from early diagnosis of their academic problems and from continuous counseling as to consequences of overly slow progress in their program. Students who are working many hours per week need an alternative way to meet minimal living expenses. They may also need more social support for making education the highest priority in their lives.

The present structure has all the aspects of a vicious circle. Students who are working many hours and making slight progress make the least use of support services that might help them to reorder priorities. Likewise, the student who is experiencing academic difficulties at this institution may not be receiving the counseling and reinforcement necessary to make the commitment to overcome these difficulties. A constructive solution for this problem might be the creation of programs that separate out the transfer students to form a cadre of high aspiring peers with assured or required access to support services. As we have suggested above, support services especially designed for older minority women would be particularly helpful for the transfer student with heavy domestic obligations and persistent problems with reading and writing English.

Future Research

The identification of these particular barriers in higher education raises issues for basic and applied research. From a basic-research point of view, the theoretical framework that has been used by earlier studies of higher education has a relatively poor fit to older minority students attending public colleges. Until we have some more abstract explanations for how these barriers operate, it will be difficult to derive useful interventions directly from the research. Domestic labor is the barrier most in need of further theoretical formulation and research. Without this basic research, the present results will function only to suggest possible experimental programs. These programs will necessarily be based more on practical wisdom than on any scientific grounds.

We need to know more about Chicanas in non-degree-granting training programs at the community college. To what extent is their present educational experience meeting their needs? The present study only reached the edges of these questions. Before recommendations can be made, we need to know more about their financial and domestic obligations, their experiences within their programs, their academic problems, and their aspirations. The present research taught us that it is not easy to obtain accurate information about the precise program or major in which a student is enrolled. These matters are often rather vague at the community college level.

Administrators in institutions of higher education with larger numbers of Hispanic students should determine whether the factors we have identified as critical operate to deter progress on their campuses as well. These results have already proved very stimulating to administrators at the campuses surveyed; they felt they had new and different ways to view the problems of the minority student within their institutions. Support service staff, in particular, were able to reexamine their programs for relevance to the different barriers we have identified. Policy research of this kind can be an effective tool for sensitizing and educating decision makers.

NOTES

1. Throughout the paper we use the term *Chicano* interchangeably with *Mexican American* and *students of Mexican origin*.

2. She used Census statistics published in the P-20 series of *Current Population Reports* (U.S. Bureau of the Census, 1968–81).

3. In all but the private university, we used registrars' lists that included self-identification on ethnicity for sampling purposes. At the urban state university the list was supplemented by selecting Hispanic-surnamed students from microfiche records. A random male sample was drawn at the private university, the community college, and the rural state university campus. We sent questionnaires to the total Mexican American female population at the private university, the UC campus, and the community college. Female samples at the other two schools were randomly drawn from the Mexican-origin population.

The initial mail questionnaire was followed by two reminder postcards and a third mailing of an additional questionnaire to two of the campuses. From the subsample of nonrespondents, we selected a 50 percent random subsample and attempted to reach them through campus liaisons, who obtained only 22 usable questionnaires. The nonrespondent sample had better skills in Spanish than the respondent sample. Otherwise, the sample appeared to be representative of the general student population of Chicanos. The total response rate was 55.9 percent; the usable sample size was 679. Of respondents born in Mexico, only those who has been in this country for more than five years were included in the final sample.

Items for the questionnaire were pretested on 102 college students and refined for the final version of the instrument. We created multiple-item indices for variables of major interest and tested their reliability with Cronbach's alpha.

4. When observed correlations between variables in the model were recomputed from the path coefficients, the result showed a good fit between observed and expected values. The zero-order correlations between the predictors and Program Progress are compared to the recomputed values from the path model below:

Predictor of Progress	r	Model	Difference
Domestic Hours	−.35	−.35	00
Freedom from Academic Difficulty	.31	.30	.01
Hours Paid Work	−.40	−.40	00
Type 1	.36	.41	.05
Type 4	−.37	−.32	.05
Age	−.46	−.47	−.01

5. See U.S. Bureau of the Census, 1981, table 5, p. 7.

REFERENCES

Alba, R. D., & Lavin, D. E. (1981). Community colleges and tracking in higher education. *Sociology of Education, 54*(4), 223–237.

Andrade, S. J. (1982). Social science stereotypes of the Mexican-American woman: Policy implications for research. *Hispanic Journal of the Behavioral Sciences, 4*(2), 223–244.

Arnold, C. (1983). The role of older students in the equalization of college participation between women and men in the 1970's. Unpublished manuscript. Stanford, CA: School of Education, Stanford University.

Astin, A. W. (1972). *College dropouts: A national profile.* Office of Research, American Council on Education, Research Report, 7(1).

Astin, A. W. (1975). *Preventing students from dropping out.* San Francisco: Jossey-Bass.

Astin, A. W. (1982). *Minorities in higher education.* San Francisco: Jossey-Bass.

Baca Zinn, M. (1980). Employment and education of Mexican-American women:

The interplay of modernity and ethnicity in eight families. *Harvard Educational Review, 50* (1), 47–62.

Berk, S. F., & Shih, A. (1980). Contributions to household labor: Comparing wives' and husbands' reports. In S. F. Berk (Ed.), *Women and household labor* (pp. 191–227). Beverly Hills, CA: Sage.

California Postsecondary Education Commission. (1980). *Equal educational opportunity in California postsecondary education.* Sacramento: CPEC.

Carter, T. P., & Segura, R. D. (1979). *Mexican-Americans in school: A decade of change.* New York: College Entrance Examination Board.

Daigle, S. L. (1979). *Attrition and retention in the California State Universities and colleges.* Long Beach, CA: Chancellor's Office, CSU.

Espinosa, R. (1975). *The impact of evaluation processes upon student effort in ethnic groups which vary in academic preparation.* Unpublished doctoral dissertation, Stanford University.

Frontiers: A Journal of Women Studies. (1980). *5*(2).

Klerman, G., & Weissman, M. (1980). Depressions among women: Their nature and causes. In M. Guttentag, S. Salasin, & D. Belle (Eds.), *The mental health of women* (pp. 57–92). New York: Academic Press.

Melville, M. (Ed.). (1980). *Twice a minority: Mexican American women.* St. Louis: Mosby.

Mirande, A., & Enríquez, E. (1979). *La Chicana: The Mexican-American woman.* Chicago: University of Chicago Press.

Muñoz, D. G., & García-Bahne, B. (1977). *A study of the Chicano experience in higher education.* The Center for Minority Group Mental Health Programs, Grant No. MN24597-01, National Institute of Mental Health.

National Center for Education Statistics. (1977a). *Transfer students in institutions of higher education.* Washington, DC: U.S. Government Printing Office.

National Center for Education Statistics. (1977b). *Withdrawal from institutions of higher education.* Washington, DC: U.S. Government Printing Office.

National Center for Education Statistics. (1980). *The condition of education for Hispanic Americans.* Washington, DC: U.S. Government Printing Office.

Nelson, L. (1980). Household time: A cross-cultural example. In S. F. Berk (Ed.), *Women and household labor* (169–190). Beverly Hills, CA: Sage.

Olivas, M. (1979). *The dilemma of access: Minorities in two-year colleges.* Washington, DC: Howard University Press.

Robinson, J. P. (1980). Housework technology and household work. In S. F. Berk (Ed.), *Women and household labor* (pp. 53–68). Beverly Hills, CA: Sage.

Tinto, V. (1975). Dropout from higher education: A theoretical synthesis of recent research. *Review of Educational Research, 45,* 89–125.

U.S. Bureau of the Census. *Current Population Reports,* Series P-20. No. 190, October 1968; No. 260, October 1972; No. 354, March 1979; No. 373 (Advance Report), October 1981. Washington, DC: U.S. Government Printing Office.

Vásquez, M. J. T. (1982). Confronting barriers to the participation of Mexican-American women in higher education. *Hispanic Journal of Behavioral Sciences, 4*(2), 147–165.

Walsh, J. (1980). Making the multi-university more multi-ethnic. *Science, 209,* 473–475.

Western Interstate Commission on Higher Education. (1980, January). *Representation of minorities in higher education in the West.* Boulder, CO: WICHE.

12 | Educational Stratification and Hispanics

RICHARD R. VERDUGO

The function of the educational system is to sort and rank individuals as they proceed through different levels of schooling. Contrary to popular belief, this sorting and ranking often is not based on achievement or merit. Instead, individuals seem to be sorted (tracked) and ranked (graded) according to such ascriptive criteria as gender, ethnicity and race, and class background. (For discussions on the relationship between class and education, see, for example, Bowles & Gintis, 1976; Collins, 1971.)

This article examines the process by which Hispanics are ranked and sorted in the educational system. To address this issue, I have integrated literatures in two research areas, educational stratification and racial stratification, with the purpose of synthesizing perspectives from both areas in order to enhance our understanding of the educational process affecting Hispanics.

There are three sections in the article. The first section presents data that describe the educational condition of Hispanics, such as dropout rates, high school completion, and college enrollment rates. The second reviews major findings from the racial stratification and educational stratification literatures. The third section synthesizes the racial and educational stratification literatures to explain the processes that affect the educational performance and outcomes of Hispanics. The article concludes with a summary and suggestions for additional research.

THE EDUCATIONAL CONDITION OF HISPANICS

There are three distinct levels in the educational system: elementary, secondary, and postsecondary. At all three levels, Hispanics fare less well

---

Michael Olivas and Naomi Verdugo provided comments on earlier drafts of this paper. I appreciate their suggestions. Any errors in the paper, however, are my own.

325

than their white counterparts. Table 12.1 presents information on the enrollment of Hispanics in public elementary and secondary schools. In 1976, approximately 2.8 million Hispanics were enrolled in elementary and secondary schools, comprising about 6 percent of the total public school enrollment. Generally, Hispanics do not progress through the educational system as consistently or as rapidly as do whites. For example, Hispanic high school seniors are older (see table 12.2)) and are more likely to drop out of high school (see table 12.3) than their white counterparts. In 1978, 18.8 percent of Hispanics aged fourteen to nineteen were not in school and had not graduated from high school, as compared to 8.8 percent of whites the same age.

Perhaps the most often used statistic about a group's educational status is high school graduation. Not surprisingly, Hispanics are much less likely to be high school graduates than are non-Hispanics. Table 12.4 presents such information. Note that at all ages, Hispanics (particularly Mexican Americans and Puerto Ricans) are less likely to be high school graduates than are whites. At the postsecondary level, Hispanics aged eighteen through thirty-four are not enrolled in college at the same rate as whites (see table 12.5). However, despite fluctuations, differences between the two groups decreased over time. Brown et al. (1980, p. 188) examined attrition rates among Hispanics and whites and found that

Table 12.1:   Enrollment in Public Elementary and Secondary Schools, 1976, in Thousands

Total	White	Hispanic	Percent Hispanic of Total
43,714	33,229	2,807	6.4%

SOURCE: Brown et al. (1980, p. 40).

Table 12.2:   Age Distribution of Hispanic and White High School Seniors, Spring 1972, by Percentage

Age	Hispanic	White, Non-Hispanic
Less than 17 years of age	0.3	0.1
17	1.5	2.4
18	49.4	77.5
19	36.0	17.4
20	10.8	2.1
21 +	2.1	0.4

SOURCE: Brown et al. (1980, p. 64).

Table 12.3: Percentage of Hispanics and Whites Aged 14 to 19 Who Were Not in School and Not High School Graduates, 1972–1978

Year	Hispanics (H)	Whites (W)	Percent point difference (H − W)
1972	15.5	7.9	7.6
1973	19.3	8.5	10.8
1974	19.1	8.8	10.3
1975	15.7	8.2	7.5
1976	17.2	8.8	8.4
1977	17.0	8.7	8.3
1978	18.8	8.8	10.0

SOURCE: Brown et al. (1980, p. 96).

Table 12.4: Percentage of Hispanic and Non-Hispanic Population Aged 25 Years or Older Who Completed 4 Years of High School or More, by Age Category and Hispanic Subgroups, March 1978

Age	Non-Hispanic	Total Hispanic	Mexican American	Puerto Rican	Cuban	Other
25-29	87.1	56.6	51.3	52.1	*	74.5
30-34	84.4	50.1	44.1	43.7	*	67.8
35-44	76.9	44.2	37.2	35.2	57.8	62.7
45-64	62.7	30.3	21.4	26.0	40.9	51.1
65+	38.6	17.3	7.1	*	34.9	28.3

SOURCE: Brown et al. (1980, p. 22).
*Percentage not shown where estimates are less than 20,000 persons.

Table 12.5: Percentage of Hispanic and White Population Aged 18 to 34 Enrolled in College, 1972–1977

Year	Hispanic (H)	White (W)	Percent point difference (H − W)
1972	8.3	16.0	−7.7
1973	10.3	15.2	−4.9
1974	11.5	15.7	−4.2
1975	12.7	16.8	−4.1
1976	14.2	16.6	−2.4
1977	11.8	16.6	−4.8

SOURCE: Brown et al. (1980, p. 138).

Hispanics are more likely to drop out of college. They also found that Hispanics who earn doctorates and bachelor's degrees tend to be older than their white counterparts (p. 42).

The data presented above point out that Hispanics drop out at greater rates and tend to be delayed in their educational attainment as compared to whites. These results are remarkably consistent at all three levels of the educational system. Clearly, then, Hispanics do not fare well throughout the educational system.

What accounts for the low educational attainment of Hispanics? Are Hispanics themselves solely responsible, or does the educational system play a role? Studies have shown that education is highly valued by Hispanics, especially the completion of high school (Coleman et al., 1966; Grebler, Moore, & Guzmán, 1970).[1] Thus, given the high value placed on education, at least through high school, it would seem that the educational system is partly responsible for the poor educational condition of Hispanics. In the following section an attempt is made at integrating two literatures, racial stratification and educational stratification, to develop a framework by which we can better understand the data presented above.

RACIAL AND EDUCATIONAL STRATIFICATION: A REVIEW OF THE LITERATURE

In this section I examine the educational and racial stratification literatures that may shed light on the educational experiences of Hispanics. Briefly, it is argued that racial stratification affects the educational system in at least two ways. First, racial stratification uses an elaborate ideological mechanism, racism, that assumes subordinate ethnic or racial groups are both biologically and culturally inferior to superordinate ethnic or racial groups. This encourages the negative stereotyping of minorities and influences school personnel in how they teach and evaluate minority students. A second way racial stratification penetrates the educational system is by segregating and tracking ethnic or racial minorities. Aside from its obvious distributional effects, tracking has other results, such as reinforcing stereotypes, reducing a student's self-esteem, and other social-psychological factors affecting school performance.

Stratification systems are complex social structures that maintain social order. They are "a way of classifying people and their functions, of prescribing which sorts of people should do what sort of things" (Hodges, 1964, p. 8). The mechanisms by which stratification systems are maintained vary by society, but two seem to be used most often: an *ideological* mechanism and, for lack of a better term, a *spatial* mechanism. Stratification systems construct elaborate ideological schemes to justify the existence of a given social order through the totality of group ideas that explain relevant aspects of life. Ideological schemes have ranged, for example, from such justifications of a given social order as the "will of God" to those alleging biological superiority. Bierstedt (1963, p. 171) has noted: "an ideology is an idea supported by a norm." Ideologies, then, encompass norms, mores, folkways, values, and theories. Thus, ideologies provide explanations for the order of things. But more importantly, they are rooted in group interests (see Mannheim, 1936, chap. 2). In addition to ideological mechanisms, there are structural or spatial mechanisms; they involve separate or unequal treatment. Structural mechanisms are such phenomena as housing segregation, occupational segregation or discrimination, or wage differentials for persons in the same job.

Ideological and structural mechanisms reinforce one another and serve to justify and maintain a given social order. Ideology is used to justify differential treatment or spatial separation, which in turn is used to perpetuate a given ideology. For example, the ideology that achievement should be based on merit is used to justify a tracking system. Those in remedial or noncollege tracks are seen to be unqualified for placement in college-track courses. And by being in noncollege tracks the notion is reinforced—to oneself and others—that one is not qualified for college. For those in college tracks, the notion is reinforced that they must, indeed, be qualified individuals—superior to those not in the same track.

Racial Stratification

According to van den Berghe (1974) modern racial stratification systems developed after a period of paternalism. Paternalistic systems are characterized by rigid stratification and large gaps between subordinate and superordinate groups in terms of power, wealth, status, and life chances. With respect to racial- and ethnic-group membership, a paternalistic system is much like a caste system. Other characteristics of paternalism include endogamy, rules of etiquette specifying appropriate deference between subordinates and superordinates, and an ideology supporting the subordination of the lower caste. Paternalism tends to develop in an agricultural economic system and often results in stereotypes about subordinate groups (e.g., that they are childlike or irresponsible).

Modern racial stratification systems are said to be competitive. As society evolved from a predominantly rural agricultural economic system to a highly industrialized one, paternalistic stratification systems (such as the American slave system) gave way to competitive ones. The basic premise of competitive systems is that one's socioeconomic position is no longer determined by such ascriptive traits as race because prejudices not only would result in a misuse of talent but would also conflict with the dominant economic ideology of an industrialized society: achievement by merit, an important inheritance derived from the rising, and increasingly powerful, middle class of the Industrial Revolution. Also, a competitive system based on the notion of a free market and race prejudice, it is argued, would raise the cost of doing business.

Modern ideological competitive systems are characterized by several features. To begin with, skill and performance are alleged to become as important as one's racial-group membership. Racial barriers are less rigid, and open competition between the races emerges. While one race is rarely completely superordinate, it is still clear that the bulk of wealth and power reside with the superordinate group. Second, in such a system, the stereotypes of the subordinate group change from being characterized as childlike to that of being violent or aggressive in nature. Finally, the emerging ideology stresses liberty, equality, and fraternity. In the modern era, racial stratification is seen as competitive as persons of different races begin to enter the same arenas and are presumed to be judged on the basis of merit alone. However, this hardly masks the control of society's major institutions by the superordinate group. Of all of society's institutions, education and the family are believed to have the most powerful effects on one's future success. Education is often viewed as an important asset for socioeconomic success, particularly for minorities.

Educational Stratification

Educational stratification denotes differentiation within the educational system. Typically, differentiation is said to be based on such criteria as tests, grades, and performance. However, social and ascriptive criteria are also employed in the differentiation process. For example, such ascriptive criteria as race, gender, and class background are often used by school personnel in their assessment of students. In a competitive system, the goal of such differentiation is to separate students at an early age in order to fill prescribed roles in larger society; the more important roles are slated to be filled by "superior" students. Thus, the primary means by which the educational system fills roles in larger society is by ranking and sorting students.

While numerous theorists, philosophers, and social scientists extol the virtues of education and the educational system, the fact remains that one of its key functions—if not the single most important function—is to sort and rank individuals (see Spring, 1976). Via testing, grades, and other criteria of performance, individuals are groomed to fill social roles in society. The primary rationale for such an objective is the need to identify the most suitable—not necessarily the most talented—individuals for important roles in society (Davis & Moore, 1945). This notion leads to the question of how individuals are differentiated, on the basis of merit or on the basis of ascription.

That talent and achievement are used in differentiating students is a predominant belief of American culture. Such measures as IQ, standardized tests, and grades are the primary means by which students are differentiated. Students are ranked and tracked depending upon their performance on these criteria. But there have been serious criticisms raised about the stratification process within the educational system, particularly regarding the accuracy of intelligence tests and about the effect and role of school personnel on student performance.

There is much debate on the meaning of intelligence and about the tests used to measure the concept. At the root of the debate is not only the concept of intelligence but also the validity of intelligence tests. For example, it was initially believed that intelligence was a universal concept; that is, ability can be found in all human groups, with only slight variation. It was also proposed that some groups and individuals are able to develop skills and abilities better than others are (Jensen, 1969). However, cross-cultural research finds otherwise; different environments lead to the development of different skills and abilities (Cole, Gay, Glick, & Sharp, 1971; DeVos & Hippler, 1969; Levin, 1970). But if intelligence is culture-bound, which groups' cultural skills are being measured by tests? Evidence suggests that IQ tests measure skills and abilities linked to middle-class culture. As Ogbu (1978, p. 36) states, "the tests are constructed to tap primarily those cognitive skills and strategies that are functional for the dominant caste."

Criticism has also been leveled against the role teachers and school personnel take in differentiating students. Rosenthal and Jacobson (1968) found that teachers label students based on such information as reported test scores. In their study, test scores were incorrectly reported to teachers, with high scores given to poor students and low scores given to good students. The teachers adjusted their behavior accordingly. Preferential treatment was given to reportedly good students while indifferent treatment was given to reportedly bad students. The result was that students performed and evaluated themselves according to the treatment they received: the self-fulfilling prophecy. Cicourel and Kitsuse

(1977) extend the analysis by conceiving "the differentiation of students as a consequence of the administrative organization and decisions of personnel" (p. 283). They found that personal and social factors (e.g., social-class background and race) are used in interpreting objective measures of a pupil's success or failure. Thus, in many circumstances, school personnel are guided by social norms and values in their evaluations of students.

These criticisms regarding tests and the subjective evaluation of students by school personnel make sense if we view the educational system as a sorting machine (Spring, 1976)—that is, a sorting process that reproduces "the structure of power relations and symbolic relations between classes" (Bourdieu, 1977, p. 487). In short, the educational system reproduces a social order stratified by class, gender, and race found in larger society. For example, Bowles and Gintis (1976) note that there is a correspondence between values, norms, and skills in the workplace and those inculcated in the classroom. Schools mirror society's division of labor and the larger class structure.

The Influence of Racial Stratification on the Educational System

Given a racial stratification system whose goal is to maintain a particular racial order, and an educational system whose objective is to distribute people in the hierarchy of labor-market roles, it is natural that the educational system becomes a primary tool in perpetuating racism and racial inequality. It is, therefore, essential to understand how racial stratification influences educational stratification.

As an ideology, racism influences educational stratification in at least three ways. First, racism leads to the negative stereotyping of racial minorities. Negative stereotyping influences the behavior and attitudes students, school administrators, and teachers exhibit toward minority students and, as has been pointed out, influences the achievements of minorities. For example, research by Rosenthal and Jacobson (1968) indicates that teachers' expectations affect student performance; and Cicourel and Kitsuse (1977) note that school personnel frequently use subjective-normative conceptions in evaluating students. There are numerous ways in which teachers affect the achievements of their students. Research has indicated that teachers' behavior toward low and high achievers has included the following:

1. Teachers are impatient with low achievers and give them less time to answer (Allington, 1980; Taylor, 1979).

2. Teachers have been shown to praise low achievers less frequently than high achievers (Brophy & Good, 1970; Good, Cooper, & Blakey, 1980; Rejeski, Darracott, & Hutslar, 1979).
3. Teachers tend to give less attention to low achievers and spend little time interacting with them (Adams and Cohen, 1974; Rist, 1970; Rubovits & Maehr, 1971).
4. It has been noted that low achievers are seated farther away from teachers (Rist, 1970).[2]

In terms of school personnel and administrators, Cicourel and Kitsuse (1977) note that though middle-class students might be average students, they are still positively evaluated because they come from the "right" families.[3] This is very important in terms of recommendations for jobs or further education.

Second, racism enters the curriculum by depicting minorities negatively, falsely, or not at all (Knowles & Prewitt, 1969). Such depictions not only perpetuate racist beliefs but also influence the perceptions minorities have of themselves and of their ethnic or racial groups. For example, the depiction of minorities solely in negative terms (e.g., coming from broken homes, violent, lazy) develops the notion among students and school personnel that all minorities are of these types and that minorities have not made important contributions to society.

Third, the use of intellegence tests may reinforce racism since they measure one's knowledge of middle-class culture. Such tests are used to label minority students and funnel them into remedial programs. As Olmedo (1977, p. 177) says, "The empirical evidence now available often leads to ambiguous and contradictory conclusions." That is, it isn't clear that such tests correctly predict academic achievement. Thus, until the predictive power of such tests is conclusively proven, they should not be used.

Structural forms of racial stratification also enter the educational system. For instance, minorities may automatically be placed in noncollege tracks because they are seen to be intellectually deficient or culturally deprived. Hence, minority students may be physically segregated, even within an integrated school, and tend to be overrepresented in noncollege vocational tracks. Residential segregation has also been linked to the inferior quality of education received by minorities.

This section has described the relationship between racial and educational stratification. First, it was noted that mechanisms of racial stratification penetrate the educational system and that the end result of such an infiltration was the maintenance of a given racial order. In maintaining this racial order, two mechanisms are at work, one ideological and the

Table 12.6:   Percentage of Hispanic and White High School Seniors, by Program, 1972

Program	Hispanic	White, Non-Hispanic
General	40.6	32.1
Academic or college prep	29.3	45.4
Vocational or technical	30.1	22.5
TOTAL	100.0	100.0

SOURCE: Brown et al. (1980, p. 60).

other structural and physical. The ideological component—racism—and the norms, mores, values, and folkways that flow from it penetrate the educational system as an elaborate justification regarding the treatment of minorities. It also appears in the curriculum by negatively stereotyping minorities and is seen in the tests used to sort and rank students. The ideology of racism involves a whole set of subtle and not-so-subtle beliefs and values. Racist structural mechanisms underlie the educational system and are expressed in such phenomena as tracking and school segregation. This often occurs as a result of prejudicial stereotypes held by school personnel. Minority students seem to be disproportionately placed in non-college-prep courses (e.g., remedial and vocational education) and steered into blue-collar trades. For example, table 12.6 shows that a larger percentage of whites are in college-prep programs than Hispanics; and in addition, a larger percentage of Hispanics are in vocational or technical programs than are whites.

The low expectations school personnel have for minority students result in labeling these students as low achievers. Because students' performance, regardless of their potential, tends to correspond to these labels, even bright minority students are often enrolled in noncollege tracks. This occurs early in the educational process because teachers (including well-intentioned teachers) do not think it is likely that minority students will attain professional occupations. The end result is to reinforce subordinate-superordinate racial relations and to perpetuate stereotypes, which lead to "them"-and-"us" distinctions. The long-term effect of such stratification processes is, inevitably, the maintenance of a given racial order.

HISPANIC STUDENTS IN THE EDUCATIONAL SYSTEM

The framework suggested above would lead one to believe that the poor educational experiences of many Hispanics are the result of racial stratification processes in the educational system, rather than any deficiencies inherent in Hispanic students or their culture. Hispanic students are subjected to racism and differential treatment. This affects the way they are sorted and ranked in the educational system. The outcomes are poor educational experiences and the perpetuation of a given racial order. Thus, Carter (1970) says:

> The fact the school fails to Americanize or raise the group status of so many Mexican Americans was evidence of its success. Local society functioned well with an easily controlled, politically impotent, and subordinate ethnic caste. School practices evolved that functioned to perpetuate the social and economic system by unconsciously encouraging the minority group to fail academically, drop out early, and enter society at the low status traditional for Mexican-Americans, thus producing the human types necessary to perpetuate the local society. Mexican-American failure to achieve well in school contributed to the Anglos' belief that they had innately inferior intelligence, that they were lazy, passive, fatalistic, and lacked initiative. This self-reinforcing circle of circumstances became well established in the Southwest and persists to the present. (pp. 204–205)

Racism, as an ideology, has played a prominent role in the education of Hispanics. Viewed as "slow" or "culturally deprived," Hispanics have been placed in remedial tracks and have had negative interactions with both students and teachers. There are many areas in which ideological racism manifests itself, but none are so striking as beliefs about language, family and culture, and curriculum.

It is commonly believed that Hispanics have a language problem. There are three components to such a perspective: that Hispanics are alingual, that their vernacular is an inferior Spanish, and that bilingualism is detrimental to cognition (Carter & Segura, 1979, p. 91). Basically, there was a belief that Hispanic students were handicapped because they spoke Spanish. However, in an effort to maintain "national unity" and a "national culture," educators refrained from employing bilingual programs or other programs that might assist Hispanics in school. It was not uncommon for educators to segregate students on the basis of language; supposedly, such segregation would eradicate their language handicap. The separation of Spanish-speaking Hispanics from English-speaking students and the refusal to carry out language training seem to have been racially motivated:

> Language educators generally advanced these points as the common sense of the matter rather than as debatable issues or, in the style of many anti-immigrationists of the 1910s and 1920s, as polemical scare tactics. To sup-

port English-only instruction in the schools was to express one's commitment to a unified polity and a common culture. (Schlossman, 1983, p. 881)

On a smaller scale, the mentality described above was played out in the daily routines of students and teachers. Thus, there is evidence regarding the punishment of Hispanic students for speaking Spanish on school grounds (U.S. Commission on Civil Rights, 1972; Moore, 1970). Such punishment has varied from merely informing the students that they should speak English to physical punishment. Carter and Segura (1979, p. 185) indicate that schools no longer forbid the use of Spanish but, instead, promote English.

Yet another target of racism is the Hispanic family. In this case, the family is blamed for the poor educational experiences of Hispanics. Perhaps the most damaging ideology along these lines has been the "culture-of-poverty" viewpoint, a perspective that argues that individuals who are poor are embedded in a cultural system characterized by low aspirations and motivations and a strong sense of fatalism, with little value associated with education and hard work.[4] For Example, Heller (1966) states:

> The kind of socialization that Mexican-American children receive at home is not conducive to the development of the capacities needed for advancement in a dynamic industrialized society. This type of upbringing creates stumbling blocks to future advancement by stressing values that hinder mobility—family ties, honor, masculinity, and living in the present—and by neglecting the values that are conducive to it—achievement, independence, and deferred gratification. (pp. 34–35)

Finally, racist ideology has entered the educational system via school curricula and textbooks depicting Hispanics in a negative manner (U.S. Commission on Civil Rights, 1972). If discussed at all, Hispanics are portrayed in a demeaning manner or are depicted in an unrealistic framework. Thus, one Hispanic educator has stated:

> Textbook after textbook supports the notion that the early settlers of the Southwest—Spanish and Indians and mixed-blood pioneers who came from Mexico, as well as Indians native to the region—wandered around in confusion until the Anglo-Saxon, with his superior wisdom and clearer vision, vaulted the Rocky Mountains and brought order out of chaos. (Cited in U.S. Commission on Civil Rights, 1972, p. 31).

Also, a study by Johnson (1966, cited in Grebler et al., 1970, p. 158) of teacher's manuals suggests that Mexican Americans devalue formal education, especially for females; consider success in terms of nonmaterial rewards; are present-time oriented; are traditionalists and do not desire change; stress patience, conformity, and apathy; view work as necessary only as a means to satisfy present needs; are imbued with a "mañana" attitude; and reject scientific viewpoints. Finally, Hispanics are depicted in a stereotypic manner. For example, those aspects of Hispanic culture stressed in California revolve around food, music, Spanish costumes, rancheros, caballeros, and señoritas. Such depictions, however, have little relation to reality, past or present.

Aside from its ideological components, the stratification process of Hispanics in the educational system has its structural or physical aspects. Two of the more obvious structural components are tracking and segregation. The tracking of Hispanic students is an important structural mechanism and, in some cases, seems to be related to the proportion of Hispanics in a local school district. Thus, Grebler et al. (1970) reported:

> In 1966 . . . 27 percent of the children in special education classes were Mexican American, though they represented only 13 percent of the total student population. . . . It is interesting to observe that the degree of concentration appears to be related to the proportion of Mexican Americans in the community's population. In the ten counties with the highest proportion of Spanish-surnamed students, almost twice as many were in special education as their overall proportion would suggest. In counties with smaller proportions of Mexican Americans, their numbers in special education come closer to their representation in the school population. (p. 158)

Data from a study by the U.S. Commission on Civil Rights (1974) show that tracking is related to the proportion of school composition that is Mexican American and leads to the following proposition: The greater the proportion of school composition that is Mexican American, the greater is their percentage in low-ability tracks. Brown et al. (1980, p. 60) point out another form of tracking: tracking by curriculum. Indeed, their data show that 40 percent of the Hispanic sample and 32 percent of the white non-Hispanic sample were in "general" high school programs; over 29 percent of Hispanics and 45 percent of whites were in "academic or college-preparatory" programs; and 30 percent of Hispanics and 22 percent of whites were in "vocational or technical" programs. (See table 12.6 of this article.)

The segregation of Hispanics in schools mirrors their segregation in larger society. Early studies indicated that Hispanics were excluded from full participation in the larger society (Cooke, 1948; Parsons, 1965; Taylor, 1934). Indeed, Parsons (1965) described the situation as "a caste-like social structure . . . in which Anglos have always been on top of the hierarchy and the Mexican Americans [have been] isolated at the bottom" (pp. 6–7). Such a social climate was also reflected in the schools, where Hispanics were isolated and processed differently from Anglos. The rationale behind such behavior was exhibited by the two forms of racism described earlier: paternalism and beliefs about racial superiority. Thus, an early study by Paul S. Taylor (1934, p. 217) quotes the comments of two Anglo school board members: "I don't believe in mixing. They are filthy and lousy—not all, but most of them." And a second, paternalistic statement points out that segregation is a protective measure against the hazing Mexican American children will receive in school by other students:

> The white child looks on the Mexican as [Southerners looked] on the Negro before the war, to be cuffed about, and used as inferior people. If you can segregate a few grades until they learn they are not inferior [except socially], then you can put them together. If [segregated in the early grades] they will learn to take their places as whites and citizens. (p. 217)

Other reasons given at that time for the segregation of Hispanics were pointed out by Strickland and Sánchez (1948, p. 22): that Mexican American students attend school irregularly, have different social habits, and are in poor health.

What, however, can be said of the present? The U.S. Commission on Civil Rights (1971) found that Hispanic students were isolated (i.e., segregated) by both school district and school. In terms of school districts, of an estimated 1,800 school districts in the Southwest with an enrollment of 300 or more students, 206 were predominantly Hispanic—accounting for 30 percent of the total enrollment. The commission also noted that "even in areas with a high Mexican American enrollment, it is not unusual to find a predominantly Mexican American district adjoining one that is largely Anglo." One might suspect discrimination as contributing to this segregation because of the close proximity of the adjacent school districts. In terms of schools, the commission found that Mexican American pupils tend to be concentrated in a small number of schools. Thus, 45 percent of Mexican American students attend predominantly Mexican American schools (50 percent or more Mexican American).

A recent study by Gary Orfield (1982) suggests that while black segregation has decreased, Hispanic segregation has increased. Orfield states:

> There was no progress on integrating Latino students in public schools in the seventies. In fact, each region of the country has become more segre-

gated for Hispanics as their numbers have rapidly grown in American society. (p. 59)

Tables 12.7 and 12.8 present Orfield's data and corroborate his statement. Though Hispanics are more likely to be segregated in the South and Northeast, the Midwest and West exhibit the greatest increase in segregation from 1968 to 1980.

Hispanics in Higher Education

Like other groups, those Hispanics successfully completing secondary education enter the military or the labor force or pursue further education or training. But once again racial stratification is set in motion. This

Table 12.7:   Percentage of Hispanic Students in Schools with More Than Half Minority Students by Region, 1968–1980

Year	U.S.	South	Northeast	Midwest	West
1968	54.8	69.6	74.8	31.8	42.4
1972	56.6	69.9	74.4	34.4	44.7
1976	60.8	70.9	74.9	39.3	52.7
1980	68.1	76.0	76.3	46.6	63.5
Change					
1968–1980	+13.3	+6.4	+1.5	+14.8	+21.1

NOTE: From Orfield (1982, p. 68). Reprinted by permission of the Joint Center for Political Studies, Inc.

Table 12.8:   Percentage of Hispanic Students in School with 90–100 Percent Minority Students by Region, 1968–1980

Year	U.S.	South	Northeast	Midwest	West
1968	23.1	33.7	44.0	6.8	11.7
1972	23.3	31.4	44.1	9.5	11.5
1976	24.8	32.2	45.8	14.1	13.3
1980	28.8	37.3	45.8	19.6	18.5
Change					
1968–1980	+5.7	+3.6	+1.8	+12.8	+6.8

NOTE: From Orfield (1982, p. 68). Reprinted by permission of the Joint Center for Political Studies, Inc.

is not to say that new mechanisms are used; rather, in higher education residues from secondary school experiences interact with stratification mechanisms peculiar to higher education. Residues that are felt in higher education are the influence of counselors in steering Hispanic students into low-prestige, vocational majors and away from academic or professional majors, and the poor academic preparation many Hispanics receive in secondary schools. Mechanisms characteristic of the higher educational system are hierarchies within and between higher educational institutions. Within higher educational systems, there are significant differences in the types of fields in which Hispanics and Anglos are concentrated, and there are important differences in the status of colleges and universities each group attends.

With the advent of mass education, increased stratification within the educational system has been observed (Jencks & Reisman, 1969). Consequently, *where* students earn degrees is as important as—if not more important than—the degrees. What seems to be involved is a hierarchy of institutions of higher education in which two-year colleges and less prestigious four-year colleges are ranked below prestigious four-year universities—both public and private (Astin, 1982; Jencks & Reisman, 1969; Karabel, 1972). The differentiation of colleges is quite evident in Karabel's (1972) analysis of the two-year community college. In a highly critical and thoughtful paper, Karabel argues that community colleges maintain class-based stratification rather than alleviating it:

> The community college, generally viewed as the leading edge of an open egalitarian system of higher education, is in reality a prime contemporary expression of the dual historical patterns of class-based tracking and of educational inflation. (p. 526)

Karabel goes on to provide evidence in support of his statement by analyzing the student composition of community colleges, by observing the flow of community college students through the educational system, by noting tracking within community colleges, and by observing the distributive effects of public higher education.

To begin with, students who attend community colleges tend to come from low socioeconomic backgrounds and are more likely to drop out. Of those remaining, a small percentage actually receive the A.A. degree. Of those that transfer to four-year institutions, few receive the B.A. or B.S. degree. Finally, Karabel finds that there is a tracking system in community colleges involving the placement of working-class students in vocational programs. Community colleges, then, are institutions that, by and large, perpetuate and reinforce existing stratification systems. If this is the case, we would expect a higher percentage of Hispanics in post-secondary education to attend community colleges and less prestigious publicly supported four-year colleges. Likewise, we would also expect Hispanics to be underrepresented in prestigious four-year universities. Table 12.9 presents data that clearly indicate that this is the case for Hispanics. Indeed, over half (53 percent) of all Hispanics enrolled in institutions of higher education attend two-year public colleges, as compared to 33 percent of whites and 39 percent of blacks. In contrast, 19.7 percent of whites, 9.7 percent of blacks, and only 8.6 percent of Hispanics attended four-year public universities in 1978.

Table 12.9: Percentage Enrolled in Postsecondary Institutions by Race/Ethnicity and Institutional Type, Fall 1978

Type and control of institution	Total[a]	White[b]	Black[b]	Hispanic
All institutions:				
Number	11,231,172	9,194,031	1,054,371	417,271
Percentage	100.0	100.0	100.0	100.0
Public universities:				
Number	2,062,293	1,807,325	102,162	36,027
Percentage	18.4	19.7	9.7	8.6
Private universities:				
Number	718,434	600,237	44,825	17,091
Percentage	6.4	6.5	4.3	4.1
Public other 4-year:				
Number	2,833.759	2,277,778	322,718	104,221
Percentage	25.2	24.8	30.6	25.0
Private other 4-year:				
Number	1,588,220	1,341,883	142,050	33,014
Percentage	14.1	14.6	13.5	7.9
Public 2-year:				
Number	3,873,690	3,050,957	414,640	222,284
Percentage	34.5	33.2	39.3	53.3
Private 2-year:				
Number	154,776	115,833	27,976	4,634
Percentage	1.4	1.3	2.7	1.1

SOURCE: Dearman and Plisko (1980, p. 110).

NOTE: Details may not add to totals because of rounding.

[a] Represents the total head count for all races of students in the 50 states and D.C.; a difference of 31,184 from the total head count of all students because some institutions were unable to identify the race of students enrolled.

[b] Non-Hispanic.

Table 12.10:   Educational Status as of October 1974 of Hispanics and Whites
in the High School Class of 1972 Who Entered Two-year
Colleges in Fall 1972, by Sex

	Hispanic		White, Non-Hispanic	
	M %	F %	M %	F %
Completed program	5	9	11	18
Still enrolled in 2-year program	38	40	24	20
Transferred to a 4-year program	11	7	27	25
Dropped out of school	47	45	39	37
Academic reasons	13	6	6	5
Nonacademic reasons	34	38	32	33
Number of respondents	102	83	1,244	1,135

SOURCE: Brown et al. (1980, p. 186).

Another result presented by Karabel concerns the flow of two-year
college students through the educational system. Karabel finds that community college students are more likely to drop out than are four-year
college students and that only a small percentage transfer to four-year
institutions.

In terms of Hispanics, some data exist that support Karabel's findings.[5] Table 12.10 shows data on a two-year follow-up of the high school
class of 1972 and indicates that whites are more likely to have completed
a two-year program, more likely to have transferred to a four-year program, and less likely to have dropped out of school than were Hispanic
students. Thus, if Karabel finds a class-linked bias in the type of colleges
attended by students, there is also evidence of a sizable ethnic-linked
bias.

Fields of Study as an Indicator
of Racial Stratification in Higher Education

Differentiation in higher education not only is associated with the type of
colleges and universities attended but also is reflected in the types of
majors students select in school. Two of the more plausible reasons why
Hispanics seem to be overrepresented in fields that pay less and have
lower prestige associated with them are their inadequate preparation for
the professions, and tracking and counseling that guide them away from
technical fields and toward the less prestigious and less lucrative fields.
Astin (1982) opts for the first reason in accounting for the lower representation of minorities in technical fields. Using mean composite SAT

scores by anticipated major in college by ethnicity and race, Astin finds that whites have the highest scores in each of the eight anticipated majors. Astin also finds that regardless of race and ethnicity, students with higher SAT scores show a preference for technical fields. From these findings Astin draws several conclusions, but certainly one of the most important is that, in part, minorities are underrepresented in technical fields owing to their poor academic preparation. There are two problems associated with Astin's conclusion. First, as was argued earlier, there is the question about the validity of tests for minorities. Second, while some might take this to mean that minorities are not qualified for participation in technical fields, one must consider the impact of the inferior education provided to minorities, largely because of racial stratification practices in elementary and secondary institutions. Hispanics might be underprepared (if one accepts the results of SAT tests) for postsecondary education, but this is the result of stratification processes at previous levels. Thus, rather than placing all the blame on an individual's unpreparedness, overwhelming structural and ideological claims must also be considered.

In summary, there is evidence that racial stratification exists in elementary, secondary, and postsecondary levels of the educational system. Racist stereotypes among students, school personnel, and school texts affect ethnic and racial interaction in school. Racial stereotypes also influence social-psychological factors that affect achievement. Stereotypes are employed to justify the differential treatment of Hispanics, tracking and overt segregation. In essence, then, racial stratification appears to have penetrated the educational system and has played a large role in the educational experiences of Hispanics.

SUMMARY AND CONCLUSIONS

That Hispanics face considerable educational difficulties has perplexed many individuals. Attempts at finding solutions to these problems have been well intentioned but less than satisfying because the target has been Hispanics themselves rather than the educational system. Indeed, there has been a failure to fully understand the educational system, or, more importantly, the relationship between the educational system and racial stratification. This paper has attempted to describe this relationship and the implications it has for the education of Hispanics. I began with a simple premise: that the poor educational experiences of Hispanics can be better understood through an analysis of the relationship between racial stratification and the educational system. It was argued that racial stratification infiltrates the educational system in maintaining a given racial order. Two mechanisms are used by stratification systems, an ideological component and a structural one. In terms of racial stratification, ideological mechanisms such as racism provide justifications for the differential treatment of Hispanics, while structural mechanisms, such as segregation, tracking, and a hierarchy of postsecondary educational institutions, separate subordinate racial groups from their more privileged counterparts. The effects of such mechanisms are to perpetuate and reinforce stereotypes, label students negatively, develop "them" and "us" feelings, and develop positions of subordination and superordination.

The educational process is demonstrably not as meritocratic as is commonly believed. Indeed, there is ample evidence suggesting that students are in large part evaluated by school personnel on the basis of their race and social-class background. What exists, then, is a system of stratification where Hispanics are sorted, ranked, and processed through the educational system in a manner that produces little or no actual intergenerational or intragenerational social mobility. In conclusion, it seems that the educational system reproduces a given socioeconomic order based, to a great degree, on ethnic- and racial-group membership. Once this is clearly understood, additional evidence can be gathered that defines the actual function of the educational system and can be used for proposed change. A few topics that can sharpen our understanding of the educational system include analyses of teacher-student interaction; stratification in higher education, especially related to the hierarchy of colleges and universities; analyses of curricula and how minorities are portrayed in school texts; and in-depth analysis of racial stratification in a given region and how it affects local schools. Additional studies are needed to examine how racial stratification in a community affects the educational experiences of Hispanics.

NOTES

1. The Coleman et al. (1966) study found that relative to other ethnic and racial minorities, Mexican Americans (a) ranked high in their determination to stay in school and attended regularly, and (b) planned in fewer numbers to attend college. In addition, Coleman et al. found that the following are associated with the achievements of Mexican Americans: family background; influence of school facilities, curriculum, and staff; teachers' characteristics; and school composition.

2. Such behavior has been noted elsewhere. See, for instance, Brophy and Good (1974), Cooper (1979), and Good and Brophy (1980).

3. Special education teachers have told me in personal conversations that

children with learning difficulties from middle- and upper-class families are labeled "learning disabled," whereas children with similar problems from poor families are labeled "retarded."

4. For the definitive statement of the culture-of-poverty viewpoint, see Oscar Lewis (1966).

5. Only 5 percent of Hispanics enrolled in community colleges in 1972 had transferred to four-year colleges by 1973 (Brown et al., 1980, p. 182).

REFERENCES

Adams, G., & Cohen, A. (1974). Children's physical and interpersonal characteristics that affect student-teacher interactions. *Journal of Experimental Education, 43,* 1–5.

Allington, R. (1980). Teacher interruption behaviors during primary-grade oral reading. *Journal of Educational Psychology, 72,* 371–377.

Astin, A. W. (1982). *Minorities in American higher education.* San Francisco: Jossey-Bass.

Bierstedt, R. (1963). *The social order: An introduction to sociology* (2nd ed.). New York: McGraw-Hill.

Bourdieu, P. (1977). Cultural reproduction and social reproduction. In J. Karabel & A. H. Halsey (Eds.), *Power and ideology in education* (pp. 487–511). New York: Oxford University Press.

Bowles, S., & Gintis, H. (1976). *Schooling in capitalist America.* New York: Basic Books.

Brophy, J., & Good, T. (1970). Teachers' communication of differential expectations for children's classroom performance: Some behavioral data. *Journal of Educational Psychology, 61,* 365–374.

Brophy, J., & Good, T. (1974). *Teacher-student relationships: Causes and consequences.* New York: Holt, Rinehart and Winston.

Brown, G. H., Rosen, N. L., Hill, S. T., & Olivas, M. (1980). *The condition of education for Hispanic Americans.* Washington, DC: National Center for Education Statistics.

Carter, T. P. (1970). *Mexican-Americans in school: A history of educational neglect.* New York: College Entrance Examination Board.

Carter, T. P., & Segura, R. D. (1979). *Mexican Americans in school: A decade of change.* New York: College Entrance Examination Board.

Cicourel, A., & Kitsuse, J. I. (1977). The school as a mechanism of social differentiation. In J. Karabel & A. H. Halsey (Eds.), *The school as a mechanism of social differentiation* (pp. 282–292). New York: Oxford University Press.

Cole, M., Gay, J., Glick, J. A., & Sharp, D. W. (1971). *The cultural context of learning and thinking: An exploration in experimental anthropology.* New York: Basic Books.

Coleman, J., Campbell, E. Q., Hobson, C. J., McPartland, J., Mood, A. M., Weinfeld, F. D. & York, R. L. (1966). *Equality of educational opportunity.* Washington, DC: U.S. Government Printing Office.

Collins, R. (1971). Functional and conflict theories of educational stratification. *American Sociological Review, 36,*1002–1019.

Cooke, H. W. (1948). The segregation of Mexican American school children in southern California. *School and Society, 67*(1745).

Cooper, H. (1979). Pygmalion grows up: A model for teacher expectation communication and performance influence. *Review of Educational Research, 49,* 389–410.

Davis, K., & Moore, W. E. (1945). Some principles of stratification: A critical analysis. *American Sociological Review, 10,* 242–249.

Dearman, N. B., & Plisko, V. W. (1980). *The condition of education.* Washington, DC: National Center for Education Statistics.

DeVos, G. A., & Hippler, A. (1969). Cultural Psychology: Comparative studies of human behavior. In A. Lindsey & E. Aronson (Eds.), *Handbook of social psychology* (2nd ed., Vol. 4., pp. 327–417). Cambridge, MA: Addison-Wesley.

Good, T., Cooper, H., & Blakey, S. (1980). Classroom interaction as a function of teacher expectations, student sex and time of year. *Journal of Educational Psychology, 72,* 378–385.

Grebler, L., Moore, J. W., & Guzmán, R. (Eds.). (1970). *The Mexican-American people: The nation's second largest minority.* New York: Free Press.

Heller, C. S. (1966). *New converts to the American dream? Mobility aspirations of young Mexican-Americans.* New Haven, CT: College and University Press.

Hodges, H. M. (1964). *Social stratification: Class in America.* Cambridge, MA: Schenkman.

Jencks, C., & Reisman, D. (1969). *The academic revolution.* Garden City, NY: Doubleday.

Jensen, A. R. (1969). How much can we boost IQ and scholastic achievement? *Harvard Educational Review* (Reprint Series No. 2), 1–123.

Johnson, K. R. (1966). *Teaching culturally disadvantaged pupils.* Chicago: Science Research Associates.

Karabel, J. (1972). Community colleges and social stratification. *Harvard Educational Review, 24*(4), 521–562.

Karabel, J., & Halsey, A. H. (Eds.). (1977). *Power and ideology in education.* New York: Oxford University Press.

Knowles, L. L., & Prewitt, K. E. (Eds.). (1969). *Institutional racism in America.* Englewood Cliffs, NJ: Prentice-Hall.

Levin, R. A. (1970). Cross-cultural study in child psychology. In P. Musson (Ed.), *Carmichael's manual of child psychology* (3d ed.) (pp. 559–612). New York: Wiley.

Lewis, O. (1966). The culture of poverty. *Scientific American, 215*(4), 19–25.

Mannheim, K. (1936). *Ideology and Utopia.* New York: Harcourt, Brace & World.

Moore, J. W. (1970). *Mexican Americans.* Englewood Cliffs, NJ: Prentice-Hall.

Ogbu, J. U. (1978). *Minority education and caste: The American system in cross-cultural perspective.* New York: Academic Press.

Olmedo, E. L. (1977). Psychological testing and the Chicano: A reassesssment. In J. L. Martínez, Jr. (Ed.), *Chicano psychology* (pp. 175–195). New York: Academic Press.

Orfield, G. (1982). *Working paper: Desegregation of Black and Hispanic students from 1968 to 1980*. Washington, DC: Joint Center for Political Studies.

Parson, T. W., Jr. (1965). *Ethnic cleavage in a California school*. Unpublished doctoral dissertation, Stanford University.

Rejeski, W., Darracott, C., & Hutslar, S. (1979). Pygmalion in youth sport: A field study. *Journal of Sports Psychology, 1,* 311–319.

Rist, R. (1970). Student social class and teacher expectations: The self-fulfilling prophecy in ghetto education. *Harvard Education Review, 40,* 411–451.

Rosenthal, R., & Jacobson, L. (1968). *Pygmalion in the classroom*. New York: Holt, Rinehart and Winston.

Rubovits, P., & Maehr, M. (1971). Pygmalion analyzed: Toward an explanation of the Rosenthal-Jacobson findings. *Journal of Personality and Social Psychology, 19,* 197–203.

Schlossman, S. (1983). Self-evident remedy? George I. Sánchez, segregation and enduring dilemmas in bilingual education. *Teachers College Record, 84*(4), 871–907.

Spring, J. (1976). *The sorting machine: National educational policy since 1945*. New York: McKay.

Strickland, V. E., & Sánchez, G. I. (1948). Spanish name spells discrimination. *The Nation's Schools, 41*(1).

Taylor, M. (1979). Race, sex, and the expression of self-fulfilling prophecies in a laboratory teaching situation. *Journal of Personality and Social Psychology, 37,* 897–912.

Taylor, P. S. (1934). *An American Mexican frontier*. Chapel Hill: University of North Carolina Press.

U.S. Commission on Civil Rights. (1971). *Ethnic isolation of Mexican Americans in the public schools of the southwest* (Mexican American Education Study, Report I). Washington DC: U.S. Government Printing Office.

U.S. Commission on Civil Rights. (1972). *The excluded student: Educational practices affecting Mexican Americans in the Southwest* (Mexican American Education Study, Report III). Washington, DC: U.S. Government Printing Office.

U.S. Commission on Civil Rights. (1974). *Toward quality education for Mexican Americans* (Mexican American Education Study, Report IV). Washington, DC: U.S. Government Printing Office.

van den Berghe, P. L. (1974). Paternalistic versus competitive race relations: An ideal-type approach. In N. Yetman & C. H. Steele (Eds.), *Paternalistic verses competitive race relations: An ideal-type approach* (pp. 64–79). Boston, MA: Allyn & Bacon.

ABOUT THE EDITOR
AND THE CONTRIBUTORS

INDEX

About the Editor
and the Contributors

ERNESTO BALLESTEROS is Director of Admissions, East Los Angeles College. He completed his Ph.D. at the University of California, Los Angeles, and his research has been in the area of Chicano student achievement.

MARÍA A. CHACÓN is Principal Administrative Analyst, Academic Personnel in the Office of the President of the University of California. She received her Ph.D. in Spanish from Stanford University and was involved in research on Chicanas at the Stanford Center for Research on Women.

ELIZABETH G. COHEN is Professor of Education at Stanford University, where she chairs the program in Education and the Social Sciences. She received her doctorate in sociology from Harvard and has published extensively on racial relations and schooling. She is the author of *Designing Groupwork for the Classroom* (Teachers College Press).

RICHARD P. DURÁN is Associate Professor in the Graduate School of Education, University of California, Santa Barbara. He holds a Ph.D. in psychology from the University of California, Berkeley and has written in the area of Hispanic education and psycholinguistics. He is the author of *Latino Language and Communicative Behavior* and *Hispanics' Education and Background*.

JOSÉ P. MESTRE is a physicist in the Department of Physics and Astronomy, at the University of Massachusetts, Amherst. He holds a Ph.D. in physics from the University of Massachusetts and has research interests in Hispanic education, technology, and cognitive development. He is the coauthor of *Language Perspectives on Mathematics Learning*.

DANIEL G. MUÑOZ is Director of Counseling, Revelle College, University of California, San Diego. He received his Ph.D. in counseling psychology from Michigan State University and maintains a counseling practice in Carlsbad, California. His research has focused upon Chicano mental health.

FRANÇOIS NEILSEN is Assistant Professor of Sociology at the Chapel Hill campus of the University of North Carolina. He received his Ph.D. from the University of Chicago and was coinvestigator of the Hispanic cohort of the High School and Beyond studies, conducted at the National Opinion Research Center.

MICHAEL A. OLIVAS is Professor of Law and Education, University of Houston, and Director of the Institute for Higher Education Law and Governance. He also is chair of the UH Higher Education Graduate Program. He received his Ph.D. from Ohio State University and his law degree from the Georgetown University Law Center. He is the author of *The Dilemma of Access* and *The Condition of Hispanic Education,* and the editor of *Higher Education and the Law.*

VILMA ORTIZ is a Visiting Scholar at the Educational Testing Service, where she is conducting research on Hispanic school achievement in the National Assessment of Education Progress. She received her doctorate in social psychology from New York University and has held research positions at the University of Wisconsin, the University of Michigan, and Fordham University. Her research has focused upon Puerto Rican schooling and Hispanic education.

MARÍA PENNOCK-ROMÁN is a Research Scientist at the Educational Testing Service, where she is undertaking research on the measurement of bilinguals. She took her doctorate in psychology from the University of California, Berkeley and was on the Graduate School of Education faculty at the University of Pennsylvania. She is a native of Puerto Rico.

RICHARD SANTOS is Assistant Professor of Economics at the University of Texas, Austin. His research is on Hispanic youth employment, and he is the author of *Hispanic Youth: Emerging Workers.* He received his doctorate from Michigan State University, and has been in residence at the Ohio State University Center for Human Resources Research.

SHARON STROVER is Assistant Professor in the Department of Radio, Television, and Film, University of Texas, Austin. She completed her doctorate at Stanford University, where she was affiliated with the Center for Research on Women. She was previously on the faculty at Western Kentucky University.

RICHARD R. VERDUGO is Mathematical Statistician, National Center for Education Statistics, U.S. Department of Education. His research interests are in racial stratification and Hispanic earnings, and he has held research positions at the Library of Congress and the National Council of La Raza. He received his Ph.D. in sociology from the University of Southern California.

Index